# Global Projects

As the world's population continues to grow, there is an ever-increasing need for huge investment in basic infrastructure: water and sewage, energy production and distribution, transportation, and telecommunication. At the same time, infrastructure systems in developed countries are deteriorating and in need of renewal. Today, many of the engineering and economic problems surrounding infrastructure construction projects have been solved, but the threat of social misalignments and political conflicts renders the development and management of such projects more challenging than ever before. This book presents a new theoretical framework that allows us to analyze the institutional and social movement processes, both negative and positive, that surround global infrastructure projects as they confront cross-national and cross-sectoral (e.g., private–public partnerships) institutional differences. The value of this framework is illustrated through a series of studies on a wide range of infrastructure projects, including roads, railroads, ports, airports, water supply, and energy pipelines.

W. RICHARD SCOTT is Professor Emeritus in the Department of Sociology with courtesy appointments in the Schools of Business, Education and Medicine at Stanford University. He is also a senior researcher in the Collaboratory for Research on Global Projects (CRGP) at Stanford.

RAYMOND E. LEVITT is Professor of Civil and Environmental Engineering and Director of the Collaboratory for Research on Global Projects (CRGP) at Stanford University.

RYAN J. ORR teaches project finance and infrastructure investment in the Graduate School of Business and the School of Engineering at Stanford University, where he is also Executive Director at the Collaboratory for Research on Global Projects (CRGP).

# Global Projects

## Institutional and Political Challenges

EDITORS

W. RICHARD SCOTT, RAYMOND E. LEVITT
AND RYAN J. ORR

CAMBRIDGE UNIVERSITY PRESS
Cambridge, New York, Melbourne, Madrid, Cape Town,
Singapore, São Paulo, Delhi, Tokyo, Mexico City

Cambridge University Press
The Edinburgh Building, Cambridge CB2 8RU, UK

Published in the United States of America by
Cambridge University Press, New York

www.cambridge.org
Information on this title: www.cambridge.org/9780521181907

First published 2011

Printed in the United Kingdom at the University Press, Cambridge

*A catalogue record for this publication is available from the British Library*

*Library of Congress Cataloging in Publication Data*

Global projects : institutional and political challenges / editors: W. Richard Scott,
Raymond E. Levitt, Ryan J. Orr.
    p.  cm.
    ISBN 978-1-107-00492-4 (Hardback) – ISBN 978-0-521-18190-7 (Paperback)
1. Infrastructure (Economics) – Developing countries.   2. Economic development
projects – Developing countries.   3. Public–private sector cooperation – Developing
countries.   4. International cooperation.   I. Scott, W. Richard.   II. Levitt,
Raymond E.   III. Orr, Ryan J.   IV. Title.
    HC59.72.C3G56 2011
    338.9009172′4–dc22

                                                                    2010050613

ISBN 978-1-107-00492-4 Hardback
ISBN 978-0-521-18190-7 Paperback

*In memory of Richard Burt*

# Contents

List of figures                                                      *page* ix

List of tables                                                              x

List of contributors                                                     xii

Preface                                                                    xv
*Raymond E. Levitt and Ryan J. Orr*

    Introduction: studying global projects                 1
    *W. Richard Scott*

    **Part I  Foundational themes**              **13**

1  Global projects: distinguishing features, drivers,
   and challenges                                               15
   *Ryan J. Orr, W. Richard Scott, Raymond E. Levitt, Karlos
   Artto, and Jaakko Kujala*

2  The institutional environment of global projects             52
   *W. Richard Scott*

3  Social movements and the growth in opposition
   to global projects                                           86
   *Doug McAdam*

    **Part II  Institutional differences and global projects:**
         **empirical studies**        **111**

4  Rules versus results: sources and resolution of institutional
   conflicts on Indian metro railway projects                  113
   *Ashwin Mahalingam, Raymond E. Levitt, and W. Richard
   Scott*

5   Institutional exceptions on global projects:
    a process model                                        135
    *Ryan J. Orr and W. Richard Scott*

6   Local embeddedness of firms and strategies
    for dealing with uncertainty in global projects        183
    *Ryan J. Orr and Raymond E. Levitt*

7   Who needs to know what? Institutional
    knowledge and global projects                          247
    *Amy N. Javernick-Will and W. Richard Scott*

    **Part III   Political conflicts and global projects**   277

8   "Site fights": explaining opposition to pipeline
    projects in the developing world                       279
    *Doug McAdam, Hilary Schaffer Boudet, Jennifer Davis,*
    *Ryan J. Orr, W. Richard Scott, and Raymond*
    *E. Levitt*

9   To talk or to fight? Effects of strategic, cultural,
    and institutional factors on renegotiation
    approaches in public–private concessions               310
    *Henry Chan and Raymond E. Levitt*

    **Part IV   Governance strategies and structures**       351

10  Network-based strategies and competencies
    for political and social risk management in
    global projects                                        353
    *Witold J. Henisz*

11  Organizations enabling public–private
    partnerships: an organization field approach           377
    *Stephan F. Jooste and W. Richard Scott*

References                                                 403

Index                                                      449

# *Figures*

| | | |
|---|---|---|
| 1.1 | Landscape of organizational scholarship | *page* 20 |
| 1.2 | Coordination and institutional costs in global projects | 38 |
| 1.3 | Four quadrants of the global projects research agenda | 39 |
| 5.1 | A generic narrative model | 173 |
| 6.1 | Strategies to succeed in foreign environments | 239 |
| 7.1 | Important types of institutional knowledge | 258 |
| 8.1 | Causal recipes for political conflict | 301 |
| 8.2 | Causal recipes for legal conflict | 303 |
| 9.1 | Positioning of current research with respect to the existing literature | 313 |
| 9.2 | Conceptual model of analysis | 315 |
| 9.3 | Relational-legal contracting performance continuum | 316 |
| 9.4(a) | Sufficient condition (factors X and Y are sufficient to cause the outcomes) | 340 |
| 9.4(b) | Necessary condition (factor Y is necessary to cause the outcome) | 340 |
| 10.1 | Chevron's integrated approach to stakeholder consultation | 371 |
| 10.2 | Chevron's incorporation of stakeholder feedback into project design | 373 |
| 11.1 | Graphic representation of South African PPP enabling field | 393 |
| 11.2 | Graphic representation of British Columbian (Canada) PPP enabling field | 395 |
| 11.3 | Graphic representation of Korean PPP enabling field | 398 |

# Tables

| | | |
|---|---|---:|
| 2.1 | Three pillars of institutions | *page* 54 |
| 3.1 | Growth and issue focus of transnational social movement organizations | 105 |
| 5.1 | Summary of informants, organizations, and projects sampled | 147 |
| 5.2 | Condensed vignette summaries | 150 |
| 5.3 | Ignorance, deviant action, and outcomes | 154 |
| 5.4 | Sensemaking, local knowledge search, and outcomes | 156 |
| 5.5 | Response, response action, and outcomes | 158 |
| 6.1 | Firm descriptions | 191 |
| 6.2 | Project descriptions | 193 |
| 6.3 | Project engagement characteristics, by firm type | 194 |
| 6.4 | Overall local relational embeddedness | 197 |
| 6.5 | Relative local embeddedness | 198 |
| 6.6 | Examples of emergent uncertainty | 206 |
| 6.7 | Indicators of local embeddedness and strategy–structure fit | 219 |
| 6.8 | Strategies to increase supply of local knowledge | 222 |
| 6.9 | Strategies to decrease the need for local knowledge | 229 |
| 6.10 | Strategies to reduce the impact of a local knowledge deficit | 234 |
| 6.11 | Summary of shortcomings of extant theory and the contribution of this article | 243 |
| 7.1 | Case study information | 254 |
| 7.2 | Relative frequency of important institutional knowledge mentioned by informants for international projects | 257 |
| 7.3 | Relative frequency of important knowledge type mentioned by informants for international projects according to company type | 271 |

| | | |
|---|---|---|
| 8.1 | List of cases | 290 |
| 8.2 | Causal conditions | 295 |
| 8.3 | Outcome conditions | 298 |
| 9.1 | Rule of law index by subfactors | 323 |
| 9.2 | Coding scheme for the relational–legalistic renegotiation approach continuum | 334 |
| 9.3 | Coding scheme for future business index (FBI) | 335 |
| 9.4 | Coding scheme for current investment activity (CIA) | 336 |
| 9.5 | Coding summary | 338 |
| 9.6 | Consistency analysis for necessity | 341 |
| 9.7 | Cases with low strategic scores | 347 |

# Contributors

KARLOS ARTTO Professor of Project Business, School of Science and Technology, Aalto University, Finland

HILARY SHAFFER BOUDET Post-doctoral Scholar, Stanford Prevention Research Center, School of Medicine, Stanford University

HENRY CHAN Ph.D. in Civil and Environmental Engineering and Consultant at the Transaction Advice Group of Arup in San Francisco, CA

JENNIFER DAVIS Assistant Professor, Department of Civil and Environmental Engineering, and Higgins-Magid Fellow, Woods Institute for the Environment, Stanford University

WITOLD J. HENISZ Deloitte & Touche Associate Professor of Management in Honor of Russell E. Palmer, Former Managing Partner, The Wharton School, University of Pennsylvania

AMY JAVERNICK-WILL Assistant Professor, Department of Civil, Environmental and Architectural Engineering, University of Colorado at Boulder

STEPHAN F. JOOSTE Ph.D. candidate, Department of Civil and Environmental Engineering will become a consultant at The Aurecon Group in South Africa

JAAKKO KUJALA Professor of Project and Quality Management, Department of Industrial Engineering and Management, University of Oulu, Finland

RAYMOND E. LEVITT  Professor, Department of Civil and Environmental Engineering and Director of the Collaboratory for Research on Global Projects, Stanford University

ASHWIN MAHALINGAM  Assistant Professor of Building Technology and Construction Management, Department of Civil Engineering, Indian Institute of Technology (IITM), Madras, India

DOUG MCADAM  Professor of Sociology and Director of the Program on Urban Studies, Stanford University

RYAN J. ORR  Instructor in Civil and Environmental Engineering in the Graduate School of Business, and Executive Director of the Collaboratory for Research on Global Projects, Stanford University

W. RICHARD SCOTT  Professor of Sociology Emeritus and Senior Research Scientist, Collaboratory for Research on Global Projects, Stanford University

# Preface

This book presents the results of research conducted by scholars in or associated with the Collaboratory for Research on Global Projects (CRGP) at Stanford University from the founding of CRGP in 2002 up to the present time. In this preface we describe the goals, origins, membership, and activities of CRGP that have resulted in this body of scholarship.

In developing countries, improving the quality and quantity of civil infrastructure – water supply, wastewater treatment, roads, railroads, ports, airports, power, and telecommunications – is one of the primary means to improve human health, reduce transaction costs for society, and thereby raise living standards. Large investments in social infrastructure – schools, hospitals, civic buildings, etc. – present another pressing set of needs. In many developed countries civil and social infrastructure built in the last century has served those countries well initially, but has subsequently failed to keep up with population growth and has been systematically under-maintained, so it needs substantial expansion and refurbishment at a time when governments worldwide are severely fiscally strained. Various estimates place global demand for infrastructure in developing and developed countries over the next decade at anywhere from $10–$20 trillion. In addition to being underdeveloped and under-maintained, civil and social infrastructure worldwide is currently being developed in ways that generate substantial greenhouse gas emissions from energy intensive materials like cement and steel, contributing greatly to pollution of land, water, and atmosphere. Moreover, development of these projects often results in harsh and inequitable social outcomes for population groups who are subject to their environmental impacts or who are forcibly displaced from their homes, oftentimes without adequate provision for compensation and resettlement. Clearly, better ways need to be found for financing, governing, constructing, and sustaining infrastructure projects over their lifecycles worldwide.

CRGP was founded to conduct fundamental and applied research, education, and outreach to enhance the economic, environmental, and social sustainability of projects that provide sorely needed civil and social infrastructure worldwide. To advance this goal, CRGP was established as a cross-disciplinary center at Stanford, cutting across many interested departments and schools in collaboration with reflective practitioners from a group of industry partners. This Stanford Center was designed from the outset to collaborate with complementary teams of scholars from universities in other regions worldwide and their government and industry partners – hence the name "Collaboratory." Since its founding, CRGP has successfully brought together teams of faculty and students from engineering, project management, political science, sociology, economics, law, finance, and history at Stanford and partner institutions to work on various aspects of the financing, governance, and sustainability of infrastructure projects around the world.

Organizational and institutional theory has provided a unifying perspective to bridge between the contributions of CRGP scholars in this effort. Key CRGP institutional scholars at Stanford in this effort to date have included: Steven Barley, organizational ethnography; Gordon Chung, institutional history; Jennifer Davis, public health and water project governance; Avner Greif, institutional economics; Thomas Heller (co-Nobel Laureate, Peace), institutional law; Raymond Levitt (CRGP Academic Director), project organization and governance; Doug McAdam, political sociology; Roger Noll, economics of privatization; Douglass North (Nobel Laureate, Economics), institutional economics; Ryan Orr (CRGP Executive Director), project finance and infrastructure investment; and W. Richard Scott (CRGP Senior Research Scientist), organizational and institutional sociology.

All of the authors of chapters in this volume have had, and most still have, strong and direct connections with CRGP as faculty members, doctoral students, or visiting scholars. Several of the papers were written or co-written by a number of doctoral students associated with CRGP. These (then) student collaborators include Henry Chan, Stephan Jooste, Ashwin Mahalingam, Ryan J. Orr, Hilary Schaffer Boudet, and Amy Javernick Will. Witold Henisz, a member of the management faculty at the Wharton School, University of Pennsylvania, spent a sabbatical year at Stanford serving as Visiting Professor of Civil and Environmental Engineering during 2008–2009. His work has focused on the impact of political hazards on international investment strategies and the design of project governance structures. Thus, all contributors are current faculty members, current or past Ph.D. students and postdoctoral fellows, current or past visiting scholars at CRGP, or members of Collaboratory partner institutions.

CRGP's first significant international research Collaboratory partner was a group of academics from Finland: Karlos Artto of Helsinki University of Technology (now part of Aalto University) and Jaakko Kujala of University of Oulu, project-based business; Kalle Kähkönen of the Finnish National Research Institute, project risk analysis; and Risto Tainio of Helsinki School of Economics, organization studies. This Finnish consortium was sponsored by the TEKES National Research Agency plus a group of Finnish companies including Kone Elevators, Nokia Networks (now Siemens-Nokia Networks), Jaakko Pöyry Corp., and Foster Wheeler.

Other international scholars with strong links to the Collaboratory have included: Giel Becker and Manfried Köster of University of Pretoria in South Africa, global project governance; Christian Brockmann of University of Bremen in Germany, global project management; Nuno Gil of Manchester University Business School, private–public partnerships for infrastructure delivery; Rahinah Ibrahim from University Putra Malaysia, project knowledge management; Ashwin Mahalingam from IIT Madras, infrastructure privatization; and Jennifer Whyte of University of Reading, UK, IT for global project collaboration.

CRGP was launched in 2002 with start-up funding from the Deans of the School of Engineering and the School of Humanities and Sciences. A significant seed grant from Stanford's Freeman Spogli Institute for International Studies made possible CRGP's first major research project on sources of conflict in global infrastructure project delivery. Aside from this initial funding, CRGP's research has been funded by a combination of Stanford internal research grants, outside research grants, and annual affiliate program membership contributions from companies involved in global infrastructure development, finance, and investment. Sponsor companies have included: Akin Gump Strauss Hauer & Feld LLP; American Infrastructure MLP Fund; Alberta Investment Management Corporation; Baker McKenzie LLP; Bechtel Corporation; Coudert Brothers; Det Norske Veritas of Norway; EMP Global Infrastructure Fund of Bahrain; Finnish Global

Project Strategy Initiative; HRJ Capital; Japan Marine Science, Inc.; KPMG; Meketa Investment Group, Inc.; Meridiam Infrastructure; Nossaman LLP; Parsons Infrastructure & Technology Group, Inc.; Qatar Economic Zones; Queensland Investment Corp,; and Zurich North America. CRGP researchers are deeply appreciative of the support we have received from all of these enterprises that has allowed us to conduct this program of fundamental cross-disciplinary research on the determinants of successful global project outcomes.

Over the years, we have learned that the most important factor for ensuring effective collaboration with industry is to identify a "reflective practitioner" within each of our sponsor companies. We thank David Altshuler, Abu Chowdhury, Julie Kim, Ross Israel, Gregory Keever, Dennis Lorenzin, Lars Erik Mangset, Barry Metzger, Shailesh Pathak, Todd Rowland, and Grant Stevens for their many extraordinary contributions to our program.

During its early days, CRGP was exceptionally fortunate to attract as a visiting scholar Mr. Richard Burt who was just stepping down as General Counsel of Bechtel Corp. and had previously played the same role for ABB, a Swiss-German global engineering and construction consortium. Rick Burt engaged enthusiastically in our interdisciplinary research program, advising both faculty and students, and providing us with the benefit of his years of practical experience and incisive intellect. Rick had a special interest in exploring the potential for large pension funds to provide pools of capital to fund regionally and sectorally diversified portfolios of infrastructure projects in ways that are mutually attractive to both sides. He argued that the relatively low risk, long term, inflation-adjusted returns from infrastructure projects could be structured in ways that would meet both the pension obligations and fiduciary requirements of pension funds, while simultaneously buttressing the legitimacy of private investment of workers' pensions in these critically needed public works projects. Rick's vision is currently being advanced through a serious of CRGP roundtables that have brought together managers of some of the world's largest pension funds with forward-looking sponsors and developers of infrastructure to explore ways in which this marriage of interests and needs can be facilitated.

Sadly, Rick was denied the chance to see his vision realized by an unexpected heart attack in the prime of his life. We, therefore, gratefully dedicate this book to the memory of our late friend and deeply admired colleague, Rick Burt, for his pivotal contributions to CRGP's nascent research program, his warm friendship, and tireless support.

It is our hope that this book will provide useful points of departure in this area, and will inspire scholars from multiple academic disciplines worldwide to join with CRGP in the pursuit of knowledge and tools to advance the development of more sustainable global infrastructure development projects and global projects of all kinds in our increasingly interconnected and fragile world economy and polity.

Raymond Levitt, Director
Ryan J. Orr, Executive Director
Collaboratory for Research on Global Projects
Stanford University
Stanford, California

# Introduction: studying global projects

W. RICHARD SCOTT

Given the fragile condition of our planet with its finite space, resources, and capabilities, we are not in favor of "development" for its own sake. Nevertheless, the likely arrival within the foreseeable future of a billion additional inhabitants on our planet will generate the need for a huge investment in basic infrastructure: water and sewage, energy production and distribution, transportation, and telecommunication, among others. At the same time, such support systems in developed countries are deteriorating and in need of renewal. Infrastructure construction projects are assuming increasing salience for both developed and developing countries. And, increasingly, those who design, fund, and build such projects are international or global in character.

Historically, the major challenges in carrying out infrastructure construction projects have been primarily technical and financial in nature, focusing on design, construction, financing, and the details of maintenance and operation. Today, many of these engineering and most of the economic problems have been solved, but the threat of social misalignments and political conflicts renders the development and management of such projects more challenging than ever before. This volume concentrates primarily on challenges confronting global projects stemming from the complexity and volatility of the political and institutional contexts within which these projects are embedded.

In this brief introduction we describe the emergence of project-based organizations, noting the origins of scholarly work on projects and the kinds of theoretical approaches currently being developed to examine these systems. Next, we comment on various conceptions of the context or environment within which projects operate, calling attention to the gradual broadening and elaboration of these frameworks. And, finally, we present a brief overview of and introduction to the chapters comprising the volume.

1

## Project organization

### *Early formulations*

Students of organizations first began to become aware of the emergence of a new mode of organizing during the late 1960s to early 1970s when, far out on the fringes of the field, a few marginal observers identified "outlier" forms which they termed, variously, "temporary" (Bennis and Slater 1968), "post-industrial" (Bell 1973), "adhocracies" (Toffler 1970) or, in Hedberg and colleagues (Hedberg, Nystrom, and Starbuck 1976) memorable simile, as organizations "camping on see-saws," resembling "tents" more than "palaces."[1] At about the same time "contingency theory" arguments were advanced that insisted that, to be effective, organizations needed to reflect in their design the complexity of their environments (Burns and Stalker 1961; Lawrence and Lorsch 1967; Thompson 1967). Such approaches suggested that, under conditions of great complexity and high uncertainty, organizations should resort to more lateral and flexible coordination strategies, such as those offered by teams and projects (Galbraith 1973;1977).

These insights and arguments were first collected and codified by Henry Mintzberg in his book, *The Structuring of Organizations* (1979), where he depicted the "adhocracy" as one of his five basic forms of organizing. Presciently, this form was described as "capable of sophisticated innovation" because it is "able to fuse experts drawn from different disciplines into smoothly functioning ad hoc project teams" (p. 432). Unlike a related form, "professional bureaucracies" that also rely on standardization of skills and vertical decentralization (see Scott 2003: 258–60), the adhocracy's distinguishing structural characteristics included: (1) organic rather than mechanical structures; (2) low levels of formalization; (3) high horizontal job specialization; (4) work organization based on projects (outcomes) rather than processes (functions); (5) coordination based on mutual adjustment; and (6) selective decentralization (Mintzberg 1979: chap. 21).

Approaching the same topic from a different direction, another wave of theorists worked to expand institutional economist Oliver Williamson's (1975) "markets and hierarchies" framework that attempted to explain the conditions under which organizations (hierarchies) were superior to market-based modes of coordination.

Scholars such as Powell (1990) and Miles and Snow (1992) proposed that a wide range of intermediate "network" forms could be identified that functioned in the space "between markets and hierarchies." These forms were viewed as based on longer-term relations rather than spot-market transactions, often crossing formal organizational boundaries, and emphasizing norms of reciprocity and a search for mutual benefits.

A final strand stemmed from a collection of scholar-practitioners associated with the Tavistock Institute in London who, working in close association with the companies they studied, developed a "socio-technical" model of organizations, focusing on the interface between "a nonhuman and a human system" (Trist 1981: 25). Rather than favoring one facet over the other, these scholars sought the "joint optimization" of the needs of both (Emery 1959). More fundamentally, they stressed the extent to which the construction of technologies did not simply follow mechanistic principles, but were the result of human choices: technologies were human constructions. The pursuit of these insights attracted a small but lively cluster of studies on the evolution of technical systems, including some very complex forms. These studies stressed "the importance of paying attention to the different but interlocking elements of physical artifacts, institutions, and their environment and thereby offer[ing] an integration of technical, social, economic and political aspects" (Bjiker, Hughes, and Pinch 1987: 4; see also, Hughes 2004).

## Defining project organizations

At the close of the twentieth and opening of the twenty-first century, scholars began to examine more closely a growing population of organizations that were a subtype of network forms: project-based firms. The larger of these forms – those engaged in large or mega-projects were typically nodes of complex systems of multiple types of actors – both organizations (e.g., firms, banks, public agencies) and individuals (Morris and Hough 1987; Hughes 1998; Miller and Lessard 2000; Whitley 2006). We describe in Chapter 1 our own conception of projects and detail their distinguishing characteristics. Suffice it to say here that such projects focus on unique or customized singular products, are conducted over long periods of time, require the contributions of a diverse set of specialized entities, and confront complex and contested environments.

Also, as we try to emphasize in the volume, the firm is no longer viewed as a solitary actor but a focal unit in a larger system or "field" of actors. Attention must be devoted to assembling a collection of participants whose composition will shift with the changing phases of the project. Whereas early organizing models relied on unified hierarchies of power and authority, supplemented as necessary by external contracting, large project-based systems, because the interests and goals of their central participants often differ, are obliged to employ a broader range of governance mechanisms, including adjudication, cooptation, participation, and mediation. Coordination mechanisms must be enhanced by governance systems.

## Theoretical approaches to project-based organizations

Because the arena of organization and management studies has become highly differentiated around axes ranging from discipline to theoretical perspective to methodology, it is not surprising that the analysis of a new form would proceed in multiple, albeit related, directions. All current approaches in business and international business studies place much emphasis on strategy – whether in terms of how to devise and produce the right engineering design, how to reduce costs and risks and maximize returns, or how to achieve sustainable, environmentally friendly solutions. Social science scholars examine the related questions, posed less explicitly and framed less prescriptively, of how varying types of organizations and organizational systems adapt, survive, and thrive under varying conditions.

Our review of the literature suggests the dominance of two theoretical approaches to large project-based organizing efforts together with the gradual emergence of a third. The first draws from and expands on the "contingency" approach to organization design. The second employs the "resource-based" view of the firm and extends it to project-based organizing. A third, emerging "institutional" perspective calls attention to the context within which these organizational systems operate.

### Contingency-based approaches

A wide range of sophisticated work is associated with a contingency-based view of the firm. This perspective had its origins in the early work of Herbert Simon (1945[1997]), developed later in March and Simon (1958), as an information-processing view of organizations. In this conception, organizations are, fundamentally, information-processing systems and, in this capacity, must find ways to adequately process the information demands posed by the environments in which they operate. As these environments become more complex, conflicted, and uncertain, if the organization is to survive, its information-processing and problem-solving capacities must respond accordingly.

This basic contingency insight, as noted, was extended by theorists such as Lawrence and Lorsch (1967) and Galbraith (1973), but has been greatly elaborated by scholars working on complex project-based organizations. Among the most creative of these was Stinchcombe (1985), who studied the organization structure of Norwegian firms managing the construction and operation of oil production in the North Sea. Stinchcombe developed an "extended definition of hierarchy" to examine the ways in which standard contracts were expanded to incorporate many elements of hierarchies to deal with high levels of uncertainty, including, dispute resolution, nonmarket pricing, and the adjustment of incentives and controls to changing conditions.

The contingency perspective underlies the sophisticated analysis of Miller and Lessard (2000), who view large engineering projects as governance arrangements devised by sponsors and leading partners to align or reconcile the divergent interests of contractors, operators, clients, and investors within a framework imposed by communities and regulators (see also, Shenhar and Dvir 2007).

Also, following subsequent theorizing by James March and colleagues (Levitt and March 1988; March 1990; Cohen and Sproull 1991), many of these approaches stress the importance to organizations of constructing systems that enable learning. Organizations learn both from their own and the experiences of others in their cohort. Some contemporary scholars argue that, in the current world, the organization with superior learning systems will enjoy a competitive advantage (Nonaka and Takeuschi 1995). This emphasis is, increasingly, being expanded into a "knowledge-based theory of the firm" (Nissen 2006). With this step, approaches that had their origin in early contingency theory begin to converge and overlap with resource-based approaches to the firm.

## Resource-based approaches

More so than contingency approaches, which emphasize the inter-dependence of organizations and their environments, resource-based approaches refocused attention on the internal attributes and capabilities of organizations. This approach to the analysis of firms began with the pioneering work of Edith Penrose (1959), who recognized that the most important asset a firm possesses is its specialized use of resources (including worker skills) and it's capacity to mobilize them as required in new and diversified combinations. Some capabilities – constellations of interdependent knowledge and skills – are difficult to imitate by other firms and hence provide a unique source of competitive advantage (Hamel and Prahalad 1994).

Nelson and Winter (1982) placed this insight into a broader evolutionary framework, suggesting that an organization's capabilities or "routines" were equivalent to the genes in a plant or animal. To survive, an organization must be able to reproduce and modify its routines in the face of changing situations. But, they cautioned, many of these routines are based on tacit knowledge, so that it is not easy for an organization to deliberately choose to modify its routines as required by changing circumstances. Indeed, many organizations do not (consciously) know what they know! Capabilities are embedded in participants and ongoing relationships, in rules and routines.

Teece (2009; Teece and Pasano 1994) emphasizes that in fast-paced industries, sustainable advantage requires in addition to "difficult-to-replicate knowledge assets", "difficult-to-replicate dynamic capabilities" – "to continuously create, extend, upgrade, protect, and keep relevant the enterprise's unique asset base" (Teece 2009: 4). Such skills include the discovery and development of opportunities, effectively combining inventions, upgrading of "best-practice" business processes, and the ability to shape new "rules of the game" in the global marketplace (p. 6).

Davies and Hobday (2005) embrace this dynamic capability framework but suggest that additional skills are required in order to successfully cope with the complexity posed by large complex projects. These complexities include: "the variety of distinct knowledge bases which need to be integrated into the final product or system"; the "intensity of user involvement and the user's understanding of final requirements"; the existence of "substantial feedback loops from later to earlier project stages"; the need to devise and coordinate an adequate "system architecture" to manage the "interconnections between components and subsystems" as the product design evolves; and the necessity to cope with a "changing regulatory environment' (pp. 31–3).

Most project analysts give some attention to the need to understand and manage the larger context within which the project is taking place. Thus, for example, Miller and Lessard (2000: 23) discuss the necessity of developing adequate strategies and mechanisms to deal with "institutional arrangements"; and, as just noted, Davies and Hobday attend to the challenges posed by "changing regulatory environments" (2005: 33). But on closer examination, the conceptions employed by these analysts appear to us to be somewhat underdeveloped. They generally hearken back to Douglass North's (1990) well-known early formulation of institutions as the "rules of the game", limiting attention primarily, in our terms, to the regulative component of institutions. (See Chapter 2.)

## An institutions-based approach

As should be clear from the above cursory summary, contemporary scholars have made progress in identifying the defining features of project-based organizations, and are successfully adapting mainstream theoretical perspectives in order to better understand the design, structure, and strategies associated with projects. Although some attention has been accorded to the importance of context, this seems to us to be the area most in need of elaboration and development, both theoretical and empirical.

As noted, mainstream approaches acknowledge the role played by political processes and institutions, although the former are treated primarily as governmental instability and the latter as regulatory restrictions (e.g., Miller and Lessard 2000). The approach we take to political processes emphasizes that important political forces are at work apart from those operating in the public sector (see Chapter 3). And, to enable a more robust conception of institutions, we adapt Scott's (1995; 2008) "pillars" framework, stressing that institutions are comprised of three elements: regulative, normative, and cultural-cognitive (see Chapter 2). While the regulative pillar has received its due, the normative has been almost completely neglected by project scholars, although the work of Whitley (1999) has begun to find its way into international business studies.

Some aspects of cultural-cognitive institutions have received more attention from international business scholars because of the influential work of Hofstede (1984; 1991). Hofstede suggest that countries differ in their modal value orientations across several dimensions, for example, how power differences are managed and whether individualism or collectivism is more favored. These dimensions have found their way into international business scholarship. For example, Kogut and Singh (1988) have employed Hofstede's value dimensions in assessing choice of entry mode by multinational firms, and an international collection of scholars assembled by House has utilized these dimensions to examine cross-cultural differences in leadership style (House et al. 2002). Recently, Binder (2007) made use of Hofstede's dimensons, together with others proposed by Trompenaars and Hampsen-Turner (1998) to suggest various modes of cross-cultural collaboration within global projects. While we find this a useful window on culture, to focus exclusively on value orientations ignores other important facets of culture, such as variations in ideas, ideologies, and identities. In brief, we believe that international business and project scholars have, to date, employed a relatively impoverished conception of institutions.

We are pleased to note that our concern with developing an expanded conception of the organization's context is shared by others. Thus, Mike Peng and colleagues have been calling for the development of "an institution-based view" of business strategy to supplement existing "industry-based competition" and "firm-specific resources and capabilities" (Peng 2002; Peng, Wang, and Jiang 2008; Peng et al. 2009). Peng suggests that an institutional approach can provide the "third leg of a strategy tripod". (Peng et al. 2009: 63) Actually, we believe that, fully developed, institutional perspectives can do more than inform the strategic decision making of project-based organizations. It can help to inform and guide the decisions that must be made by a wide range of actors – including host governments, oversight bodies, consumers of services, community members, and interest groups – all those who have a stake in the effective and sustainable operation of vital civic infrastructures.

## Guide to volume chapters

As noted in the preface, all the chapters of this volume report work that has been carried out by scholars associated with the Collaboratory for Global Projects at Stanford University. About half of the papers included were written expressly for this volume. The others have been previously published and are reprinted here.

In Chapter 1, Ryan J. Orr and colleagues offer a general overview of and introduction to the concept of project-based organizations operating within a global context. The chapter asks why global projects (GP) have emerged at this time, and examines the challenges they confront. It focuses in particular on the strategic implications for companies and host countries posed by the new types of organizations.

W. Richard Scott discusses in Chapter 2 the conception of institutions which guides and informs the papers collected in this volume. In addition to offering a relatively expansive definition of institutions, the chapter also describes its application to multiple levels, ranging from the global to the local field.

In Chapter 3, Doug McAdam explains why social movements have become relevant to the study of GPs, as recent projects have become increasingly subject to opposition from social movements – local, national, and transnational. The activities of public authorities are described, both in the way in which they influence projects, but also in the ways they shape other modes of political activity.

These first three chapters are intended to supply a general intellectual context for all of the remaining chapters, providing a broad theoretical palate on which the empirical research can draw.

Chapter 4, by Ashwin Mahalingam, Raymond E. Levitt, and Scott, describes results from a study of two projects that comprised part of the construction of a metro railway project in India. Although international teams were involved, much of the conflict observed was related more closely to the institutional conflicts developing between public bureaucrats and representatives of private firms rather than between broader cultural communities, such as religious or national groups.

Chapter 5, by Orr and Scott, reports the results of an inductive study examining 23 cases of misunderstanding arising from institutional differences on GPs. The bases of such conflicts are examined, as are the mechanisms devised to deal with them.

In Chapter 6, Orr and Levitt examine the extent to which varying types of firms – developers, contractors, consultants – are involved in or exposed to the complexities of the local context. They develop measures to assess this exposure or "embeddedness," and examine the strategies available to firms for coping with varying degrees of local embeddedness.

Involvement in a global environment is not simply a matter of extent of exposure to new classes of risk. In Chapter 7, Amy Javernick-Will and Scott explore the opportunities for learning afforded by these contexts. Utilizing data from interviews from informants for fifteen projects from three types of firms (developers, contractors, engineering consultants), they examine what types of knowledge are most important for each.

In Chapter 8, Doug McAdam and colleagues examine what types of factors affect the likelihood and magnitude of political opposition to GPs involved in constructing oil and gas pipelines. Factors considered range from the political structure and economic conditions of the host country and community, nature and size of project, characteristics of project participants, nature of funding and oversight regimes, to activation of local and transnational movement organizations. They also ask whether the factors that give rise to more institutionalized forms of conflict such as lawsuits, differ from those associated with more informal, grassroots forms of social protests.

Chapter 9, by Henry Chan and Levitt, examines a collection of cases drawn from the transportation and power sectors in order to ascertain what factors account for the nature of the renegotiation process utilized in revising infrastructure concession agreements. What factors determine the extent to which parties engage in more formalized, legal approaches or are able to proceed by means of more trust-based, relational approaches?

Taking a step back from the direct analysis of sources of political opposition to or modes of negotiation undertaken by projects, in Chapter 10 Witold Henisz examines the ways in which organizations can take advantage of recent developments in network analysis to construct a more informed portrait of the social and political contexts in which they operate. He argues that those concerned with assessing the political and social risks confronted in their environments would do well to employ recent analytic tools developed to assess the networked structure of their environments.

Stephan Jooste and Scott explore, in Chapter 11, newly developing configurations of organizations that attempt to enable the development and successful completion of infrastructure projects involving partnerships between public and private organizations. To date, a number of "field-level" enabling structures have been developed. Three of these, in Canada, South Africa, and South Korea, are described and compared.

It is our hope that the theoretical frameworks being developed here, together with examples of their empirical application, will stimulate others to pursue this research agenda so that both the study of global projects as well as the broader study of international business will benefit from an enlarged understanding of the role that "culture" and "politics" plays in the construction of the systems that will undergird our twenty-first century world.

## Endnote

1 It should be noted that "craft" modes of production have been in use for several centuries. Such modes were viewed, however, as alternatives to bureaucratic organizations rather than as possible components of such hierarchical forms (see Stinchcombe 1959).

# PART I

# Foundational themes

# 1 | Global projects: distinguishing features, drivers, and challenges

RYAN J. ORR, W. RICHARD SCOTT,
RAYMOND E. LEVITT, KARLOS ARTTO,
AND JAAKKO KUJALA

## Introduction

Today it is taken for granted that firms, governments, and nongovernmental organizations (NGOs) will participate routinely in initiatives involving partners and resources from multiple world regions and time zones. For example, firms such as Google routinely undertake software development projects with teams of globally-distributed employees working together in real-time via web-enabled collaborative work-space applications. After the Asian tsunami in 2004, private firms, government agencies, NGOs, and international volunteers from more than thirty nations came together in a disaster relief effort of unprecedented transnational proportions. The Channel Tunnel constructed between England and France was a cross-border, public–private partnership among two governments and multiple private sector firms from around the world – including legal advisors, financiers, designers, contractors, and equipment vendors.

Few, if any, major projects in the modern era rely exclusively on people or resources from a single host country or sponsor. The new strategic environment for such projects is global, technology-enabled, interconnected, and dynamic.

Globally networked organizational arrangements are underpinned by technologies that have emerged since the 1970s for rapid human travel, information sharing, and interpersonal connectivity. Today a FedEX package can be delivered anywhere in the world in just 24 hours. The standard Windows–Intel personal computer system enables instant file sharing across boundaries of nation, language, and race. Mobile telephones enable instant communications without heed to physical proximity.

Technological progress has altered the relative efficiency and competitiveness of different organizational structures and strategies. Large, slow-moving, industrial-era hierarchies are losing their dominance (Walsh, Meyer, and Schoonhoven 2006). Smaller, nimbler, global-born firms are emerging as successful players (Oviatt and McDougall 1994; Knight and Cavusgil 2004). Loosely affiliated networks of companies working across industries and borders have also gained in influence and importance (Powell 1990; Child 2005).

Generally, with higher mobility and connectivity, the cost of coordinating and integrating specialist providers and services from outside the firm has fallen, enabling more networks, partnerships, and alliances. As such, it has become relatively less attractive for firms to internalize noncore functions or to commit to the fixed costs of a large internal staff. This trend was foreseen by Malone (Malone, Yates, and Benjamin 1987) more than two decades ago. Employment relations have become more flexible. This is true even in Japan, which has long-standing conventions of lifetime employment that do not change easily. Professional, managerial, and technical employees expect to work for several firms over the course of a career; and organizations are reconfiguring themselves more rapidly with changes in the technology and competitive environment (DiMaggio 2001).

With more involvement of external partners and faster-paced change, the relative frequency of "one-off" projects with unique networks has also risen, and, with it, the importance of the discipline of project management, which has diffused from the curriculums of engineering schools into business schools. Another discipline to gain prominence under the conditions of the new technology environment is supply chain management (Gereffi and Korzeniewicz 1994). As more firms procure more subcomponents from low-cost providers, supply chains or, in the more recent terminology, "global value chains," have grown to have longer and longer tails (Bair 2009).

No field has been unaffected by the new technological landscape. The design of organizations and teams for research, healthcare, government, peace-keeping, information technology (IT), construction, pharmaceuticals, movies, and international development have all been impacted.

Traditional organization theory, although still foundational, has been to this point unable to satisfactorily accommodate the multi-organization, globally networked systems enabled by the last quarter century of technological innovation (Aldrich and Ruef 2006). For example, in Qatar, new eGovernment systems outsource traditional governmental functions to specialized networks of consultants in other countries. Joint-forces command simulation exercises engage thousands of officers and soldiers at computer terminals from militaries around the world. Globally networked research projects in physics and medicine involve investigators and science equipment at universities across several continents.

Of course, coordination of these complex initiatives occurs not only by means of intentional forms of coordination but also via the invisible hand of the market through global supply chains. For example, minerals from Africa are formed into electronics components in Taiwan that are assembled into electronics devices in Japan which are plugged into pieces of heavy equipment made in America that are purchased by Australian mining companies that are operating in countries like Peru, Indonesia, and Romania.

Today's major airport, seaport, or high-rise building construction project is likely to involve thousands of organizations from dozens of countries. Although the assembly of resources happens locally, the supply of resources flows through a set of supply chains that resemble an octopus with tentacles stretching around the globe. Not even the head of the octopus – i.e. the company executives and project administrators who are in charge – actually know where all of the components originate, or who is employed at the ends of the tentacles. It is possible to map supply chains to the second-, third-, and fourth-tier, but not without a concerted research effort to trace financial and material flows.

Throughout this volume, we refer to this new organizational phenomenon as a "global project". *A global project is defined as a temporary endeavour where multiple actors seek to optimize outcomes by combining resources from multiple sites, organizations, cultures, and geographies through a combination of contractual, hierarchical, and network-based modes of organization.*

This definition recognizes global projects as complex organizational systems, with distinctive challenges posed by distance, dispersion, and network complexity. By *distance*, we refer to differences in institutions – beliefs, traditions, and rule systems – between project participants. By *dispersion* we acknowledge that project participants are seldom collocated and often distributed across multiple sites. By *network complexity* we recognize that project participants are interconnected through complex webs of formal and informal relationships.

Note that this definition is broader than that employed in the other chapters of this volume, which concentrate attention on *global infrastructure construction projects*. Infrastructure construction projects are a subset of global projects. (We describe the distinctive features of global infrastructure construction projects in a later section of this chapter.) The broader formulation developed in this chapter is applicable to such projects and identifies the general features distinguishing this complex new mode of organizing.

Although global projects can be large enough to have regional, national, and even transnational economic, environmental, and social impacts, scale is not a core part of our definition. A global project may in fact be small, for example, an R&D project with three scientists located in different countries. The purpose of this first chapter is to identify, describe, and situate global projects as a relatively distinctive organizational mode and to review its drivers and risks. Despite the underlying benefits that have led to the proliferation of this mode of organizing, it is beset by real challenges posed by attempting to manage dispersion, distance, and network complexity.

Even though we observe many nuanced differences – in scope, scale, and sector – global projects are now everywhere. And yet, scholarly work to examine the compound effect of low-cost communications, multi-site collaboration, and globally reaching supply chains on the strategy and structure of projects remains thin and fragmented at best. The relevant literatures span several disciplines – economics, international business, sociology, anthropology, and political science. As we attempt to demonstrate, scholars of organizations, project management, and multinational enterprise are well positioned to investigate this new organizational mode and to begin to expand and revise theory to reflect the evolving nature of organizational practice.

The precise origin of the term global project is not known, but the widest usage up to this point in time has perhaps been in the legal profession. Today most top-ranked international law firms have a "Global Projects Group," specializing in the development and financing of energy and infrastructure projects that involve cross-border transactions. International law firms with established global projects practice areas include Allen & Overy, Baker Botts, Baker & McKenzie, Clifford Chance, Coudert Brothers, Linklaters, and Paul Hastings.

However, by employing the term global project, we do not mean to restrict our analysis to a narrow legal perspective; indeed, we actively seek to flesh out a much wider view. Nor do we mean to imply that some projects have evolved to become multi-firm, multi-site, and networked while others have remained strictly domestic, conventional, or traditional. Instead, we want to suggest that the nature of organizing has changed fundamentally for projects of all kinds, and that this significant trend warrants deeper investigation.

The remainder of the chapter is organized around the following set of interrelated research questions:

- What are the distinctive features of global projects? How are all global projects similar; that is, what distinguishes them as a category that can be classified and compared?
- What are the drivers of global projects? Why have global projects emerged as an organizational phenomenon? What motivates efforts to integrate human and physical resources from multiple organizations, sites, geographies, and countries?
- What are the challenges that accompany an organizational system with resources being drawn from a global pool? In particular, how do distance and dispersion impede efforts to generate value?
- What are the strategic implications – for companies and host countries – now that global projects have come to loom large on the organizational landscape? And what new approaches and types of research are needed?

We hope this chapter helps develop new conceptual thinking as well as inform managerial practice at a time when the effects of technological innovation and globalization are generally known and accepted, but also at a time when organizational theory and scholarship have not yet fully adapted their conceptions and methods to accommodate these changes (Walsh, Meyer, and Schoonhoven 2006). Over the next decade, it is expected that these trends will become even more pronounced as rapid innovation continues with smart phone devices, the mobile internet, and social networking tools.

## Theoretical background

Theoretical formulations and empirical studies of organizations, project organizations, and the multinational enterprise all offer considerable insight into the global project phenomenon, and yet, all fall short of illuminating its distinctive features. From the perspective of organization theory, global projects are clearly a new phenomenon. Organization theory has focused on stable organizations undergoing incremental change over sustained periods of time, and has only recently begun to attend to more temporary and flexible modes of organizing (Aldrich and Ruef 2006; Scott and Davis 2007). There are also still very few studies of organizations that cross over multiple national settings (King, Felin, and Whetten 2009). While theoretical conceptualizations and studies of the multinational enterprise do exist (e.g., Dunning 1993; Ghoshal and Westney 1993; Nohria and Goshal 1997), this work has not been centered on the unique challenges of project work, including one-of-a-kind constructions; nor has it examined the fundamental alteration of the business environment caused by multiple firms internationalizing together and forming temporary project networks and permanent multinational business networks. Also, scholars are just beginning to discover the importance and rapid growth of transnational institutional structures (Djelic and Quack 2003; Martin 2005). Finally, whereas theories and studies of project organization have begun to appear (e.g., Stinchcombe and Heimer 1985; Miller and Lessard 2001), they have not directly focused on global or cross-national aspects of organizing. Thus, global projects as a category represent what is shown in Figure 1.1 as a relatively unexplored cell in the contemporary landscape of organizational analysis.

## Four arenas

### *Scholarship on organizations*

Theory and research on organizations originally addressed neither the temporary nor the multicultural aspects of organizing. At the dawn of

**Figure 1.1** Landscape of organizational scholarship

this work in the early twentieth century, the focus was on how to plan, control, and administer the tasks performed by individuals to form a coherent whole. Early work by engineers and social psychologists stressed the rationalization of individual tasks and the control and motivation of individual workers and work groups. Later efforts by sociologists and economists focused on organization structure and the structure of wider systems of organizations (Baum 2002; Scott and Davis 2007; Shenhav 1999). While exceptions to this trajectory have arisen more recently that do address the temporary and the multicultural dimensions of organizing (e.g., Eccles and Crane 1988; House et al. 2004), there have been few investigations that address both of these dimensions at the same time. During the past decade, increasing research attention has been devoted by organization scholars to the construction of temporary systems such as network organizations (e.g., Child 2005; Harrison 1994) but most of these represent new approaches to accomplishing standardized undertakings such as the manufacture of garments or computer chips rather than the creation of one-of-a-kind facilities or customized social change or service projects. There is not yet a coherent body of knowledge for practitioners and scholars to rely on that explores the phenomenon of temporary, global, network-based organizing, despite the fact that all three of these individual areas of scholarship have advanced in recent decades. Perhaps the most promising work for understanding global projects within organization theory has been on patterns of organizing at the field or industry level. "The notion of a *field* connotes the existence of a community of organizations that partakes of a common meaning system and whose participants interact more frequently and fatefully with one another than with actors outside the field" (Scott 1994). The view of global project arrangements that we set out to develop herein is consistent with the field approach. (See also Chapters 2 and 11).

## Scholarship on project management

Early research on project management focused on the emergence within organizations of teams or project groups that relied on more complex lateral rather than hierarchical modes of coordination to manage more complex and uncertain tasks (Galbraith 1973; 1977). An important stream of this work, which was based on a conception of organizations as information-processing systems (March and Simon 1958), was pursued and elaborated by research pursued mostly by scholars in engineering schools. For example, Levitt and colleagues (Jin and Levitt 1996; Levitt et al. 1999) designed computation models to simulate varying levels of information-processing demands and the response of varying structural designs to them. Scholarship was available and growth of the practitioner community was sufficient by the mid-1980s to support the formation of the *Project Management Journal*. Practitioners of project management have defined projects as temporary endeavors undertaken to create unique products or services or related processes, or, more broadly, as organized undertakings, limited in time to achieve specific objectives (NPMT 1985).

While helpful, these definitions and prior studies are insufficient to describe the new organizational order. We must recognize that global projects – by their very nature – assemble individuals, teams, and organizations from multiple socio-cultural systems and/or geographical settings, which creates the need for a new dimension of management expertise. There are not only issues of coordination and management but of governance. Recently, many students of project management have been quick to move into the study of international project management from the perspective of the quantitative increases in the pressures and challenges of project management when carrying out projects in foreign countries (e.g. Voropajev 1998; Richards 1999). For example, the *International Journal of Project Management* has been dedicated to providing scholarship along these lines of analysis ever since the time of the publication of its first issue in 1983. Looking at project management literature, however, a remaining research gap is a lack of attention to the qualitative shift in the anatomy and structure of the projects themselves, which increasingly contain complex stakeholder networks and supply chain linkages touching down in countries and cultures spanning the entire globe.

One of the specialized branches of project management scholarship includes a set of empirical and conceptual studies on large engineering and megaprojects (Morris and Hough 1987; Kharbanda and Pinto 1996; Miller and Lessard 2000, 2001; Williams 2002; Flyvbjerg et al. 2003; Grün 2004). This literature uses terms such as *complex projects*, *major projects*, *giant projects*, and *megaprojects*. Examples include naval bases, transportation systems, Olympic Games, and aircraft development programs. In fact, based on our definition above, we can conclude that this large engineering project literature is mainly about global projects even if not framed as such explicitly. The large engineering project literature incorporates several characteristics not confronted by conventional organizations or projects:

- the involvement of multiple organizations with different, sometimes contradictory, subgoals which introduces the need for coordination;
- changes in the prioritization of project objectives over time;
- changes in the involvement and/or relative influence of varying organizations over time; and
- the impact of wider socio-political environments on projects.

The multiple organizations include engineering firms, contractors, financiers, equity investors, public organizations, regulators, NGOs, and political decision-making bodies. Each collaborates to pursue a joint objective, but each also pursues its own specific objective, which may come into conflict with the wider purpose. According to this literature, the track record of large-engineering and mega-projects is poor, many being abandoned before completion. The low success rate is at least partially a testament to the unique challenges posed by distance, dispersion, and network complexity.

## Scholarship on multinational enterprise

Research on multinational enterprise, which branched off from organization theory, economic theory, and management theory in the early 1970s, addresses the interaction of multicultural and geospatial aspects and organization design. Many studies in the *Journal of International Business Studies*, for example, have looked at the evolution, spread, and organization of the multinational enterprise, the assessment of cultural differences and political risk, and varying entry strategies (Kobrin 1979; Kogut and Singh 1988; Shenkar 2001; Witt and Lewin 2007). These studies have represented the 'eclectic' paradigm of locational advantage (Dunning 1988, 1993), depicting the process of 'internationalization' as one of incremental and adaptive learning in moving across locations until an enterprise is fully "globalized" (Johansson and Vahlne 1977). Global projects are an arena of action in which the assumption (so often posited in mainstream work on the multinational enterprise) that a single firm will fan out beyond its home base and declare dominion over foreign markets, is further weakened. The concept of global projects recognizes that with technological innovations, not only has it become easier for individual firms to outsource work around the planet, but that dozens of firms have done so simultaneously such that the overall milieu of specialized and globally interlinked players has become radically more diverse and complex, altering the composition and dynamic of the business environment itself. Scholarship on the multinational enterprise has relatively little to say about new ways of temporary organizing characterized by more highly fragmented, interdependent, multi-site, multi-firm, collaborative initiatives, stitched together with a combination of contractual, hierarchical, and network-based arrangements.

## The challenge: updating organization theory

In sum, we need to recognize that the forces of globalization have given rise to a relatively novel form of organizing – one that challenges current understanding in organization theory and utilizes project-based approaches in a multinational context. Dubbed the "major story of our lifetime," globalization is a trend that refers to the increased mobility of ideas, goods, services, labor, technology, and capital in terms of velocity and volume of cross-border exchange (Levitt 1983; Sassen 1998; Friedman 2005).[1]

Scholars have recognized that economies and societies are becoming more globally interconnected (World Bank 2005) and that institutions and organizations within and across the boundaries of nation-states have converged in many respects in contrast to a time but a few decades ago (Krücken and Drori 2009; Meyer, et al. 1997; Drori, Meyer, and Hwang 2006; Djelic and Quack 2003).[2] At the same time, scholars recognize that societal and cultural differences remain and that due to closer interactions may actually be increasing in salience (Guillén 2001; Hall and Soskice 2001; Hancké, Rhodes, and Thatcher 2008; Whitley 1999). Recognizing the changes brought about by globalization, scholars of organizations, project management, and international business have all incrementally adapted their theories of organization. And yet, there has been little attention paid to the systemic effects: the unintended – and little understood – consequence of thousands of organizations worldwide "going global" and outsourcing noncore activities during a fairly narrow window in time. Project structures and business environments themselves have become fundamentally altered, with resources and roles disaggregated across boundaries of various kinds.

The organizational landscape of today versus the one of thirty years ago is so different that the changes are more akin to a change in *kind* rather than one of *degree*. Rather than continuing to refer to the era of globalization, it may now make sense to begin to refer to the era of post-globalization, to underscore the point that the business environment has become so consistently multicultural, multi-organizational, multi-tiered, and multi-site that we are witnessing the beginnings of a new organizational order. Global projects are everywhere. This trend has vast implications both for the firms that consistently participate in these interlinked endeavors, and for the design and strategy of projects themselves.

In summary, global projects are a relatively new, and yet already pervasive organizational phenomenon. This mode of organizing is not yet well recognized or accounted for by existing theories of organization, project organization, or the multinational enterprise; nor are the strategic implications understood by the individual firms that have contributed to this collective-level phenomenon. Thus, although widespread in practice, the global project remains inadequately studied or theorized. In this chapter, we endeavor to advance organizational theory in this exciting new direction. Considering the under-theorized nature of this phenomenon, we devote this and the next two chapters of this volume to develop new conceptual ideas and arguments. Subsequent chapters link these ideas to empirical research.

## Toward a theory of global projects

### The emergence of a literature on global projects

The global projects concept has slowly but steadily developed in the organizations, project management, and international business literature over the past decade. Global project-related phenomena have been studied across most sectors of the modern economy, including *software development* (Herbsleb et al. 2000; Carmel and Agarwal 2001), *oil industry* (Solomon 1995), *automotive industry* (Manheim 1993; Hoegl et al. 2004), *pharmaceutical industry* (Mendez 2003), *power industry* (Jonsson et al. 2001), and *construction industry* (Chan and Tse 2003; Mahalingam and Levitt 2007). There have been studies of *global R&D initiatives* (Chiesa 1995), *multi-university collaborations* (Teasley and Wolinsky 2001; Corley, Boardman, and Bozeman 2006; Cummings and Kiesler 2007), *large-scale international science projects* (Hameri 1997; Shore and Cross 2005), and *military command and control initiatives* (Cebrowski 2003).

A number of scholars have employed the term global projects in their writings directly (van Fenema and Kumar 2000; Mahalingam and Levitt 2007; Orr and Scott 2008 [see Chapter 5]) while others have adopted related and parallel terminology. Rubrics and labels applied to this or closely related phenomena include *virtual organizations* (Ajuha and Carley 1999), *distributed work systems* (Hinds and Kiesler 2002), *geographically distributed teams* (Hinds and Mortensen 2005), *geographically dispersed organizations* (Boh et al. 2007), *multi-team projects* (Hoegl, Weinkauf, and Gemuenden 2004), *multi-company collaborative engineering projects* (Kano, Sriram, and Gupta 2003), and *complex multinational projects* (Jonsson et al. 2001).

Several recurring themes occur in these studies:

- challenges of coordination and integration due to distance, dispersion, and interdependence;
- problems of misunderstandings, misjudgments, and conflicts due to differences in values, beliefs, expectations, work practices, conventions, and social, economic, legal, political, and financial institutions;
- benefits of shared identity and history, periodic face-to-face meetings, and other synchronous forms of communication to reduce coordination challenges and conflicts;
- strategic approaches to reduce coordination challenges including standardization of procedures, standardization of module interfaces, work partitioning, and division of responsibilities;
- opportunities for innovation and learning afforded by cross-fertilization of varying traditions and exposure to new ways of thinking and working;
- the utility of examining the wider network of organizations or the structure of the field of organizations.

Much of the literature has a negative slant, emphasizing challenges of dispersion, distance, and network complexity. And yet, multi-site, multi-organization modes of organizing persist; suggesting that benefits can outweigh costs. Elaborating a more optimistic view, military command and control scholars envision a day when information technologies might fully enhance sensemaking, shared-awareness, self-organization, self-synchronization, and orchestration of coalitions for network-centric operations (Alberts and Hayes 2005; Nissen 2006).

## Drivers of global projects

### Self-interested firms "going global"

What explains the rise of global projects? We propose that global projects are the natural consequence of technological innovations that have altered the economics of organizing by reducing inter-organizational coordination costs. Reducing coordination costs has had two profound implications: (1) more specialized forms of organization have arisen with noncore activities being outsourced to more specialist providers and lower cost locations; and (2) multi-site and global collaboration activities have blossomed. As thousands of firms have outsourced noncore activities and have gone global during a relatively short time frame over the past three or four decades, global projects have emerged, somewhat endogenously, as the nexus of inter-organizational cooperation in a global marketplace. Today, many products and services are created and assembled by an interdependent network of highly specialized suppliers, manufacturers, and systems integrators. While global projects were not consciously designed, they have emerged as the new organizational reality across many sectors – aerospace, industrial systems, software, development, and peace-keeping – where cross-functional teams collaborate on large initiatives.

The rationale for individual firms to "go global" is multidimensional (see Ghemawat 2007; Dunning 1988). Reasons for internationalizing include:

- developing new resources – opening up undeveloped markets and untapped natural resource supplies; for example, oil and gas exploration projects in Angola have been made possible with geological, drilling, and subsurface expertise from international players;
- global arbitrage – exploiting low cost resources; for example, inexpensive land, abundant and low cost energy, cheap and dependable

labor, low-interest rate financing, manufacturing capacity, shipping capacity, and engineering capacity are examples of factors of production that are priced at differential rates worldwide;

- offering specialized products – aggregating demand for unusually rare or precious products or services; for example, Kone Elevators offers a highly specialized product for which its investments in R&D and manufacturing capacity would not have been justified had it only been focused on serving the domestic market in Finland;
- saving time – supporting continuous workflow across time zones; for example, Arup, Fluor Sun Micro Systems, and other engineering firms use "24 hour around the world engineering" to compress design cycle times with offices spaced at eight-hour intervals in cities like Manila, London, and Palo Alto;
- circumventing regulation – avoiding restrictive rules and legal codes; for example, in Norway, strict labor law discourages lay-offs, and thus several Norwegian firms are known to hire temporary staff outside of Norway as a way to avoid taking on fixed costs in research and development programs;
- meeting labor imbalances – supplying workers to mega-projects; for example, large-scale development efforts underway in the United Arab Emirates would never have been possible were it not for thousands of expatriate designers, engineers, and superintendents, and millions of Chinese, Indian, Pakistani, and Filipino construction workers, who seized upon the opportunity to live abroad and earn a higher expatriate salary;
- testing new markets – exploring emerging opportunities in international markets – companies like Microsoft have situated research and development projects in China as a way to learn about the local players, culture, and business environment with an eye towards eventually expanding into software sales and other lines of business.

Thus, new technologies have enabled individual firms to internationalize for many reasons as noted above, and as they have done, so global projects have arisen as a field-level phenomenon.

## Rationalized modes of organizing

Another prerequisite for the emergence of global projects has been the rationalization of organization forms through the latter half of the twentieth century. In recent decades social processes have compelled all organizations, including firms, governments, and NGOs, to become more rationalized – formally organized as instrumental systems linking systematic means to ends. Organizations have become more similar in form and in operating logics – partly as a result of competitive pressures, partly in response to cultural imperatives regarding the "appropriate way to organize." In modern societies, the cultural imperative of organizing the pursuit of goals in a rationalized manner is strongly entrenched. (DiMaggio and Powell 1983; Dobbin 1994; Meyer and Rowan 1977; Scott 2004). The rationalization and standardization of organizational forms is another factor that has worked to reduce coordination costs among organizations. As technological advances enabled global communication, new kinds of project forms were created by organizational and institutional entrepreneurs who were familiar with the earlier models (Aldrich 2005; Hardy and Maguire 2008). Once a handful of models had developed, other firms were quick to copy and learn from these pioneers. Successful modes of organizations diffuse quickly through an organizational field, as described below and in Chapter 2.

In sum, a global project has characteristics of a federated enterprise of actors, each one seeking advantages of assembling resources and functions across socio-cultural, geographic, and temporal settings, while at the same time working together to achieve a common objective – whether it be building a metro, providing humanitarian aid, or launching a space mission. Global projects have arisen in response to a combination of technological/economic and cultural forces, in response to new conditions and as rationalized modes of organizing have been created and widely diffused.

## Global projects confront new risks

Although internationalization offers the prospect of promising gains, it also introduces a new set of risks due to the increased coordination and institutional costs associated with these arrangements. The irony is that, as more organizations have sought to internationalize and outsource, project networks have become more diverse and complex, and fundamentally new kinds of systemic risks have been introduced.

## Coordination costs

Coordination is defined as the "synchronization of actions" (Wittenbaum, Vaughan, and Stasser 1998) and the "the linking together of resources and processes to achieve desired outcomes" (Jennings 1994: 53). Coordination costs include time and resources spent in integrative activities that involve communicating, translating, measuring, specifying, reviewing, testing, and monitoring. In global projects, these types of costs are increased because of the greater diversity encountered and the wider distances covered. In a project network, the overall level of coordination and coordination costs have historically been driven by such factors as complexity, scale, uncertainty, interdependence, and time pressure. We discuss these causal factors briefly below as a basis for understanding where coordination costs come from and how they are amplified in the face of distance, dispersion, and network complexity.

## Complexity and scale

The fundamental source of coordination in project-based work is the product itself – the office building, science experiment, or space mission as it may happen to be. In an important sense, the structural blueprint for these systems is object- rather than person- or organization-centered (Knorr-Cetina 1999). As the product involves more and/or different elements, it becomes more complex. Complexity is produced by a large number of parts that interact in a non-simple way (Simon 1969). Complex products are not necessarily vague or unpredictable, but the vast number and variety of elements and relationships is not easily coordinated (Campbell 1988). Project administrators facing complexity must apply appropriate expertise and skills to simplify, restructure, and render these problems more manageable (Baccarini 1996; Galbraith 1977). The typical organizational response to complexity is differentiation, subdividing the work into simpler, more tractable components. But, the greater the complexity of a project in terms of component parts, pieces of software code, or touch points with the natural environment – and, hence, the greater the organization's structural differentiation – the greater the need for coordination of interfaces and interrelationships. Complexity and scale are closely related for obvious reasons – as a project becomes larger it tends also to become more complex in terms of number of parts and relationships (Blau 1970; Galbraith 1973).

## Interdependence

Several varieties of interdependence have been defined in organization research, including workflow/task interdependence (Thompson 1967; Van de Ven, Delbecq, and Koening 1976), outcome interdependence (Wageman 1995), goal interdependence (Tjosvold, Andrews, and Struthers 1991), and resource interdependence (Thibaut and Kelley 1969; Pfeffer and Salanick 1978; Tjosvold et al. 2001). Generally speaking, the concept of interdependence describes the situation where individuals, departments, and, increasingly, organizations must coordinate with one another to achieve success. For example, on complex construction projects specialized technicians and craftsmen must coordinate together to assemble hundreds of subcomponent parts in the proper arrangement in physical space and time. If the design of one component changes or if the components do not fit together within the appropriate tolerance of error, one or more of the interdependent components must be modified and responsible parties must communicate and adjust with one another. It is realistic to expect that the greater the level of interdependence, the higher will be the coordination costs on a project.

## Uncertainty

According to Stinchcombe and Heimer (1985), the primary challenge of project administration is to manage *uncertainty,* the two sources of which are the environment and technology. They argue that "the central difference between project administration and the administration of repetitive processes is the role of uncertainty about what to do in projects, which must be resolved by decisions." Traditional organization theory is of little use in project administration because projects have neither a stable repetitive process nor an organization chart with stable positions and authority relations, but more recent theorizing has begun to address these issues (Nohria and Eccles 1992; Powell 1990; Child 2005). Stinchcombe and Heimer observe that the primary practical tool of project administration is the PERT diagram which drives what they call an "activities approach to organization."

Activities to resolve uncertainty include: collecting information, making decisions and plans, and then measuring and comparing the outcome to the plan. Under conditions of strong uncertainty, ambiguity, and change, approaches such as experimentation, trying multiple solutions simultaneously, sensemaking, and learning become just as important as planning and executing (March 1991; Weick 1995; Meyer, Loch, and Pinch 2002; Pinch, Loch, and Meyer 2002). Resolving uncertainty has obvious implications for the need for coordination. Uncertain events in one part of a project can trigger chain reactions of unanticipated, interconnected events that further amplify coordination costs.

## Time pressure

On top of complexity, interdependence, and uncertainty, project administrators are faced with the management of workflow in the face of schedule constraints. When facing tight deadlines, project administrators may seek to compress design and implementation schedules by overlapping sequential activities. However, gains from overlapping tasks must be evaluated against sometimes exponential increases in coordination and rework that are caused by greater reciprocal interdependencies, information sharing, and error frequencies (Jin and Levitt 1996; Loch and Terwiesch 1998). Generally speaking, the more truncated the schedule and the more managers perform interdependent tasks concurrently, the greater the total costs of overall coordination.

## Dispersion and distance

When cross-functional teams work in global structures multiple forms of distance impede attempts to communicate and coordinate between the "virtual archipelago" of partners and sites (Carmel and Agarwal 2001). Cross-site work introduces delay (Herbsleb et al. 2000). Travel and shipping costs are not insignificant, especially in an environment of rising energy prices. Time-zone differences disrupt work–life balance and upset sleep schedules, and make it difficult for a team to get into a "deep rhythm." Communication at a distance by email and telephone masks underlying local contextual conditions and eliminates informal "corridor talk" and "coffee breaks" that seem to be crucial for group coordination (Damian and Zowghi 2002).

Challenges do not end with physical distance. What has been termed "cultural distance" or "psychic distance" or "institutional distance" also poses a special set of challenges. These are sufficiently complex and significant as to deserve separate treatment. For clarity, we use the terms "institutional differences" and "institutional distance" because we feel that these represent the broadest constructs (see also, Chapters 2, 4, 5, 6, and 7).

## Institutional differences

Project participants from various socio-cultural backgrounds inevitably inhabit different "thought worlds" that create frictions even when team members are co-located. A number of scholars have attempted to develop conceptual frameworks to categorize various dimensions of cultural and institutional environments that condition how individuals think, act, and interact in different countries and world regions (Hofstede 1984; 1991; Trompenaars 1993; Ghemawat 2001; Xu and Shenkar 2002; House 2004; Ionascu, Meyer, and Erstin 2004; see also Chapter 9), and in Chapter 2 of this volume, we introduce our own schema. Each of these frameworks represents an effort to distill complex differences in human-constructed institutions shaping cognitive processes that enable, guide, and constrain human behavior into a simplified typology. The following list suggests the variety and complexity of dimensions underlying institutional differences:

- cognition and language – differences in meanings associated with terms, phrases, categories, concepts; differences in systems of reading, writing, speaking, and listening (Brannen 2004);
- emotional patterns – differences in emotions invoked by different situations (Gordon 1990); degree to which group decisions are driven by cognitive calculation versus emotion (Thagard and Kroon 2006);
- space-time orientation – differences in orientation towards sequential versus parallel usage of time; differences in need for space and territoriality (Hall 1966; 1976; Trompenaars 1993);
- belief systems – differences in basic beliefs about ethics, morality, purpose, good, evil; differences in conceptions of individual, group,

authority, obligation, rights (Hofstede 1991; Geertz 1983; see also, Chapter 9);

- values and preferences – differences in preference for affiliation, power, wealth, equality, harmony; differences in values related to aesthetics, style, and hygiene (Hofstede 1984; 1991; Trompenaars 1993; Hall 1976; Kluckhohn and Strodtbeck 1961);
- leadership styles – differences in acceptable styles of leadership – i.e. authoritarian, consensual, collegial (House et al. 2004);
- technological standards – differences in standards for units of measurement, currency denomination, voltage capacity, and wireless authentication (Bijker, Hughes, and Pinch 1987; Brunsson and Jacobsson 2000; Tate 2001);
- work practices and protocols – differences in filing a timecard, expensing a receipt, performing an inspection, conducting a performance evaluation (Orr and Scott 2008 [Chapter 5];
- financing, accounting, and corporate governance standards – differences in principles of audit, valuation, mark-to-market, transparency; differences in cash versus accrual accounting, treatment of options, nonfinancial reporting (Clark and Wójcik 2007);
- organization structures – differences in organization size, managerial span of control, depth of hierarchy, horizontal interaction, unity of chain of command (Hall and Soskice 2001; Whitley 1992b);
- personal vs. impersonal enforcement of agreements – differences in whether agreements are enforced through reputational or legal mechanisms (is it safe to do business with complete strangers?) (North 1990; Greif 1994; MacMillan, Johnson, and Woodruff 2002);
- industry organization – differences in how functions are organized across public and private sectors and how they interact; differences in authority of regulatory agencies; differences in fragmentation of the market into specialist firms versus large conglomerates (Hall and Soskice 2001; Whitley 1999);
- professional roles – differences in the role of an architect, quantity surveyor, professor across societies; differences in the presence or absence of roles in society (see Chapter 4);
- legal, regulatory, and policy environment – differences in existence of laws and enforcement related to health, safety, worker rights, discrimination, environment, intellectual property, etc. (Hall and Soskice 2001; Henisz 2000; Oxley 1999; see also Chapters 7 and 9).

Each of the elements in the framework, such as belief systems, could be further unpacked into dozens of more specific sub-dimensions. Although categorization schemes are helpful as analytic aids, they have limitations. The rich and nuanced differences between socio-cultural systems are innumerable and evade being fully captured by abstract categorizations. Key groups and institutions that exist in one culture may not be present in another, making elements and entire systems incommensurate and difficult if not impossible to compare. Moreover, even when multiple abstract frameworks are combined, as in the broad framework described in Chapter 2, there will still be large gaps and many points of disagreement among those familiar with specific cultures. Nevertheless, most authors agree that mental models of individuals within a culture tend to mirror the surrounding matrix of beliefs, traditions, and rules in the broader human-constructed environment, and thus when individuals across cultures interact, misalignments, frictions, and misunderstandings will occur (Zaheer 1995; Petersen and Pedersen 2002; Evans 2004; Nachum and Zaheer 2005; Orr and Scott 2008 [Chapter 5], and, hence, useful predictions can be made regarding problems likely to be encountered.

Institutional differences are a poorly understood concept, but relate both to the differences in patterns of interaction between groups, and also to differences in individual-level knowledge and assumptions about the existence, salience, and appropriateness of various institutions across groups. Institutional differences lead to complex problems in the context of cross-border collaborative ventures. Oftentimes it is the subtlest of differences that leads to the most vexing of challenges (O'Grady and Lane 1996). For example, there are persistent problems with recognizing, interpreting, and reconciling:

- contextual cues and symbols – can conventions attached to gestures, body language, and meaning-laden cues in the broader environment be interpreted?
- influential groups – can influential social, political, and economic organizations be mapped? (See Chapter 10.) Can rules, traditions, and jurisdictions of enforcement be deciphered for these different organizations? (Cummings and Doh 2000)
- differences in grammar and syntax – is it possible to understand the multiple ways in which words are used and put together to communicate meaning in varying cultures? Can the structure of human

utterances and the ordering of nouns, verbs, and adjectives into sentences be understood?

- subtle meanings – can the intended meaning associated with certain words, characters, and phonetic sounds that carry multiple meanings be accurately communicated? Do understatement, sarcasm, and compliment translate across cultural systems?
- unconscious expectations – are there taken-for-granted assumptions and expectations that lie beneath the surface of interactions? Are they observable?
- conflicting beliefs – are points of deep moral, ethical, or religious belief fundamentally misaligned across cultures? Do beliefs – and civilizations – clash (Huntington 1996)? Is it possible to reach consensus, ever?
- cultural contradictions – do complex contradictions exist between what is illegal and what is common practice, such as is often the case with corruption and lobbying (Rose-Ackerman 1999; Doig and Theobald 2000)?

Frictions come in the form of misjudgments, miscommunications, and misunderstandings that are largely accidental, and that can be surprising even for the most seasoned project executives, and that can have costly consequences (see Chapter 5). When points of view are strongly at odds, more overt tensions, disagreements, and conflicts can occur. Working across differences in "thought worlds" can ultimately lead to a wide range of unexpected monetary and time costs and reputational and relational frictions that silently erode globalization's value proposition. These pervasive hidden costs have been under-emphasized or even ignored by most proponents of globalization (e.g., Friedman 2005).

Most of the differences in mental models between participants in a project network are latent – that is, they are not activated and do not cause problems (Shenkar, Luo, Yeheskel 2008). Institutional differences become particularly problematic when project participants are required to communicate and coordinate intensely – i.e. sharing resources, resolving interdependencies, defining interfaces, integrating subsystems, and diagnosing errors – or when misunderstandings in simple everyday communications have big downstream effects. Subtle differences in language, individual, and organizational expectations, and work practices can lead to misunderstandings that become further compounded and difficult to resolve due to time pressure and basic misalignments in emotional conditioning. If mistrust takes root, relationships can quickly spiral into unproductive cycles of suspicion, blame, and conflict.

In summary, it is a well-known fact that coordination costs increase as projects involve greater scale, complexity, uncertainty, interdependence, time-pressure, and physical distance. This assertion is noncontroversial; many generations of projects have been constrained by these factors. What is new is that technological advances and cultural forces producing higher levels of similarity among organizations during the past three decades have resulted in projects becoming consistently more multicultural, multi-organization, multi-site, and multi-tiered (from a supply chain standpoint). From an evolutionary standpoint, the proliferation of global projects suggests that on the margin the production cost savings of these new organizational arrangements have been sufficient to offset the growth in coordination costs. Nonetheless the new frictions of distance, dispersion, and network complexity are not insignificant, and represent a new layer of costs that have never been so severe on conventional projects. Moreover, the new institutional costs associated with differences in rules, assumptions, and beliefs further complicate matters. We expect that as the number of organizations, contracts, legal systems, external stakeholders, regulatory environments, tax codes, office locations, time zones, cultures, leadership styles, and languages increase, then so do the coordination and institutional costs of administering global projects – perhaps exponentially – as illustrated in Figure 1.2.

In our research over the past decade, we have labeled this new layer of coordination costs due to differences in thought worlds "institutional costs." We suggest that these costs are a form of transaction cost, arising not from the classic problems of measuring and enforcing agreements (North 1990) or from overcoming opportunism (Williamson 1979), but from basic problems of misunderstandings when institutions are misaligned (see Chapters 2, 4, and 5). It is not yet known exactly how this new class of transaction costs interacts with more conventional kinds of coordination costs associated with traditional project work.

Our early research building on more than a decade of simulation experiments conducted with the Virtual Design Team (VDT) simulation model (Levitt et al. 1999; Jin and Levitt 1996; Carroll, Burton,

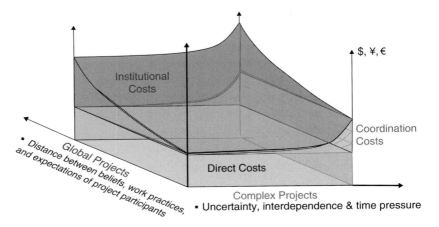

**Figure 1.2** Coordination and institutional costs in global projects

and Levitt 2004) suggests that interaction effects are significant and nonlinear. In the VDT modeling environment, as we increase task complexity, uncertainty, interdependence, and time pressure, there is an exponential increase in coordination work that exceeds the sum of the coordination work caused by increasing each of the variables individually, a result which can overwhelm the organization's information processing capacity. Based on these results, we have reason to believe that organizations involved in global projects face an ever-increasing compounding of coordination costs due to the added coordination complexity of multiple dimensions of distance, dispersion, network complexity, and institutional differences that cause institutional costs (see Figure 1.2). Research on multi-organization project teams in the Intelligent System Engineering Laboratory at MIT provides confirmatory evidence: with a linear increase in the number of organizations and the distance between organizations in the project, there is an exponential rise in coordination costs (Kano, Sriram, and Gupta 2003: Figure 6).

## Studying global projects: a research agenda

The global project perspective calls for new concepts, terminology, strategic thinking, management tools, risk management approaches, and success metrics. We begin to consider how to approach some of these challenges below.

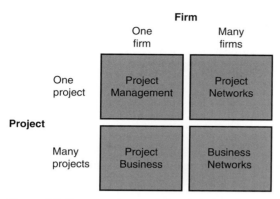

**Figure 1.3** Four quadrants of the global projects research agenda

In particular, we discuss the rise of firms that specialize in *project business*, and that interact with other firms in temporary *project networks* and *permanent business* networks in the context of a larger global project undertaking. Together these concepts underpin an exciting new set of research areas that fall under the broader global project umbrella (see Figure 1.3).

We have previously discussed the emergence of research on project management during the mid-twentieth century as requiring new methods for coordinating highly interdependent tasks within organizations. Here we describe several prominent conceptual distinctions that have been employed to examine these systems of coordination.

## Varieties of global projects

### Project business

The concept of project business recognizes that many organizations engage in projects on a recurring basis for their business purposes (Artto and Wikström 2005; Whitley 2006). Instead of entering a country and setting up a permanent presence, as described in much of the international business literature, many engineering consultants, systems suppliers, and contractors follow globally distributed airport, port, and metro projects as their ongoing business strategy. Project supplier firms such as Alcatel, ABB, Kone, Mitsubishi, and Svendala may engage in several sequential or parallel global projects with different delivery scopes (Cova et al. 2002): deliveries of parts, sub-projects, packaged complete subsystems, and turnkey deliveries of complete final products with tested and assured functionalities. From this viewpoint, the firm's portfolio of delivery projects is at the core of the analysis (Artto et al. 1998).

## Project networks

The concept of project networks recognizes that constellations of international firms tracking serious business development opportunities move together, almost in unison from country to country on a "hit-and-run" basis looking for the greatest risk-adjusted returns. It is increasingly common for public sector agencies soliciting bids for the design, finance, construction, operations, and maintenance of major public infrastructure systems to list "international experience" as one of the criteria for the selection of the winning consortia. As a consequence, oftentimes the largest international players can be found partnering together – and doing so repeatedly as they travel throughout the world seeking opportunities for business. Market participants are not alone in organizing in cross-border networks; alliances among like-minded government agencies, departments within multilateral institutions, international nongovernmental organizations (INGOs), and export credit agencies are widely distributed.

## Business networks

The concept of business networks calls attention to the fact that even though firms enter and exit projects on a "hit-and-run" basis, often it is the same players working alongside one another in a more permanent constellation. Despite the word "business" in this term, the business network may include nonbusiness actors as well. For example, a major oil developer initiating a new oil exploration project in a foreign country brings not only a database of hundreds of international vendors and suppliers but also, increasingly, partnerships with operational INGOs and international governments who handle capacity-building, healthcare, and institution-building functions. Participation in the short-term project network can be a means for actors to reshape their position in the underlying permanent business network. Business networks may also be useful in overcoming liabilities of foreignness, reducing costs of market entry, and buffering political risk. For example, by entering into an inhospitable country on the coattails of a major oil company, smaller firms can utilize temporary office trailers, electricity, and customs-expediting procedures set up by the lead oil firm.

Once we turn our attention to "field" level phenomenon (see Chapter 2) – project and business networks – research is generally scarce. For example, little is known about collective-level interactions of entire fields of "global players" with fields of "local players." For example, in smaller countries such as Iceland and Qatar, large-scale aluminum and gas developments have recently eclipsed national GDP and expatriate workers exceed the national population. The impact of these developments on broader societal change are dramatic and unprecedented, as international values and practices permeate and challenge local beliefs and ways of life (see MIGA, 2006).

Interesting strategic questions reside in the dynamic interplay between the short-term project network and the more permanent business network. Actors cannot always be expected to behave "rationally" within the purposes of the project at hand when there are longer-term reputational effects and contradictory and hidden agendas among actors within the business network.

Our subject, global projects, stresses the additional complexity entailed in moving from one project to many, and from one firm to many, and from single business interactions to repeated games in the business network. The complexity of the current scene is posed by the recent growth of project networks and business networks.

## Global project analysis

For executives to more fully comprehend the complex, dispersed, interdependent systems of actors within which their organizations are now embedded, it will be necessary that they map out and analyze global project networks more explicitly. To obtain this type of information, executives need at their disposal analysts with a new set of skills and tools. Building computer-based methods to model the topology of global project networks at different scales would be one productive direction of future research. The conceptions and tools that dominate organizational practice today, such as *organization charts* based on reporting relationships within the hierarchy, are no longer sufficient in a globally networked world, driven more by a focus on a common object or knowledge networks and less by authority relations. Organizational boundaries have become increasingly weak, perforated, and interdependent. Many of the relationships in a global project constellation are not based on employment contracts and formal hierarchy, but instead on inter-organizational collaborations, subcontract relationships, supply chain relationships, joint ventures, and other interpersonal connections.

New modeling tools must reflect not only formal organization and networks within the hierarchy, but also various external partners who provide information and resources, perhaps tracked in terms of financial and/or information flows (see Chapter 10). As these less formally constituted networks can be very large, an ability to "zoom-in" and "zoom-out" to show the network at different scales would be crucial. In an effort to accelerate research in this direction, we propose a skeletal modeling framework in Appendix 1 to this chapter, built around the core concepts of actor–work nodes, relationships, interdependence, distance, complexity, and vulnerability. This skeletal approach recognizes that failure of the global project can occur either if a task carried out by an individual actor is unsuccessful due to uncertainty, complexity, or time pressure, or if the relationship between two actors is compromised due to errors and conflicts that originate because of institutional distance. We propose that the product of interdependence and distance can be one useful proxy for institutional costs between nodes in the project network. Additional layers of detail overlaid on such a model could reflect creditworthiness, balance sheet strength, and market share of participants in the network, which would be useful to understand the vulnerability of the various nodes. Calibration would require further empirical work.

Efforts to formalize the representation of global project constellations at a single point in time should lay the footwork for understanding complex supply chain linkages and inherent vulnerabilities and for developing more dynamic models to visualize network evolution over successive project stages. Organizations equipped with futuristic network topology and change-mapping tools will be better equipped to understand the systemic risks of participating in a dispersed and interdependent system over distance. Analysts who are taught to think about mapping the project network will have a greater awareness of systemic level risks.

## Success metrics for global projects

Project managers emphasize success in terms of "project outputs": delivery on-time, on-budget, and on-specification. Business executives track "strategic outcome" metrics such as gross margin, net profit, and return on equity. All of these metrics continue to have their place, but new metrics are needed for organizations in the permanent project business. These may include:

- *Collaborative advantage* – Is the firm making the most of global strategic partnerships to deliver innovative products and services at superior quality and low cost in the most exciting markets?
- *Constellation quality* – Who are the top strategic partners of the organization? How do these players rank within their industries? How global are their businesses?
- *Counterparty exposure* – What is the organization's exposure to counterparties in the network?

Making a diagnosis of the overall network of players that come together for a global project is another area where new metrics are needed. We propose several candidates:

- *Network integration* – To what extent are all of the providers of major inputs to the global project effectively synchronized? Does the membership of mailing lists and web-based groups match the need for integration of components, systems, and services?
- *Network distance* – What is the average level of physical and institutional distance across all of the significant relationships in the network? How does this compare to other projects?
- *Network experience* – What is the average level of prior experience of major actors in the network with one another? with similarly scaled networks? with similarly diverse, dispersed, and complex networks?
- *Network vulnerability* – To what extent do various nodes and relationships within the network face risk of failure? Can this be quantified? Are sufficient redundancies built in?

## Distinctive characteristics of global infrastructure projects

The remainder of this volume is dedicated to a special class of global projects – infrastructure construction projects to develop transportation, energy, social, communications, and water infrastructure. There are a number of attributes associated with this class of projects that make it rather unique within the wider landscape of global projects. As a preface to the remainder of the volume, we describe some of these unique characteristics as follows:

- *Infrequent undertakings involving global and local participants* – For the most part, large-scale transportation, energy, and social change projects are undertaken on an infrequent basis. A large metro in a downtown area is a once-in-a-century activity for local government officials, INGOs, and business firms. Locals tend to defer to the judgment, experience, and scale of specialist consultants, developers, and equipment providers for the planning and execution of these initiatives. The effect is that whenever a major project is announced, a network of global players will descend into the local planning and political arena (see Chapter 2). A relatively small set of firms currently exist that roam the world on a "hit-and-run" basis with executives traveling from project-to-project who have deep comparative advantages with the technologies, business processes, and human resources to deliver large-scale infrastructure in the different sectors. With globalization, this trend has been reinforced, and this cluster of globe-trotting firms has developed what might be described as an "international culture" and "international protocols"; and they tend to get on fairly well together. There are recurring business relationships between these firms from projects undertaken together in many different parts of the world. Personnel often move from one of these firms to another. However, complex relational dynamics tend to arise between the field of "outsiders" and the cast of "locals" in terms of who has superior knowledge, who has long-term liability, and how much tension and co-adaptation there is at the edges of this interface.
- *Complex interfaces* – In addition to the "global-vs.-local" interface, the wider network of actors involved in a global project also involves many complex public-to-private and cross-functional interfaces. The public sector tends to have a logic that is informed by

concepts such as accountability, transparency, and due process. The private sector tends to be more oriented towards efficiency, innovation, and the achievement of goals. Tensions often emerge (see Chapter 4). Cross-functional interfaces also invoke salient differences. Professionals from engineering and construction tend to have different priorities than professionals in finance and law, and so on. Across different organizational interfaces and professional boundaries there are differences in language, mindset, and work practices, rule systems, and metrics of success. These often subtle differences, which we describe throughout this volume as *institutional differences*, can lead to tensions, frictions, and conflicts, which are a common challenge for the participants in most, if not all, global projects. Our research shows that the potential for conflict is exacerbated when there are substantial differences in how the professions are practiced. For example, the roles, responsibilities, and work hours of an architect or an electrician in France vs. the US differ considerably.

- *High levels of local embeddedness* – A third recurring feature of global projects, is that they involve high numbers of contact points between project participants and the local community, much more so than other standard business activities. For example, a large metro running through the downtown core of a city is going to bring project participants into contact with dozens of local residents, commuters, businesses, government agencies, NGOs, slum dwellers, and the like. The federated enterprise of specialized firms tasked with delivering a metro consists of a wide range of consultants, general contractors, subcontractors, and technical systems providers – many of them "outsiders", as noted above. Each of these players, depending on the nature and size of their assignment, will have a different number of financial and informal relationships with the local field of players and exposure to the local culture and institutional arrangements. As we will show in Chapter 6, a general contractor can have upwards of 3,000 local relationships. In contrast, an elevator installer probably has fewer than 50 local relationships. Activities such as buying land, hiring local labor, importing goods through customs, and seeking permits are deeply intertwined with local institutional arrangements. The high levels of embeddedness faced by outsiders, who may come to a project with technical superiority, creates a large potential for cultural and institutional frictions.

- *Significant social and political complexity* – On top of the issues with complex interfaces, institutional differences, and high levels of local embeddedness, most large-scale infrastructure projects are situated in urban or semi-urban areas and tend to have considerable social, environmental, and distributive impacts. The potential for social and political conflict is enormous and difficult to predict. A toll-road project may have impacts on endangered species, local waterways, and native burial grounds. Resettlement of thousands of community members can be invoked by an order of eminent domain to assemble land for a new airport. A water project may divert agricultural water to residential dwellings. A high-speed rail project may cause noise, dust, and vibrations that reduce property values for those living next to the right-of-way but improved property values for those who hold land near the stations. Some stakeholders will be winners and others will be losers; some will be advocates and others will be opponents. Almost by definition, large infrastructure projects invoke vested interests, heated emotions, political tensions, lawsuits, and media wars. This social and political complexity adds yet another challenge to management (see Chapter 3).
- *Irreversibility due to physical nature of constructions* – Most large infrastructure projects are more or less irreversible due to the physical nature of the excavations and structures that are erected. As such, decisions and their effects are consequential, and stress levels can be quite high on days when dynamite is exploding, concrete is being poured, and steel beams are being hoisted. This irreversibility further exacerbates relational dynamics. A somewhat different but related aspect on this theme is that simple misjudgments and miscommunications due to language differences, communication patterns (i.e., styles of nodding the head or motions of waving the arm), or work practices (i.e. familiarity with wearing steel-toed safety boots) on a construction site can translate into catastrophic accidents and serious injury and death. As such, institutional differences are not simply an inconvenience, or a deterrent to effective work habits and communications, but a serious latent liability. Many global infrastructure projects today involve participants from twenty, thirty, or even more countries, cultures, and languages,

and it is a wonder that an even greater number of serious and costly glitches do not result.

- *Close attention to budget and schedule* – Most large infrastructure projects are planned and managed against the metrics of budget, schedule, and technical performance specifications. As such, it is relatively straightforward to measure the impact of relational frictions and to pinpoint situations in the project where expectations between parties have proven incompatible and unanticipated delays have been created. This makes it possible to assign a dollar value on the "transaction costs" that arise from institutional differences and relational misalignments. From a research standpoint, this makes global infrastructure projects a promising arena for the empirical measurement of the costs of cross-institutional differences and misalignments. Several of the chapters of this volume are devoted to this task. At the same time, it is essential that we recognize that some aspects of life that individuals and communities value are not readily reduced to economic metrics.

## Conclusion

### Contribution and limitations

This chapter has addressed four general themes. First, we emphasize that global project arrangements have become pervasive in the twenty-first century driven largely by simultaneous organization-level decisions to "go global" and to "outsource" work by thousands of organizations. We have argued that these developments were driven by both technological and institutional forces. Second, we have suggested that these new forms confront systemic risks of dispersion, distance, and network complexity. Third, we have proposed new conceptual approaches for the analysis and management of globally networked initiatives. Finally, we have discussed the distinctive characteristics of infrastructure construction projects, as a relatively unique class of global projects, and as a preface to the remainder of this volume.

An inherent challenge in our conceptual approach is that we are working at a level of analysis that is much broader than traditional studies in transaction cost and organizational analysis, which typically focuses on two-party dyads and single hierarchies. Future researchers will need to find new ways of representing multi-organizational

structures with analytic computer models that permit scaling to varying levels of detail. Nevertheless, we believe that modern day evolution of organizational practice necessitates that scholars develop
multidisciplinary and multi-level approaches to understand the proliferation of activity at the network and field levels.

## Areas for future research

The global project phenomenon is pervasive, disruptive, and complex.
It has all of the hallmarks of a major research arena calling for further
conceptual and empirical study. In addition to the topics noted in the
discussion above, additional promising areas for a long-term research
agenda under the general rubric of global projects research include:

- *Structural variations* – To what extent do global projects vary in
  scale and inter-organization topology across sectors? Is it possible to
  identify structural typologies that recur on a more frequent basis?
  How many actors, supply chain tiers, teams, and sites are involved?
  What does the network look like? Who within the network drives
  decision making with respect to overall structure of nodes and
  linkages in the network?
- *Project strategy* – What are the strategic management implications
  of global project arrangements for various classes of actors who
  may be involved – public sector agencies; INGOs; decision-making
  bodies; contractors; investors; financiers? What is the strategy for
  the overall global project endeavor given the diverse composition of
  actors in the network?
- *Leadership* – What makes for an effective leader within the context
  of a global project network? How do leaders create shared vision
  and common purpose across multiple organizations that may have
  contradictory project and business objectives? When leaders lack
  formal authority that exists in the hierarchy, what are the alternative bases of influence?
- *Teams* – What is the definition of a team in the twenty-first century?
  How do the dynamics of fully co-located teams differ from those of
  distributed, semi-permanent teams? What are the ingredients for
  high performance teams in complex, networked environments?
- *Risk management* – How does physical and institutional distance
  translate into frictions, errors, conflicts, and costs across linkages of

the network? How do time pressure, interdependence, and actor–work attributes further amplify these problems? How are risks managed in networks and through networks? Can network vulnerability be assessed and measured?

- *Collaborative advantage* – Which organizations in practice have achieved the greatest benefit of taking a network-centric approach to business and project management? What are the lessons learned from these cases?
- *Constellation management* – Which organizations in practice are the epicenters of the most powerful constellations of business partnerships? Who are the other constellation members?
- *Trust and shared project culture* – When global project participants lack prior shared experience and come together from multiple languages and cultural backgrounds, what approaches can be taken to engender trust and shared culture? How can conflicting social representations be framed in ways to create bridges to new group identities, symbols, and collective meanings specific to the project and the group of people? How long does this process take? How can it be accelerated?

Our long-term research objective is to allow the design of global projects to become more intentional and less a phenomenon of improvisation and reliance on "dumb luck." We hope to create a knowledge base that will enable us to train a new cadre of managers who are conceptually equipped to manage systemic risks and enhance performance of these complex multi-organizational systems.

Below is a basic modeling framework to provide a starting point for future researchers to map and assess risks in global project networks.

- *Level of analysis:* The global project constellation, including the full set of formally and informally connected actors contributing to the initiative – i.e., launching the space shuttle, building the high-speed rail system, or running the peace-keeping mission.
- *Actor–work nodes:* Organizations, teams, or individuals engaged in goal-oriented tasks.
- *Actor–work node attributes:* For simplicity, nodes of the network have both actor and work attributes:
  - actor competency (index of task experience, skill level, slack resources);
  - task difficulty (index of task novelty, task complexity, uncertainty, time pressure);
  - actor solvency (creditworthiness, balance sheet, market share).
- *Relationships:* Actors are connected by ties that designate information, financial, or other resource flows.
- *Relationship attributes:* Relationships between actors have two primary attributes:
  - interdependence (measuring organization dependencies, schedule dependencies, product dependencies);
  - distance (measuring multiple dimensions of distance).
- *Model outputs:*
  - Node level

  Node vulnerability = actor competency − task difficulty

  - Relationship level

  Relationship vulnerability = interdependence × distance

- Cluster level

> Cluster vulnerability = if statement: if three or more adjacent actor-work nodes and relationships have medium to high vulnerability, then network cluster is vulnerable

- Network level

> Network complexity = number of nodes, number of relationships
>
> Average node vulnerability = weighted average of vulnerability of individual nodes
>
> Average relationship vulnerability = Weighted average of vulnerability of relationships

## Endnotes

1  According to globalization discourse, people worldwide are linked more densely than ever before. International communication and travel are commonplace. Money and information flow freely between countries; goods and services created in one city are increasingly available throughout the world. Businesses are able to work as if national borders did not exist. Human rights activists, labor organizers, academics, journalists and others are able to work in the spotlight of the global theater.

2  The Globalization Index, published annually in the Foreign Policy magazine, tracks the comparative advancement of globalization across 62 countries along four key components: economic integration, person-to-person contact, political engagement, and technological connectivity. The Globalization Index aggregates indicators such as trade and investment flows, movement of people across borders, volumes of international telephone traffic, internet usage, and participation in international organizations (Kearny 2005).

# 2 | The institutional environment of global projects

## W. RICHARD SCOTT

Since the 1960s, students of organizations have increasingly recognized the extent to which organizations are creatures of their context – social actors affected by and, simultaneously, shaping the environments within which they operate. Beginning with the insights of "general" or "open" system theorists (Bertalanffy 1956; Katz and Kahn 1966), organizational scholars have labored to:

- extend the levels of analysis employed – from approaches focusing on individual behavior within organizations that treated the organization as context, to viewing organizations themselves as collective actors, to examining organizations as components of wider systems, whether organizational populations or organization fields; and to
- expand the facets of environment considered – from technical and resource-based exchanges, to political processes, to involvement in relational systems, to institutional forces (Scott and Davis 2007: chap. 5).

Studies of systems of organizations operating in diverse institutional environments are, hence, in the forefront of the most recent phase of organization studies. To exemplify and explore this dual focus, it is difficult to conceive of a better object of empirical analysis than that presented by global infrastructure construction projects, which involve the temporary collaboration of multiple independent organizations, operating under diverse regulatory and financial authorities in varied national contexts. Chapter 1 has described the basic characteristics of global projects, emphasizing their operation as a temporary system of component organizations and individuals operating in diverse sites, geographies, and cultures. This chapter concentrates on the institutional environments in which they operate, beginning with a brief discussion of how we understand this concept and then turning to consider its application to and relevance for the study of global projects.

## Conceptualizing institutional environments

### Background

Institutional arguments are a late-comer to the dialogue on organizations but they have a long history in the social sciences. Indeed, they dominated social science discourse during the decades surrounding the turn of the nineteenth to twentieth century, during what is regarded as the classical period of social theory. Influential scholars such as Charles Horton Cooley, Emile Durkheim, Karl Marx, Herbert Spencer, Thorstein Veblen, and Max Weber are appropriately characterized as institutional theorists, although their interests and emphases varied (Adler 2009). However, for a variety of reasons, including the ascendancy of positivism, behavioralism, and methodological individualism, institutional arguments were subordinated and marginalized in the social sciences during the first half of the twentieth century (see Hodgson 1996; Thelen 1999; Scott 1995/2008: chap. 1).

During the 1950s, however, a renaissance in institutional theory took place, importantly fueled by linkages to organization studies (e.g., Selznick 1949; Parsons 1956). And, characteristic of its origins, institutional ideas and approaches rapidly spread to find recruits across all the social sciences, from cognitive psychology and ethnomethodology to economics, management studies, political science, and sociology. While range and breadth are desirable, they often connote diversity, and so it is with institutional scholarship. Current efforts encompass such varied approaches as the bounded rationality arguments of March and Simon (1958); the transaction cost approach of Williamson (1975; 1985); the rational choice arguments of Moe (1984) and Weingast (2002); the macro-sociological work of Meyer and Rowan (1977) and DiMaggio and Powell (1983); and the micro-foundational cognitive approaches of Zucker (1977) and Barley and Tolbert (1997). How to tame this cacophony?

### An inclusive conception of institutions

Since the mid-1990s, I have been devising and extending an inclusive conception of institutions (Scott 1995/2008).[1] In my view:

Institutions are comprised of regulative, normative and cultural-cognitive elements that, together with associated activities and resources, provide stability and meaning to social life (Scott 2008: 48)

**Table 2.1** *Three pillars of institutions*

|  | Regulative | Normative | Cultural-cognitive |
|---|---|---|---|
| Basis of compliance | Expedience | Social obligation | Taken-for-grantedness Shared understanding |
| Basis of order | Regulative rules | Binding expectations | Constitutive schema |
| Mechanisms | Coercive | Normative | Mimetic |
| Logic | Instrumentality | Appropriateness | Orthodoxy |
| Indicators | Rules Laws Sanctions | Certification Accreditation | Common beliefs Shared logics of action Isomorphism |
| Affect | Fear Guilt/ innocence | Shame/honor | Certainty/ confusion |
| Basis of legitmacy | Legally sanctioned | Morally governed | Comprehensible Recognizable Culturally supported |

*Source:* Table 3.1, p. 51, W. Richard Scott, *Institutions and organizations: Ideas and interests,* 3rd edn. Thousand Oaks, CA: Sage (2008). Reprinted by permission of the publisher.

This conception attempts to recognize and incorporate much of the existing complexity of extant approaches and to emphasize that institutions are multifaceted structures, made up of varied elements that work in different ways to order social life. A distinguishing feature of all institutional arguments is the importance accorded to the symbolic dimensions of society – regulative, normative, and cultural-cognitive – but such formulations insist that, if they are to exert effects, these symbols cannot be disembodied but must be connected to human activities and resources, both human and material. It is important that we view institutions as being "inhabited" by social actors (Hallett and Ventresca 2006).

As summarized in Table 2.1, the three types of institutional elements – constituting three "pillars" of institutions – embody different logics, employ different mechanisms, conjure up different emotions, and evoke different bases of legitimacy. We consider each pillar in turn.

## Regulative elements

Regulative institutional elements rely on relatively explicit rules reinforced by surveillance activities and backed by sanctions. In this conception, institutions provide "the rules of the game" (North 1990: 3). Actors comply out of expedience – to achieve rewards or to avoid pain. The basic mechanism underlying compliance is coercion. The institutional logic at work is an instrumental one; the accompanying affect involves either fear or hurt, on the one hand, or the satisfaction of being innocent, the pleasure of being rewarded, on the other.

Economists and rational-choice political scientists emphasize a regulative conception of institutions. Lawyers and managers are at home in this world. Rules are, without question, a critical component of most institutional frameworks. Organization and management theorists have long privileged the importance of formal, rule-based systems of authority, and political scientists and economists stress the value of the "rule of law" in providing predictability and order in the world of politics and enterprise. Such elements also enjoy the advantage of being more visible, easier to study, and more readily codified and modified. More nuanced scholars recognize that "the enactment of a social rule is never perfect and that there always is a gap between the ideal pattern of a rule and the real pattern of life under it" (Streeck and Thelen 2005b: 14).

Nevertheless, to restrict attention to this more formalized aspect of institutions is problematic. Formal rule systems, characterized by Roland (2004) as "fast-moving institutions," are more likely to be shallow or superficial in their effects, encouraging actors to "game the system" or decouple their behavior from what is required. Regulatory systems rely on the use of abstract categories and prescriptions which leave out much of the "complex, illegible, and local social practices" which constitute the social worlds to which they refer (Scott 1998: 2).

As for our current focus, global projects, they – much more than their domestic counterparts – are likely to confront varied, unexpected, and, potentially, conflicting regulatory regimes. Although there does not exist a unified "coercive sovereign" comparable to a nation-state at the global level, an ever-increasing number of international bodies have been granted the right to devise various rules that specify with precision what types of conduct by states or other organizational actors are required, and that possess the capacity to enforce these rules, if necessary, by exacting sanctions (Abbott et al. 2001). For example, the World Bank is able to establish and enforce a wide range of policy and procedural requirements on those projects it is funding.

## Normative elements

Normative elements introduce "a prescriptive, evaluative, and obligatory dimension into social life" (Scott 2008: 32). Some types of norms arise out of and function through the interaction of small groups or larger communities. In work systems, norms emerge in the give-and-take of individuals in work groups and operate through occupational and professional communities (Homans 1950; Van Maanen and Barley 1984). Prescriptions for behavior evolve, are internalized by participants, and mutually reinforced. But norms can also be more consciously constructed to deliberately provide guidelines for behavior. Within societies, professional associations and religious bodies formulate and promulgate prescriptions for behavior. Although they are often quite explicit, like rules and regulations, they are not backed by coercive power.[2] At the transnational level, various types of international professional groups and nongovernmental organizations (NGOs) formulate prescriptions and standards to specify appropriate behavior for organizations and individuals in areas ranging from environmental protections to human rights to quality control (see Brunsson and Jacobsson 2000).

The basis of compliance to norms does not rest in the instrumental calculation of rewards versus punishments but on an internalized sense of obligation, a belief that the guidelines are scientifically or morally grounded, and a regard for the good opinions of others whom one respects. In March and Olsen's (1989) terms, an actor's compliance rests on the application of a logic of "appropriateness." Participants ask: What is the nature of this situation? Given my role, what is my appropriate response to it? Affective responses to norm violation are different from and stronger than are those to rule-breaking, involving feelings of shame or dishonor on the one hand, or moral rectitude on the other.

Global projects bring together managers and workers from varying work traditions. Most of the participants have no previous experience with one another. Expectations regarding work roles may differ;

standards for behavior may conflict; and the customary practices, even the way in which labor is divided, may vary (Taylor and Levitt 2007). These expectations and customs are less likely to be known, and are less easily knowable, in advance: they are less likely to be recorded or to be codified in consultant reports on local conditions. And, because they are admixtures of convention, routine, and habit, they are less easily managed from above or changed by administrative directive. They help to comprise the more "slow-moving" institutional elements (Roland 2004), and such elements carry great sway in shaping both expectations and behavior.

## Cultural-cognitive elements

The hyphenated term, "cultural-cognitive," is employed to emphasize the shared nature of the beliefs (culture) as well as the role they play in individual cognition. Thus, Hofstede (1993: 89; 1991:4) defines culture as "the collective programming of the mind which distinguishes one group or category of people from another"...; "the software of the mind." Cultural beliefs include the most deep-set and "slow-moving" of the institutional elements. Whereas in some cases, they entail a conscious commitment to more explicit ideologies or policies, they also connect to deeper "background" assumptions that are taken for granted by their adherents (Campbell 2004: chap. 4).

Moreover, more so than the other two types of institutional elements, cultural-cognitive elements operate via *constitutive* mechanisms: they enable the construction of fundamental social categories. Rather than regulating existing activities, as do rules and norms, constitutive efforts "create the very possibility of certain activities" (Searle 1995: 64). Constitutive work creates distinctions, categories, typifications, templates for organizing, and scripts for acting (Greenwood and Hinings 1993; Schank and Abelson 1977). In this sense, the most basic mechanisms of the cultural-cognitive pillar provide the foundation on which regulative and normative forces operate.

Although cultural-cognitive elements provide underpinnings for the two other elements and, in this sense, operate in combination with them, they are also capable of providing a basis for social order independent of normative or regulative mechanisms of control. Shared beliefs in themselves are a sufficient basis for social order. For example, in her analysis of a basic science laboratory, Knorr-Certina

(1999) describes the manner in which a shared conception among laboratory personnel of the nature of the work – what is a "problem"; what is a "solution" – provided the core foundation of their social order.

The institutional logic underlying the cultural-cognitive pillar is one of "orthodoxy": a concern not to "stand out" or to be found "out of step." One physician does not want to act too differently from his/her colleagues; and one school attempts to adopt the characteristic structures and curricula embraced by other schools (Meyer, Kamens, and Benavot 1992). And while each firm may attempt to be somewhat distinctive in order to gain competitive advantage, they all will want their structures and practices to be "state of the art," as defined by their relevant reference groups. Actors out of step with prevailing cultural-cognitive systems feel confused and disoriented (see Chapter 5); those in conformity experience reinforcement and enhanced confidence. Cultural-cognitive elements are undoubtedly the most "sticky" and are among the slowest to undergo change.

Given the continuing diversity in economic, political, religious, and ethnic systems with their associated conceptions of reality and understandings of "how things work," global projects may expect to encounter substantial differences in cultural-cognitive belief systems carried by varying types of participants. Such differences not only reside in broader societal systems but will be encountered among project participants working in different sectors (e.g., public/private, manufacturing/commerce) or in different occupational worlds (e.g., finance, law, engineering), or in different companies. Individuals embedded in these diverse social worlds will frame events in somewhat different ways, bring to bear different lenses in assessing situations, and are likely to utilize varying repertoires of actions in responding to them (see Chapters 4, 5).

It is important to stress that our identification of three types of institutional elements is meant to point to analytic distinctions – differences in the underlying ingredients that make up institutional environments. Most existing systems are composed of complex mixtures of these elements. One will find regulatory systems, normative frameworks, and cultural-cognitive schema – all of them simultaneously at work in any social setting. Health care, public administration, higher education, and the various commercial industries all have their unique institutional make-up. Still, since the elements – regulative, normative, and cultural-cognitive – work in different ways and are marked by somewhat different indicators, we believe that awareness of their distinctive properties and ways of acting enables analysts to keep before them the rich admixture of forces and processes at work in an institutional complex.

## Institutional elements and legitimacy

The institutional environment constitutes one important facet of the context within which a global project must operate. Other important facets include economic or market features and political structures and processes. (For a discussion of the latter, see Chapter 3.) Of course, economic and political features are themselves institutionally structured, but also have independent effects via the exchange of goods and services and the play of power. To date, the lion's share of studies has emphasized economic aspects of projects (e.g., Miller and Lessard 2000; Davies and Hobday 2005). Whereas an economic analysis of an organizational system, such as a project, calls attention to its performance – the relative efficiency and effectiveness of a given system in its setting – and points to the importance of a cost/benefit assessment, an institutional approach focuses on its legitimacy – its social acceptability and creditability. It should be obvious that, no matter how successful the economic performance of an organization, to be viable and sustainable, the organization needs to be seen as operating in ways that are viewed as acceptable both in its wider and local context. In short, economic and political analyses are essential, but do not address all of the contingencies confronted by global projects.

Legitimacy is important for all organizations. However, like performance, the concept is complex and fraught with issues and trade-offs. At the most general level, legitimacy refers to the degree of alignment between the organization's structures and procedures and the dictates and assumptions of its institutional environment (Scott 2008: 59; Suchman 1995: 574). But, as we would expect, this condition will vary depending on which elements are most salient (again, see Table 2.1). A regulative focus stresses legality – conformity with prevailing laws and rules. A normative approach favors a deeper, moral basis of justification, rising above a rule-based framework to one looking toward "equity" or "justice." A cultural-cognitive view stresses the extent to which an organization's structure and activities are recognizable, are culturally supported, and appear to "make-sense" within its context.

Moreover, in our complex modern world, there is likely to be dissensus and conflict around each of these assessments. There exist multiple "authorities" and "audiences" – varying legal jurisdictions and agencies, diverse reference groups, and numerous, conflicting "stakeholders" proffering alternative bases of legitimation (Ruef and Scott 1998). Such circumstances are particularly likely to occur in the institutional environments surrounding global projects. Kostova and Zaheer (1999), for example, point out the difficulties posed for multinational organizations in attempting to operate in a number of different environments. Multiple criteria and diverse authorities and audiences will be present and are likely to offer conflicting alternatives for going forward.

The ensuing challenges and dilemmas provide the context within which project participants must operate. They are sources of problems and costs, but also offer possibilities for innovation and learning. Subsequent chapters in this volume attend to both costs and benefits of operating in a transnational institutional environment.

## Institutions and agency

Before elaborating on ways of conceptualizing the institutional environments of global projects, it is necessary to counterbalance the thrust of this initial discussion of institutions. Although consistent with the early formulation of institutional theorists of the 1970s and 1980s (e.g., Meyer and Rowan 1977), the view presented above will seem to many contemporary readers to be overly determinant, depicting institutional forces as all-powerful and as unduly constraining social action. It appears to leave little or no room for *agency* – the ability of human actors to intervene and to make a difference in the institutional scaffolding that underpins and overarches human affairs. We must correct this impression. While environments, including institutional components, do shape human behavior, they themselves are shaped and altered by the actions of social actors. Moreover, institutions operate not only to constrain, but also to provide resources for and empower actors.

A salutary corrective to an overly determinant model of social order has been provided by Anthony Gidden's (1979; 1984) *structuration* theory, which posits the duality of social structure: social structure as both context for and product of social action. All social behavior takes place within an existing social structure; but what is that structure? It is the patterned actions and beliefs of the social actors (including organizations as collective actors) themselves. Social structures, to exist, must continually be produced and reproduced by social actors, who, in the process, can introduce departures from previous actions – through errors and misunderstandings, but also through learning and creativity. In structuration theory, actors are viewed as knowledgeable and reflexive beings, capable of monitoring ongoing situations and intervening in systems of interdependent activities and relations. They are shaped, surrounded by, and situated in these social structures, but also empowered and informed by them. As they experience and interpret these symbolic systems and respond to them, in the process institutions – which are "by definition, the more enduring features of social life" (Giddens 1984: 24), the more resilient aspects of social structure – are, variously, maintained and altered, eroded and constructed. Thus, institutions evolve endogenously from within spheres of social action but once in existence take on a life of their own to support, influence, and constrain future episodes of social action (Berger and Luckmann 1967; Greif 2006).

## Constructing institutions

The construction of institutions is necessarily a complex process but, following the early ideas of Sumner (1906) and the more recent language of Strang and Sine (2002), it can be crudely subdivided into two strands. The first, termed an *agent-based* account emphasizes intentionality and conscious intervention by actors. Purposeful actors work to construct rule-based frameworks – such as constitutions, contracts, and policies – to support and channel future actions. This view emphasizes not only purposeful design but also social power. As DiMaggio (1988: 13) states:

Put simply . . . institutionalization is a product of the political efforts of actors to accomplish their ends . . . the success of an institutionalization project and the form that the resulting institution takes depends on the relative power of the actors who support, oppose, or otherwise strive to influence it.

Institutions are consciously shaped by individuals having access to more valued resources, connections to more central networks, and possessing superior social skills (Fligstein 2001b).

The second process by which institutions are constructed is termed a *naturalistic* approach. Sociological students of institutionalization, such as Berger and Luckmann (1967) and Tolbert and Zucker (1996), stress the unconscious ways in which "activities are habitualized and reciprocally interpreted" during social interaction (Strang and Sine 2002: 502). In this view, institutions are not created by the purposeful actions of interest-based agents, but emerge from the collective sensemaking and problem-solving behavior of many actors confronting similar situations who, collectively, find ways to "muddle through" (Lindblom 1959).

While each of these approaches can explain episodes of institutional construction, on reflection, both are stylized accounts, omitting and/or emphasizing one or another dimension of the behavior of those who construct institutions. Thus, in the first account, agents are viewed as rational actors, but it is essential to recognize that such actors are never sufficiently prescient to take into account all of the factors that affect the creation and development of a given institutional framework, nor do they have the capacity to accurately predict their outcomes (see Pierson 2004: 108–22). Designs are launched, but have multiple, often unanticipated effects, conditions change, as do the "interests" and participation of the attendant parties, so that expected benefits may not be realized, or are differently valued when they arrive. As for the second account, while those "unintentional" naturalistic institutional entrepreneurs may be unaware of the larger project in which they are involved, they are pragmatically interpreting changing situations and making choices that make sense under the conditions they confront (see Emirbayer and Mische 1998).

The naturalistic view of institutional construction shifts attention from the regulative elements to emphasize the normative and cultural-cognitive. Social actors operate in a world of mutual obligations and within "webs of significance [they themselves] have spun" (Geertz 1973: 5). Norms are less easily designed than are rules, and the most influential and enduring cultural-cognitive frameworks – languages, religions, philosophies, ideologies – are constructed and shaped over time by the interpretations of many witting and unwitting users and believers.

In addition to constructing new institutions, agents are active in diffusing existing forms across time and space. Institutional *carriers*, including immigrants, salesmen, and consultants, spread existing models from one place to another (Jepperson 1991; Scott 2003; Scott 2008: 79–85). For global projects, important types of carriers include international consultants, investment bankers, contractors, expatriate employees, and international NGOs. Carriers are never simply neutral conveyers of ideas and practices, but work to translate, adapt, and modify existing models to fit new circumstances (Czarniawska and Joerges 1996).

A capacity for agency and for learning and innovation is valued by most participants in modern organizations, and so a happy circumstance for members of global projects is that these types of settings afford unusual opportunities for these to occur. The richer and more diverse are the institutional environments from which actors originate, the greater their opportunities for choice and for learning, but, on the other hand, the greater the potential for conflict and confusion. Being expected to work and cooperate with those holding different ideas and exhibiting different modes of acting and relating both challenges our own assumptions and provides alternative modes of thinking and working. International business scholars such as Peng (2003; Peng et al. 2009) emphasize the ways in which institutional change affords organizations many opportunities for strategic choices. Of course, some participants will be more open to these opportunities than others (see Chapter 5). And, organizations vary in both the extent to which they require "local" knowledge and in their capacity for retaining and learning from others in this context or from past projects (see Chapters 6 and 7.)

## Institutional environments and global projects

In addition to considering the multiple types of institutional elements at play in the environments of global infrastructure development construction projects, we believe that it is also helpful to parse them by distinguishing between environments at varying organization levels and in terms of differing organization fields.

*Levels*

Organizations are penetrated by institutional environments operating at numerous levels, so that it is helpful to be clear as to the level of concern. We briefly consider four levels: local, sectoral, national, and transnational.

### Local environments

All organizations operate in some "local" environment – a context within which their operations are conducted. Hence, those charged with managing or operating organizations are well advised to acquire "local knowledge" (Geertz 1983). Participants are drawn from specific communities; exchanges occur with specific suppliers and purchasers; and local packages of regulations, regarding taxation, hours of operation, health and safety of participants, pollution controls, and related sets of locally enforced – or locally ignored – rules apply. However, some newer types of organizations, such as multinational corporations (MNCs) operate in not one but many localities. This is true not only because they locate their subsidiaries in differing international locations, but because, as legal entities, many choose to locate one or another function in the most favorable legal jurisdiction. Thus, some corporations have located their headquarters in New York or Chicago but choose to incorporate in a state such as Delaware or New Jersey because of their permissive corporate laws (Romano 1985). More imaginatively, newer corporations such as Tommy Hilfiger, based in Hong Kong, is incorporated in the Virgin Islands, lists its shares on the New York Stock Exchange, holds its annual meetings in Bermuda, and licenses its trademark to producers around the world (Scott and Davis 2007: 365). Modern organizations are less likely today to adapt to the environment they are in and more likely to seek out the most favorable environment for each business function!

This assertion certainly applies to global projects. Most sponsors will not consider a project unless it is situated in an environment in which they have sufficient experience to feel comfortable. Sponsors desire tax havens, a business climate without too many irregularities, and a region operating under the "rule of law" to protect their property rights. If local conditions are not favorable, sponsors may decide to locate their special project vehicle – the legal entity that enables the flow of capital to the various project parties – in the jurisdiction of their home country or a third country. Much effort and expense – "due diligence" – is typically devoted to selecting a favorable local environment in which to operate and finding locally knowledgeable partners with whom to navigate that environment. In addition to this local environment in which the project is carried out, other localities will play a role, including the location of the lead firm, prime partners, and subcontractors. The "institutional distance" among these participants – the difference or similarity between the regulatory, normative, and cultural-cognitive environments of the home and host countries (Kostova and Zaheer 1999: 68) – will affect the processes and outcomes of the project (see also, Eden and Miller 2004; Xu and Shenkar 2002).

But more so than many other types of global projects, infrastructural construction projects are literally "grounded" in a local environment – a building, a bridge, a transit system, or a pipeline is attached to a specific location. Once a site is chosen, it is difficult – and always costly – to relocate. Even though each project is connected to a location, the degree of local embeddedness – the extent to which particular organizational participants are affected by and must take into account local conditions – varies substantially among the various project participants (see Chapter 6).

## Sectoral environments

The sector within which a project operates constitutes a distinctive and influential institutional environment. It makes a palpable difference whether one is constructing large dams, airports, mass transit systems, or water sanitation and distribution projects. Comparative research by Schmitter (1990) and Campbell, Hollingsworth, and Lindberg (1991), among others, points out that differences in institutional governance systems across sectors within a society are often larger than those occurring across societies. Each sector is associated with a distinctive mix of public and private organizations, particular regulatory regimes, different professional and occupational groups and associations, and distinctive language and ideology. For example, in the transportation sector in California, it is not common for drivers on highways to pay user fees, but in the power and water sectors, it is much more acceptable. Related to this, there has been little public opposition or resistance to privatization of electric power generation in California, but there has been and continues to be fierce opposition from public engineers' unions, such as the Professional Engineers in California Government – a public employees' union representing 13,000 CalTrans engineers, architects, land surveyors, and related professionals – to the use of public–private partnerships (PPPs) for developing and operating any kind of civil infrastructure (e.g., roads, bridges, ports, airports, water and sewer systems) or social infrastructure (e.g., schools, hospitals, courthouses, prisons) in the state.

Sectors also differ in terms of their ability to garner international funding and in the amount of attention they receive from international nongovernmental organizations (INGOs). For example, water supply projects are much more likely to depend on more localized financial instruments and to work below the radar screen of INGOs. And, as a consequence of these and other differences the determinants of conflict associated with these projects is found to vary (see Chapters 3, 8, and 9).

Especially at the sector level, it is necessary to soften and blunt the sharper notion of public (vs. private) governmental structure and to substitute the broader and vaguer concept of *governance* system in order to recognize the varying, but often substantial, role played by "private" actors, such as professional and trade associations, in setting and enforcing rules and norms of practice. For example, in the European Union, rule-making in major fields was delegated to private expert organizations such as the European Commission for Electrotechnical Standardization and the European Telecommunications Standards Institute. These associations lack formal regulatory authority, but exercise control through the setting of standards, establishing monitoring systems, and creating forums within which activities and reforms can be debated and promulgated (Jacobsson and Sahlin-Andersson 2006). In many sectors, private actors share with, and even substitute for, public agencies in the exercise of legitimate authority. The advantages of such arrangements – insider knowledge, enhanced legitimacy accorded to one's peers – are well known, as are the disadvantages – lack of objectivity and inattention to the public interest (Streeck and Schmitter 1985).

Numerous scholars have proposed conceptual schema for parsing the complex governance arrangements operating at the sectoral level. For example, Schmitter (1990) proposes a generalized framework contrasting economic and sociological models devised to create either spontaneously equilibrating, self-reinforcing, or externally enforced modes. And Campbell, Hollingsworth, and Lindberg (1991) develop an evolutionary model within which sectoral actors pursue their interests within a historically shaped framework that constrains their selection of new governance regimes.

The infrastructure development projects sector is apt to be associated with numerous salient factors, including the environmental impact, the "social footprint" (the composition and size and nature of the populations affected), how likely are local and international NGOs to be activated, the strictness of regulatory rules, the nature of the enforcement machinery, and the willingness of users to pay for end services. These types of factors help to determine the degrees and types of opposition and resistance that may confront the project (see Chapters 8 and 9).

### Societal environments

In a time when globalization is much in vogue, it would nevertheless be wrong not to recognize the continuing importance of individual societies and their associated nation-states. National institutions have been for several centuries the most salient structures for guiding and structuring economic and political projects. Beginning with the Treaty of Westphalia in 1648 and continuing into the present, the nation-state has come to be regarded as the appropriate way in which to organize societal systems. This treaty replaced the Holy Roman Empire in Europe with a system of sovereign, autonomous states (Krasner 1993) which, although punctuated by a period of imperialistic colonialism, gradually became the model for subsequent nation-building.

Historical and organizational institutionalists, in particular, emphasize that societal systems, while sharing broad features in common, vary in their distinctive institutional arrangements. In his earlier work, Whitley (1992b), for example, argues that considerable variation exists across societies in the characteristics of firms as economic actors, the nature of authoritative coordination and control systems within firms, and the structure of markets, including the extent of interdependence and in the role of competitive vs. cooperative ties among firms. More recently, he has identified six types of "business systems" ranging from fragmented to state-organized, depending on such factors as the strength of the nation-state's coordinating and developmental role, the extent to which the state encourages the establishment of intermediary economic associations, and whether the state directly or indirectly regulates market boundaries, entries and exists, and the activities of economic actors (Whitley 1999; see also, Van Dijek, Jules, and Groenegegen 1994). These historically generated systems provide a set of "organizing logics that inform action and meaning" (Biggart and Guillén 1999: 726). Economic and managerial practices not consistent with these logics – those "plopped and dropped" on a community from outside – will be less likely to be effective. For example, French water development companies were well known for exporting their *affermage* model of private water project development throughout the 1990s with a legacy of failed projects in many countries (Vives, Paris, and Benavides 2006). Similarly, US independent power producers tried to export private sector models of power development with little success – seven of ten companies exited the business (Woodhouse 2005).

Whether at the local, sectoral, or societal level, the lion's share of scholarly attention has been accorded to the *allocative* and the *regulatory* roles of governments. Taxing systems, grants-in-aid, subsidies, and various forms of corporate welfare are familiar examples of allocative powers. Regulatory systems are often viewed as motivating evasion or "capture" by firms rather than compliance (Stigler 1971; Wilson 1980), but recent studies by scholars of law and society suggest that such programs may have larger effects through the normative and cultural-cognitive processes they set in motion rather than by means of their coercive mechanisms (Dobbin and Sutton 1998; Edelman and Suchman 1997).

Less attention has been accorded the nation-state's *constitutive* powers. These structures, more than other social units, possess the capacity to create and legitimate organizational forms, such as for profit- and nonprofit corporations, sovereign wealth funds, and, more recently, public–private partnerships (PPPs) for the development and operation of specific civil or social infrastructure assets. Some societies have created national or regional frameworks to enable PPPs to function more effectively, assisting them to overcome the capacity challenges faced by state governments as well as defend the private firms from governmental opportunism (see Chapter 11). More generally, the state also determines the nature and distribution of property rights – "rules that determine the conditions of ownership and control of the means of production" (Campbell and Lindberg 1990: 635). For example, the rights accorded to workers and unions by the Wagner Act in 1935 were greatly restricted by the Taft-Hartley Act of 1947 which eliminated previously constituted rights for workers. States not only provide the constitutive legal framework within which contracts are written, but also organize and staff the multiple types of forums within which disputes are adjudicated (see Hult and Walcott 1990: chap. 3).

## Transnational environments

Like others, including Hannerz (1996) and Djelic and Sahlin-Andersson (2006), we prefer the more modest and, we believe, accurate term "transnational" to the more widely used and, in our opinion, grandiose term "global" to refer to developments above the societal or national level. The "big" news regarding institutional environments during the last few decades is the flurry of activity occurring at the transnational level, which has produced a profusion of new institutional forms – such as the European Union, OECD, World Trade Organization, multilateral lending institutions, regional banks, and bilateral investment treaties. Whereas earlier political scientists treated nation-states as the "real actors" and national institutions as of preeminent importance, more recent developments and scholarship "take into account seriously the space in between nations" (Djelic and Quack 2003: 3). This space, "traditionally conceived as anomic" (p. 25), has become during the past half-century, an arena of intensive and extensive institutional building.

Djelic and Quack suggest that these developments have occurred at two levels: (1) changes in national systems that impact transnational systems; and (2) developments at the transnational level itself. With regard to the first, the conduct of many national activities involving cross-border trade and investment creates connections to firms, governments, and customers in other nations. As such trade and investment increases in volume and scope, these transactions are associated with a growing number of problems and disputes that must be resolved by the development of transnational rules and agencies to oversee them. Hence the rise of the World Trade Organization and the proliferation of bilateral investment treaties and international protocols, such as the OECE, IMF, ICSID, UNCITRAL, and the Paris Club for the settlement of investment disputes. As an example, Dezalay and Garth (1996) record the history of the emergence of a collection of governance systems to handle international commercial disputes, including such associations as the International Chamber of Commerce and the American Arbitration Association. Such transnational institution building may also be sector-specific, but it is often the case that the firms located in the stronger states determine the rules and procedures adopted by the weaker.

The second institution-building process, by contrast, does not originate from the actions of organizations within nation-states, but is generated by actors and processes situated at the international level. Admittedly, some actors originated at the national level and subsequently became transnational, but others began as transnational creatures. Such transnational agencies as the United Nations (and its various commissions) and the World Bank have been joined by a wide array of professional associations and INGOs, which have increased from a few hundred at the beginning of the twentieth century to many thousands as we enter the twenty-first century (Boli and Thomas 1997). As already noted, these include the efforts of many types of scientific associations seeking to promulgate a variety of standards, structures, and conceptions of "best practices," as well as a growing number of transnational social movement organizations (TSMOs), pursuing causes ranging from human rights to environmental protections to global justice issues (Brunsson and Jacobsson 2000; Cohen and Rai 2000; Djelic and Sahlin-Andersson 2006; Smith 2005; Smith and Johnston 2002; see also, Chapter 3).

Many of these organizations exercise legal authority. Institutions that are "legalized" score high on three independent dimensions: *obligation*: the extent to which "states or other actors are bound by a rule or commitment"; *precision*: the extent to which "rules unambiguously define the conduct they require"; and *delegation*: when "third parties have been granted authority to implement, interpret, and apply the rules" (Abbott et al., 2001: 17). The extent of legalization varies from high to low on each of these dimensions – marking the difference between various combinations of "hard" and "soft" law (Abbott and Snidal 2001; Goldstein, et al., 2001).

However, most INGOs and TSMOs must rely primarily on normative and cultural-cognitive elements – "soft law" – since they lack financial incentives or coercive sanctions to enforce their programs. As Boli and Thomas (1997: 172) point out: they "are more or less authoritative transnational bodies employing limited resources to make rules, set standards, propagate principles and broadly represent 'humanity' vis-à-vis states and other actors." Given their large and growing numbers and situations in which their claims of expertise and jurisdiction often overlap and conflict, coordination and adjudication among these bodies pose a challenge. It is often difficult to know whose interests a particular INGO represents and how it arrives at and justifies its position. Hence, increasingly INGOs confront the challenge of establishing their legitimacy and accountability in an arena of conflicting interests (Fox and Brown 1998). Lacking an overarching hierarchy or structure of decision-making, differences among these organizations are often resolved by differential resources or influence or by the formation of coalitions among interested parties.[3]

Although we insist on the value of identifying various levels at which institutional forces operate, that should not prevent us from recognizing the extent to which the various levels intersect and interact. Transnational events and processes affect and penetrate sectoral, societal, and local structures and processes. Macro-level influences enter into the performance of multicultural teams (Jelinek and Wilson 2005). Conversely, what happens within these teams, as they confront and deal with each challenge, works over time to transform institutional frameworks at higher levels.

## Organization fields

### Defining fields

A widely used concept employed by students of organizations and institutions is that of the organization field. First defined by DiMaggio and Powell (1983: 143), an *organization field* refers to:

those organizations that, in the aggregate, constitute a recognized area of institutional life: key suppliers, resource and product consumers, regulatory agencies, and other organizations that produce similar services or products.

Fields include both relational systems, linking organizational participants into networks of exchange, information and funding flows, status and power relations, as well as shared symbolic systems, including the presence of a cultural-cognitive and normative framework and a common regulatory regime. In the world of firms, fields are often formed around specific products or services; in the world of politics, around some specific issue, policy, or interest. Organizations thus play varying roles in a field, but together constitute and participate in a common "local social order" (Fligstein 2001b: 107); they share a common meaning system and they "interact more frequently and fatefully with one another than with actors outside of the field" (Scott 1994: 207–8).

As with all social structures, organization fields are subject to processes of structuration, and vary in terms of the degree of their development – the stability of their networks, the clarity of field boundaries, and the extent to which common conceptions, norms, and rules prevail (DiMaggio and Powell 1983; Scott 1994). Three of the most important building blocks of field structures are organizational archetypes, institutional logics, and governance systems (Scott et al. 2000).

*Organizational archetypes* are "set[s] of [organizational] structures and systems that consistently embody a single interpretive scheme" (Greenwood and Hinings 1993: 1055). "Structures" refer to such features as differentiation and mode of integration of economic, social, and political relations within the organization; "systems" are the procedures for control and decision making; and the "interpretive scheme" refers to dominant values and beliefs. These schema are, of course, comprised of cultural-cognitive elements. A more highly structured field will contain several populations of organizations adhering to a small number of archetypes; e.g., the law firms and commercial banks in New York and London that participate in global projects all follow a prototypical pattern of organizing.

*Institutional logics* are defined by Friedland and Alford (1991: 248) as "a set of material practices and symbolic constructions which constitutes its organizing principles and which is available to organizations and individuals to elaborate." That is, in addition to a limited collection of organizational archetypes, organizational fields exhibit a shared conception of the work to be accomplished and a limited repertory of activities for carrying it out. Institutional logics are made up of both cultural-cognitive and normative elements. As discussed below, the institutional logics associated with global projects include those associated with transnational legal firms, construction companies, and host governmental agencies.

*Governance systems* are regimes that exercise oversight and enforce compliance at the field level. As defined by Scott and colleagues

(2000: 172–3), "governance structures refer to all those arrangements by which field-level power and authority are exercised involving, variously, formal and informal systems, public and private auspices, regulative and normative mechanisms." Governance structures are invariably shaped by the views and interests of the more powerful field participants. These organizations work to craft rules and logics so as to preserve the stability of the field as well as their own dominant role within it (Fligstein 2001a). Among those participating in the governance of global projects, multilateral agencies such as the World Bank provide extensive oversight over the projects in which they are involved, and INGOs attempt to influence the standards established for projects within their areas of interest.

## Fields and global projects

The concept of organization field developed in studies of systems of organization operating within a single society and, often, operating under fairly stable environmental conditions. Hence, it is appropriate to ask whether the concept has applicability to or relevance for global projects set in more diverse and volatile environments. We think it has, but only if we recognize that these project organizations function in a number of interrelated fields. Indeed, we discern at least three important organization fields to take into account in studying global infrastructure projects: (1) the field of global infrastructure players – e.g., transnational law firms, banks, developers; (2) the field of local organizations comprising the host community; and (3) the "new" field created by the appearance and actions of the specific global project as it interacts with its host environment.[4]

### (Field 1) The field of global infrastructure players

It is useful to distinguish between the *organization set*: the focal project company and its immediate exchange partners (Evan 1966) – including sponsors/developers, contractors, lenders, end users, and operators that together comprise the project organization – and the larger *organization field* within which this temporary network of organizations is situated. The larger field is centered around a finite collection of multinational corporations (MNCs) who constitute the major players in global infrastructure projects. Key players are drawn from several major populations of organizations involved in the core tasks. *Law firms* structure contractual relations between the host government concessionaire, lenders, fuel suppliers, contractors, and other parties. *Bankers* play roles both as lenders, issuing debt financing to support a project's cash needs, and as financial adviser, representing host governments as they define key attributes and risks of the project being developed. *Developers*, sometimes also called sponsors, are responsible for all stages of the project, including exploring feasibility, site selection, securing permissions and funding, managing the construction, and overseeing start-up and operations of the completed project. Major development firms include corporations such as AES Corporation in the power sector, Veolia in the water sector, Hutchinson in the ports sector, and GMR Group in the airports sector. *Contractors* are those more technically specialized firms engaged to carry out specified construction tasks, including site clearing and preparation, procurement, assembly of component systems, and managing cost, schedule, and quality control activities. *Project consultants*, including lawyers, financial advisers, planners, architects, and engineers, provide expert advice and guidance to the developers and/or host communities.

Students of organizations have been slow to recognize the increasingly international character of organizations and organizing processes. Only recently have scholars begun to examine the somewhat distinctive structures associated with MNCs or to consider the complex environments within which they operate (Bartlett and Ghoshal 1987; Ghoshal and Westney 1993; Hennart 1982; Kostova and Zaheer 1999; Nohria and Ghoshal 1997). Unlike many MNCs, corporations engaged in infrastructure construction do not typically "straddle" fields – that is, engage in a portfolio of diversified activities that cross industry or sector boundaries – but they are confronted by many of the same basic strategic choices as other MNCs regarding extent of centralization of decision making, standardization of policies, and mobility of human resources (Westney 1993).

Apart from the major types of developers and construction companies, other types of players in this global field include the multilateral banks and other types of private equity investors, in particular, the multilateral agencies such as the World Bank and Asian Development Bank and infrastructure funds such as Alinda Capital Partners; international labor representatives, such as International Federation of Chemical, Energy, Mine and General Workers' Unions (ICEM), nongovernmental advocacy organizations operating at the national and/or transnational level, such as Friends of the River, The International Accountability Project, Amazonwatch, Rainforest Action Network, EarthAction, and a number of professional associations, such as the Construction Industry Institute (CII) and the Collaboratory for Research on Global Projects (CRGP), providing information and training services to the key players (see Brunsson and Jacobsson 2000; Cohen and Rai 2000; Keck and Sikkink 1998).

In terms of our conception of field structures, we observe the presence of a number of organizational *archetypes* that differentiate the various types of organizational populations involved – for example, developers, contractors, funding agencies, and INGOs.

The *governance systems* operating in this field include (1) more traditional nation-state enforced treaties such as the legal systems of the European Union (EU) or the World Trade Organization (WTO); (2) a dense web of bilateral investment treaties between states that have proliferated over the past two decades; (3) the standards and procedures enforced by various multilateral agencies, such as the World Bank, that make their funds conditional on adherence to them; and (4) the use of "softer" governance mechanisms, such as the Equator Principles, that involve the creation of normative frameworks promulgated by INGOs, conformity to which is voluntary, mutually reinforced, or overseen by a network of advocacy organizations (Keck and Sikkink 1998; Mörth 2006; Jacobsson and Sahlin-Andersson 2006). A variety of professional associations, including International Accounting Standards (IAS), the International Organization for Standardization (ISO), and the International Federation of Consulting Engineers (FIDIC) also set, promulgate, and enforce standards in their areas of expertise, such as quality, environmental safeguards or safety, encouraging compliance by appealing to scientific evidence, or global "best practice."

The *institutional logics* at play in this global field include, principally, those associated with the primary players: banks and financial interests that utilize and defend the importance of economic logics; law firms which negotiate the contracts and endeavor to protect the interests of their respective clients in terms of legal frameworks; specialized construction companies that embrace a variety of technical and occupational logics concerning how the work is to be done and by whom; and INGOs who variously craft and espouse the protection and advancement of widely shared norms and values concerning human rights and environmental concerns.

In short, the organizational field within which global infrastructure projects operate is extraordinarily complex. It is also dynamic, with the entry of new kinds of players – e.g., the recent rise of "south-south" investors and companies – the emergence of new kinds of institutional logics – e.g., increasing attention to sustainable projects, environmental safeguards, and "green" accounting – and the invention of new kinds of governance structures and mechanisms.

### (Field 2) The organizational field of the host community – time 1

Infrastructure projects must be conducted at a particular time and in a particular place, although sometimes components, such as turbines for a dam, may be prefabricated elsewhere in advance and delivered to the site for installation. The project is typically designed for a setting in which an established organizational field is already in place at the onset of the project. In short, we return to consider the "local environment" confronted by any organization, described above when we identified various levels of interest. However, in order to embrace a broader "field" definition, we augment the local set of interorganizational relations that exists at any community level and consists of the horizontal relations connecting competitors and allies with those vertical relations that connect local with more distant funding, regulatory or managerial units (Warren 1967; Scott and Meyer 1991).

Even if the project is sited in a relatively remote area, an organized field of actors and beliefs will already be in place. The size of the "local" field affected by the project is, necessarily, a function of the nature, size, and reach – the "footprint" – of the project envisioned, including its outputs and outcomes. In the case of a water treatment system, for example, the area that is economically, environmentally, and/or socially affected may be confined to a relatively small region; if a large dam or airport is to be constructed, the affected area will extend far beyond the area where the project is sited.

The composition and structure of a host community field varies greatly but, in most cases, will include the following categories of actors:

- *Relevant governmental organizations* – These may include governmental units at the local, state, or national level. Such units vary

along many important dimensions, including extent of democratization, involvement in larger geo-political structures and processes, and extent of state and local autonomy. They may include
units with planning or regulatory jurisdiction over the type of
infrastructure involved, customs agencies that must clear imported
components or materials, tax agencies, inspectors enforcing labor
or environmental standards, and building officials who must issue
permits for construction.

- *Individuals and organizations residing in the project area* – The
  socio-demographic and relational characteristics of the populations –
  of both individuals and organizations – vary greatly and will affect
  interest in and response to a given infrastructure project. Residents
  will be particularly sensitive to its effects on quality of life, traffic
  patterns, and taxes.
- *Those who are currently employed in the affected sector* – Workers
  and associated professional groups such as unions will have an
  important stake in the project proposed and will be sensitive to its
  implications for jobs and wages.
- *Social movement organizations* – SMOs exist in most contexts,
  although their characteristics and degree of activism differs
  according to the openness of the political system. Local SMOs
  may be independent entities or affiliates of state or national organizations, but even if independent may develop important political
  connections with other SMOs, both local, national, and transnational (see below).
- *Potential beneficiaries and end users* – Most projects are promoted
  by a set of sponsors and advocates, including those who will profit
  from, operate, or use the products/services of the completed project.

## (Field 3) The new field created by the project – time 2

Perhaps the most unusual organization field associated with global
projects is that created by the arrival and operation of the project
in the selected host community. New organizations will arise to
pursue and support – and to oppose – the project. Depending on the
nature and scale of the project, an existing local field is subject to
disruption and to re-structuration, reordering itself to accommodate
or to resist the newcomer. In many instances, the local field may be
permanently transformed.

Principal actors in the field at time 2 will include:

- *Project company* (PC) – Some specific combination of companies – including developers, financial backers, contractors and consultants – comes together to form a temporary private consortia, coordinated by the PC, to carry out and manage the work.
- *Project management unit* (PMU) – In some, but not all cases, the host government will establish its own entity – a PMU – to deal with and oversee the project to protect the interests of the host. In many cases, the PMU will employ expatriate consultants who attempt to bridge the cultural and institutional divide between the host government and the cadre of international contractors and consultants (see Mahalingam 2005; and Chapters 4, 6, and 7).
- *Those adversely affected by the project* – Groups residing in the area will come to recognize that their interests may be adversely affected by the project. Such groups may include those who currently supply similar or related services or those who are sponsoring competing project concepts or alternative services. These groups will attempt to mobilize to protect their interests and may seek to form alliances with others outside the affected area, including TSMOs (see Chapter 9).

Selected aspects of the global field (Field 1) and the host community field (Field 2) will be activated, but as these fields come together, they are likely to be altered, forming Field 3. The actors, logics, and types of governance systems that come into play will depend on the location of the project in time and space and the unfolding interaction of the principal players. Existing organizations and coalitions may be disrupted; selected local players will rise to new positions of power, and reactionary entities, such as protest movements, may emerge.

The success of the project will be affected by many factors since a large number of actors and forces are at play, but will depend critically on the type of project governance structures and mechanisms put in place to manage the relation between the PC and PMU as well as that with central stakeholders. And while the information requirements posed by these complex environments are daunting, data sources and strategies for analyzing them are being strengthened (see Chapter 10).

Our interest in global infrastructure projects may be seen as an aspect of the broader topic of changing business systems and practices in a time of increasing globalization. In the final section of this chapter, we briefly discuss the parameters of this larger debate, including the effects of globalizing forces on institutional differences, and the various categories of social actors and types of institutional logics at play.

## Globalization and institutions

We have largely avoided using the term globalization to this point, preferring, as noted, the more modest concept of transnational systems and processes. But globalization is one of the most commonly employed – some would say over-employed – concepts of our age: a mantra for our times. There is no dearth of commentary, in both the popular and scholarly literature, on the topic, in part because there exists great controversy over such fundamental issues as how recent a phenomena it is, to what extent it undermines the authority of nation-states, whether it is simply another name for "Westernization," and whether its effects are primarily beneficial or adverse (see Berger and Dore, 1996; Guillén 2001).

### *Globalization: toward greater homogeneity?*

While these are interesting and important issues, most salient for our purposes is the question of whether trends toward increasing globalization are causing institutions at all levels to become more homogenous, more similar over time. In Tom Friedman's (2005) colorful language, is the world becoming "flat"? In discussing a "flat" world, Friedman's emphasis is on the creation of a more level playing field: more competitive markets. But such leveling necessarily entails the smoothing over of many types of institutional differences which create barriers to the free exchange of goods and services. Hence, it is appropriate to ask: Are the kinds of institutional differences which we have described, and which are a major focus of this volume, disappearing before our eyes?

If we examine Friedman's list of "flattening forces" – the mechanisms he argues to be at work in bringing about increased similarity among companies and countries – it is notable that 9 of the 10 forces he discusses involve new technologies and/or related changes in production and distribution systems. (The lone exception, a political event, was the fall of the Berlin Wall in 1989.) Friedman discusses such information-technology breakthroughs as the invention of the web-browser, "Netscape," and the development of workflow software. Other, organizational, innovations cited as important include the development of open-sourcing collaborative communities, outsourcing, and of supply chains that link production processes across companies (Freidman 2005: chap. 2). There is no disputing that these are significant developments currently underway and that they affect important features of the production and flow of goods and services. Nevertheless, the arguments made rely on a kind of technological and economic determinism: technological and economic forces shaping society – an argument not unlike Karl Marx made more than a century ago. Like others (e.g., Gay 2005), we believe it important to consider the play of other types of forces active in fashioning the modern world. We should not overlook the importance of cultural elements – symbolic systems such as ideas, beliefs, and ideologies that guide and justify our actions. We consider five conceptions of the types of forces at work.

**World system**
John Meyer and associates (Drori, Meyer, and Hwang 2006; Krucken and Drori 2009; Meyer et al. 1997) largely support Friedman's view of increasing homogeneity among societies, but emphasize cultural rather than technological forces as inducing the process. This approach argues that the global expansion of similar nation-states and organizations is less a function of increasing exchanges and information technology than of the diffusion of a cultural model stipulating the structural features of modernity and rationalization. They document that modern state and organizational structures are less dependent on economic development or trade relations than on the rise of scientific and professional connections carried by the spread of globalized educational institutions.

Agreeing that cultural and political forces play a central role, Berger (2002) points out that the messages carried are by no means consistent and uniform: while some push toward increased homogeneity, others support divergence and variety. He identifies a number of competing conceptions and their associated "carriers":

**"Davos" culture**
Following Huntington (1996), we employ this term, which refers to the annual World Economic Forum meeting held in the Swiss

mountain resort Davos, to label the recently dominant international culture of business and political leaders. Supporters of this belief system include representatives from the major MNCs and their political allies. Although cloaked in the neutral language of economic analysis, the Davos culture espouses an ideology of corporate liberalism, calling for more openness of markets and fewer political restrictions on corporate decision making. The belief advanced is that if governments do not unduly interfere and attempt to restrict the movement of capital and labor, thereby allowing these resources to flow freely and find their best (most productive) use, then all will prosper. Clearly, such ideas have been a "flattening" force, reducing institutional differences in political and economic systems among societies in recent years (Streeck and Thelen 2005a).

A number of international governance structures were created to advance this ideology, including the World Bank, International Monetary Fund, and World Trade Organization. These financial institutions/governance structures receive support from associations of corporate executives, banking interests, and investors groups, as well as sympathetic governments.

Obviously, however, this point of view has suffered a serious setback with the onset of the recent global financial crisis. Governmental intervention and stricter regulatory regimes suddenly enjoy widespread support. However, it remains to be seen to what extent the governance arrangements devised to reform the system will continue to rely on market-based mechanisms near and dear to adherents of the Davos culture.[5]

### Intellectual and professional culture

This multi-vocal culture is made up of ideas advanced by academics and other professionals, foundations, and various INGOs. While many of the ideas advanced, such as those based on scientific evidence or on broadly shared humanitarian principles, may be viewed as having a flattening effect since they assume a universalistic institutional logic as the world system perspective emphasizes, others emphasize the value of protecting and advancing difference and diversity. Such is the case for biologists seeking to stress the value of biodiversity, of theologians and philosophers advocating the value of multiple religious traditions, or of social scientists and activists stressing the advantages of cultural diversity and of protecting the rights of indigenous peoples. Moreover, many of the arguments made by these agents conflict with and challenge the relatively narrow, neoliberal Davos culture by insisting that in addition to advancing economic development, it is important to attend to the rights of workers, consumers, and environmental concerns.

The claims made by this diverse professional community and advocacy groups are backed by a wide range of foundations, associations, and associated governance structures, including international organizations such as agencies of the United Nations and World Health Organization, as well as a growing collection of INGOs. As already described, these groups rely primarily on normative pressures, but also attempt to gain the ear of government authorities so that their concerns can be built into laws and treaties.

### Popular culture

We refer here, of course, to the many varieties of mass media: movies, television, newspapers, magazines, music videos, and, increasingly, the internet. Appadurai (1996) refers to these types of cultural products and carriers as "media-scapes" that provide us with a large and rich repertory of images, narratives, and worldviews, increasingly shared by viewers throughout the world.

The transmission of population culture is not associated with governance structures in a conventional sense, but it clearly has its champions and disseminators in organizations such as MTV and other broadcast networks and in the giant media corporations, including Time Warner, Disney, and Viacom. As Appadurai (1996: 53) points out:

The imagination – expressed in dreams, songs, fantasies, myths, and stories – has always been part of the repertoire of every society, in some culturally organized way. But there is a peculiar new force to the imagination in social life today. More persons in more parts of the world consider a wider set of possible lives than they ever did before. One important source of this change is the mass media, which present a rich, ever-changing store of possible lives.

Again, while it would seem that the widespread dissemination of mass media would operate to advance flattening and homogenization of institutional differences, a number of studies show that while the mass media penetrates widely, it sets in motion processes termed "indigenization" that adapt these messages to local circumstances and combine them with elements from the local culture creating hybridization and fusion rather than cultural uniformity (Appadurai 1996; Hannerz 1996). Appadurai (1996: 11) concludes, "globalization is not the story of cultural homogenization."

### Critics and skeptics
Another voice in the discourse on globalization is supplied by a large subset of vocal and increasingly influential activist organizations, ranging from the Sierra Club and Greenpeace to the Rainforest Action Network and the Alliance for Global Justice. These advocacy groups have been quick to take advantage of the new technologies, including the cell phone and the Internet, to mobilize large numbers of people on short notice to dissent from and disrupt global projects (Cohen and Rai 2000; Smith and Johnston 2002). In some cases, disparate and isolated SMOs, have come together to forge a powerful, unified coalition, as exemplified by the success of the World Commission on Dams, which since the late-1980s has reduced greatly the number of large dams constructed (Khagram 2004).

All of these, as well as other voices shape globalization processes.

## The persistence of institutional differences

A number of empirical indicators suggest that the pervasiveness of globalization as a flattening process which levels cultural/political/ social differences has been much exaggerated in popular media accounts. Thus, Ghemawat (2007) has amassed data from a variety of sources that indicate that, on average, only about 10 percent of economic activity at the beginning of the twenty-first century – e.g., telephone calls, direct investment, stock investment – involved inter-national exchanges. As a consequence, he prefers to talk of "semi-globalization" and insists that we need to take into account not only geographic and economic distance in examining cross-societal trans-actions, but also administrative and cultural distance in assessing transnational connections.

In a similar vein, Campbell (2004: chap. 5) has compiled data that contradicts the thesis that national economies are rapidly converging in their industrial policies to adopt neoliberal approaches to tax policies or regulative regimes. Rather, he finds the continuation of a variety of societal approaches to managing the relations between the economic sectors and the polity. There continue to exist, narrowly, a variety of forms of capitalism (Berger and Dore 1996; Hall and Soskice 2001; Hancké, Rhodes, and Thatcher 2008), or, more generally, a variety of socio-economic structures (Whitley 1992b; 1999) and cultural systems (Hofstede 1991; Huntington 1996) which have radically different effects on the ways in which local business is conducted – and hence have important implications for infrastructure projects.

It is also clear that institutional change is a complex process, manifesting itself in different times and places as displacement (the emergence and diffusion of new models replacing old), layering (as new patterns are added, but do not supplant existing practices), drift (the gradual erosion of existing practices), conversion (the redirection of existing institutional practices to new purposes), and exhaustion (gradual collapse of an institutional regime) (Streeck and Thelen 2005b).

In sum, at least in the "short" run – for the next several decades or so – it appears that "institutional differences" will continue to be salient, affecting, among many other endeavors, the success of global projects. Indeed, somewhat ironically, given the many technological innovations that conquered physical distance and increased interaction and interdependence among peoples around the world – the flattening forces – persisting institutional differences are likely to become of even greater salience. These differences, which induce psychic distance among individuals, have formerly been buffered by physical separation. When individuals from different traditions, cultures, and cognitive worlds find themselves engaged in face-to-face, highly interdependent project groups, the latent differences suddenly become manifest. In a flattened world, the frictions and clashes that are caused between actors that are imbued with interpretive schemes from competing and conflicting institutional frameworks create a whole new set of challenges for those who design and manage organizations. Institutions matter, perhaps now more than ever!

## Endnotes

1 Other efforts to construct conceptual frameworks for understanding institutional forces include those of Aldrich and Fiol (1994), Campbell (2004), Greif (2006), Hall and Taylor (1996), Peters (1999), and Suchman (1995). Still other frameworks focus primarily on cultural differences – a subset of institutional differences – (e.g., Hofstede 1984; 1991).

2 In earlier times, and in some societies today, religious authorities are able to exercise regulative control.

3 On the Camisea pipeline project in Peru, which we studied, two NGOs both claimed to represent the same "uncontacted" indigenous group that would potentially be impacted by a planned – and now constructed – energy pipeline project. One NGO was in support of the project; the second NGO was implacably opposed to it.

4 For a related discussion of types of fields together with a description of fields surrounding public–private partnerships (PPPs), see Chapter 11.

5 Some analysts suggest that governmental officials in the US charged with designing the "bail-out" and other recovery programs underway are the victims of "cognitive regulatory capture" – having spent too many years of their career on Wall Street.

# 3 | Social movements and the growth in opposition to global projects

DOUG McADAM

## Why social movements?

At first blush it might seem odd to accord a prominent conceptual spot to the study of social movements in a volume on "global projects." And indeed, if this volume had been put together thirty to forty years ago, it would not have been necessary. But the world was a very different place in, say, the mid-1970s. In much of the developing world at that time the main challenges to large infrastructure projects remained primarily technical and/or engineering in nature. Not so anymore. Today virtually all the big technical challenges to such projects have been solved. The primary threats to global infrastructure projects now take the form of misunderstandings and conflicts resulting from conflicting institutional frameworks or from the reactive mobilization by grassroots groups and/or nongovernmental organizations (NGOs) opposed to construction. This chapter details the challenges posed by the latter source: collective movements resistant to development.

The emergence of reactive mobilizing groups mirrors an earlier shift toward resistance to infrastructure projects that occurred in the democratic West. Such projects were almost invariably completed in the first five to six decades of the twentieth century, but resistance to such projects increased substantially in the 1960s, and especially in the 1970s, as the rise of the New Left in the US and the "new social movements" in Western Europe, dramatically increased the general levels of social movement activity in those countries. We see the same pattern unfolding in the developing world, only beginning some fifteen to twenty years later than in the industrialized democracies. This second trend is now very much in evidence. Big dams were perhaps the first sector to fully embody the trend (Khagram 2004), but all manner of large infrastructure projects now appear to be increasingly "at risk" of catalyzing mobilized opposition.

We are drawn to this phenomenon by motives beyond our professional interests as social movement scholars. This trend has important implications far beyond the study of social movements. The issue of infrastructure and infrastructure projects is both vitally important and exceedingly complex. The importance of the issue derives from the massive infrastructure needs projected for the developing world over the next twenty to thirty years. Consensus estimates for population growth predict that there will be another billion people on earth by 2015, almost all of them born in developing countries with minimal existing infrastructure (Sachs 2005). Providing these people with affordable and sustainable housing, safe drinking water, sewage, energy, transportation, and communication generates a demand for about $1 trillion in infrastructure development over the next five years in East Asia alone, and upwards of $3 trillion worldwide (Asian Development Bank, Japan Bank for International Cooperation et al. 2005).

The complexity of the challenge becomes clear when we simultaneously recognize the right of local communities to exercise voice over the siting of these projects and the fact that, in the past, a good many of these facilities were built to satisfy Western political and financial priorities, with correspondingly little regard for the well-being of either the host country or the peoples directly affected by the projects (Karl 1997). In short, while respecting the rights of local communities to respond to legitimate environmental, human rights, and other threats, we will have to find ways to press ahead with critical infrastructure projects or consign the developing world to ever more severe levels of poverty and deprivation in the years to come. Understanding the dynamics of reactive resistance to such projects and, eventually, the kind of enlightened governance arrangements that give communities a meaningful voice in their design and operation will be critical, not only to reducing Western exploitation in the developing world, but if we are to break through the infrastructure gridlock that is coming to characterize much of the globe.

## Social movement theory

To better understand the mobilization of opposition to global projects we turn to that body of scholarship – social movement studies – that has most concerned itself with such matters. We begin with a brief history of the field.

## From "collective behavior" to "social movements"

Until roughly 1975 there was no body of work devoted exclusively to the study of social movements. Indeed, to the extent that they were studied at all, social movements were seen as but one type of a more general social phenomenon known as *collective behavior.* The other forms of behavior that comprised the category were panics, crazes, fads, crowds, and revolutions. The list betrays the underlying view of social movements. These collective behaviors were seen as reflecting the unusual, the aberrant, the irrational in social life. But from whence did they arise? All forms of collective behavior were held to be responses to rapid social change and the breakdown of social order. It is important to emphasize, though, that the response was not seen, even in the case of social movements and revolutions, as a form of rational, instrumental politics, but rather a kind of psychological coping behavior. Rapid social change encouraged mobilization, not by altering power relationships or creating new grievances, but by engendering feelings of alienation, anomie, frustration, etc. that supplied the underlying motive force for collective action. In short, social movements were seen as collective attempts to manage or resolve the psychological tensions produced by social change and the resulting breakdown of social order.

This emphasis on the psychological functions of social movements was also reflected in the more micro-level accounts of movement participation. Particular personality types or states of mind, rather than instrumental rationality, were held to dispose individuals to movement participation. Writing in 1959, William Kornhauser, one of the major proponents of this approach, argued that "mass movements are not looking for pragmatic solutions to economic or any other kind of problem. If they were so oriented, their emotional fervor and chiliastic zeal . . . would not characterize the psychological tone of these movements. In order to account for that tone, we must look beyond economic interests to more deep-seated psychological tendencies" (1959: 163).

Yet another key theorist in this tradition, Neil Smelser, concurred, offering a more starkly Freudian account of movement participation. Wrote Smelser (1973: 317):

The striking feature of the protest movement is what Freud observed: it permits the expression of impulses that are normally repressed . . . The efforts – sometimes conscious and sometimes unconscious – of leaders and adherents of a movement to create issues, to provoke authorities . . . would seem to be in part efforts to "arrange" reality so as to "justify" the expression of normally forbidden impulses in a setting which makes them appear less reprehensible to the participants.

The emphasis is clear: at both the macro and micro levels of analysis, social movements are more properly viewed as a psychological, rather than political, phenomenon. Accordingly, they are better left, in Gamson's wonderful phrase, to "the social psychologist whose intellectual tools prepare him to better understand the irrational" (1990: 133).

In an era in which social movements are ubiquitous and appear to be such a consequential *political* phenomenon, this older psychological perspective may seem odd or quaint. It becomes more comprehensible, however, when we think about the touchstone movements the older generation of scholars was seeking to explain. For them, writing as they did in the post World War II period, it was the rise of the Nazis in Germany and Soviet-style Communism that begged explanation. And while more recent scholarship has suggested that even these "extreme" movements are not adequately accounted for by psychological explanations, at the time such accounts seemed plausible given both the horrors associated with the movements and the liberal/left values of the scholars who took them as their subject matter.

The progressive movements – civil rights, peace, feminist, environmental – of the 1960s and 1970s in the US and Western Europe were quite a different matter. With the values of a younger generation of scholar/activists clearly aligned with these movements, the older psychological accounts of protest fell quickly out of favor. In their place, came newer perspectives that shifted the focus from psychological factors to the organizational and/or political dimensions of protest. In the US the *resource mobilization* (McCarthy and Zald 1973; 1977) and *political process* (Tilly 1978; McAdam 1999[1982]; Tarrow 1983) perspectives held sway. In Europe, *new social movement* theory (Kriesi 1989b; Melucci 1980, 1985, 1989; Touraine, 1981) was dominant. Whatever their differences, all of these perspectives defined social movements as a form of *rational politics*, practiced primarily by traditionally powerless or marginalized segments of society. By asserting this view, the newer generation of scholars redefined the study of social movements as the proper province of political sociologists and organizational scholars.

This reframing of the field and the popularity of the "new left" movements in the US and the "new social movements" in Europe led to a broad outpouring of work on the topic. Over the past quarter century, the study of social movements has emerged as a major sub-field within sociology and an important topic for study within a number of other social science fields, most notably political science. If anything, interest in the general topic and the pace of work in the field has only increased with time. And with the escalating advance of scholarship has come an expansion in research topics and the application of social movement theory to a much broader range of cases – historically and geographically – than the ones typically taken up by the pioneer generation of scholars active during the 1970s and 1980s. And yet within this profusion of work we think it is still possible to discern a general analytic consensus concerning the broad factors that shape the emergence, development, and decline of social movements.

## Opportunities and threats, mobilizing structures, framing processes

Three broad sets of factors continue to structure a great deal of theorizing and empirical research in the study of social movements. These three factors are (1) the evolving structure of political opportunities and threats that movement groups (as well as other actors) confront; (2) the density and forms of organization (informal as well as formal) available to insurgent groups; and (3) the collective processes of interpretation, attribution, and social construction that mediate between opportunity/threat and action. It will be easier to refer to these factors by the conventional shorthand designations familiar to movement scholars: *political opportunities/threats, mobilizing structures*, and *framing processes*. We take up each in turn.

## Political opportunities and/or threats

While it is now common for movement scholars to emphasize the central role of the broader political system in shaping the prospects for emergent collective action, the theoretical influences underpinning the insight are not all that old. In the United States it was the work of such *political process* theorists as Tilly (1978), McAdam (1999[1982]), and Tarrow (1983) that first asserted the link between institutionalized politics and social movement activity. Drawing inspiration from these works, a number of European scholars began to craft the *new social movement* tradition which brought a comparative dimension to the study of *political opportunity structures*. Among the first Europeans to explore the link between institutionalized and movement politics were Kriesi (1989a), Kitschelt (1986), Koopmans (1995), and Duyvenkak (1995).

Though sharing a general theoretical point of departure, the earliest US and European scholars working in this tradition tended to be oriented to slightly different research questions. While most US scholars were interested in how political environmental *changes* set particular movements in motion, their European counterparts tended to emphasize differences in the more *stable* features of political systems as a way of accounting for variation in the rates and forms of movement activity within Europe. This difference no doubt stemmed in part from the fact that most US scholars focused attention on a single case and relied on longitudinal data to measure shifts in political opportunity. By contrast, European scholars engaged in comparative work that sought to link changes in the character and pace of movement activity to the differences in national governance arrangements.

Over time an important distinction has emerged in this literature. Initially, scholars were overwhelmingly attuned to the role of expanding *political opportunities* as catalysts of movement activity. By political opportunity, we simply mean any significant change in (a) the formal institutional structure, or (b) the repressive capacity of the state, or (c) the informal set of alliances within a polity that either grant new leverage to movement groups or weaken the power/influence of their opponents. Virtually all initial work in this tradition emphasized the catalytic effect of favorable changes in political opportunity on the rise and/or success of particular social movements (McAdam 1999 [1982]; Costain 1992; Tarrow 1989).

Gradually, however, other analysts came to question the exclusive stress on opportunities. Richard Flacks (1988) was among the first to argue that *threats* were as likely to set movements in motion as opportunities. Subsequently, a number of other theorists joined Flacks in calling for equal attention to the role of threats and opportunities in shaping movement activity (Goldstone and Tilly 2001; McAdam 1999[1982]). When combined with the extensive, empirical literature on "Not in My Backyard Movements" (NIMBYs), it is now abundantly clear that movements can arise from perceived threats to group interest as well as opportunities to advance those interests. Current speculation holds that most rights-based movements or liberation struggles are triggered by expanding opportunities, while most other kinds of movements – including the kind of opposition to global projects that is of interest here – are more responsive to perceived threats to group interests or identities.

There is another sense in which movement scholars have come to grant more equal analytic attention to the concepts of threat and opportunity. In recent years, critics have argued that the field has become too "movement-centric," focusing exclusively on the behavior of insurgent groups and ignoring the interactive dynamics that shape the broader "episodes of contention" in which movements are typically embedded. In their book *Dynamics of contention*, McAdam, Tarrow, and Tilly (2001) urge scholars to redefine the central phenomenon of interest as contentious episodes rather than movements per se. What does all of this have to do with "threat" and "opportunity?" When one moves from studying a movement to the broader episode of contention of which the movement is but a part, one invariably finds that threat *and* opportunity are both implicated in the case as experienced by the contending parties. Similar to organization theory's concept of "field" (see Chapter 2), a broader focus on episodes encourages attention to the wider array of collective actors at play.

Consider the following "revisionist" account of the episode of contention that gave rise to the US Civil Rights Movement. Most conventional analyses of the *movement* begin the story with the onset of grassroots civil rights activism in Montgomery, Alabama in 1955–56. A mix of political opportunities – including the growing importance of the "black vote," the progressive judicial philosophy of the Warren Court, and the onset of the Cold War, which made American racism a significant foreign policy liability – are normally credited with setting the movement in motion by granting increasing leverage to civil rights forces (McAdam 1999[1982]). If, however, we focus not on the movement per se, but the broader episode of contention of which the movement is but a part, the story looks very different. In this retelling, the broader episode begins almost ten years earlier with the onset of the Cold War. And it is various kinds of threats, not opportunities, that set the episode in motion.

It begins with Truman's limited advocacy of civil rights reform. As modest as these initiatives seem to us now, they were infused with extraordinary political and cultural significance at the time, marking, as they did, the first federal initiatives on race since the end of Reconstruction. As such they represented the very public abrogation of the long-standing federal/southern "understanding" on race that had ceded control of the "Negro question" to the white South. The question is what prompted Truman to take such a momentous step? Though his initiatives would seem to fall under the heading of "domestic politics," they make little sense when analyzed in that context. As I wrote in 1999 (p. xx):

> . . . Truman's status as a non-incumbent made him uniquely vulnerable to challenge as he headed into the 1948 [presidential] election. Moreover with black voters now returning solid majorities for his party, Truman had seemingly little to gain and everything to lose by alienating that strange, but critically important, New Deal bedfellow: the southern Dixiecrat. And that, of course, is just what his advocacy of civil rights reform did. Angered by his proactive support of civil rights, the Dixiecrats broke away from the party in 1948 and ran their own candidate, Strom Thurmond, for president. The electoral votes of the once "solid" south were now in jeopardy.

Truman's otherwise puzzling behavior becomes entirely comprehensible, however, when we realize he was motivated much more by foreign policy considerations than domestic politics. Locked in an intense, ideological struggle with the Soviet Union for influence around the globe, Truman saw American style racism as a significant foreign policy liability. In embracing the need for civil rights reform, Truman was motivated by nothing so much as the postwar Soviet *threat* and the obvious propaganda weapon which Jim Crow afforded the USSR. And in breaking with Truman and the national Democratic Party in 1948 the Dixiecrats were also motivated by threat rather than opportunity. In Truman's actions they saw a profound *threat* to the "southern way of life," not to mention the Democratic Party's political dominance in the South. Of the major protagonists involved in the postwar conflict on race, then, only civil rights forces were responding to opportunities rather than threats. And at that, they were relative latecomers to the conflict. The onset of the mass movement in Montgomery may have represented a crucial escalation of the conflict, but not its point of origin. Indeed, rather than Montgomery sparking the conflict, the reverse is true. It was the reopening of the *national* debate on race between 1946 and 1948 that granted the *local* struggle in Montgomery heightened significance, both on the national and the world stage.

From an initial preoccupation with opportunities and a narrow focus on movements, scholars in the field are increasingly attuned to the need to study contention rather than movements per se, to consider the wider field of factors and forces at play, and to see a mix of opportunities and threats motivating action by the various parties to the conflict. In thinking about opposition to "global projects," we too will adopt this broader analytic framework.

## Mobilizing structures

If destabilizing changes to systems of institutionalized politics set movements in motion, their influence is not independent of the various kinds of *mobilizing structures* through which groups seek to organize. By mobilizing structures we mean those collective vehicles, informal as well as formal, through which people organize and engage in emergent collective action. This focus on the meso-level groups, organizations, and informal networks that comprise the structural building blocks of social movements constitutes the second conceptual element in the analytic framework shared by most movement scholars.

As was the case with the work on political opportunities, theory and scholarship on the organizational requirements and dynamics of collective action drew its initial inspiration from two distinct theoretical perspectives. The most important of these was *resource mobilization* theory. As formulated by its original proponents, McCarthy and Zald (1973, 1977), resource mobilization sought to break with the grievance and strain-based conceptions of social movements and to focus instead on the mobilization processes and the organizational manifestations of these processes. This approach departed substantially from earlier work which viewed social movements as almost the converse of formal organizations. However, McCarthy and Zald called attention to the fact that social movements that persisted for any length of time did so by becoming *social movement organizations* (SMOs). If they are to be sustained, movements, like all organizations, must find a reliable supply of resources, devise a division of labor, develop some sort of incentives and controls, and tend to its boundaries. In some ways, theirs was less a theory about the emergence or development of social movements than it was an attempt to describe and map a new social movement form – professional social movement organizations – that they saw as becoming increasingly dominant in the US in the 1970s.

The second theoretical tradition to encourage work on the organizational dynamics of collective action was the *political process model*. Scholars working within this tradition, in general, dissent from resource mobilization's equation of social movements with formal organization, instead devoting more attention to the processes and mechanisms by which movements emerge and evolve. Charles Tilly and various of his colleagues (Tilly et al. 1975; Tilly 1978) laid the conceptual foundation for this second approach by documenting the critical role of various established social settings – work and neighborhood, in particular – in structuring contentious collective action in nineteenth-century Europe. Drawing on Tilly's work, others in the newer generation of social movement scholars sought to apply his insights to various New Left struggles in the US. So Morris (1984) and McAdam (1999[1982]) analyzed the critical role played by local black institutions – principally churches and colleges – in the emergence of the US civil rights movement. Similarly Evans's (1980) research clearly located the origins of the women's liberation movement within informal friendship networks forged by women who were active in the southern civil rights struggle and American New Left. In turn, these early studies spawned a vibrant tradition of research on the role of network-based recruitment processes very much in the spirit of the political process model's emphasis on informal, grassroots mobilizing structures (Gould 1991, 1995; Kriesi 1988; McAdam 1986; McAdam and Paulsen 1993; Snow, Zurcher, and Ekland-Olson 1980).

While some early proponents of these approaches initially treated the two models of movement organization as mutually exclusive, over time the profusion of work inspired by both has led to a growing awareness among movement scholars of the diversity of collective settings in which movements develop and of the organizational forms to which they give rise. So instead of debating the relative merits of these "opposing" views, movement scholars have increasingly turned their attention to other research agendas concerning the organizational dynamics of social movements. Among the more interesting of these agendas have been (1) the evolving population ecology of specific movement "industries" or entire movement "sectors" (Minkoff 1993, 1995);

(2) the mapping of interorganizational networks within particular movements (Anheier 2003; Broadbent 1998; Diani 1995; Osa 2003a, 2003b; Passy 2003) or between movement groups within urban settings (Baldassarri and Diani 2007; Diani and Bison 2004; McLaughlin et al., 2009); and (3) the rapid expansion in transnational social movement organizations, which we will elaborate below (Smith 1998, 2005).

The other exciting development in this area has been the increasing volume of work at the intersection of social movement studies and organizational theory. In developing the resource mobilization perspective, McCarthy and Zald sought self-consciously to apply organizational theory to the social movement phenomenon. For some twenty years after that the borrowing remained distinctly one-sided, with social movement scholars making far more use of insights from organizational studies than the reverse. In the last ten years, however, this has changed as organizational scholars have come to see social movement theory as a fruitful perspective for helping to understand the processes of change and conflict that are increasingly ubiquitous in organizational life (Clemens 1996, 1997; Davis and McAdam 2000; McAdam and Scott 2005; Schneiberg 2002; Strang and Soule 1998; Vogus and Davis 2005). Indeed, in many ways, just as movements have come more and more to resemble organizations, organizations, with their shifting boundaries and more flexible structures, increasingly resemble social movements (Davis et al., 2005).

## Framing and other subjective processes

If the combination of political opportunities and mobilizing structures affords incipient insurgent groups a certain structural potential for action, they remain, in the absence of one other broad set of factors, insufficient to account for emergent collective action. Mediating between opportunity/threat and organizing activities are the shared meanings and emotions that people bring to their situation. At a minimum some critical mass of individuals must feel both aggrieved about some aspect of their lives and optimistic that, by acting collectively, they can redress the situation. Lacking the necessary mix of cognition and emotion that supports these two perceptions, it is highly unlikely that people will mobilize even when afforded the objective opportunity and organizational capacity to do so. Conditioning the presence or absence of these shared meanings/emotions is a host of complex social psychological and cognitive processes that movement scholars have only recently begun to explore. We refer to these under the general heading of *framing processes*, but in truth framing is only one of four types of subjective processes that appear to be implicated in emergent collective action. Moreover, of the four, framing may well be the one least critical to initial mobilization. Still, because of its prominent place in the social movement literature we take up framing first.

**Framing**

Snow and colleagues (1986) coined, or more accurately, first applied Goffman's (1974) term to the study of social movements. This contribution helped to crystallize and articulate a growing discontent among movement scholars over how little significance proponents of the resource mobilization and political process perspectives attached to ideas and shared meanings in their models. In sharp contrast to McCarthy and Zald's (1973) assertion that grievances were ever-present and therefore largely irrelevant to movement emergence, Snow and colleagues argued persuasively that even if one could identify *objective* grounds for discontent in society, how these conditions were understood *subjectively* was highly variable and therefore critically important to an understanding of movement dynamics. Reflecting this premise, scholars in this tradition have sought to highlight the self-conscious efforts of movement actors to strategically frame issues in such a way as to convert and motivate activists, appeal to bystander publics, attract media attention, garner allies, and, ultimately, influence policymakers (Babb 1996, Cress and Snow 2000, Diani 1996, Noonan 1995, Rohlinger 2002). However, this emphasis on self-conscious, strategic framing implies the existence of a relatively mature movement guided by self-styled movement leaders or activists. In short, as a form of ideational work, framing applies primarily to the ongoing development of a movement, rather than its beginnings. Three other processes would seem better suited to this latter challenge.

**"Cognitive liberation"**

Besides the stress on political opportunities and existing supportive social systems, proponents of the political process model also emphasize the need for some kind of transformation in group consciousness as a requirement of movement emergence. This process is referred to as "cognitive liberation" (McAdam 1999[1982]: 48–51). This may be viewed as a specific type of ideational work in which individuals attempt to collectively make sense of their situations (Weick 1995). As long as group members see their fate as legitimate or feel powerless to change it, collective action is almost certainly not going to take place. At a minimum a critical mass of group members must either begin to view some aspect of their life as unjust or illegitimate and/or come to believe in the efficacy of group action if a movement is to develop. While the political process perspective is typically seen as synonymous with the "political opportunity" concept, much of the causal force of those opportunities depends upon the subjective impact they have on the perceptions of potential participants. The argument is that as favorable changes occur in the environment the cognitive underpinnings of the status quo are undermined, helping to set in motion the transformation of group consciousness so critical to movement emergence.

### Emotion work and the affective requirements of contention

Even as movement scholars began to explore the subjective dimension of collective action, the stress remained resolutely on cognition and shared meanings. The concepts of "framing" and "cognitive liberation" reflect this bias. By contrast, until very recently, the role of emotion in social movements remained largely unexplored (although, in a sense, it resonated with the formulations of those early students of collective behavior). With the work of such scholars as Aminzade and McAdam (2001), Gould (2002, 2009) and Goodwin, Jasper, and Polletta (2001) this has begun to change. Motivating these works is the shared view that emergent collective action turns as much on the play of heightened emotions as on any set of new cognitions or shared meanings. The emotions most often thought key to movement emergence are either anger or fear, though without sufficient belief in the power of collective action (read: hope), even these powerful emotions are not likely to produce sustained collective action.

Less work has been done on the sources of such emotions, but that which has been done has tended to emphasize either the role of dramatic events in sparking widespread anger or fear as a catalyst for mobilization or the strategic efforts at *emotion work* by movement activists. As examples of the former, one could point to the outrage sparked by the very public death of Emmett Till as a catalyst for civil rights activism, or the fear aroused by the accident at Three Mile Island as a spur to environmental activism in the wake of the incident (Walsh and Warland 1983). Gould's groundbreaking 2009 book on the origins, development, and decline of ACT-UP includes any number of fascinating examples of emotion work in the context of the organization's activism in combating AIDS.

### Collective identity

It is from the work of European scholars associated with *new social movement* theory that another helpful concept as been added to these subjective, "culturalist" perspectives on movement emergence. In the eyes of such scholars as Alain Touraine (1981) and especially Alberto Melucci (1980, 1985, 1989), the defining quality of social movements is their capacity to generate new sources of *collective identity* to bind their adherents together. For these scholars, emergent collective action implies the presence of a new, unifying identity. Thoughtful applications of this emphasis have been crafted by Armstrong (2005), who studied the gradual coalescence of a field of gay/lesbian organizations in San Francisco from 1950 to 1990. Although some of these groups organized around "issues" (e.g., equal rights), others mobilized in order to create more space within which they could more fully express "who we are." And Rao and colleagues (Rao, Monin, and Durand 2003), examined the rise of "upstart" chefs in France during the 1960s who challenged the hegemony of *haute cuisine* to create *nouvelle cuisine*. In doing so, they turned their backs on existing institutional logics – conventional ideas about how to define and carry out one's work – and adopted a new conception of the chef's role which involved increased autonomy to experiment with recipes and reconfigured modes of relating to waiters and other members of the staff.

## Social movement theory and global projects

Having provided a brief account of developments in social movement scholarship over the past few decades, we turn now to connect them to the primary topic of this volume: global infrastructure development projects. It is not just construction firms, professional services corporations offering legal and other business services, and financial institutions that have reorganized their operations in order to work more effectively in a global environment. Social movement organizations, mobilized around a diverse set of issues affected by infrastructure development, have also elevated their operations so that they can exercise influence more effectively across multiple countries. While fewer than 200 transnational SMOs existed in the 1970s, by the year 2000 almost 1,000 such organizations were in existence, working on issues such as human rights, the environment, development and empowerment, and global justice (Smith 2005). Hence, social movement processes occur at three levels: at the local level in response to a specific proposed project, at a national level, often in support of local movements, and at a transnational level, as established movements attempt to intervene directly to affect developments of concern wherever they occur around the world as well as to provide resources for and assistance to local movements.

While important differences remain among specific nations and local movements, scholars have identified a number of forces conducing to greater similarities among countries and projects. Giugni (2002) suggests that the processes at work to increase greater homogeneity among countries include: (1) globalization phenomena that work to "disembed" social relations from local contexts together with the creation of transnational structures that support convergence in mobilization processes employed by national movements; (2) an increase in structural isomorphism: the tendency for national structures – both nation-state and other organizations – to become more similar over time; and (3) the diffusion of practices from one context to another as innovations, tactics, and techniques travel from one area to another.

We can build and elaborate on these processes by employing the opportunities/threats, organization, framing perspective previously outlined. In a later chapter (Chapter 8), we discuss some of the types of factors that affect the likelihood and extent of movement activities in relation to pipeline and water projects across a number of countries. We organize the argument around the three broad causal factors discussed above to offer a general account of why anti-project movements have become so ubiquitous. In this discussion, however, we reverse the order and begin with what we see as arguably the most important of the three factors: the subjective meanings associated with events that animate anti-project activists.

## Human rights, environmentalism, and the spread of other insurgent frames

It is conventional to criticize the "political process" perspective for its "structural bias" and inattention to subjective, "culturalist" processes (Goodwin and Jasper 1999; Gould 2009). This critique seems valid at least when applied to the perspective as it evolved and came to be associated almost exclusively with the concept of "political opportunity structure." In its original formulation, however, meaning making and shared understandings were central to the theory. Consider the following quote from an initial sketch of the perspective (McAdam 1999[1982]: 48):

> While important, expanding political opportunities and indigenous organization do not, in any simple sense, produce a social movement ... Together they only offer insurgents a certain objective 'structural potential' for collective political action. Mediating between opportunity and action are people and the subjective meanings they attach to their situations.

This is why we begin our application of the theory with a consideration of the origins and spread of various "insurgent frames" that have encouraged growing opposition to infrastructure projects in many parts of the world.

Most of these movements frame their opposition to the projects in the language of human rights (including the rights of indigenous people) and/or in environmental terms. For John Meyer and his colleagues these two issues – along with a concern for women's rights – are among the central normative "requirements" for gaining standing among nations in the current global order (Drori, Meyer, and Hwang 2006; Meyer, Boli, Thomas, and Ramirez 1997; Meyer et al. 1997). A concomitant of modernization, this Western-dominated world order began to take shape at least 300 years ago, but with a more accelerated pace since World War II and especially over the past two decades. These scholars argue that, beginning with the Enlightenment period, Western conceptions of individuals as not simply "subjects" but "actors" – persons entitled to fundamental rights – has gradually assumed dominance in the modern world. The early carriers of these Western notions included merchants, missionaries, and the military (Abernethy 2000). These "modernizing" movements have been markedly advanced by recent globalization trends in which nation-states and organizations increasingly coexist and compete in a highly inter-connected, transnational system of communication and exchange (Djelic and Quack 2003). More recent types of carriers include professional and trade associations (Brunsson and Jacobsson 2000) and international nongovernmental organizations (INGOs) (Boli and Thomas 1999).

While critics have complained that the perspective elides causal mechanisms and pays insufficient attention to local variation in, and resistance to, adoption of Western policies and normative regimes, the general trends Meyer and colleagues adduce in the data seem clear enough. These trends include the spread of Western institutional forms, convergence in a host of policy and regulative regimes, and, most relevant for our purposes, the diffusion of normative support for human rights, environmentalism, feminism, and respect for the rights of indigenous peoples (Berkevitch 1999; Drori, Meyer, and Hwang 2006; Frank, Hironaka, and Schofer 2000).

The expanding geographic salience of and widening normative support for these issues serve as the ideational backdrop to the story of growing opposition to global projects. But these Western-inspired norms are not the only sources of the opposition. There is another, rather ironic, ideological trend that also fuels anti-project sentiment in the developing world. We refer to a very general anti-Western back-lash that has developed in the recent period. One can discern harbin-gers of this resistance in nationalist revolts in the 1920s and 1930s, the push for decolonization after World War II, the movement of "non-aligned" nations in the 1960s, and a host of other precursors. Acknowledging these precedents, we think the intensity and geo-graphic breadth of these sentiments has grown dramatically since 1980, not coincidentally the year that marked the solidification of Islamic authority in Iran.

The recent upsurge in anti-Western and, especially, anti-American sentiment (Katzenstein and Keohane 2007) has economic, cultural, and political components. Cultural opposition takes the form of resistance to the spread of a Western-dominated global culture and the corres-ponding decline of local ways of life. In truth, much of this opposition is directed at *American* culture in particular, with France and other Western countries among the severest critics of the homogenizing, debasing effects of the Americanization of their own cultures.

The economic form of the anti-Western backlash can be seen in strident and growing opposition to the kinds of neo-liberal practices that were everywhere stressed in the wake of the collapse of the Soviet system. While never entirely absent (even at the zenith of neo-liberal thought in the early 1990s), opposition to these practices built steadily during the 1990s, becoming broadly normative throughout the developing world by the end of the decade. Nor has this opposition only been expressed in strictly normative or narrow economic terms. Instead, shading into our last category of opposition, resistance to neo-liberal practices has increasingly found intense and consequential *political* expression in the past decade or so. Among the more noteworthy examples of this political backlash is the ascendance of anti-Western leaders in many Latin American countries, rioting and other forms of popular opposition in the wake of the collapse of the "Asian Tigers" in the late 1990s, and a discernible cooling in the relationship between Russia and the democratic West since the onset of the twenty-first century. Demonstrations on behalf of "global justice" have routinely been launched in connection with the meetings of finance ministers and multilateral funding institutions such as the World Bank in cities ranging from Seattle to Washington DC to London (Davis and Zald 2005).

Even more recently, with the collapse of the Western (American)-dominated global economy and the meltdown of credit systems, opponents to the Western version of unfettered capitalism find themselves vindicated as they call for new, more transparent models and more rigorous oversight.

Finally, we would be remiss if we did not mention the single most dramatic and consequential source of anti-Western sentiment in the world today. We refer, of course, to the various strands of Islamic fundamentalism that currently fuel global opposition to Western political, economic, and cultural practices. Although the ideational origins of these oppositional strands are much older (Tosini 2008), the significant behavioral "moment" that loosed this particularly virulent form of anti-Western opposition on the world is the Iranian Revolution. To say that this form of anti-Western opposition has grown over the past quarter century would be a gross understatement.

Taken together, all of these ideational/ideological trends have dramatically increased the "discursive opportunities" (Koopmans and Olzak 2004) to frame global projects in oppositional terms. Fueled by a paradoxical mix of support for Western civic norms and anti-Western sentiments, these anti-project movements betray both the *empirical* salience of the ideas reviewed above and the *theoretical* importance attributed to "framing and other subjective processes" as they mediate between events and reactions to events in the modern world.

## The proliferation of domestic and transnational mobilizing structures

As noted above, one of the principal objections to the "global civil society" perspective sketched by Meyer and colleagues is their failure to specify the processes and/or agents held to be responsible for the empirical trends they report. More attention needs to be devoted to the agents and the processes by which ideas about individual rights or desirable institutional practices spread – the mechanisms of their dissemination. There is, charge critics, a disembodied, "hand of God" quality to the argument, as if the emerging global norms were some-how spreading of their own, inevitable accord. From the perspective of social movement theory, however, there would appear to be no shortage of actors implicated in this process. This brings us to the second component of the perspective sketched above and a consider-ation of the domestic and transnational "mobilizing structures" that have proliferated over the past three to four decades.

Growing public sentiment and support for the kinds of civic norms stressed by Meyer and colleagues isn't the only clear empirical trend in evidence over the past several decades. Smith (2005) offers clear evidence of a dramatic increase between 1973 and 2000 in the found-ing of "transnational social movement organizations" attuned to the normative issues stressed here. Table 3.1 reproduces the main sum-mary table from Smith's 2005 publication.

According to Smith's data, the number of human rights and women's groups rose by 600 percent over this period of time, while environmental transnational SMOs increased by a factor of ten. While not surprised by these kinds of dramatic increases, proponents of the "global civil society" perspective tend to interpret them as *expressions* of the underlying normative trends they observe rather than their cause. But new ideas and policy innovations require carriers. The perspective proposed here sees social movements as one of several major carriers of these norms and, indeed, vehicles for the broader process described by world system theorists. SMOs, however, differ from the carriers described above in that they do not simply convey ideas, norms, and standards – interpretive frames – but also carry

**Table 3.1** *Growth and issue focus of transnational social movement organizations*

|  | 1973 N=183 | | 1983 N=348 | | 1993 N=711 | | 2000 N=959 | |
|---|---|---|---|---|---|---|---|---|
|  | No. | % | No. | % | No. | % | No. | % |
| Human rights | 41 | 22 | 89 | 26 | 200 | 28 | 247 | 26 |
| Environment | 17 | 9 | 43 | 12 | 126 | 18 | 167 | 17 |
| Peace | 21 | 12 | 37 | 11 | 82 | 11 | 98 | 10 |
| Women's rights | 16 | 9 | 25 | 7 | 64 | 9 | 94 | 9 |
| Development/Empowerment | 8 | 4 | 15 | 4 | 52 | 7 | 95 | 10 |
| Global justice/Environment | 7 | 4 | 13 | 4 | 30 | 4 | 109 | 11 |
| Multi-issue organizations | 18 | 7 | 43 | 12 | 82 | 12 | 161 | 17 |
| % change from prior decade | 30 | | 90 | | 104 | | 42 (est. to 2003) | |

*Source:* Table 8.2, p. 233, Jackie Smith, "Globalization and transnational social movement organizations," in Gerald D. Davis, Doug McAdam, W. Richard Scott, and Mayer N. Zald (eds.), *Social Movements and Organization Theory.* Cambridge University Press, 2005. Reprinted by permission of the author.

information about mobilizing routines, repertoires for organizing, and resources to aid in implementing them (Clemens 1997). In their study of water supply projects, Davis, Boudet and Jaya (in press) found that a relatively high number of memberships in international NGOs among citizens of the host country was a necessary condition for the emergence of legal conflict.

Space constraints prevent a full treatment of the obvious chicken-and-egg problem at the heart of the "world order" framework. The spread of new norms surely does encourage the founding of new organizations, but obviously the presence of these organizations also speeds the diffusion process. So the processes are reciprocal and mutually reinforcing. The real question is what sets this reciprocal dynamic in motion? Or, to put it another way, how did *these* particular norms get adopted by the Western powers and diffused so broadly?

The standard story highlights the proactive role of the Western democracies in embracing these norms at the close of World War II by encoding them in the founding documents of the United Nations. What that story elides, however, are two significant sources of pressure on the Western allies to make good on their own ambivalent embrace of this human rights agenda. The first were the Cold War pressures the Western allies were under to put their own colonial and, in the case of the US, "internal colonial" houses in order to blunt the threat of Communist propaganda (Dudziak 2000; Layton 2000; McAdam 1999[1982]; Skrentny 1998), as described above. The second source of pressure was the powerful postwar nationalist struggles in Asia and Africa pressing for an end to colonial dominion. Likewise, within the US, the civil rights movement pressured an otherwise ambivalent and deeply divided federal government to embrace at least limited civil rights reform. This is hardly the last word on the subject. What should be clear, however, is that the spread of these norms owed at least as much to the pressure brought to bear on the Western states by movement groups as by any proactive advocacy of human rights by the states themselves.

The rapid expansion of transnational SMOs we see revealed in Smith's data suggests that these reciprocal processes remain central to the spread of norms in the contemporary period. Nor are these the only organizational carriers of these norms. It is much harder to measure with any precision the growth, during this period, of national or local movement groups or NGOs in the developing world who were attuned to human rights, environmental, or feminist issues. The magnitude of the increase, however, is almost certain to be far greater than that seen in Smith's data because of the almost total lack of awareness of these issues in the developing world in the early 1970s.

For anyone interested in understanding the growing opposition to global infrastructure projects during this same period, the relevance of these organizational trends should be obvious. Not only did the spread of new norms – to say nothing of a diffuse anti-Western sentiment – discussed in the previous section increase the likelihood that proposed projects would be viewed negatively by the public at large, but the organizational trends documented here increasingly insured that there would be movement groups and NGOs in place to help encourage this "oppositional" framing. In some cases, local grassroots groups would mobilize first, with the attendant publicity later attracting national and transnational NGOs to the conflict. In others, the announcement of a project in the Western press would attract the attention of transnational NGOs who would then descend on the site to help mobilize more grassroots opposition through the provision of resources and collective action frames (see Cohen and Rai 2000; Khagram 2004;

Smith and Johnson 2002). Either way, the organizational piece of the causal story should be clear. As forms and levels of movement organization grew apace of oppositional ideologies, the chances of organized reactive mobilization against global projects increased dramatically.

## *Opportunity and threat in relation to global projects*

In bringing our general theoretical discussion of threats and opportunities to a close we embraced the tendency among movement scholars to attend to the *mix* of threat and opportunity (rather than the earlier emphasis on opportunity alone) that almost always shapes "episodes of contention." When we consider the anti-project movements that are at issue here, it is clear that this broader focus on opportunities *and* threats is essential to an understanding of the phenomenon. First and foremost, these movements are motivated by the shared sense of *threat* the projects are thought to pose. The importance of the "oppositional" ideas and organizations discussed in the previous two sections is that their presence in the developing world has greatly increased the likelihood that large infrastructure projects will be defined, not as sources of jobs, or community pride – as they well might have been thirty to forty years ago – but as threats to human rights, indigenous groups, and/or the environment. Advancements in science from anthropology to zoology have increased recognition and awareness of potential dangers to human or biological diversity. The increasing salience of these constructed "threats" has ushered in a form of NIMBYism (not-in-my-backyard) that is increasingly common in the developing world.

The central importance of *threat* in these cases does not, however, make *opportunity* irrelevant. The central conceptual question is: what *forms* of opportunity would seem to be most relevant to the appearence of opposition movements? We emphasize three such forms, each of which is associated with a major dimension of political opportunity long recognized by social movement scholars.

### New allies

The first form of opportunity is tied to the availability of *new allies*. The central premise underlying the political opportunity argument is that, absent some significant reduction in the power disparity between state authorities (or certain non-state elites) and challenging groups, the likelihood of successful collective action is going to be very low. Various factors or processes can affect this reduction in power. One of them is the availability of new allies; allies whose resources, influence, connections, etc. increase the movement's capacity and leverage.

In the case of these anti-project movements, various allies could be identified, but we will confine ourselves to only the most obvious. This is the rapidly expanding network of transnational SMOs and INGOs discussed in the preceding section. These groups have the potential to aid local resistance movements in at least three ways. First, mirroring the primary function ascribed to domestic SMOs by *resource mobilization* theorists, they can provide resources that greatly enhance the organizational capacity of groups that might not be able to mobilize on their own. Second – steeped in the "oppositional ideas" touched on above – these outside organizations can bring compelling collective action frames to the struggle to help mobilize the local community. And finally, the presence of these groups – with their connections to policymakers in other countries – can facilitate an innovative form of transnational pressure politics described in detail by Keck and Sikkink in their influential 1998 book, *Activists beyond borders*. Dubbed "the boomerang effect" by the authors, this form of politics allows local movements to bring pressure to bear on recalcitrant national authorities by using their transnational allies (and perhaps their connections to other outside elites) to directly lobby the authorities for redress of grievances.

### Increasing elite vulnerability

The power disparity between established authorities and movement groups can be reduced either by enhancing the capacity and influence of the latter or rendering the former more vulnerable and/or receptive to challenge. These anti-project movements would seem to benefit from this form of opportunity as well. The clearest example of this concerns the growing controversy that has engulfed and hamstrung the World Bank, and to a lesser extent other Western-based multilateral sources of project funding. Flush with the heady sense of an ascendant neoliberalism, the World Bank operated relatively free of constraints in the early to mid-1990s. But as the anti-Western, anti-neoliberal backlash built steadily through the decade, the World

Bank found itself vilified as the embodiment of neoliberal abuses and under enormous political pressure to change its operating philosophy and procedures (Davis and McAdam 2000).

This has had two practical effects regarding the kind of opposition movements on offer here. First, because of its visibility and generally negative image, World Bank involvement in a project is virtually guaranteed to spark opposition. Second, once that opposition has mobilized, it confronts an objectively more vulnerable institution in the World Bank than would have been the case some fifteen to twenty years ago.

### New forms of institutional access

Challenging groups can also benefit from the creation of new forms of institutional access or entrée. Not only do these procedural changes grant movement groups more voice in policy setting, but they also create a general opportunity for insurgents to disrupt or threaten to disrupt "business as usual" should they feel their interests are being ignored.

In response to the heated criticism of the past decade or so, the World Bank and other multilateral lenders have created new, transparent procedures that are designed to grant local stakeholders much more of a voice in the planning of global projects. While the "facility siting" literature has long viewed this kind of increased voice as key to reducing opposition to projects, we argue the opposite. Consistent with the expectations of political process theory, we see this kind of institutional access as another form of political opportunity, encouraging mobilization on the part of opposition groups. But, it is also possible that early success by resistance groups in shaping a project may over the long run eventuate in a more successful and sustainable project.

### Forms of conflict

As noted above, we are not only interested in the *sources* of conflict but also in the various *forms* they take – specifically the extent to which participants rely on relatively formalized, legal mechanisms as compared to those that employ other, more informal, approaches. These latter approaches may be further subdivided into two related continua.

On the one hand, we have (1) those that vary from more peaceful expressions of grievance – e.g., rallies, demonstrations – vs. those that resort to more overt forms of confrontation and violence. Chapter 8 explores factors conducing to the choice of one or another of these approaches, as does a related study by Davis and colleagues (in press). Alternatively, we have examined a second continuum: (2) those that vary from legal mechanisms (litigation) to rely on more relational mechanisms based on mutual confidence and trust. Institutional and cultural factors affecting this choice are explored in Chapter 9.

## Conclusion

We have sought, in this chapter, to do two things. First, recognizing that most of the readers who have been drawn to the volume by its focus on global projects will be unfamiliar with scholarship on social movements, we have sought to provide a brief summary of the evolution and current state of knowledge within this area of study. Our second goal has been to use that framework to offer a general analytic account of why we see global infrastructure projects as increasingly vulnerable to challenge in the contemporary world. To reiterate, the spread of various oppositional frames – anti-neoliberalism, indigenous rights, environmentalism, radical Islam – have dramatically increased the likelihood that global projects will be viewed as threatening by local stakeholders. Simultaneous to these cultural trends, the dramatic expansion in the transnational social movement and NGO sectors over the past two to three decades has granted local groups increasing access to the material resources, oppositional frames, and political allies needed to mobilize and sustain opposition movements.

Finally, the increasing controversy around such projects has prompted the key sources of multilateral funding (e.g., the World Bank, Asian Development Bank) to grant local stakeholders more opportunities for consultation on proposed projects. But far from defusing conflict, these procedural reforms would seem to have only encouraged greater resistance by affording local groups the perfect opportunity to mobilize and the venues in which to do so. Later in this volume (see Chapter 8), we will use this general theoretical perspective to structure our empirical investigation of opposition to pipeline projects in the developing world. Here we have simply sought to provide a more general analytic lens through which to view such cases.

# PART II

# Institutional differences and global projects: empirical studies

# 4 | Rules versus results: sources and resolution of institutional conflicts on Indian metro railway projects

ASHWIN MAHALINGAM, RAYMOND
E. LEVITT, AND W. RICHARD SCOTT

As indicated by previous chapters, an increased need for public facilities and infrastructural improvements of all kinds – transportation, energy production and distribution, clean water, and sanitation – has led to a rapid rise in the volume of activity in the international construction industry in recent times – in particular, in developing countries. As a consequence, we observe an increase in the number of large "global projects" that involve collaboration among participants from multiple companies and countries.

In addition to the complexities present in most large engineering projects, global projects are distinct from nonglobal projects in that the former involve the necessity to interact with individuals, firms, and agencies from diverse national and cultural backgrounds. As a consequence, participants confront a variety of institutional differences – including regulatory, normative, and cultural-cognitive disparities with which they must attempt to cope (see Chapter 2; Scott 2008). The existence of these differences presents substantial challenges to global projects, imposing associated "institutional transaction costs" requiring time, attention, and the expenditure of additional resources (see Chapters 1 and 5).

A case study was carried out to investigate the types of challenges posed by institutional differences in one large construction project. In addition to examining institutionally based conflicts, we identified some of the ways in which these conflicts were resolved and, in particular, the types of actors who were instrumental to their resolution.

## Research setting

The first author conducted a study of two engineering projects in India that were part of a single metro railway system being built by a regional government (see Mahalingam 2005). The rail system was

113

financed partially by a multilateral finance institution as well as by the Indian government. A client's organization, the Management Unit (MU), was set up to manage and monitor the construction of the entire urban rail system. The MU was staffed by public sector employees from the Indian Railways, a government entity. The overall rail system consisted of several sections, of which we studied two, that were awarded as separate Design-Build project contracts. They included the construction of stations and installation of some of the electrical and mechanical equipment. Both projects were nearly identical in terms of physical size, work volume, complexity, and type of work required. The expected duration of the projects was four years. Both were started at the same time, and three years had elapsed when we conducted our study.

The MU awarded the contracts to two different international joint venture (IJV) groups, one between a Swedish, a Japanese, and an Indian company, and the second involving a German, a Korean, and an Indian contractor. In addition, the MU employed a single private sector consulting organization – an IJV composed of participants from three Japanese firms, one American firm, and one Indian public sector firm affiliated with the Indian Railways – to provide expertise in the building of the system and to help manage the relationships with the contractors. Most of the consultants supplied by the Japanese and American companies were experienced consultants, primarily from the UK, and recruited to fill their roles for the duration of the project. Subcontractors and laborers were recruited primarily from the local Indian private sector.

This design fulfilled several study criteria. First, the project groups involved participants from several different companies and multiple countries, allowing us to observe institutional conflicts across a variety of interfaces: professional, organizational, and national. Second, the nature of global project work is such that most participants will rarely have worked with each other on a previous project, so that there was little possibility that whatever conflicts existed had been previously resolved. Third, selecting two comparable engineering projects involving the same MU and consultants but different contracting parties provided the possibility of comparison and control in interpreting results and generalizing from the data collected.

## Research methods

A qualitative research approach was selected since this method is particularly well suited to support exploratory inquiry into areas in which little previous research exists (Scott 1965; Eisenhardt 1989). The first author spent a total of four months physically on the two project sites. A variety of methods was employed to collect data including:

- unstructured open-ended interviews with informants from all of the participating parties – client representatives in the MU, consultants, contractors, and designers. Interviews ranged from a few minutes to over three hours;
- semi-structured interviews, focusing on specific topics relating to the institutional conflicts uncovered during unstructured interviews;
- archival data were collected concerning the project, including copies of contracts, minutes of meetings, progress reports, and organization charts; and
- direct observation of activities, including meetings between the MU and contractors, and accompanying project personnel on site visits.

Qualitative research often involves the blending of data collection with data analysis (Eisenhardt 1989; Strauss and Corbin 1998). Analysis always reveals gaps in the data – issues not addressed—so that by combining the two phases, it is possible for investigators to redress issues of missing data. The analysis methods also involved the creation of "codes" or categories of interest. Reviewing the data collected often revealed possible analytic codes, which then were applied to evaluating subsequent events. The codes and subcodes were revised in the light of additional information, but eventually settled into a framework for viewing (1) the major sources of conflict, and (2) the methods employed in their resolution.

## Types of institutional conflicts

Initially we had expected to observe instances of institutional conflicts and misunderstandings arising from differences in the cultures associated with the varying corporate organizations and differing national backgrounds of the participants. These types of conflicts have been widely reported in previous studies of global firms (e.g., Chan and

Tse 2003; Cramton and Hinds 2005; Henisz 2000; Hofstede 1991; Javidan and House 2002; Mahalingam and Levitt 2007; Mol 2003; Orr and Scott 2008 [see Chapter 5]; Salk 1996; Shenkar and Seira 1992). However, very few such conflicts involving non-Indian international participants were described by respondents or observed in our study of participants' interactions. We did learn of differences that developed between Swedish and Japanese participants on one of the projects. The Swedes were observed to be more willing to accept risks than the Japanese, who were more "uncertainty avoidant," in Hofstede's (1991) terms. As one Swedish project manager put it:

Swedes tend to be a bit more informal and relaxed about things – especially about procedures. Japanese try more to follow the procedures and like to have rules. It's quite stressful. Particularly if you have people not used to working in a regimented way, working for someone that likes it that way. That creates stress and friction.

But such conflicts were rare. Perhaps whatever problems of this type emerged had been resolved prior to our study, which commenced three years after the projects had begun. In addition, the international contracting organizations and consultants all had many years of experience in working alongside people of different nationalities.

The types of conflicts that surfaced stemmed primarily from differences in work practices and from differences between the more professional stance of the contracting groups vs. the bureaucratic orientation of the Indian client. In short, there were important institutional differences in the ways in which the Indian bureaucracy works – the institutional logics it employs – and those that guide the actions of international firms.

Two general types of institutional conflicts were observed on the metro railway projects: (1) conflict between a "rules" and a "results" orientation; and (2) conflict between an "hierarchial" and a "collegial" orientation. We define and describe examples of each type.

## Rules versus results

The client organization was a local public sector organization. Most of the members of the MU were local Indian civil servants, but the MU also employed several expatriates from the UK, working as freelancers, to assist them in managing the contracts. Civil servants in charge of the MU adopted what we term as primarily a "rules" orientation and insisted that contractors conform to the precise "letter of the law" as spelled out in the official project documents.

Members of the MU were contractually entitled to conduct periodic inspections of the work on site to determine if the contract specifications were being followed. In addition to regularly scheduled inspections, they would also conduct special inspections before the start of certain activities, such as concrete pours, to make sure that the contractors were following the correct procedures. During several of these inspection visits, MU participants detected errors and omissions from the terms of the contract. For instance, they insisted that the spacing between steel reinforcing bars should conform precisely to design specifications and not deviate even by a small amount. In practice, such precision was almost impossible to achieve and, the engineers argued, would have no effect on the performance of the structure. Nevertheless, when such "defects" were detected by investigators, they ordered that the entire reinforcing assembly was to be redone.

In contrast, contractors adopted a "results" orientation, striving to complete the work in a timely manner and to the general satisfaction of the design and contract guidelines. They insisted that it was not possible to conform exactly to design specifications all of the time and that a certain amount of "engineering judgment" and tolerance could be used so that the contract could be met in a timely manner. As one engineer explained:

Now what we would do is we would inspect the area ourselves and if the inspector has a genuine grievance then we would have to rectify it, because that's the only way we are going to be allowed to go forward. We have to address it. But in many cases you must employ common sense in construction. When you say you have a longitudinal rebar and they are going to be at 150 mm. centers, it doesn't matter if one is at 149 and another is at 151. What is the real impact of that other than it has to be tapped one way or the other? That sort of thing, if it stops your progress, you would rightly be annoyed. So there were lots of issues and lots of adjustments to approaches to the work.

This complaint was only one of many similar ones we recorded. Much tension and conflict was reported around the issue of how strictly to follow design specifications.

In addition to problems associated with deviations from contract specifications revealed by inspectors, conflicts were also observed in connection with the granting of approvals to proceed with project work. Because the contracts were Design-Build, the contractors had to submit the detailed design for each phase of the project for client approval. In one situation, the contractors had selected a design firm with whom they were already working to design the lighting system for the station. The MU had approved these specifications. The contractor then selected an equipment supplier and, in conjunction with this supplier, made modifications in the proposed design in ways they believed would enhance the system. The supplier was a world-renowned light company with sophisticated systems, and the designer provided e-mail approval of the design changes to the contractor. The contractor was anxious to move forward on schedule with the installation.

However, MU officials insisted that the contractor needed to obtain signed approval from the design firm accepting responsibility for the changes before they would grant their approval. Obtaining the design firm's approval, however, required days of delay since paperwork detailing the changes had to be prepared and transferred to Australia, the location of the design firm. The contractor was forced to postpone work until signed approvals had been obtained. A representative of the contractor complained:

There is a tendency in the Indian system that before something can happen you have to dot all the i's and cross all the t's. In common sense in any construction project, that can't be. It's not possible to dot all your i's and cross all your t's and have all the paperwork in place.

In these examples, we observe two different approaches: two contrasting logics. Contractors, dominated by engineers and designers, were trained to concentrate on results: on meeting international standards and getting the work done. MU officials were primarily concerned with ensuring conformity to the contracts they were paid to enforce. Since the latter orientation may appear to be arbitrary and indefensible, it may be useful to briefly consider the wider context surrounding Indian civil servants.

### The Indian civil service

Historically, the Indian civil service was put in place by and modeled on the British system – first through the East India Company and then through the British Government. In an attempt to root out corruption and maintain control over a large number of extremely heterogeneous territories – there were 562 princely states and provinces in India – the British introduced a highly centralized, bureaucratic, and rule-based system of governance in India (Misra 1986; Nair and Jain 2000). Even after India gained its independence in 1947, the existing model of administration persisted. As Das (2000) points out:

> The nature and type of public administration in India has not changed very much since the colonial days. In essence it is a rule-based administration, at least the way it is designed on paper, and a number of control systems, both internal and external, are in place.

Contemporary Indian civil servants were therefore trained in a system that encouraged and has institutionalized a highly bureaucratic and rule-based form of administrative behavior.

### The Central Vigilance Commission

In addition to this lasting historical legacy, a system that reinforces these tendencies can be traced to the financial scandals involving the purchase of shares by Indian officials belonging to an industrialist named Mundhra in 1957. The resulting scandal led to the establishment of a Committee on the Prevention of Corruption which created an "anti-corruption agency" labeled the Central Vigilance Commission (CVC) in 1964. The CVC was conceived to be the apex vigilance institution, free of control from any executive authority, monitoring all official activity conducted by or with the authority of the central government, and advising other authorities in the government on planning, executing, reviewing, and reforming oversight work.

In essence, the CVC was created to overcome the evils of corruption within the Indian administrative bureaucracy. The CVC would either directly monitor or create a separate task force to oversee every public-sector undertaking in India. The duty of this task force was to ensure that all the processes undertaken on a given project were free of corruption. Every task force was set up as an independent entity, and therefore reported only to the central CVC commissioner, not to anyone on the project. The CVC had established a task force to oversee the metro railway projects that we studied, and we observed their visits to various sites to evaluate design changes, purchase orders, and related decisions as the projects proceeded.

In November 2003, the CVC sent a message to the project that started with these lines:

Corruption is the biggest evil of our society. It has reached such serious proportions that we cannot choose to sit and lie back. Persistence and determination alone would enable us to eradicate the evil of corruption.

Indeed, this was not much of an overstatement. At the time of our study, corruption in India, especially in the public sector, was still rampant. A World Economic Forum survey ranked India 45th out of 49 countries on the honesty of its officials, and 44th in the effectiveness of laws protecting shareholders.

The CVC officers adopted two strategies: preventive and punitive. In the interest of prevention, they attempted to identify corruption-prone locations in the organization, and planned and carried out both regular and surprise inspections to detect system failures or malpractice. On the punitive side, if an official was found guilty of suspected corruption, the Vigilance officer's responsibility was to collect all incriminating evidence and to assist the Central Bureau of Investigation in prosecuting the offender. Punishments were severe: While an official was under investigation, she was not eligible for pay-raises or promotions. Even if, in the end, the official was exonerated, she could not reclaim these losses and suffered a social stain on her career thereafter. Such measures motivated officials to make decisions completely in line with contract specifications.

Thus, for reasons of both historical tradition and fear of reprisal from a strong surveillance system, Indian representatives within the MU were strongly motivated to adhere closely to contractual rules. A concern with being considered inflexible or overly rigid, for most, did not offset normative and coercive pressures to strictly enforce "the letter of the law."

## Hierarchical versus collegial orientation

We also observed conflicts between MU administrators and contractors over the ways in which the project was administered. Because they had been awarded a Design and Build contract, international contractors thought that they would be allowed to exercise full control over the construction decisions once the designs had been approved. Since the performance risks associated with not finishing the contract on time or the construction failing to meet desired quality standards fell on the contractors, they believed they should have considerable latitude in carrying out the work on a daily basis. In this sense, they adhered more to a "professional" or "craft" mentality (Stinchcombe 1959), expecting to be allowed substantial discretion over the actual conduct of their work. This approach is characteristic of most construction projects where, due to extensive division of labor and high specialization, the members of each trade are expected to possess distinctive expertise and skills and, hence, manage their own work processes.

MU administrators were expected by international contractors to limit their role to the approval of design and the inspection of work once completed to determine that it met design requirements. However, MU officials insisted on playing a more active role, attempting to control or influence choices made by the contractors in the way in which the work was conducted, which equipment vendors were selected, and to participate in similar process decisions. As one Indian design engineer who had worked with the Indian government for many years commented:

Most of the Indian people are from the Government organizations and bureaucratic set up. So you will find that it is a very hierarchical structure – especially railways is very hierarchical. Whatever the boss says has to be obeyed, whereas these [international] people who are coming in from other companies have a work culture that is completely different. They are oriented more toward a horizontal type of setup where the experts are working there and they are responsible for whatever they see. They take care [of issues that arise]. Because of this, there are conflicts. We experienced lots of conflicts because of the differing mindsets of the people – because of their differing backgrounds.

MU administrators sometimes required contractors to provide them with information, such as on the contractors' internal decision-making processes, that contractors deemed inappropriate. MU officials' responses to queries or requests for approval from contractors were sometimes overly slow, in the eyes of contractors, because administrators wanted the information to be scrutinized by multiple levels of the hierarchy before responding. MU officials would sometimes question the contractors' right to select a supplier or subcontractor, believing that they should be involved in making these choices. A Swedish project manager on one of the projects vented his frustration:

The client's involvement in this project is very hands-on. They are involved in every minor detail of this project. This is a Design-Build contract and their (the MU's) task is to ensure that we comply with the contract requirements, specifications, drawings, and such matters – but I think they are trying to control the job rather than to monitor it. To me, a Design-Build project should involve monitoring, not controlling. If we are not complying with the document, then OK: it's their job to point this out and push us into complying with the contract. But there are other occasions where they are trying to push us in their direction rather than to let us go on when everything is in compliance with the contract.

On some occasions the MU's proclivity to involve themselves in the details of contractor activities, spilled over into an expectation that they could ask contractors for extra services or equipment free of charge. Although contractors were amenable to making minor modifications in their work, they expected to be reimbursed for incurring extra costs if new features were desired that were not part of the original contract specifications. In one instance, Indian officials insisted that the contractors buy pumps with special corrosion-resistant lining, although this was not required by the contract. A British design consultant working for the MU voiced his opinion on this situation:

It's just like a kid going into a sweetshop and saying, "I want this and this and this." The [Indian] officials will just say: "I do not approve of these pumps unless you can provide the coating." This represents a kind of chink in the armor of commonsense. The client will say that coating produces a superior pump, and you can't argue with him. It does. The question then is, "Are they entitled to that superior pump?" And in my opinion, the answer is "no".

The ensuing debate lasted many weeks, during which time this phase of the project was delayed.

For some of the contractors, such behavior by MU officials was unacceptable. They expected more of a partnership relationship but found themselves in a hierarchical one – a superior–subordinate relationship; and, even occasionally, in a "master–servant" relationship, where they were simply expected to conform to demands irrespective of their justification. A British contracts manager commented:

A contract like this is a partnership between two parties. It cannot be a master–servant situation that India is used to. The [Indian client's] thinking was: "I am the master and you are the servant. You do what I say." Then, we have to say politely, "Well, no. I don't do what you say. I do what I am obligated to do under the contract, and here is the contract that you signed." It can't be a dictatorial regime . . . The client seems to believe: "Here's a normal Indian contract. It's a normal Indian project: master–servant." Obviously, international contractors come to India and they have to respect the culture and try to fit in and not be too disruptive. But at the same time, there needs to be reciprocation from their culture to accommodate to what's there in the contract and to deal with the international contractor.

By contrast, MU officers were critical of the behavior of international contractors. They could not understand why the contractors were so upset at being asked to perform some extra work. They viewed them as refusing to agree to perform even the smallest of extensions without additional payment. As one senior Indian electrical engineer remarked:

Even if they are asked to put in two more screws, they will ask for more money – in a contract of Rs. 1000 crore ($225 million), they will ask us.

MU officers took a broader and more diffuse, but also differentiated, view of their relation to the international contractors who were performing the work. On the one hand, they wanted to hold contractors strictly to the contract specifications, especially if they believed that the exercise of autonomy by contractors might put themselves in jeopardy – so that MU officers would be held accountable for deviations from the contract. On the other hand, they viewed contractors as their employees, hired and compensated by them, and thus expected to do their bidding, expected to be responsive to their demands as project overseers. Contracts were regarded as specifying the baseline of expectations: what must be done. But, because contractors were "subordinate," taking orders from MU officials, they were expected to acquiesce to demands made of them.

These general differences in institutionalized norms and understandings gave rise to an ongoing series of disagreements, disputes, and standoffs among the contending parties. How were they resolved? We describe five strategies employed in dealing with differences on the railway projects.

## Conflict resolution strategies

Different approaches were described by participants or observed by the investigator in attempting to resolve disagreements. They include:

## Role reallocation

On one project, we learned of a dispute over whether or not the work had progressed sufficiently to warrant release of the payment as specified by contract: whether or not a "milestone" had been reached. Missing a milestone meant that the contractors would have to wait for another month to be paid. MU officials were required to sign off that the milestone had been met. The specific case in question involved a concrete pour that was supposed to be 50 percent complete for the release of payment. An informant reported that the MU official inspected the work and concluded:

The pour is 48.9 percent completed – the milestone for 50 percent is not achieved. This involved a payment of 20 or 30 million rupees. The contractor needs to pay for his sand and aggregate and for his workers. If we delay him and pay him next month then he has no cash coming in and some cash going out. The [MU officials] were really stupid on this – they wouldn't sign off if they thought there was any possibility for it to come back to them.

In this case, the international consultant to the MU stepped in to help resolve the issue. He suggested that the MU official only needed to recommend whether or not payment should be authorized, not actually approve it. The consultant continued the story:

So what we did was tell them they could write on their report "Only 48% achieved – milestone not achieved" and it will come to me and I'll write "This milestone substantially achieved, and we can issue payment now." And I sign it and it goes to the MU department that issues payment.

In this instance, an international consultant circumvented the existing process by reallocating roles and responsibilities. The MU officials, in effect, became the "consultant" and the consultant the decision maker. The impasse was resolved and the project was allowed to go forward on schedule.

The responses of MU officials to this strategy varied. In some cases, we observed instances where they were upset at their authority being usurped. In others, they appeared to be willing to be "let off the hook" and allow the international consultant to assume more responsibility. Thus, in another incident, a MU official expressed relief:

Hats off to [this consultant] – the way he handled this. He does not complain; he is always ready to step in to solve this. If you are not ready to draft a letter – and this has happened to me also – he will say: "OK, leave it. I will draft a letter." He will draft it himself. All those gestures really move me.

## Appealing upstairs

In several cases of institutional conflict, project participants would raise a contentious issue to a more senior level in the hopes of obtaining a resolution. In some cases, senior MU officers were very progress oriented and eager to see contracts completed as scheduled. In one instance, the contractors were making very slow progress on the contract because lower-level MU officials continuously demanded various documents and additional details before they granted approval. Eventually, the construction manager brought the matter to the attention of a senior MU director. This director wanted the work to progress on schedule and instructed less senior MU officers to be more lenient toward the contractor. Because the order came from their own senior officers, subordinate officers reduced their demands on contractors, and the pace of work quickened.

Senior MU directors did not side with contractors on all disputes: in some cases junior MU demands were supported. But in both types of cases, because the senior directors, and the managing director in particular, were held in high esteem by both parties, his decisions were followed. A German engineering consultant working for one of the contractors commented:

These [senior MU] officers are not the typical Indian railway officials. That's why the project is moving forward – because of [the MU director] and his deputy: that's what keeping it running. A job of this magnitude in five years is a huge effort for any country, and it's a bigger effort in India since these people are not used to getting things done on time. But the top management has played a role in pushing things along. They do not fiddle around with small details.

And on other side, one junior-level MU official stated:

I feel that because of [the MU managing director], things were clearer. The [director] has made it clear that the project is to come in on time – the target is clear. He also knows how to handle these matters because he is like god. Whenever he comes, his word becomes like a law. Nobody argues with him because nobody doubts his decision.

In other cases, we observed conflicts being appealed to higher level MU consultants, who could help work out solutions because they not only held a high staff position in the MU but also were often held in high esteem by project personnel.

Although appealing disputes to higher level officials worked in some situations, it was not a universal solution. It appears that only a minority of the senior MU officials exhibited the qualities required to earn the respect and esteem of both their own staff and of the contractors. Moreover, even these unusual senior officials did not have the time to address all of difficulties that arose lower in the hierarchy. For everyone, both rationality and capacity are "bounded," as we have learned from March and Simon (1958).

## Translation and education

In many cases, MU officials summarily rejected proposals or documents submitted by contractors without informing them of their reasons or what they needed to do to receive approval. In many of these situations, contractors would turn to the MU's international consultants for information, advice, and assistance. In one instance, a contractor's choice of a vendor for an electrical part was rejected on the grounds that the vendor did not meet the specifications, although the nature of the shortcoming was not made clear. Approached again, the MU official simply reiterated that the required criteria were not met. Approached for his help, the international consultant reviewed the documentation and realized that the contractor had failed to supply adequate detail on the proposed manufacturer's facility. He listed out for the contractor the required information, and although it required additional time and effort, the contractor was able to resubmit his proposal and receive approval from the MU official. Here, consultants helped to resolve the impasse by making clear why the choice was being rejected: by "translating" the MU's behavior to make clear to the contractor the underlying reasons for rejection.

In another situation, the contractor obtained bids from a variety of vendors in the local market to determine their charges for flooring for some of the station facilities. The MU officers rejected the contractor's calculations regarding appropriate rates for these materials, indicating they were not in line with local rates for flooring. The contractors pointed out that the rates were higher because the contracts specified marble floors which necessarily cost more than conventional flooring. MU officials had not taken into account the special flooring required, but resisted exceeding their customary rate structures. Again, the contractors turned to the international consultants for assistance – to help the MU officials understand why customary rates needed to be exceeded. An Indian consultant described the ensuing process:

Initially, the [MU officers'] response was: "Why? It should cost only this much. This is how flooring is done." So we had to sit down and explain to them why it was going to cost them more. Because there is water there, and we are talking about underground structures, and if we are using cheaper material, it will deteriorate, and wear out and fail – and it if fails, and someone is injured, then you are in big trouble. And with the cheaper stones, you may have to take it out and redo it, if they are of poor quality. Your stone, instead of lasting 25 years will just last you 10 years. So at that time, there may be the cost of doing the same work again and you have added cost in the long run. So slowly, very slowly, they were getting convinced, and the [senior MU] management was very clear that they wanted international quality stations. So, eventually, they decided, "Yeah, OK: we'll approve the new rates." But it took us quite some time and some convincing.

This strategy involved both translation and education – helping to make clear to MU officials the reasons why the requested rates were higher than normal involving both information about the reasons for special materials, as well as explaining the possible adverse consequences of utilizing cheaper materials. Voices were not raised nor did either part lose face. Neither power nor authority was applied: neither party was forced into pursuing a particular path of action.

## Changing the cast or the forum

Situations occurred when participants were unable to resolve a conflict because of insufficient information or expertise. In one meeting we observed, a conflict occurred over the performance of generators. Contractors claimed that they were reporting performance data that came directly from the manufacturer, but MU officials did not accept the contractor's performance data. A British design manager who was presiding over the meeting proposed a meeting for the following day, asking that the contractor bring along both a representative from the manufacturing company and a copy of their calculations. Additional, better informed actors were asked to participate in the decision process.

In other cases, meetings would be dominated by rigid and dominating Indian officials. Rather than attempting to reach a decision in these meetings, consultants would suggest that the decision be post-poned and that both the cast of participants and the forum be changed. In the words of one of the consultants:

We've got to try and mediate and smooth the waters. It's like pouring oil on troubled waters, and there are various ways of trying to do that. One is actually to try and keep people away, so in other words, we actually try and arrange our meeting to exclude certain [MU officials], sort the problems out with the contractors and move along. We've done that in several areas.

## Superior power

However, in other instances, conflicts were resolved by the Indian's administrator superior position. The client organization, staffed by Indian railway employees, controlled the flow of money: They had legal authority to hire or dismiss the contractors. When other avenues to resolve conflict proved ineffective, we observed instances where MU officials forced their decisions on to contractors. Contractors some-times grudgingly complied with MU directives, but typically planned to file a legal claim for additional costs incurred at the end of the project.

Contractors had to weigh two types of costs: the costs of compli-ance vs. growing institutional transaction costs in the form of add-itional documentation and accompanying delays. At some point, many decided to "cut their losses" and comply with MU demands. Because we did not pursue data collection to the end of the project, we were unable to assess the relative costs of continuing to haggle vs. compliance followed by attempts at legal redress.

In one instance, a disagreement occurred over the safety standards to be adopted for the design of underground stations. Indian building codes did not extend to include safety standards for underground build-ing, but several of the international contractors, who had previously built underground structures, proposed a set of standards they believed appropriate. However, MU officials insisted that more conservative (i.e., higher) standards be set. For a time, there was a standoff, but the MU standards were adopted. A structural consultant commented:

In this case, I don't think anybody did come to a compromise – the con-tractors were told in effect by the MU that these were the standards the client was prepared to accept, and if they didn't want to do it that way, then the MU would not accept the work. So in order to get on with their job, the contractors submitted designs [to comply with the higher standards]. I think contractors recognized the importance of getting on with the job . . . and they didn't want to spend a long time having a stalemate and said, "OK, we'll do it." Now, if the contractors were instructed to do it in a more conservative way [meet even higher standards], and if they had to redo some of the work, then I think they would claim an exception and seek payment later via a claim.

Superior power has its advantages.

Among the various strategies we observed, there appeared to be, in many, a common factor – or, more specifically, a common actor: the international consultant.

## International consultants

One of the most interesting and unexpected benefits of our field work was the recognition of the existence and importance of a community of freelance expatriates who performed a range of tasks on the international projects we studied. These consultants were employed by both the international contractors and the client, some serving as independent, short-term contractors for limited time periods of a few months, others for the full duration of the project, in this case, four years. They constituted a significant proportion of the employed skilled workforce on the projects we observed, ranging from 10 to 50 percent of the manpower employed by contractors or by the client organization at various points in time over the duration of the project. On the Indian projects, roughly one-third of these expatriates were employed by the MU as consultants while two-thirds were employed by contractors.

### Background

A large proportion of these freelancers came from the UK. (This was the case not only for the Indian projects but for a related set of projects we studied in Taiwan.) This group was advantaged because the official language of most international projects is English, but in India in particular, the legal systems and Indian bureaucracy were strongly influenced by British colonial rule. A typical freelancer was trained as an engineer and began their career as an employee in the country of their birth, often the UK. After several years of experience working for domestic firms, they accepted an offer as a project employee on a global project located outside their home country. Some of these individuals then spent the remainder of their career hopping from one global project to another, working as freelancers for limited periods of time on each project. Some others returned to their country of origin after a few years, only to "reenlist" later. Most were specialists in an engineering discipline – structural engineering, geotechnical engineering, construction, tunneling – and had built up a substantial résumé working on large construction projects over the course of their careers.

**Lifestyle**

We observed the lifestyle of this rather large, loosely knit community both in India and in Taiwan. Most of those with whom we talked had worked in several different Asian countries and had grown accustomed to an itinerant mode of life. For example, one freelance British expatriate working in Taiwan as a contracts administrator for a Korean contractor had worked for more than twenty years on highway, tunnel, and bridge projects in Singapore, Malaysia, Indonesia, Vietnam, Japan, and Korea. Another British expatriate who was a consultant to the MU on one of the India railway projects was originally from London but had spent the last thirteen years overseas, including working on projects located in Pakistan, Oman, Singapore, Hong Kong, and now in Delhi.

This was obviously not an easy lifestyle and it placed a considerable burden on spouses and children, who had to change schools every three or four years. Many were motivated by the relatively rich style of life they could enjoy. They earned the same amount of money that they would have received had they been doing similar work in the home countries, and, given the lower cost of living in Asian countries, could live very well. Furthermore, freelances from countries such as the UK were not required to pay taxes for earnings abroad provided they were overseas for nine months out of a given year. Others emphasized the challenging and exciting nature of their jobs. One British expatriate who was working as a consultant for the Indian MU said:

I like big projects. There's a certain satisfaction in being part of a big project – seeing it in all the stages of its life. When I first went abroad – I was 26 when I went to Hong Kong – I'd left the University and I was determined to be Isambard Brunel the Third[1] – very high aspirations! Working overseas, you had more responsibilities and more exposure to interesting large-scale projects than would be the case in the UK. For example, the Jubilee line extension [in London] had a project team of over 1200 people – so there would be no way that I would have been Project Director of Jubilee line – I'd be five levels down; and certainly, as a young engineer, I would be one of many looking after a tiny little part of the work. So there's much more job satisfaction and scope for personal enhancement by going abroad.

Then, too, working in many different countries and experiencing different cultures and peoples was an adventure that most freelancers found appealing.

Most freelancers with whom we talked were married. Some had married women from their countries of origin, but a significant number – almost half of those we interviewed – were married to Asian women. More than half of the expatriate freelancers preferred to have their spouses with them as they traveled from country to country; the others chose to work alone while their families led relatively stable lives in their home countries. For those whose families and children accompanied them, most preferred to send their children to a British school or to an International School in the nearest city of the country in which they were currently working.

## Networking

Obviously, being a freelancer on projects in a foreign country is a rather uncertain and risky profession. Job security is low, and the contracts are relatively short – at most a few years of duration, after which time, one is unemployed. Freelancers obtained job information primarily by word of mouth and by keeping in touch with other expatriates with whom they had worked in the past. The freelance community was much too large for every member to be acquainted, and there was no formalized system for notifying freelancers of jobs now or soon to become available. So, the freelancers relied "on the strength of weak ties" (Granovetter 1973), relying for job information not only on close friends but a wider circle of work associates and past acquaintances. The mutual ties – both strong and weak – with other freelancers – past and current – helped them to find out about work opportunities.

Our interviews suggest that informal ties worked through both a "push" and "pull" mechanism. On the "push" side, one freelancer whose current position was nearing an end would proactively contact another to inform him he was looking for work. The colleague would then advise him about any openings of which he was aware and, if a position was applied for, would provide a recommendation. However, our informants reported the "pull" mechanism to be a far more common method of recruitment on the projects in India. Here, an expatriate who was already working in India would contact others in their network to see if they were available to fill an opening on their project. One British expatriate working in India remembered:

One of the guys – an Australian guy who was very much involved in the project – I knew him and was in touch with him. So he sent me an e-mail when I was in Hong Kong to say that the contract (in India) was being signed, and as the contract moved on, he sent me another e-mail to say that he was looking for a commercial manager.

As is suggested by the interview data, these informal networks were greatly abetted by the widespread use of e-mail. Given the loose connections, the great mobility of participants, and the global stage on which the players operated, e-mail would seem to be a near-indispensable tool for the freelancers. Each collected a set of e-mail addresses from their project associates. Most relied on two e-mail addresses: a temporary address for the project on which they were currently employed, and a permanent address – typically a hotmail account – on which they could always be reached.

Not all of the ties, however, were based on work. We learned of, and participated in, some of the more playful associations based on a common British heritage and male culture centered around sports – cricket and soccer matches – and liquid refreshment. Some of these sporting and social clubs were occasional and episodic, based on a pick-up game or a shared viewing of an important match on TV. Others were more institutionalized – such as the Hash House Harriers, a venerable sports and drinking club that was well known in Asian circles. These types of activities and associations built valued community for expatriates in distant and foreign lands.

### Project role

In the Indian rail project we studied, roughly one-third of all the expatriate freelancers were employed as consultants to the Indian MU while the other two-thirds were employed by one of the contractors. Considering all of these freelancers, almost half were employed in "boundary-spanning" roles – occupying positions such as contract administrator, overall project managers, quality control managers, etc. The remaining freelancers occupied technical or managerial functional positions such as tunneling engineer, design manager, electrical expert, and so on.

Those involved in the boundary-spanning positions were of particular interest, given our focus on institutional conflicts. Although hired for their technical qualifications, many of the freelance expatriates brought along another valued, but often unrecognized, expertise: multi-institutional intelligence. This expertise was based on years of experience in surviving and maneuvering within the contested terrain of global projects. A continuing theme that surfaced again and again in our discussion of how conflicts were resolved, was the central role played by these expatriate freelancers. They were, more often than not, the ones who stepped into the middle of disputes to assume responsibility for a contested decision (role reallocation), work to translate client demands to contractors or client needs to contractors, attempt to educate client officials on technical requirements, or work to revise the cast of characters assembled to make a decision or the forum in which that decision would be made.

## Summary and concluding comment

A case study was carried out to identify the types of conflicts stemming from institutional differences that arose during the construction of a metro railway system in India. We had expected to observe altercations resulting from the differences among the several types of international contractors in their beliefs and work conventions. However, most of the conflicts witnessed involved disputes between public officials charged with overseeing the project on behalf of the Indian client, on the one hand, and the design and construction engineers working for the international contractors, on the other. The government officials tended to embrace what we have termed a "rules" orientation, viewing their primary responsibility as insuring that contractors precisely conform to the work specifications of the project contracts. They also were more likely to exhibit a "hierarchical" orientation, in which contractors were to be closely supervised as the work proceeded and would conform to the demands of their "superiors."

For their part, because the contracts called for the international firms to both design and build the project, international contractors assumed that they would be allowed to exercise some leeway in interpreting the contract, exercising their professional judgment on matters that would not, in their view, jeopardize the quality of the outcome. They assumed a "results orientation," expecting to be judged on the quality of the finished project. Moreover, because of their specialized expertise, they expected to be deferred to in matters involving the details of design and construction and to enter into a more "collegial" relation with the representatives of the client.

We observed that many of the resulting conflicts arising from these differing orientations were resolved or at least mitigated by the intervention of a collection of freelance expatriate contractors working for either the client organization as consultants or for one of the international contracting firms. Various strategies and tactics were observed, including role reallocation – in which the expatriate would assume responsibility for approving a departure from the contract, assisting the client representative to better understand, through education and translation, why a departure was necessary, and adjusting the cast of characters or the forum in which decisions were made in order to exclude participants viewed as overly rigid. In other cases, high officials within the client organization would step in to insure that the project moved forward in a timely manner.

Although hired for their technical expertise, we observed the freelance expatriates to also be a source of institutional expertise. They were often able to adjudicate and resolve institutional conflicts because of their experience in living and working overseas with multiple international firms and in diverse national contexts.

We learn, then, that institutional conflicts assume many forms. On this project, they appeared to stem primarily from two sources:

- a difference in the work cultures of public officials in contrast to those of private firms; and
- a difference in the assumptions made about the prerogatives attending client–contractor relations – superior–subordinate vs. client–professional.

As we have attempted to show, these differences were embedded in and reinforced by differing incentive systems, varying governance structures, different participant identities, and different historical and personal experiences.

### Endnote

1 Isambard Kingdom Brunel was a legendary nineteenth-century British engineer who pioneered the design of steel bridges and steel-hulled steamships.

# 5 | Institutional exceptions on global projects: a process model[1]

RYAN J. ORR AND W. RICHARD SCOTT

When you hear hoof beats think Horses, not Zebras – unless you're in Africa.

There is an ever-growing body of scholarly research to assess and categorize differences in cross-national cultural values (e.g., Hofstede 1984; House et al. 2004) and social institutions (e.g., Hall and Soskice 2001; Busenitz, Gomez, and Spencer 2000) as they affect business practice and economic performance. Within this corpus of research, terms like liabilities of foreignness (Hymer 1976; Zaheer 1995), psychic distance (Johansson and Vahlne 1977), cultural distance (Kogut and Singh 1988), institutional distance (Xu and Shenkar 2002), and institutional idiosyncrasies (Henisz 2003) have become increasingly common. Although there is considerable variation in terms and rubrics, these studies typically draw out a general hypothesis that differences between cultures and social structures impede the success of cross-societal collaborative ventures. In the words of Javidan and House (2002), "From a practical point of view, the complexity of cross-national negotiations, mergers, assignments and leadership probably depends on the extent of the difference between the two cultures." Despite widespread support for this premise, there has been relatively little empirical effort to examine the underlying processes – the actual dynamics and conditions – by which cross-societal variations in rules, norms, and cultural beliefs are translated into the kinds of complications and costs that have been documented by mainstream researchers (Shenkar 2001).

To enhance understanding of how cross-societal friction actually arises, we analyzed a set of 23 case studies collected from cross-border contractors and investors, such as Bechtel, Walt Disney, and the World Bank, involved in large-scale global projects. The considerable volume of cross-border business carried out in large-scale global projects has only recently begun to be explored in the international business literature. Such projects offer a promising context for researching what happens in encounters across institutional systems. All of the case studies examined here involve an *institutional exception*, which we define as *an episode that involves an entrant first being surprised by, then making sense of, and then adapting to institutional differences arising between it and local project players or external stakeholders.* Our analysis explores the dynamics by which these situations of accidental deviation from established institutions unfold and the conditions under which they have more or less costly consequences for the entrant organization.

Utilizing a broad view of institutions as encompassing three general classes of socially constructed elements – cognitive-cultural, normative, and regulative (Scott 2008; see also Chapter 2) together with an examination of 23 empirical cases, we propose a set of propositions and a generic narrative model to address four research questions: (1) How are institutional exceptions triggered? (2) How are they resolved? (3) How are the consequences manifested? and (4) What conditions increase the likelihood that institutional differences will negatively impact cross-societal collaborations? Through this work, we hope to contribute both to theoretical development of the nature and implications of institutional exceptions and to practical knowledge of how managers learn to navigate – and can be trained to better cope – within an unfamiliar institutional milieu.

## Background

As Kobrin (1976) observed thirty years ago, "The development of international management as a distinct field is based upon an assumption that the problems of conducting simultaneous operations in a large number of varied environments are different in kind rather than degree from those encountered in a single society or polity." Studies during the intervening years have explored interactions among three kinds of variables: (1) the types of societal differences that are relevant to firm performance; (2) the types of firm-level decisions that are affected; and (3) the strategies and structures that firms employ to cope with the differences encountered.

### *Societal–institutional differences*

Viewed in the aggregate, investigators have explored a wide range of societal differences (see Henisz 2003). A number of scholars have examined cultural differences, with a majority employing Hofstede's

(1984, 1991) value dimensions to calculate cultural distance (e.g., Kogut and Singh 1988; Park and Ungson 1997; Beamish and Kachra 2004; Barkema et al. 1997; Horii, Jin, and Levitt 2005; see a review by Robson, Leonidou, and Katsikeas 2002). Others have concentrated on various facets of host government policies or behavior, including laws and regulations surrounding the acquisition of property (Djankov et al. 2002), the protection of intellectual property (Lee and Mansfield 1996), propensity of the government to invest in technological development (Mahmood and Rufin 2005), and fairness of processes for acquiring government licenses. More general attributes or capacities of governments have also been examined, including overall stability of a regime (Kobrin 1979), policy/political alignment across branches (Heinsz 2000), adequacy of the court system (McMillan, Johnson, and Woodruff 2002), and extent of corruption (Johnson et al. 2000; Doh et al. 2003). Broader conditions affecting the business climate in a society would include the level of goodwill or trust among firms operating in the same field or sector (McMillan and Woodruff 1999), the number and quality of specialized intermediary organizations providing supportive business services (Khanna, Palepu, and Sinha 2005), the prevalence of contractual hazards such as technological "leakage" where proprietary knowledge is usurped by alliance partners or subsidiaries (Oxley 1999), and the hazards associated with free-riding on brand name and reputation (Gatignon and Anderson 1988).

Broader, comparative work deals with many of these and other societal differences. For example, studies by Whitley and associates in both Europe (1992a) and Asia (1991) point to differences among countries (and regions) in what are termed "business recipes" and include firm structures and the modes in which firm interdependencies are managed (Whitley 1992b); and variations in the regulation of work systems (Whitley and Kristensen 1997). In a similar vein, Hollingworth and Boyer (1997) describe differences in what they term "social systems of production" which vary because of differences in resource base and human capital, historically specific development processes, and the actions of governmental entities, trade unions, employers, and business associations. Another research team with a long tradition of utilizing a more broadly devised institutional theory and research program is the Uppsala School (Johanson and Vahlne 1977; Melin 1992; Eriksson, Johanson, Majkgård, and Sharma 1997). At a more macro level, scholars Hall and Soskice (2001) categorize societies more generally into those that rely principally on competitive markets, characterized by arms-length relations and formal contracting among firms (liberal economies) versus those relying on strategic modes of coordination characterized by denser networks of cross-shareholdings among firms, the activities of industrial trade associations and labor unions (coordinated economies), and the actions of a more intrusive state. Their approach stresses the importance of history and culture, shared experience, informal rules, and understanding. This and related work emphasizes that firms and industries in different countries will react to the "same" stimuli – e.g., global competitive pressures – in different ways (for an empirical test, see Biggart and Guillén 1999; Guillén 2001).

Considered together, these works signal a strong resurgence of interest in the nature of institutional factors affecting business practice and economic performance. That is, cross-societal differences are increasingly being viewed as instances of variations in institutional environments – a formulation that helps us to replace "place" names with more abstract (and general) concepts that are more readily translated into specific variables and indicators (Przeworski and Teune 1970). More particularly, it usefully connects research on international business with theoretical developments in neoinstitutional theory. Eleanor Westney (1993) was a pioneer in making this connection to the sociological variant by recognizing the utility of viewing multinational companies as enterprises operating in multiple institutional fields operating under varying rules, norms, and cultural frameworks. And, on the economics front, Oliver Williamson (1994) recognized the value of embedding his transaction cost approach to the design of corporate structures in a wider institutional environment, noting that these macro differences could influence the parameter settings affecting the comparative costs of governance structures (see also Henisz and Williamson 1999).

## Types of firm decisions

Turning more briefly to the kinds of firm-level decisions affected by institutional differences, we see studies on a wide range of behaviors including efforts to assess the stability of the policy environment (Henisz, Zelner, and Guillen 2005); choice of country, sector, and location (Henisz and Delios 2001); mode of entry, including acquisitions, joint ventures, and greenfield investments (Kogut and Singh 1988;

Doh et al. 2003); responsiveness to host cultural routines and preferences (Prahaldad and Doz 1987); and legal recourse to international arbitration in order to avoid domestic courts (Wells and Ahmed 2006).

## Types of firm structures and strategies

Earlier institutional theorists (e.g., Meyer and Rowan 1977; DiMaggio and Powell 1983) tended to portray organizations confronting institutional pressures as passive conformists, but subsequent research has demonstrated that firms are by no means helpless when confronting institutional differences and challenges. Theoretical formulations have been revised to consider the ways in which firms play an active role in their fate, and researchers have examined firm-level characteristics, such as size, sector location, and linkages to other organizations, that mediate response to institutional pressures (Scott 2008: chap. 7). Firm attributes that have been examined in international business research include extent of previous experience in a given, or related, societal context (Delios and Henisz 2003; Guillén 2002); whether a company is organized as a domestic or multinational entity (Henisz 2003); whether the firm is affiliated with a business group (Khanna and Palepu 2000); and whether the firm brings distinctive knowledge or has ties to powerful allies (Henisz, Zelner, and Guillén 2005). More experienced firms, multinational companies, and firms connected to business groups were more likely to be able to capture "local" knowledge, including ways to be effective in local economic transactions and political contests.

## Intended contribution

Our study offers a somewhat different emphasis and perspective from previous work on institutional environments and efforts by firms and their managers to cope with unexpected differences encountered.

- Unlike most empirical research, we purposely embrace a broad conception of institutions, emphasizing that cultural, political, legal, or normative differences may be activated. Our conception of institutions is elaborated in the following section.
- Rather than focus simply on varying attributes of institutions and firm-level choices, we develop a process model that shifts attention

from outcomes and impacts (what happened?) to social process (how did the observed effects occur?)

- And unlike many scholars doing research in this arena who embrace a rational choice conception of managerial decision making, we explore an intendedly rational, but more cognitively circumscribed, sense-making perspective to consider how institutional exceptions are experienced and managed, or mismanaged.

## Institutions and institutional exceptions

Our study is grounded in a relatively broad conception of institutions, which we view as symbolic frameworks that provide guidelines for behavior and lend stability, regularity and meaning to social life (Scott 2008; Campbell 2004). For analytic purposes, it is helpful to sort the universe of institutional elements into three general categories: regulative, normative, and cultural-cognitive – three types of "pillars" constraining and guiding social behavior (Scott 2008; see also, Chapter 2).

*Regulative elements* include formal regulations and rules that govern behavior such as constitutions, laws, and property rights (Scott 2008; North 1990). The regulatory pillar "is distinguished by a prominence given to explicit regulatory processes: rule setting, monitoring, and sanctioning activities. In this view, regulatory processes involve the capacity to establish rules, inspect another's conformity to them, and, as needed, manipulate sanctions – rewards or punishments – in an attempt to influence future behavior" (Scott 2001: 52). Regulations may be created and maintained by transnational authorities, nation states, or provinces and local regimes with power to create rules and sanction deviance (Djelic and Quack 2003). Individual organizations such as firms and unions also issue rules, monitor behavior, and attempt to enforce compliance of their participants. Economists and rational choice political scientists direct most of their attention to regulative elements (e.g., Aoki 2001; Weingast and Marshall 1988).

*Normative elements* include the informal norms, values, standards, roles, conventions, practices, taboos, customs, traditions, and codes of conduct that guide behavior and decisions (Scott 2001; North 1990). "Emphasis here is placed on normative rules that introduce a prescriptive, evaluative and obligatory dimension to social life. Normative systems include both values and norms." (Scott 2001: 54) Values are conceptions of the preferred or the desirable. Norms specify how things should be done; they define legitimate means to pursue valued ends. Normative systems define goals and objectives (e.g., winning the game, making a profit) but also designate appropriate ways to pursue them (e.g., rules specifying how the game is to be played, conceptions of fair business practices). Many occupational groups, both professional and craft-based, generate and enforce work norms and actively promulgate standards and codes to govern conduct (Van Maanen and Barley 1984; Brunsson and Jacobsson 2000). Emphasizing normative rather than regulative features of institutions shifts attention from employing a "logic of consequentiality" to a "logic of appropriateness" (March and Olsen 1989: 23). Sociologists are particularly likely to emphasize normative aspects of institutions.

*Cultural-cognitive elements* – the "operating mechanisms of the mind" (North 2005) – include shared beliefs, categories, identities, schemas, scripts, heuristics, logics of action, and mental models (Scott 2001). These elements are cultural in the sense that social reality is referenced and rationalized against external symbolic frameworks and cognitive in the sense that social reality is interpreted and constructed through internalized frames of meaning-making. Thus, both external cultural benchmarks and internalized interpretive processes shape perceptions and explanations of social reality (Sen 2004). Some of the most important cultural-cognitive elements provide archetypes for dividing labor, constructing organizations and project teams, and crafting recipes and routines for conducting work (Greenwood and Hinings 1993; Whitley 1992b). Cultural anthropologists and organizational theorists emphasize cultural-cognitive elements (Douglass 1986; Geertz 1973; Powell and DiMaggio 1991).

The overarching construct guiding our study is the *institutional exception*. This construct employs the vocabulary of organization theory, where the concept of an "exception" has a long history. In the information-processing view of organizations pioneered by March and Simon (1958), "exceptions" describe situations where an actor lacks some or all of the information necessary to perform a task and therefore must forsake existing conventions and routines and engage in search behavior in order to formulate a response (Galbraith 1974, 1977; Saastamoinen 1995; Jin and Levitt 1996). Building on this line of thinking, the term institutional exception describes an occasion when a knowledge void about pertinent institutional elements interferes with task completion and requires troubleshooting.

Institutional exceptions come in many forms, but *differences among institutional elements* create some characteristic forms. Ignorance of local regulative elements – laws, rules, requirements – often lead to missteps and embarrassing misunderstandings. Encounters with divergent normative frameworks – conventions, structured expectations, work practices – are not easily resolved. Also difficult are the exceptions grounded in differing cultural-cognitive elements, when the framings of situations conflict, basic values are challenged, and entrant and host find themselves "on a different page" or "on a different wave length." While many exceptions involve combinations of elements, we employ these categories to broadly categorize the types of exceptions encountered.

A defining characteristic of institutional exceptions is the naivety of the offending actor. To use a sport's analogy, consider for a moment what would happen if a football player were put out onto a basketball court, and told to play, never having watched a basketball game, never having touched a basketball, never having been taught the rules. The result would be a classic institutional exception, characterized by the player blundering around on the playing field trying to learn to play the game while the game was in motion, causing delay of game violations, angering members of the opposing team, certainly looking ludicrous from the perspective of the fans in the crowd, and experiencing penalties and fines from the referee.

Thus, because they are accidental, institutional exceptions are not like other kinds of institutional conflicts that are intentionally confrontational – i.e., bigotry, racism, and intolerance between Muslims and Christians (Huntington 1996); contests of jurisdiction between professionals in corporate mergers (Greenwood and Hinings 1993); disputes over environmental and business priorities in multilateral forums (Mol 2003). Nor do institutional exceptions involve intentional deviations from established rules and norms that are calculated by rational economic actors to be personally beneficial, as in a game theoretic framework where actors choose either to cooperate with institutions or to cheat, defect, renege, shirk, or transgress (Greif 1994, 2000, 2006; Weingast 1996). On the contrary, institutional exceptions tend to be more born of ignorance, arising out of a lack of familiarity with the existence, applicability, or salience of the novel institutions encountered. Basic misjudgments and misunderstandings of a more accidental and unexpected nature give rise to misconceptions, confusion, and false impressions, and, as we will see, generate a host of unanticipated institutional transaction costs – that is, money costs, time costs, relational friction, and reputational damage.

## Methods

### Method selection

A case-based method was selected for four reasons. First, case-based methods provide a level of in-depth scrutiny that survey methods miss and permit the analysis of rich multivariate phenomena (Eisenhardt 1989; Glaser and Strauss 1967; Yin 2003). Second, there have been calls in prior literature to use case studies to examine the high incidences of failure and instability in global ventures (Parkhe 1993; Parkhe and Shin 1991). Third, case-based methods contrast with and complement earlier quantitative methods that were intended to explain the performance of cross-national ventures based, for example, on measures of political instability or corruption (Hines 1995) or abstract cultural distance measures (Kogut and Singh 1988). Finally, the case-based method is an ideal mode of inquiry for addressing research questions regarding "how" things occur – the investigation of social processes (Yin 2003).

### Data collection

**Data sources**
The primary mode of data collection was by interviews conducted by the first author. The interviews, which occurred during the 18 months between May, 2003 and November, 2004, lasted one to two hours and were digitally recorded for subsequent transcription and review. Informants also provided extensive secondary archival data relevant to the projects described that enriched the contextual background surrounding many of the institutional exceptions, including newspaper articles, project briefs, internal memos, e-mail, organization charts, budgets, schedules, and other project documents.

**Informants**
In total, 39 managers were interviewed. The managers had all worked on projects, in areas including management, engineering, design, and

supervision of construction. The managers were affiliated with 29 unique organizations ranging in size from small consulting firms to the US Navy. In combination, the collection of informants had experience on projects in over 60 countries across various sectors, including oil and gas, power, heavy civil and commercial construction. The goal of interviewing informants from many unique organizations, in many industry sectors, across many projects and countries was to develop a model that was general rather than a model that was overly fitted to a single industry or project type.

### Informant selection

The selection of informants was guided by several factors. As a basic prerequisite, it was necessary that informants have direct experience on a project involving participants from diverse societal systems and that their experience be sufficiently recent, within the previous ten years, to permit adequate recall of events. It was also necessary that they agree to have the interview digitally recorded. A practical consideration was access. Leads to alumni and industry affiliates were obtained through the authors' personal contact network and through the engineering program at their university.

### Starting point of investigation

Although we had institutional theory in mind as a conceptual guide for fieldwork and a strong sense from reviewing the literature that institutional differences would lead to conflicts and costs, we did not know *how* these situations would actually unfold. Thus, we made every attempt to begin our interviews with a *tabula rasa* – an open mind, as recommended by established methodology texts. Glaser and Strauss (1967: 37) advise:

An effective strategy is, at first, literally to ignore the literature of theory and fact on the area under study, in order to assure that the emergence of categories will not be contaminated by concepts more suited to different areas. Similarities and differences with the literature can be established after the analytic core of categories has emerged.

### Interview questions

The interviews followed an open-ended format. Informants were encouraged to talk about challenges their organization had faced on a recent global project. These interviews started out with open-ended questions such as, "Take me on a grand tour of the project" or, "Tell me about the challenges on the project that were surprising." There are two key points to note about these broad questions. First, by requesting a broad overview of a project, including many challenges beyond the scope of the study, such as challenges with an unfamiliar natural environment or a new technology, we could direct later stages of the interview toward specific challenges that had arisen from the unfamiliar social world – such as differences in beliefs, informal protocols, or formal rule systems. Second, while these general questions created opportunities for spontaneous discussion around emergent topics, they were not so specific as to prime the informants to talk only about problems in coping with the institutional requirements of the host country. Once a story about a specific institutional exception did emerge, we encouraged respondents to give more details about the associated chain of events, resolutions, and costs with questions like, "I see – what happened next?", or, "Oh – there was a meeting?", or, "Really – how much did that cost?"

## Data analysis

### Unit of analysis
Given the project focus and the nature of the data – individual interviews based on personal experience – this article relies on the individual manager's interpretations and actions. But although the individual manager appears to be the unit of analysis, in virtually all cases, this person served as an informant to describe the experiences of a project team or organizational unit. Hence, the unit under study is best described as an organizational subsystem, with information provided by an officer responsible for, or associated with that component.

### Inductive method
Data analysis followed the approaches variously known as grounded-theory building (Eisenhardt 1989), analytic induction (Robinson 1951; Znaniecki 1934), and the constant comparative method (Glaser and Strauss 1967:105). The constant comparative method entails:

first, coding each incident in the data into as many categories of analysis as possible and comparing incidents [in] each category; second, integrating categories and their properties . . . resulting in a unified and . . . developing theory; and third, delimiting the theory . . . and reformulating it with a smaller set of higher level concepts.

This approach differs from enumerative induction, which applies statistics to assess the strength of relationships between variables. Instead, through constant comparison, "Cumulative growth and development of theory is obtained by formulating a generalization in such a way that negative cases force us either to reject the generalization or to revise it" (Lindesmith 1947: 12).

### Iterative analysis

Within this method, vignette preparation, random-member checks, analysis, concept development and follow-on interviews were performed in a highly iterative and dynamic process. Institutional exceptions, where an unforeseen challenge on a global project could be traced back to a lack of familiarity with pertinent institutions, were transcribed in vignette format with a chronological story-like summary of key details and events (Miles and Huberman 1994: 81). As vignettes were completed, random member checks (Lincoln and Guba 1985) were conducted by e-mail to ask informants to verify accuracy and approve the disguise of potentially sensitive details,[2] such as dollar values and names of geographical locations. As analysis progressed, brief follow-up interviews – from 5 to 30 minutes – were conducted by telephone to clarify facts, thicken data and better ground the emerging conceptual framework.

### Vignette selection

Of the 39 informants, 19 were able to confidently describe details surrounding an institutional exception in enough detail to support the preparation of a vignette. Four informants provided data for two vignettes. In total, 23 vignettes were developed and for each, Table 5.1 displays major characteristics of the informant, their organization and the project. Interviews with the other 20 informants did not yield a detailed vignette describing an institutional exception. Many of these informants talked primarily of technical challenges, unforeseen problems posed by the vagaries of the natural environment, or discussed in vague terms culture, management styles, or local customs, but did not share in-depth, specific examples of divergent institutional understandings and the resulting dynamics. Hence, these interviews did not generate vignettes.

Table 5.1 *Summary of informants, organizations, and projects sampled*

| ID No. | Number of interviews | Informant's position in the entrant organization | Entrant organization type | Entrant nationality[a] | Local host nationality | Project type | Project value[b] | Project phase[c] when incident occurred |
|---|---|---|---|---|---|---|---|---|
| 1 | 3 | Vice President | AEC[d] Prime Consultant | US | Korea | Transportation | <1B | Design & Eng. |
| 2 | 2 | Anthropologist | Environmental Consultant | US | Uganda | Hydroelectric | <1B | Feasibility |
| 3 | 2 | Engineer | Design Consultant | US | China | Manufacturing | <100M | Commissioning |
| 4 | 2 | Project Manager | Steel Manufacturer | Japan | US | Bridge | <100M | Implementation |
| 5 | 2 | Assistant Ops Officer | US Navy | US | Albania | Road Building | <10M | Procurement |
| 6 | 4 | Vice President | Developer | US | Europe[e] | Real Estate | <100M | Feasibility |
| 7 | 2 | Senior Project Manager | Developer | US | China | Soccer Stadium | <100M | Implementation |
| 8 | 3 | Project Director | AEC Prime Consultant | US | Israel | Transportation | <1B | Implementation |
| 9 | 2 | Vice President | Contractor | Canada | Russia | Fiber Optic | <100M | Feasibility |
| 10 | 3 | Vice President | AEC Prime Consultant | US | Korea | Transportation | <1B | Design & Eng. |
| 11 | 1 | Project Manager | Steel Manufacturer | Japan | US | Bridge | <100M | Implementation |
| 12 | 4 | Vice President | Developer | US | France | Real estate | <100M | Design & Eng. |
| 13 | 2 | Project Engineer | AEC Prime Consultant | US | Tajikistan | Dam Construction | <100M | Implementation |
| 14 | 2 | Director of Operations | US Navy | US | Spain | Building | <100M | Implementation |

Table 5.1 (*cont.*)

| ID No. | Number of interviews | Informant's position in the entrant organization | Entrant organization type | Entrant[a] nationality | Local host nationality | Project type | Project value[b] | Project phase[c] when incident occurred |
|---|---|---|---|---|---|---|---|---|
| 15 | 3 | Project Manager | General Contractor | Japan | US | Manufacturing | <100M | Implementation |
| 16 | 4 | Project Engineer | Nonprofit | Canada | Cameroon | Development | <100K | Implementation |
| 17 | 2 | General Superintendent | Sub Contractor | Canada | Malaysia | Transportation | <100M | Implementation |
| 18 | 2 | President | Consultant | US | Phillipines | Water Diversion | <1B | Implementation |
| 19 | 3 | Project Manager | US Navy | US | Japan | Building | <1M | Design & Eng. |
| 20 | 4 | Vice President | Developer | US | Spain | Real Estate | <10M | Design & Eng. |
| 21 | 3 | Project Manager | US Navy | US | Japan | Base Construction | <1M | Implementation |
| 22 | 3 | Vice President | AEC Prime Consultant | US | Vietnam | Infrastructure | <100M | Design & Eng. |
| 23 | 1 | Project Executive | Chemical Plant Developer | US | Canada | Chemical Plant | <100K | Feasibility |

[a] In each of the cases, the informant and the entrant organization share the same nationality.

[b] Approximate overall project values in US$. Note that in each case, the informant's organization was responsible for only a percentage of the overall project value, depending on the size and nature of their specific contractual responsibilities.

[c] Projects phases occur in the following sequence: feasibility, design & engineering, procurement, implementation, and commissioning.

[d] AEC stands for architecture, engineering, and construction. This acronym is standard jargon in the construction industry.

[e] This case represents business partners in France, Germany, Russia, Poland, and Czechoslovakia.

## Sample vignettes

Table 5.2 summarizes important details of the 23 vignettes analyzed in the present study. Due to length constraints, full-length versions of the vignettes are not included in this article, but they are available in Orr's (2005b) dissertation.

## Cross-vignette analysis matrix

In order to compare and contrast institutional exceptions, we "stacked comparable cases" in a condensed tabular format (Miles and Huberman 1994: 69). This cross-vignette analysis matrix provides a factual basis for the "generic narrative model," or "typical story" that emerged from the analysis (Abbott 1992).

## Concept development

A hallmark of case study research is the use of multiple methods and sources of evidence to establish the development of new concepts (Miles and Huberman 1994). In our study, the cross-vignette analysis matrix introduces a number of concepts to enable comparative analysis of the cases. The concepts that we employ are cobbled together from a variety of sources, including informants, scholarly works, and conventional usage. Conceptual clarifications of the three umbrella constructs – ignorance, sensemaking, and response – and all other sub-constructs are provided in the text as they appear.

## *Limitations*

### Isolation of institutional elements

In the real world, it is both naïve and arbitrary to isolate beliefs, norms, or rules from other co-occurring and inter-reliant institutional elements (Hirsch 1997). Indeed, full-fledged institutional systems are comprised of a tangled web of mutually reinforcing elements. Tacit beliefs uphold and are shaped by informal norms, which in turn give rise to and are influenced by formal rule creation and maintenance (Greif 1994, 2006; North 2005; Giddens 1979). Thus, our differentiation of elements – cultural-cognitive, normative, and regulative – is an analytic attempt to identify the main element at work, although we recognize the interdependence of these elements and acknowledge the complexity of real world systems.

Table 5.2 *Condensed vignette summaries*

| ID No. | Key sequence of events |
| --- | --- |
| 1 | A US architect reported design progress by a US reporting convention that unintentionally mislead a Korean client to interpret design was progressing faster than was the case; this hurt the relationship |
| 2 | A foreign proposal to dam a river for hydroelectric power generation infuriated locals who believed in an ancestral spirit in a waterfall on the river that would cease to flow; this caused a public outcry |
| 3 | A US firm offered a Chinese workforce a performance incentive that failed because of local beliefs that an excellent employment record might attract government harassment; this damaged productivity |
| 4 | A US manager's patterns of informal conversation confused a Japanese manager who misinterpreted a sarcastic statement as an urgent request; he commited resources to a losing course of action |
| 5 | A US manager in charge of procuring local materials violated norms of personal exchange in Albania; he faced unexpected extortion from clan members who were responsible for sanctioning deviants |
| 6 | A group of US investors imposed a standard US format for the preparation of pro forma financial statements on several European partners who at first were unwilling to comply; this hurt the relationship |
| 7 | A US project manager threatened to reject a subcontractor's beam installation on a Chinese holiday associated with good luck and good fortune; this damaged the relationship |
| 8 | Joint venture partners had diverging cultural philosophies towards pursuing change orders to return a project that was losing money to profitability; a long-standing dispute destroyed the relationship |
| 9 | A Canadian contractor evaluating a project in Russia failed to understand the locally accepted function of paying bribes to secure work; they failed to win a contract they thought had been promised to them |
| 10 | A US design team held "working design meetings" with a Korean client whose unfamiliarity with this practice led them to be uncooperative and question the US team's technical ability; this soured relations |
| 11 | A Japanese firm's focus on technical excellence and professional duty caused them to fall victim to a US firm's intentional attempts to delay a project by refusing to pass quality inspections; this cost millions |

**Table 5.2** (*cont.*)

| ID No. | Key sequence of events |
|---|---|
| 12 | A US firm's standard design for a high-rise office building was unacceptable to a local partner who refused to collaborate unless the plan was modified; this caused friction in the relationship |
| 13 | A US contractor was unfamiliar with protocols of negotiation in Turkey and went ahead with a project without obtaining the necessary local approvals; this hurt the relationship and delayed the project |
| 14 | US designers expected a Spanish contractor to prepare shop drawings but the Spanish industry is organized such that contractors do not normally prepare shop drawings; a one-year delay was incurred |
| 15 | A Japanese firm failed to understand the US process of submitting formal change orders when they overran the budget on a guaranteed maximum price contract; they lost 15% of the contract value |
| 16 | A Canadian engineering team failed to comply with the local protocol of meeting with the village chieftain to approve of village projects; they faced sabotage and other mysterious barriers to productivity |
| 17 | A Canadian firm violated the local taboo of promoting employees of a particular ethnicity to positions of management; they faced ostracism and ridicule by other locals |
| 18 | A US contractor failed to consider the tribal traditions of a Phillipine patriarchal society; their project was sabotaged and they faced costly delays |
| 19 | A US design team tried to persuade a Japanse client to change an expensive, but customary, building material listed on a blueprint; this cost several months of negotiation |
| 20 | A US team had a Spanish subcontractor sign a standard contract document; it was deemed unenforceable by Spanish legal counsel and ended up costing the US firm many hundred thousand dollars |
| 21 | A US organization forced a Japanese firm to comply with US safety regulations that violated a long-standing Japanese workpractice; this created friction in the relationship |
| 22 | Several US organizations tried to invest in projects in Vietnam but were unable to sign exlusive contracts with Vietnamese agents for lack of a modern legal system; they fled Vietnam and wrote-down the investment |
| 23 | A US firm developing a new chemical plant in Canada was unaware of a provincial government requirement that called for a local engineer to certify project design drawings; this added unexpected costs and delays |

It is equally difficult to unpack and disentangle institutional and technological effects. For example, it is problematic whether differences in work practices between US and Chinese scaffold workers reflect differing institutions or differing technologies. While the scaffolding technologies differ in obvious ways (i.e., steel vs. bamboo), it is also true that across the two societies there is great variation in the logics and work practices of vendors, workers, and safety inspectors in the scaffolding industry. This is but one example of how technologies are shaped by social structures and conventions and vice versa (Bijker, Hughes, and Pinch 1987; Orlikowski 1992). Here we attempt to defocalize or bracket the effects of technological differences in order to concentrate on institutional aspects.

Finally, some conflicts arise out of relatively straightforward differences in the economic interests of the parties involved. These are excluded from our analysis, which attempts to focus on that subset of disagreements that arise because of institutional disparities. However, even this is an artificial distinction since, in our view, all interests, including those based in economic differences, are grounded in an institutional matrix of beliefs, assumptions, norms, and rules.

### One-sided perspective

All of the cases were constructed from interviews with a respondent from an entrant firm – admittedly a one-sided point of view. One of the dangers of gathering data from a single informant in a cross-cultural encounter is that of assuming the informant's perceptions of the "other" are an accurate or fair account of the situation encountered. However, because our approach was intentionally designed to assess the sensemaking and interpretive processes employed by foreign entrant firms, we felt justified in relying on their account of events. Any discussion as to how a host perceived, interpreted, or responded to an entrant's contested actions reflects our own inferences based on the entrant's recollections.

### Simplication of interactive process

The evolution of cooperative teamwork is known to be a complex, iterative, feedback-driven process (Doz 1996). When teamwork processes involving multiple participants and interests are examined over time, instances of confusion, sensemaking, and assessment will occur and reoccur. In the present analysis, we linearize this process, compartmentalizing these interactions into discreet, ordered stages. While this dissection involves simplification – reality is less linear – it captures the general trajectory of temporal development from problem recognition to response.

## Findings

How are institutional exceptions triggered? How are they resolved? How are costs manifested in this process? What conditions increase the magnitude of these costs? Can these costs be avoided? Analysis of the 23 vignettes revealed a three-phase generic narrative model. Each phase has three parts: a mindset, an associated behavior, and an outcome. In our account, the factual basis of the generic narrative model is displayed in the three-part cross-vignette analysis matrix, shown in Tables 5.3, 5.4, and 5.5, and propositions are presented both to challenge and fortify extant theory.

## *Phase 1. Challenging a host's institutions*

The evidence employed is summarized in Table 5.3, arranged to show how the first phase of all 23 institutional exceptions is described by a three-step sequence: (1) an entrant in a mindset of ignorance, (2) acts in a way that deviates from local institutions, which (3) results in cues of disapproval and accompanying costs originating from the host.

### Institutional ignorance

*Institutional ignorance* has two key conceptual aspects: lack of knowledge about applicable institutions in the action arena and reliance on nonlocal institutional knowledge that crowds out sensemaking processes. The term is not intended in the pejorative sense, as when ignorance denotes deliberate intent to ignore certain facts in order to suit one's needs or beliefs. Instead, it implies a more neutral state of being unaware of institutional systems differing from one's own, and, consequently, a reliance on previously scripted mental models that do not reflect the new context.

Table 5.3, column 3a attempts to classify the 23 vignettes in terms of the primary sort of institutional difference encountered. For example, problems were triggered on a project in Albania when a US manager lacked knowledge about local trading protocols of personal exchange

Table 5.3 *Ignorance, deviant action, and outcomes*

| ID No. | 3a Ignorance | | 3b Deviant action | | 3c Results of ignorance | | | Legend |
|---|---|---|---|---|---|---|---|---|
| | ID | RN | IA | FT | I | ET | MC | |
| 1 | c | X | c,am | | s | m | rl | ID = institutional differences |
| 2 | c | X | v,a | | so | w | rl, of, s, rp | c = cultural-cognitive |
| 3 | c | X | v,s | | s | d | rl, of | n = normative |
| 4 | c | X | c | | o | h | rl, of | r = regulative |
| | | | | | | | | RN = reliance or pre-scripted mental models[a] |
| 5 | c,n | X | c | | so | w | e | |
| 6 | c,n | X | c | | s | w | rl, of | **Deviant Action** |
| 7 | c,n | X | a | | s | h | rl | IA = take inappropriate action |
| 8 | c,n | X | v | | so | d | rl, of | FT = fail to take required action |
| 9 | c,n | X | am,a | | s | w | rl, of | c = confuses LH; a = angers LH |
| 10 | n | X | c | | s | d | rl, of | v = violates LH; s = angers LH |
| 11 | n | X | | po | s | w | of | am = accidentally misleads LH |
| 12 | n | X | c | | s | h | rl, rp | po = creates predatory opportunity for LH |
| 13 | n | X | c,v | | so | d | rl, of | |
| 14 | n | X | c,am | | s | m | rl, of | **Results of ignorance** |
| 15 | n | X | | po | s | m | rl, of | I = intensity of cues from LH |
| 16 | n | X | a | v | o | d | rl, of, s | s = subtle; o = overt; so = subtle building to overt |
| 17 | n | X | v,a | | o | w | rl, s, rp | ET = elapsed time to receive cues from LH |

**Table 5.3** (*cont.*)

| ID No. | 3a Ignorance | | 3b Deviant action | | 3c Results of ignorance | | | Legend |
|---|---|---|---|---|---|---|---|---|
| | ID | RN | IA | FT | I | ET | MC | |
| 18 | n | X | | a | so | m | rl, s, or, e | h = hours; d = days; w = weeks; m = months |
| 19 | n | X | c | | s | w | rl | MC = major associated costs |
| 20 | r | X | po | | so | m | rl | rl = relationship damage; s = sanctions |
| 21 | r | X | v | | o | d | rl, s | of = opportunity forgone; e = extortion |
| 22 | r | X | c,s | | so | m | rl, of | rp = reputation damage |
| 23 | r | X | c | | o | w | of | |

[a] such as institutional presumptions, experiences, expectations, judgments. and rules of thumb.

and assumed, incorrectly, that US trading practices would be agreeable to local vendors (5; i.e., see Case ID no. 5 in Table 5.2). In other cases, the entrant's knowledge deficit and assumptions variously concerned: keywords marking design milestones (1), beliefs in ancestral spirits (2), preferences for traditional building materials (12), habits of hiring and promotion (17), and norms of contract enforcement (20). A knowledge deficit occurs when an entrant is unfamiliar with local institutional elements and arrangements. Table 5.3, column 3a indicates that in six cases, the entrant's knowledge deficit primarily related to cognitive-cultural institutions; in 13 cases, to normative institutions; and in the remaining four cases, to regulative institutions.

The existence of an institutional exception, by definition, points to the presence of a knowledge deficit on the part of the entrant (see Table 5.3, column 3a). (Although the deficit may well involve both interacting parties, we focus on the entrant, because the situation is

Table 5.4 *Sensemaking, local knowledge search, and outcomes*

| ID No. | 4a Sensemaking | | | 4b Local knowledge search | | 4c Results of sensemaking | | | Legend |
|---|---|---|---|---|---|---|---|---|---|
| | CM | IB | OM | HM | SA | ET | NC | AC | |
| 1 | | X | | i,e | | w | 2 | m,ct | CM = close-minded & rigid adherence |
| 2 | | | X | i,e | g,p | m | 1 | m,c,ct | to pre-existing mental models |
| 3 | | | X | i,e | g,p | w | 1 | m,c,ct | OM = open-minded inquiry & adaptation |
| 4 | X | | | i,e | | h | 3 | m,ct | of pre-existing mental models |
| 5 | X | | | i,e | | w | 3 | m,ct | IB = inbetween |
| 6 | | X | | i,e | g | m | 2 | m,ct | |
| 7 | | X | | i | | h | 1 | m,c,ct | **Local knowledge search** |
| 8 | X | | | i,e | | m | 3 | m,ct | HM = hold meetings |
| 9 | | X | | i,e | g | d | 2 | m,ct | i = internal; e = external |
| 10 | X | | | i,e | | w | 2 | m,ct | SA = seek answers from third-party locals |
| 11 | X | | | i,e | | m | 3 | m,ct | g = general public; p = consultants |
| 12 | | X | | i,e | g | m | 1 | m,ct | **Results of sensemaking** |
| 13 | | X | | i,e | g | d | 2 | m,ct | |
| 14 | X | | | i,e | | m | 3 | m,ct | ET = elapsed time in mindset of sensemaking |
| 15 | | X | | i,e | p | m | 1 | m,c,ct | h = hours; d = days; w = weeks; m = months |
| 16 | | | X | i,e | g | w | 1 | m,ct | NC = new clarity of knowledge of local institutional code |
| 17 | | | X | i,e | g | w | 1 | m,ct | |

**Table 5.4** (*cont.*)

| ID No. | 4a Sensemaking | | | 4b Local knowledge search | | 4c Results of sensemaking | | | Legend |
|---|---|---|---|---|---|---|---|---|---|
| | CM | IB | OM | HM | SA | ET | NC | AC | |
| 18 | | X | | i,e | p | w | 2 | m,c,ct | 1 = high; 2 = med; 3 = low |
| 19 | | | X | i,e | g,p | w | 1 | m,c,ct | AC[a] = associated costs |
| 20 | | X | | i,e | g,p | d | 2 | m,c,ct | m = managerial effort; |
| 21 | | X | | i,e | g,p | d | 1 | m,c,ct | c = consultant fees ct = communication & travel |
| 22 | X | | | i,e | p | m | 3 | m,c,ct | |
| 23 | | | X | i,e | p | d | 1 | m,ct | |

[a] A fourth cost is project delay. It is not shown explicitly, as the durations listed under the "ET" category are indicative.

viewed from his/her perspective.) The entrant must perforce rely on *nonlocal institutional knowledge* constructed from prior experiences in an institutionally dissimilar setting. Unquestioned reliance on nonlocal institutional knowledge is detrimental because it crowds out sensemaking and leads to inadvertent overconfidence (see Louis 1980).

Several of the critical incidents involved an entrant who was confused by the absence of expected social actors or the presence of unanticipated new types of actors (16, 18, 22). "Social actors" refer to either individuals or organizations that occupy, in the former case, specified roles, or, in the latter, standardized organizational forms and routines within a given society (Scott et al. 2000; Cummings and Doh 2000). In the US, familiar social actors include "lawyers," "venture capitalists," "corporations," and "501(c)3 not-for-profits." Across societies, however, there is substantial variation in the forms and functions assumed by legitimate social actors – in the rule-sets, logics, and expectations that they embody, and in the relative positions in the organizational fields in which they exist and operate. Some of the

**Table 5.5** *Response, response action, and outcomes*

| ID No. | 5a Response | | 5b Response action | | | | | | 5c Results of response | | Legend |
|---|---|---|---|---|---|---|---|---|---|---|---|
| | FL | W | Ac | C | D | M | Av | E | IR | C | |
| 1 | on | 1 | | X | | | | X | i | n | FL = formulate response relying on: |
| 2 | n | 3 | | | | X | X | | i | r, e | o = prior and inappropriate mental models |
| 3 | n | 3 | X | | | | | | i | n | n = new mental models fitted to local institutions |
| 4 | o | 1 | X | | | | | | w | n | on = mix of bto |
| 5 | o | 1 | | X | | | | | w | n | W = weigh costs & benefits |
| 6 | on | 2 | | | | X | | X | w[a] | r, e | 1 = one alternative considered |
| 7 | n | 2 | X | | | | | | I | r | 2 = two ore more alternatives considered |
| 8 | o | 1 | | | X | | X | | w | w | |
| 9 | o | 1 | | | X | | X | | w | w | **Response action** |
| 10 | o | 1 | | X | | | | X | w | w | Ac = acquiesce D = defy |
| 11 | o | 1 | X | | | | | | w | w, r | M = manipulate |
| | | | | | | | | | | | Av = avoid |
| 12 | n | 3 | X | | | | | | i | n | C = compromise |
| | | | | | | | | | | | E = educate |
| 13 | n | 2 | X | | | | | | i | w | |
| 14 | o | 1 | | | X | | X | | w | w, r | **Results of response**[b] |
| 15 | on | 2 | | X | | | | | w | w | IR = impact on relationship with LH |
| 16 | n | 2 | X | | | | | | i | r | W = worsens; |
| | | | | | | | | | | | i = improves |
| 17 | on | 3 | | | X | | X | | w[a] | n | C = associated cost |
| 18 | o | 1 | X | | | | | | i | r | w = write-down costs of ignorance |
| 19 | n | 2 | X | | | | | | i | r | r = further resource commitment |

**Table 5.5** (*cont.*)

| ID No. | 5a Response | | 5b Response action | | | | | | 5c Results of response | | Legend |
|---|---|---|---|---|---|---|---|---|---|---|---|
| | FL | W | Ac | C | D | M | Av | E | IR | C | |
| 20 | n | 2 | X | | | | | | i | r | e = programs to educate local host |
| 21 | n | 2 | | | | X | | X | i | r, e | n = no additional cost |
| 22 | o | 1 | | | | | X | | w | w | |
| 23 | n | 3 | X | | | | | | i | w, r | |

[a] Note, negative relational impact was carefully selected by the entrant as the best possible response given the unique circumstances of the situation.

[b] Although not shown explicitly, all informants indicated some amount of experiential learning.

most intractable institutional exceptions occurred when an entrant manager was unable to locate a social actor that had been expected, or encountered a social actor that was both unexpected and extremely influential in the local context. For example, a US manager on a soccer stadium project in China reported surprise in the absence of bonding agencies and trade unions; as well as the unwelcome discovery of a government design institute and a government inspection company. This discrepancy between entrant and host in the assumed field of actors and in the matrix of routines and logics that each embodies led to many unbudgeted project costs. This represents, in a broad sense, an important class of cultural-cognitive sources of divergence.

### Deviant act

The term *deviation* has been used in the institutional literature to describe the act of departing from an established norm, standard, or cultural belief (Weingast 1996; Dalton 2005; Witt and Lewin 2007). In our study, being guided by nonlocal institutional knowledge, the entrant in each case committed an act of deviation – either by commission or omission – that provoked negative feelings and reactions from the host. *Commission* is an act of perpetrating an offense against the beliefs, norms, or laws of a host. For example, in Uganda, a US bank enraged locals when they proposed a project that would have destroyed a waterfall that was said to house an ancestral spirit (2).

*Omission* is an act of leaving something out or failing to take an action that is required under the host's institutions. For example, in Cameroon, a Canadian engineering team angered a village chieftain by initiating a community development project without at first seeking his direct consent, as is customary in that society (16).

In other cases, contested acts ranged from applying a new pay incentive system, which violated local norms and alarmed a host (3), to mandating an obligatory format for pro-forma financials, which confused a host (6), to failing to pay usual bribes, which misled and angered a host (9), to failing to submit contractual change orders, which created predatory opportunities for a host (15).

From the entrant's frame of reference, few of these actions would have been viewed as deviant – generally speaking, the entrant was acting in a way that would have been perfectly acceptable and appropriate within the norms and conventions of their own societal context. Yet, although not violent or criminal, they were viewed as inappropriate by the host. Of the 23 cases, 18 were classified as acts of commission, three as acts of omission, and two were counted in both categories (see Table 5.3, column 3b).

From the host's perspective – as reported by the entrant – these contested acts were the source of negative emotions and responses. Table 5.3, column 3b indicates that in 13 cases, feelings of confusion were triggered; in 9 cases, the local host felt violated; and in 2 cases each, feelings of fright, deception, and exploitation were provoked. These emotions, along with a complex of other factors – such as the apparent centrality of the institution broken by the entrant, the host's culturally preferred styles of communication and conflict resolution, and the host's level of sensitivity and tolerance towards the entrant's institutions and interpretive schemes – influenced the host's response. For example, when a US engineering team proposed to dam a river that would disrupt a waterfall containing an ancestral spirit, an angry chieftain in the Cameroon sabotaged equipment and materials that belonged to the entrant engineering team. The inadvertent proposal by the entrant was viewed by the host as a deliberate disregard of its core cultural values, requiring a vigorous response of protest. Several cases reveal this dynamic (5, 11, 12, 15, 16, 18).

### Outcomes of ignorance

An entrant's deviation from local institutions triggers cues of disapproval from the host and unexpected costs; these are the *outcomes of ignorance.* The fact that the host is experiencing negative emotions towards the entrant is communicated through *cues of disapproval*, including verbal statements, body language, facial expressions, and other communicatory signals and reactions. For example, at a design meeting on an airport project, a Korean client showed visible displeasure – through pained facial expressions – at a design consultant's lack of progress on a set of architectural drawings (1). The cues were sufficiently overt that the consultants became instantly aware that there must have been a misunderstanding. But by the time these signals were received and interpreted, the trust relationship between the design consultant and the client had been "crippled beyond repair."

In other cases, cues of disapproval ranged from a client verbally stating that a tugboat had been ordered for the wrong day (4), to an angry sponsor demanding a project be halted (13), to a client simply failing to respond to escalating cost reports within a reasonable time period (15). Associated costs included strained relations and a fee for a tugboat and crew (4), several days of project delay with senior managers locked in heated debate (13), and $20 million in cost overruns (15).

When the entrant finally begins to perceive the host's cues of disapproval, they act surprised or confused, because at that point they are still unaware of having failed to comply with a local institution (13, 11). In many cases, this point of realization starts with a "gut-feeling" that things are not going according to plan (14, 11). As one informant noted, "the project just wasn't working out, we knew we had to change our tack" (19).

*Cue intensity* is a term that describes the explicitness and observability of the host's verbal and nonverbal reactions to the entrant's deviant action. (Such differences in mode of response also reflect differences in underlying institutionalized conventions.) Across the cases, cue intensity varies considerably. Table 5.3, column 3c indicates that when a host's signals were more frequent or overt, the entrant perceived them more rapidly than when they were more subtle. Overt responses occurred when a host was frightened and acting in a mode of self-protection (18, 2), or angered and acting in a mode of retaliation (17). In contrast, subtle responses, such as passive silent treatment (12), or steady pressure to conform to local expectations (6), typically resulted when a host was troubled or uncertain about how to react (14, 19), or afraid to react at all (3). Cue intensity was classified as subtle in 8 cases; as overt in 7; and as subtle escalating to more overt in 8.

Each deviant action is accompanied by different kinds of costs, which we refer to as the *costs of ignorance*, and which fall into four general categories identified from the data: relationship damage, reputation damage, resource costs, and time loss (Table 5.3, column 3c). Relationship damage occurs when an entrant's trust relationship with local players deteriorates (1). Reputation damage happens when an entrant is publicly ostracized, ridiculed, or defamed and thereby loses legitimacy amongst a group of its peers or in the public spotlight (2). Resource costs result when an entrant faces monetary penalties, fees, or fines as punishment for its deviant action; when property or capital equipment are vandalized or damaged; or when rework is necessary because a mistake has been made; or when investments must be written-off or abandoned (18, 21). Time costs occur when scheduled work is delayed (11). From an entrant's outlook, these costs – which are not budgeted for in advance – are unforeseen, unpredicted, and surprising.

Several authors hypothesize that deep-seated cultural-cognitive institutions lead to the most irreconcilable challenges in cross-cultural encounters (e.g., Hofstede 1984). However, the projects in our case analysis afford a different view. In our sample of cases, the large majority of institutional exceptions stemmed not from national value differences, but from a mismatch in normative elements. Moreover, when entrants misjudged normative and regulative elements, the costs were just as severe as when cognitive-cultural elements were the culprits (see Table 5.3).

A more useful indicator of cost severity proved to be the *elapsed time to perceive cues*, which is defined as the elapsed time between an entrant's contested action and their "point of realization" – or first awareness that an institutional difference was the cause of problems. This elapsed time varied greatly: in three cases, it could be measured in hours; in 7, days; in 8, weeks; and in 5, months. The data indicate that the longer this time period, the more irrevocable are the entrant's decisions and resource commitments and the more difficult it is to correct mistakes and repair relations (see Table 5.3, column 3c). There was no obvious link between the type of element underlying the exception – cultural-cognitive, normative, or regulative – and the length of this time lag. One factor that did seem to be associated with time lag was the level of intensity of the hosts' cues. Relational dynamics were also crucial. Another factor that appeared to be indicative, but that we could not assess effectively with our interview data, was the level of sensitivity or perceptiveness of the entrant in recognizing the hosts' cues. To summarize more formally and tie to the next stage,

> *Proposition 1: The more ignorant an entrant is of local institutions, the more prone the entrant will be to engage in acts of omission and acts of commission that deviate from the host's institutions.*
>
> *Proposition 2: When an entrant's behavior is viewed as deviant, then host will react in a manner that sends cues of disapproval to the entrant.*
>
> *Proposition 3: The more subtle a host's cues of disapproval, the longer the elapsed time for the entrant to perceive those cues.*
>
> *Proposition 4: The longer the elapsed time to perceive cues, the greater the costs of ignorance incurred by the entrant.*

## *Phase 2. Making sense of a host's institutions*

What happens after an entrant perceives cues of disapproval from the local host? Table 5.4 depicts a three-part process of sensemaking that applies to all our cases: (1) with a mindset of sensemaking, (2) an entrant begins to search for local knowledge, (3) which results in a new level of understanding of local institutions, but at the cost of investing time and resources in sensemaking activities.

### Sensemaking

Once an entrant perceives a host's reactionary cues, then they become aware of an exception and enter a mode of sensemaking. Weick (1995) conceptualizes *sensemaking* as a thought process whereby active agents construct meaning by placing stimuli into frameworks that enable them to "structure the unknown" (Waterman 1990: 41), "comprehend, understand, explain, attribute, extrapolate and predict" (Starbuck and Milliken 1988: 51) surprises based on retrospective accounts (Louis 1980). Our analysis indicates that cross-cultural sensemaking operates on a continuum between two polar extremes – being open- and closed-minded, where *open-mindedness* is an attitudinal disposition of being more receptive to divergent views and more sensitive to the possibility of one's own bias.

For example, upon realizing that local natives worshipped a spirit in a waterfall, a US bank that was developing a dam project that would eventually submerge the waterfall said to house the spirit was largely open-minded and spent several months attempting to decipher the intricacies of the native religious beliefs and way of life (2). In contrast, the US Navy was closed-minded on a project in Spain; even after a one-year delay and after much time and effort devoted to troubleshooting the situation, they remained unable to understand why a Spanish contractor was unable to complete the required shop drawings (14).[3]

The entrants that we coded as being open-minded exhibited greater curiosity and interest in explaining the specifics of the institutional differences that they encountered (3, 16).[4] By contrast, entrants that we categorized as closed-minded stubbornly denied responsibility for their mistakes (10, 11, 22), wrongly blamed the host (4), or were irritated that a host did not respond favorably to their repeated attempts to "rectify" the situation (10, 11, 14). Despite recognizing cues from the host, it was evident that the more closed-minded entrants were not able to alter their pre-existing mental models, so that their interpretations continued to be inaccurate and dysfunctional. Other entrants exhibited a mindset that was in-between these two polar extremes (6, 15, 20).

By and large, the informants and their teams were intelligent and experienced personnel. Many had advanced degrees and specialized training in cross-cultural management and foreign languages. Almost all had done their homework and engaged in what might be called anticipatory sensemaking to ready themselves for their international assignments. All recognized considerable variation in the contexts in which they worked. And yet, strikingly, many still encountered institutional elements of a totally unexpected nature.

In general, the cases confirm that greater *international experience* – both in terms of duration and diversity – led to more open-minded sensemaking and better diagnosis of new institutional elements (2, 3). In contrast, entrants working abroad for the first time tended to be inflexibly closed-minded (4, 12). This is consistent with the international business literature on the role of international experience in reducing the liability of foreignness (Zaheer 1995; Reuber and Fischer 1997).

The cases also indicate that open-ended sensemaking processes occur at a more conscious level of awareness as opposed to closed-minded sensemaking processes that are more likely to be more subconscious and guided by preprogrammed scripts. Open-minded entrants actively question, ponder, and discuss within their teams the events, conversations, and decisions leading up to an exceptional incident; they introspectively examine the origin and applicability of their own expectations and routines; and they more often evaluate and adapt their behaviors to be more compatible with the local institutional code. By contrast, closed-minded entrants persist in opposing local institutions, even after recognizing that relations with the host have become awkward or started to falter, justifying their actions by employing internal reference frames (10, 22). None of our informants admitted to a fundamental distaste for the local way of life or business practice, but, in many of the vignettes, it was obvious that prior mental models were at odds with local institutions and blocking open-minded reflection and adaptation.

### Local knowledge search behavior

The *search for local knowledge* is the behavioral outcome that arises out of an attitudinal disposition of open-mindedness and includes any active effort to gather intelligence information or decipher the local institutional codes (March and Simon 1958; Cyert and March 1963; Geertz 1983). For example, when a US bank became aware that locals were concerned about a project that was going to destroy an ancestral spirit, they engaged in local knowledge search – they sent a cultural anthropologist to investigate religious practices and beliefs, they held "town-hall" meetings to listen to concerns, and they met internally to discuss facts, opinions, and possible courses of action in a collective process of mutual learning and consensus building (2). In other cases, entrants sought advice from consultants (15), held formal and informal meetings with colleagues (12) and local stakeholders (14), spoke with friends (19) and members of the local population (16), and sought out background materials about local culture, language, and history (13).

Entrants used meetings with the local host and consultations with unconcerned third parties to gather information about unanticipated institutional elements. *Meetings with the local host* included personal, small, and large group meetings between the entrant and host to troubleshoot problems. In some cases, this was merely a short conversation (4). In other cases, multiple meetings on multiple continents took place involving dozens of individuals (6). In one case a local staffer within one of the entrant's joint venture partners recognized the cultural *faux pas* and quickly made the offending entrant manager aware of his gaffe, obviating the need for such a meeting (7). *Consultations with unconcerned third parties* included private discussions with individuals outside of the institutional exception who were trusted as sources of independent advice. Several informants reported going to close friends, university alumni, and other local acquaintances (3). One described the key role of a joint venture partner (7). In several of the more costly, complicated, and confidential exceptions, entrants reported the engagement of local legal advisors, management consultants, and accounting firms (3, 15, 18). Finally, many entrants relied on translators to play the role of intermediary and to assist in clarifying communications. Several informants noted that, due to disputes with local entities, they could not fully trust the translation provided by their counterparty, and thus they retained their own translator (7). Generally, the case data indicates that entrants that were more open-minded also tended to use multiple sources of local advice and opinion, as well as published books and online sources, to increase the breadth and validity of their understanding (3, 16, 19).

### Outcomes of sensemaking

The *outcomes of sensemaking* are two-fold: changes – sometimes modest – in the entrant's state of knowledge about local institutions, and the incurrence of costs associated with local knowledge search. For example, on a dam construction project in Turkey, an entrant reported that the sensemaking period lasted several days, involving tense negotiations with the project sponsor, internal meetings, reading a book "The Arab Mind," and a string of sleepless nights (13). In other cases, sensemaking resulted in new insight into local building codes (23), a clearer conception of tribal traditions and values in an indigenous community (18), a new awareness of a traditional Japanese work-practice to wear soft-toed shoes for scaffold work (21), a new knowledge of Chinese beliefs about good luck (7), and new awareness of how payments to political officials are applied to secure work in Russia (9).

Not all sensemaking efforts brought clearer understandings. In several cases the entrant remained confused, even after perceiving cues, recognizing an exception, and attempting to understand the situation. For example, a Japanese contractor was never able to decipher the use of sarcasm in US conversation (4), the US Navy did not seem to comprehend the division of labor in Spain (14), and a US manager could not fathom the norms of personal exchange in Albania (5) (see Greif 1994).

The key outcome of the sensemaking process – when it goes well – is a *new clarity of knowledge about the institutions* under scrutiny, which serves to reduce the entrant's initial institutional ignorance. The more open-minded entrants, who had aggressively inquired about local institutions, were generally able to recount specific details and explain subtle nuances of the local institutional elements in question. For example, when we asked a Canadian manager why he had been ridiculed on a project in Malaysia for promoting Indian employees to management positions, he launched into a 25-minute explanation of 100 years of Malaysian history, telling how the balance of power had historically been divided between Chinese, Malays, and Indians and how long-standing Malaysian traditions had influenced the norms and expectations that had penetrated into his specific project (17). In contrast, the entrants who were closed-minded were unable to give similar clear or coherent accounts (14). Our cases indicate that an entrant's open-mindedness is linked to the amount of effort that they expend to acquire local knowledge, but that this is not without its costs.

The *costs of sensemaking* include time spent both in meetings and in seeking information from third-party agents; money spent on communications, travel, and consultants; as well as significant opportunity costs and delays that result when senior executives and entire project teams with hundreds of local staff are tied up for extended time periods (1, 2, 8, 15, 20). To summarize more formally,

> Proposition 5: *The greater an entrant's global experience, the greater their open-mindedness in sensemaking.*
>
> Proposition 6: *The greater an entrant's open-mindedness, the more extensive is their search for local knowledge.*
>
> Proposition 7: *The more extensive an entrant's search for local knowledge, the greater the reduction of their initial institutional ignorance, but also the greater the costs incurred in sensemaking.*

## Phase 3. Responding to a host's institutions

After sensemaking, an entrant moves into a mindset of response. Table 5.5 depicts a three-step process: (1) an entrant formulates and compares response alternatives, (2) enacts a response, (3) and experiences some outcome, a process that is typically associated with further costs (see Table 5.5).

## Response

The final phase of an institutional exception commences when the entrant evaluates and then selects a *response* to minimize the impacts of its earlier deviant act. Many studies of decision making describe how agents select responses from among alternatives (see Tversky and Kahneman 1974; Cyert and March 1963). Weighing response alternatives is a process that entails comparing the expected costs and benefits of each alternative against preferences (March 1994). Our analysis suggests that an entrant enters a mindset of response after having become convinced, whether rightly or wrongly, that they understand the institutional elements at play and the range of feasible response possibilities.

For example, a US manager on a soccer stadium project in China was angered when a Chinese contractor erected a truss that failed to meet quality standards. But, after threatening to have the contractor eliminated from the project, he learned from a Chinese staffer that this particular day of the year was a Chinese holiday associated with good luck and that the truss had only been erected to show "symbolic progress" (7). Armed with this new knowledge, the US manager was able to consider several alternative responses other than firing the contractor. In other cases, the entrant's mindset of response focused on repairing a strained relationship (16), recovering an unpaid fee (15), avoiding the payment of bribes (5, 9) improving the productivity of a Chinese workforce (3) and negotiating an agreeable work plan (13).

The cases also suggest a link between an entrant's clarity of local knowledge at the end of their sensemaking efforts and the number of alternative responses considered. Indeed, in all ten cases where an entrant's clarity of knowledge at the end of sensemaking was classified as high (Table 5.4, column 4c), the entrant consciously considered and weighed the costs and benefits of multiple response alternatives. On the other hand, in all six cases where the entrant's clarity of knowledge at the end of sensemaking was low (Table 5.4, column 4c), the entrant appeared to consider only a single mode of action (Table 5.5, column 5a). This suggests that a greater clarity of local knowledge enables greater flexibility in considering innovative response alternatives.

As with sensemaking, the mindset associated with response ranges between two extremes: conscious and unconscious. This familiar dichotomy distinguishes decisions made by intuition – fast, effortless, automatic and associative – from those made by reasoning – more deliberate, controlled, effortful and rule-governed (Kahneman 2003; Smith 2003). Although the case data were limited in this regard, it appeared that when sensemaking was closed-minded, decisions were made more likely to be intuitive. Intuitive decisions were less likely to take into account local institutions (see Louis 1980).

### Response strategies

Response behavior is the enactment of a mindset of response. A typology proposed by Oliver (1991) consists of five *response strategies* to institutional pressure: acquiesce, defy, compromise, avoid and manipulate. This typology was employed to sort out the range of responses enacted across the 23 cases. For example, after trying for months to get European partners to adopt a standard format for pro-forma financials, a US developer sent their CFO to manipulate – negotiate with and change – their partners' practices to ensure that future pro-format reports would be prepared in the necessary format (6).

In other cases, the entrant's response was to acquiesce, by meeting a village chieftain to seek approval and give gifts (16); to compromise, by negotiating to have 50 percent of a cost overrun passed on to a foreign client (15) or by re-designing a pay system to better conform to Chinese workers' expectations (3); to avoid, by foregoing a project altogether, because paying bribes was deemed intolerable (9); or to defy, by terminating a soured relationship with a partner after refusing to acquiesce or compromise (6).

The case evidence reveals that acquiesce or compromise strategies generally reduce damage to host relations while avoidance or defiance approaches entail further damages (Table 5.5). For example, in the six cases involving an acquiescent strategy, relations improved in four; and in the eleven with a compromise strategy, relations improved in seven. In contrast, in the five cases with a defiance approach, relations worsened in four, and in all four cases with an avoidance approach, relations deteriorated. In three cases involving a manipulation strategy, relations worsened in two and improved in one.

There is always dynamic and iterative interaction between an entrant's end strategy and a host's end response (Doz 1996). Acquiesce and defiance strategies typically come in pairs: if an entrant acquiesces, for all intents and purposes, the host is able to defy; likewise, if an entrant defies, the host must acquiesce or relations will undoubtedly worsen. A compromise strategy only works if both sides can communicate effectively and agree on a mutually beneficial alternative. A manipulation strategy requires the entrant to provide incentives, or sanctions, to motivate a host to alter its underlying institutions or, perhaps, to alter the host's understanding of which interests and issues are of most importance to the host (Bazerman and Neale 1992). An avoidance strategy severs interaction, typically terminating relations.

While Oliver's typology was useful for understanding entrant responses, we did find it helpful to include a sixth category: "educate". Since institutional exceptions are of an accidental or unintended nature, an important part of their resolution often involves education (1, 6, 10, 12, 21). While education may be viewed as a subtle form of manipulation, it does not have the same coercive undertone, particularly if both parties participate in the teaching as well as the learning. Education, especially when it is mutual, can frequently result in a win-win situation for both parties.

### Outcomes of response

The *outcomes of the response process* include reductions in – or the writing-down of – the original costs of ignorance; additional costs of response; and/or overall advances in experiential learning. For example, on a dam construction project in Turkey, after US managers learned to negotiate in a manner that better fit the cultural and historical setting, their relations with the project sponsor improved dramatically, and the project moved forward. The informant recalled, "We did it the local way – you know, sat and had 5 cups of tea – and there were no more problems." (13) However, the "local way" turned out to be more time-consuming than had been budgeted, costing several weeks of unplanned delay to make allowance for the protracted negotiation process. In other cases, relations with a village chieftain improved, but at the cost of numerous gifts and lengthy meetings (16); relations with a US client were critically damaged and a $5M overrun incurred (15); relations with a Russian client were terminated and many months of project feasibility planning written-down as sunk costs (9); and relations with a joint venture partner were terminated causing the "largest losses in recent history" for one entrant firm (6).

An important aspect of the final outcome of each case study was whether or not the initial costs of ignorance were lessened through the response process, or whether they could not be altered. For example, the response of one Japanese manager, who had delivered a tugboat and crew to a jobsite on the wrong day, was to re-plan delivery for the following week and to beg forgiveness from a US project manager (4). Or in the case of another Japanese firm, which had missed the legal window of opportunity to submit change orders, the end response was to admit a misjudgment and to request partial recovery for a US $20M cost overrun (15).

While money costs, time costs and reputational damage prove difficult to recoup, the cases indicate that damaged relations can be improved dramatically. In the cases where a deviant action had irreversible consequences, the mindset of response was more about impact minimization than about damage reversal. Table 5.5, column 5c shows that in eleven cases relations were improved; in eight they worsened; and in four they did not noticeably change. A significant finding of the study is that end relational outcomes are closely associated with the entrant's degree of open-mindedness in the sensemaking process. Comparisons across the columns in Tables 5.4 and 5.5 suggest that there are clear causal linkages between an entrant's sensemaking mindset, breadth of local knowledge search, clarity of new understanding about local institutions, selection of a response strategy, and end relational outcome. When sensemaking was open-minded, more often than not, this causal chain led to a positive relational outcome.

*Costs of response* were sorted into three types: absorbing initial costs of ignorance when an act of deviance had irreversible consequences (2, 23); committing time resources to educate a host (6); and expending other resources to execute responses (20).

For each case, we estimated the *elapsed time in sensemaking and response*, which is measured from the point of first recognition of an institutional exception to the point of response implementation. This period varied substantially across the cases: in two cases, it was measured in hours; in five, days; in eight, weeks; and in eight, months.

Longer sensemaking and response formulation durations tended to involve situations where an entrant was closed-minded and complacent (8, 11, 14, 22) or when the stakes were very high (2, 6, 15).

Finally, the cases indicated that the longer the elapsed time between an entrant's deviation and selection of an end response, the more locked-in are costs and irreversible are relational damages and other costs of ignorance (8, 11, 14, 15). To summarize more formally:

> *Proposition 8: The greater an entrant's clarity of institutional knowledge, the more likely they are to weigh alternative responses to fit local institutional constraints.*
>
> *Proposition 9: The greater an entrant's clarity of institutional knowledge, the more likely they are to select a compromise or acquiesce response strategy.*
>
> *Proposition 10: The poorer an entrant's clarity of institutional knowledge, the more likely they are to select an avoidance or defiant response approach.*
>
> *Proposition 11: Use of an acquiesce or compromise strategy is more likely to result in the mending of a damaged relationship; use of an avoidance or defiant approach, is more likely to result in greater damage.*
>
> *Proposition 12: The greater the elapsed time between sensemaking and response, the less likely it is that relationship damage and other costs of ignorance can be reversed.*

## Toward a generic narrative model

This study has explored how differences in institutions lead to unforeseen costs for foreign firms. The findings do not take the form of a set of verified propositions but a collection of hypotheses to be tested and the generation of a generic narrative model, depicted in Figure 5.1.

### How common are institutional exceptions?

Of the 39 informants, 19 reported institutional exceptions in their cross-border projects. The high number of cases where we could not explicitly identify this same pattern implies that while pervasive, institutional exceptions do not afflict all global projects. A quantitative approach examining a more representative collection of cases would

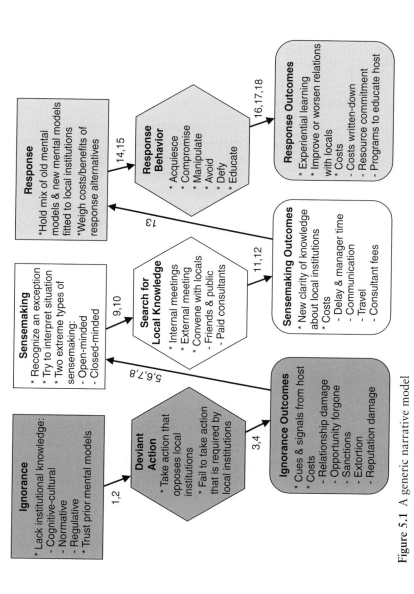

**Figure 5.1** A generic narrative model

be necessary to ascertain the frequency and variety of institutional exceptions encountered in cross-border projects and the extent of reputational, relational, time, and money costs associated with these exceptions. Of course, frequency, type of cost and magnitude would no doubt vary by firm type and sector, and such comparisons would also be interesting.

### How do institutional exceptions arise?

The findings suggest that institutional ignorance – a knowledge deficit concerning local institutions together with overconfidence in one's nonlocal institutional knowledge – is the condition that triggers an entrant to unintentionally deviate from local institutions – either by commission or by omission – which provokes negative feelings – confusion, violation, deception, fright, and anger – and cues of disapproval from the host. When the entrant perceives these cues, they recognize an exception and enter a mode of sensemaking.

### How are institutional exceptions resolved?

The findings indicate that sensemaking, which varies in degree of open-mindedness, is a process of examining the host's institutions. Meetings with the local host and external parleys with trusted third-party advisors can bring an entrant to a new clarity of understanding about logics and rules. Once the entrant is confident that accurate knowledge has been acquired, a response must be selected. Options include acquiesce, compromise, manipulation, defiance, avoidance, and education. Depending on how the response is evaluated by the host, the end result is either an improvement or worsening of relations with the host and learning, or failing to learn, of how to cope with host institutions.

### How are costs manifested in this process?

Costs are incurred in each phase of an institutional exception. These *so-called institutional transaction costs* include costs of ignorance (reputation damage, relationship damage, money costs, and time costs); costs of sensemaking (time spent in meetings, delay, communication and travel expenses, and consultant fees); and costs of response (further resource commitments, recognition that costs of ignorance may be irrecoverable). And of course, there are costs that the host incurs that are not captured here due to the limitations of the one-sided nature of the data. Indeed, it is not always the entrant who learns, adjusts, and absorbs costs; often the host is forced to bend, especially when power is asymmetric.

## How are these costs different from other kinds of transaction costs?

In the writings of North (1990) and Williamson (1979), transaction costs are defined as the costs of measuring the value of what is being exchanged (overcoming the problem of a human agent's limited ability to retrieve, store, and process data) and enforcing agreements (overcoming the problem of human agent's opportunism). But the transaction costs observed here are of a different nature. They are the costs of creating common understanding (overcoming the problems of misalignments in beliefs, informal institutions, and formal institutions). As such, institutional transaction costs are argued to be an important additional type of transaction costs, a type that is likely to become more prevalent in an era of globalization with increasing numbers of global projects and cross-border transactions.

## What conditions lead to the greatest costs?

The evidence from the case studies indicates that there are five conditions that increase the costs of institutional exceptions:

- High levels of task and outcome interdependence between entrant and host.
- An entrant that is exceedingly closed-minded or arrogant and defies the host's core institutions repeatedly over a long period of time.
- An entrant that, despite being relatively open-minded, misinterprets the host's institutions in its sensemaking processes over a long period of time.
- An entrant that must select a response under time pressure without having the luxury to fully investigate the cause of an exception.
- An entrant that is in the business of operating machinery, ships, or aircraft with possibilities of costly and irreversible glitches.

## How salient are these costs?

The magnitude of institutional transaction costs across the 23 cases varied enormously – from less than 1 percent to more than 100 percent of a firm's expected project profits on a project. Due to their unexpected nature, these costs quickly erode profit margins and are seldom easy to quantify because of the great variation across the three phases in the types of costs incurred. While increased monetary expenditures, such as airfare, consultant fees, and liquidated damages can be captured in existing cost accounting systems, it is next to impossible to calculate opportunity costs, for example, the value lost when a key executive is distracted from his normal responsibilities to take part in crisis management. Nor is it easy to estimate the cost of a tarnished image or soured relationship.

## Can these costs be avoided?

The kinds of costs that result from institutional exceptions are largely unanticipated. The question is, can they be predicted *a priori* and avoided? For the most part, the informants that we interviewed were thoughtful, intelligent, competent managers, many of whom had advanced degrees, most of whom had attempted to prepare themselves to undertake the particular international assignment. Moreover, many of them had prior experience abroad. Nevertheless, a substantial number encountered institutional exceptions and faced institutional transaction costs. We offer the following explanation.

Institutional systems are products of social construction, varying over time and space. Moreover, they are subject to change – both incremental and abrupt, with nonlinear variations, oscillations, spirals, and branching developments (Sorokin 1964; North 2005) providing an opaque and shifting target. Conventional approaches for addressing exceptions arising from these systems rely on expert assessments of probabilities and consequences of *known knowns* and *known unknowns*, but do not address the set of *unknown unknowns*. Unfortunately, many institutional exceptions fall into the latter category. And many of these uncertainties emerge only as the project unfolds; after initial plans and investments have been committed. We conclude that without recent and relevant country and sector experience, and without specific knowledge of people and place, it is extremely difficult to anticipate the full set of institutional idiosyncrasies at play – each society has its own version of the "spirit in the waterfall" that we discovered in vignette 2! Thus it is very difficult, and it may be impossible, to wholly predict or avoid these kinds of institutional transaction costs *ex ante*.

The question becomes, then, how far should firms go in trying to reduce these costs? Firms can engage in preventive activities such as collecting local intelligence, attending "charm school," studying the local language, hiring local agents, partnering with local firms, etc. However, it is important to note that these preventive activities are not costless. From an economic perspective, firms should only engage in knowledge-acquisition activities up to the point that their benefits exceed their costs (North 1990). Thus some threshold level of unanticipated institutional transaction costs may actually exist as an efficient outcome.

## Constraints on responsiveness

The exceptions described range greatly along the dimensions discussed – institutional elements involved, sensemaking approaches utilized, costs incurred. Another critical dimension, which we have not considered within our framework, involves ethical issues (Kline 2005). Conventional wisdom says "when in Rome, do as the Romans do," but in many situations responsiveness to local practices could undermine one's business code of conduct or, more seriously, violate the entrant's ethical commitments, with repercussions in the firm's wider institutional environment with spillovers to its other activities both local and international. Consider a few examples. While it may be prudent and necessary to use bamboo scaffolding to comply with national building codes, it may be questionable or even illegal to mimic local norms of embedded racism, corruption, and the use of child/slave labor. In such cases, entrants must weigh the costs of acquiesence – which may include feelings of wrongdoing or guilt and the possibility of legal sanctions from their home country – with those associated with educational efforts to make clear to the host why acquiesence is not possible or desirable. Indeed, firms need *some* global standards in order to avoid serious moral conflicts and to integrate subsidiaries, create global efficiencies, and capture knowledge (Doz, Bartlett and Prahaldad 1981; Prahaldad and Doz 1987;

Bartlett and Ghoshal 1987). Thus, while acquiesce and compromise strategies generally produce better relational outcomes with host entities, they are not always appropriate.

## Links to theory

The "institutional exception" concept presented here offers a way to strengthen the linkage between institutional theory and the international business literature. Institutional theory, particularly the game-theoretic view, suggests that an individual who deviates unilaterally from a stable set of institutions – which exist within a social system as a Nash equilibrium where all players earn a maximum payoff so long as they abide within the established rules – will be punished or sanctioned (Greif 2006). The liability of foreignness view common in international business suggests that a foreign entrant will face challenges and costs upon entering an unfamiliar market setting if they lack local institutional and business knowledge (Hymer 1976; Zaheer 1995). The "institutional exception" perspective bridges these two views, recognizing that an entrant's liability of foreignness is at least partially a result of costly deviations from the stable set of institutions in a host societal system. Thus, the "institutional exception" concept makes it possible to better connect the ways in which differences in institutional understandings between foreign entrant and local host lead to real, quantifiable transaction costs.

International business scholars may find that the "institutional exception" concept is useful to understand the challenges of foreign market entry and internationalization, because a great many of these challenges originate from institutional exceptions of one variety or another. International business theory suggests that with global experience, a firm develops a "know-how," or tacit ability, to acquire relevant local knowledge upon entering a foreign environment (Eriksson et al. 1997; Melin 1992). The findings here support this view. Each institutional exception is like a learning episode. As experience grows, managers become both more skilled at avoiding exceptions and more adept in troubleshooting and resolving exceptions when they arise.

Finally, scholars of institutional theory who are interested in the determinants and processes of institutional conflict will find a treasure trove of potential conflicts to study by moving into the international arena. Moreover, they may find that the generic narrative model developed here will have utility in describing other kinds of institutional conflicts beyond merely those of a cross-societal nature.

## Conclusions

### Contributions to science

There has been little agreement among scholars who have tried to explain the performance of cross-cultural collaborative ventures using cultural distance as a predictive independent variable (Robson, Leonidou and Katsikeas 2002; Shenkar 2001). Other scholars have concentrated attention on legal and regulatory aspects of institutional differences. Our effort responds to calls to adopt a broader institutional framework in empirical studies. The perspective advanced here describes how all three facets of institutional differences – cultural-cognitive, normative, and regulative – are translated into the kinds of intercultural frictions and costs that beset cross-border projects and collaborative ventures. We propose a process model that depicts this translation by identifying the specific conditions that affect how institutional exceptions are triggered and explores how managers react in a way that is intendedly rational, but within the limits of a cognitively circumscribed sensemaking process.

### Agenda for future research

Institutional theory holds much potential to shed light on the performance of global projects that involve participants from multiple societal contexts. To unlock this potential, more work is needed to examine how institutional exceptions vary across settings, phases, and subsystems as a given project proceeds from planning to completion stages; to identify coping mechanisms – at interpersonal, inter-team, project, firm, and wider levels – to deal with exceptions; to examine attributes of project leaders who best mollify conflicts; to identify managerial interventions – in organization structures, contracting practices, staffing policies, and administrative procedures – to help bridge across institutional gaps; and to trace evidence of organizational learning that supports improved performance within and across projects and firms.

Data for our project came from a single manager. We recognize the limitation of this approach. Additional research should rely on multiple participants and should be expanded to include not only the project but the firm and corporate levels. For example, how did the project's top management team get involved and react? Was there variation across individuals within the team? Is the "international experience" that facilitates "open-mindedness" necessarily that of the project manager, or can it be provided by others on the team, or by the capabilities of the firm? Is the manager able to draw on resources and knowledge outside of the project but elsewhere in his/her organization? A further limitation of this study was that the host's perspective has been largely ignored. Additional research needs to take into account the perceptions and behavior of the multiple types of participants involved in and impacted by global projects.

## Advice to managers

A divisional president at Bechtel with more than 45 years of experience in more than 80 countries ended one of our interviews with the following sage advice, "The toughest and most important thing [on global projects] is to train expats to see the world differently." This simple statement has two profound implications: it is crucial that expatriate managers adapt their thinking to accommodate local institutions and interpretive schemes; however, the task of fostering such a transformation in mental programming is a huge challenge!

Our advice to managers is four-fold. First, it is important to anticipate an almost infinite diversity of cultural-cognitive, normative, and regulative institutions on cross-border projects; and to inquisitively investigate these new elements with an openness of mind as to how they might bear on your operations in stunning and unimagined ways. The faster managers can identify institutional idiosyncrasies, the sooner they can diagnose their potential impacts. Second, managers should be aware that moving outside their own cognitive-cultural code is not easy; the most difficult part is getting past gut instincts and biases that were scripted during earlier experiences. Clearly, the cases reveal that even when entrants have convinced themselves that they are adhering to a rational course of action, in many instances, their intuitions are rooted in nonlocally applicable interpretive schemes and mental models. Indeed, when navigating unfamiliar institutions, past experiences may be invalid, assumptions may break down, rules of thumb may require recalibration, and previous knowledge may not bring advantage. Third, managers must learn to improve their exception-handling capabilities. Exceptions are not always preventable, so skills and processes to quickly troubleshoot, mediate, and reconcile are vital. Finally, managers must come to understand which of their own institutional norms and prescriptions are not simply matters of habit or convention or preference and which are sufficiently central to their moral core so as not to be compromised. Western companies are too often prone to assume that *all* of their beliefs and practices are superior to those of other countries (Evans 2004). While this overreaching stance is incorrect, that does not mean that all standards should be set aside when institutional exceptions arise. Managers must learn when to acquiesce, when to educate and compromise, and, if necessary, when to manipulate, defy, or avoid.

## Endnotes

1 Ryan J. Orr and W. Richard Scott, "Institutional exceptions on global projects: a process model," *Journal of International Business Studies* (2008) 39: 562–88, © 2008 Academy of International Business, reproduced by permission of Palgrave Macmillan. Financial support for this research was provided, in part, by the National Science Foundation under Grant No. IIS 9907403. Any opinion, findings, and conclusions or recommendations expressed in this material are those of the authors and do not necessarily reflect the views of the National Science Foundation.

2 Excerpt from e-mail to informants: "I would like to publish a story from our interview in a scientific publication. It is important to verify two criteria: (1) that all factual details are accurately represented; and (2) that the content is appropriately disguised to ensure confidentiality of the parties involved. Please read the story and let me know if it meets these criteria. If it needs modification, please suggest appropriate changes."

3 This exception, we think, based on discussions with non-Navy managers who had Spanish country experience, stemmed from the fact that the US and Spanish AEC industries are organized differently. In Spain, contractors do not have in-house designers, architects, or engineers to prepare shop drawings. But the Navy, exhibiting closed-minded tendencies, could not pinpoint the root cause of this exception, even after a full year's delay.

4 One prior study to operationalize the concept of open-mindedness did so with two items: "It concerns me that I might have biases of which I'm not aware"; and "It's important to me to understand what other people think

about things" (Facione, Sánchez, Facione, and Gainen 1995). Future researchers might operationalize this variable by counting the number of questions asked by the entrant of the host, or the proportion of time spent by the entrant listening vs. talking to the host during meetings and discussions; likewise, laboratory researchers might build on methods used to assess emotional intelligence.

# 6 | Local embeddedness of firms and strategies for dealing with uncertainty in global projects

RYAN J. ORR AND RAYMOND E. LEVITT

*What is called foreknowledge cannot be elicited from spirits, nor from Gods, not by analogy with past events, nor from calculations. It must be obtained from men who know the situation.*     – *Sun Tzu (500 BCE)*

## Introduction

A CEO went to Okinawa for the first time. He was on vacation – to see the beaches, to experience the local culture, and to play golf. After the trip, a researcher asked him a question: "How much did the success of your trip depend on your knowledge of the local Japanese context: the language, history, culture, economics and politics?" His answer was: "Gee. Not very much. I had to count local currency, book a hotel room and I even learned a few words of Japanese and it was a good holiday."

A second CEO also went to Okinawa, also for the first time, but with a different objective. He went to buy land, obtain permits, and develop a beachfront hotel and resort. Two years into the project, he was asked the same question and he offered a far more elaborate reply:

It was impossible to know all the risks going in. And even the risks that we thought we knew, it didn't mean we knew what to do about them. Our success owes more to our [adaptability] than it does to our ability to predict the risks. And we adapted by making friends with locals and by tapping local knowledge for each key decision ... [Local knowledge includes] all manner of facts and trends about the local theatre – about real estate activity, capital markets, city bylaws, building codes, contract protocol, the gray area between the written law and what is enforced ... health and safety standards, the credibility of suppliers, the needs of our customers and so on and so forth. We made good decisions because we had a steady stream of local knowledge.

Why are the two CEO's responses so different? In this chapter we argue that, just like the two CEOs, managers and firms that enter global projects need local knowledge specific to the purpose of their entry (Geertz 1983). We provide evidence that this so-called *local knowledge requirement* is determined largely by the embeddedness of an entrant's activities in local institutions and relations. Visiting the beach as a tourist turns out to be a lightly embedded activity, whereas developing a beach hotel and resort turns out to be a deeply embedded activity. The implication is that global project participants that are heavily embedded face greater challenges as they jump from country to country on a hit-and-run basis than firms that are lightly embedded, and even more so if they take on projects with fixed-price budgets and tight time frames.

Prior research has shown that the performance of entrant firms in foreign markets is linked to the depth of local learning engagement (Petersen and Pedersen 2002), but there has been little effort to explore how the depth of learning engagement is linked to local embeddedness (Melin 1992; Jones 1993; Luo and Mezias 2002) or to investigate how entrants cope with a local knowledge shortfall (Sinkula 1994).

In this chapter, we set out to empirically assess the link between level of embeddedness in the social and institutional environment that surrounds a global project, level of need for local knowledge, and strategies that firms adopt to cope when they lack sufficient local knowledge. In doing so, we seek to take early steps in developing a grounded theory by integrating the experiences of managers engaged in the planning, design, and management of large global projects such as airports, oil refineries, and water treatment facilities.

The concept of embeddedness is central to this study. Introduced in 1944 by Polanyi, the concept was developed and popularized by Granovetter (1985) to emphasize the extent to which economic activities take place within a supporting and constraining social structure. Granovetter's thesis is that neoclassical economists have tended to understate the importance of social relations in market interactions – the so-called "under-socialized view" – preferring instead assumptions of rational, self-interested behavior affected minimally by social structure. By contrast, sociologists and reformist economists have moved to the opposite extreme – assuming an "over-socialized view" – which overstates the centrality of social structure. He concludes by proposing a middle ground – an "embeddedness view" – to "stress the role of concrete personal relations and structures (or networks) of such relations, in generating trust and discouraging malfeasance" (p. 490). He argues that "most economic behavior is closely embedded in networks of interpersonal relations and that an embeddedness approach avoids the extremes of under- and over-socialized views of human action" (Granovetter 1985: 504).

Our approach subscribes to the general view of the importance of the specific manifestations of the surrounding social context on economic behavior, but we are interested in the variable extent to which economic actors are embedded in a given context. Social structure is a general condition, but extent of embeddedness varies for different players engaged in different activities in a project. We seek to assess the extent to which different types of firms in global projects are embedded in the *local context:* affected by the social and political conditions of the host societies in which they operate.

For a working definition, we define *local embeddedness* as the overall number of relationships and the level of interaction, coordination, or negotiation between an entrant and other entities in the social and institutional environment that surrounds a global project. This implies that an entrant's level of local embeddedness is also linked closely to the entrant's degree of exposure to host institutions – the formal rules and regulations, informal norms and customs and tacit beliefs and values that support, guide and constrain all aspects of social action (Scott 1995/2008; North 1990, 2005; see also, Chapter 2). The present study is organized around two core questions: What challenges does local embeddedness create for international entrants? And what strategies do entrants actually use to cope with different levels of embeddedness? Clearly, these questions are closely allied to the "big question" on the international business (IB) research agenda: What determines the international success and failure of firms? (Peng 2004). By responding to these questions, we take a small step towards injecting the concept of local embeddedness into the sphere of IB research, by examining the effect of variations in its level among firms of differing types with differing business models.

The findings tell a dynamic story. The empirical evidence suggests that different firms do indeed face different levels of local embeddedness, determined dually by the type of work engagement, and the key strategic decisions of management. The evidence indicates three generic strategies that managers adopt to cope with high levels of local embeddedness: increasing the supply of local knowledge; decreasing the demand for local knowledge; and reducing the impact of a local knowledge shortfall. By adopting these generic strategies – which apply to any country or foreign market entry situation – firms learn to minimize unforeseen costs and improve performance. The evidence indicates that while experiential learning is crucial to success in international markets, it has been overemphasized in the literature, since it fails to recognize other key strategies such as circumventing or avoiding the need to climb the proverbial country learning curve.

## Related theory and research

### Challenges in foreign markets

Despite differing pragmatic aims and the use of a variety of terms and nuanced definitions, IB scholars who write about entering foreign markets repeatedly employ key terms that are conceptually similar. The terms "liability of foreignness" (Hymer 1976; Ghoshal and Nohria 1989; Zaheer 1995; Hennart, Roehl, and Zeng 2002), "liability of newness" (Li and Guisinger 1991; Lu and Beamish 2004), "cultural distance" (Kogut and Singh 1988; Barkema et al. 1997; Sim and Ali 1998; Hennart and Zeng 2002), "institutional distance" (Kostova 1999; Kostova and Zaheer 1999; Xu and Shenkar 2002), "psychic distance" (Johanson and Vahlne 1977), and "political or social risk" (Goodnow and Hansz 1972; Kobrin 1979; Agarwal and Ramaswami 1992; Barkema and Vermeulen 1998; Chua, Wang, and Tan 2003) each have a long and rich history in the IB literature. Yet all of these terms imply a common assumption: that foreign firms face challenges and, perhaps, outsider disadvantages, when they enter new or unfamiliar market settings.

Although there are many variations in these views,[1] none deals with a key real world fact. As noted by Melin (1992), they ignore any notion of variation in depth of embeddedness in the local context. Too many studies suggest, albeit implicitly, that two firms from Country A who enter Country B will suffer equally from "liabilities of foreignness," "cultural distance," "psychic distance," "institutional distance," or other forms of "risk," such as country risk or political risk. For example, many scholars have discussed the concept of "foreignness" in a language that implies a generalized disadvantage or liability that affects all entrants equally (e.g., Zaheer 1995; Luo and Peng 1999; Delios and Beamish 2001; Guillén 2002). Similarly, in previous analyses of the performance of foreign-invested affiliates, scholars have expected to find that "cultural distance," "psychic distance," or "institutional distance" would encumber all foreign entrants to the same extent (e.g., Park and Ungson 1997; Beamish and Kachira 2004; Barkema et al. 1997). Likewise, many discussions of "country risk" or "political risk" imply a cloud of misfortune that floats down to plague every venture uniformly within the boundary of a given nation-state (e.g., Kobrin 1979; Agarwal and Ramaswami 1992; Barkema and Vermeulen 1998). But is it really true that entrants to a foreign market all face the same exposure to host country institutions and the same local knowledge requirement?

## Coping with challenges in foreign markets

Within the corpus of IB research, from the earliest studies to the present day, scholars have reached almost universal consensus concerning the premise that entrants into foreign markets improve performance as they adapt, learn, and accumulate experience (Cyert and March 1963; Johanson and Vahlne 1977; Erramilli 1991; Eriksson et al. 1997; Barkema et al. 1997; Autio, Sapienza, and Almeida 2000; Barkema and Nadolska 2003). This pervasive view is clearest in studies that recognize entry into foreign markets as processes of internationalization (e.g., Anderson 1993; Welch and Luostarinen 1988), organization learning (e.g., Luo and Peng 1999; Lord and Ranft 2000), and the evolutionary development of strategy (e.g., Melin 1992). Despite considerable variance across these views, the dominant perspective is that entrants learn to maneuver and transact effectively and efficiently within the context of an unfamiliar market environment as they iteratively acquire market information, adapt to unexpected conditions, amend mental models, and encode lessons learned into strategies to guide future action (e.g., Sinkula 1994: chap. 1).

However, these views fail to address two key realities. First, there has been virtually no acknowledgment that different types of firms face different levels of local embeddedness that affect the depth of their learning engagement. According to Melin (1992), who quotes (Jones 1992: 13) "mainstream theories of the MNC [multinational corporation] are unable to access the institutional and social environment 'due to their undersocialized construction'." Second, the *content of what is actually learned* has rarely been adequately described, and learning is inferred, rather than empirically investigated (e.g., Makino and Delios 1996; Barkema et al. 1997; Luo and Peng 1999). Lord and Ranft (2000) provide the following critique:

In this literature ... the organizational learning process is typically discussed in broad, illustrative terms and is usually inferred rather than directly and empirically measured. Learning processes that are described as being complicated and arduous in theory most often are operationalized and measured using simple proxies – firms are treated as singular, homogenous entities that 'learn' about a new international market as a function of the overall elapsed time or resources spent in a new country context.

This prevailing paradigm of "content-free learning" – i.e., abstracting out the content of what firms actually learn – can be traced back to general management science where the "learning curve" or "experience curve" was first developed (Wright 1936). The learning curve model stems from the observation that as organizations produce more units of a product (e.g. airplanes) the unit cost of production typically falls (e.g., labor-hours per unit produced), but at a decreasing rate (Epple, Argote, and Devedas 1991). This mathematically definable relationship has frequently been cited as evidence for learning (e.g., Wright 1936; Hirschmann 1964; Ghemawat 1985; Epple, Argote, and Devidas 1991; Levin 2000). Further support for learning curve models comes from psychological research (e.g., Lave and March 1975; Huberman 2001), where experiments show that a rat learns to navigate a T-maze according to a similar mathematical learning curve relationship (e.g., Tolman and Honzik 1930; Seward 1949).

Several IB scholars have implicitly embraced "content-free" models of learning and have suggested that organizations follow a similar curve as they learn to work in a particular host-country environment (Child and Yan 2003; Isobe, Makino, and Montgomery 2000). However, this notion may be misleading. The reason is that "learning curves" only evolve when the "learner" is engaged in a standard task. For example, they only evolve in manufacturing production when the manufacturer has a standard product (Abernathy and Wayne 1974) or in rat studies when the rat has to negotiate a standard maze. However, the task of navigating the foreign market environment involves many nonstandard activities. Furthermore, organization environments are dynamic and turbulent (Scott and Davis 2007: chap. 10); and in emerging markets volatility is generally of greater significance (Luo and Peng 1999). Thus, speculations that suggest a mathematical learning curve relationship between length of experience and performance for entry into a particular country are questionable.

In addition to having problematic theoretical roots, extant "content-free" theories of learning fail to address two key questions. The first is: What is actually learned? Scholars suggest that learning to succeed in foreign markets involves the accumulation of at least three distinct types of experience: general, country, and business activity (Kogut and Singh 1988; Benito and Gripsrud 1995). A number of scholars linked to the Uppsala school corroborate this view, drawing a similar distinction between international experience, institutional knowledge, and business knowledge (Johanson and Vahlne 1977; Eriksson et al. 1997; Petersen and Pedersen 2002). They define "institutional knowledge" as knowledge of the institutional framework: rules, norms, and values in a particular market. And "business knowledge" as knowledge on counterparts (customers, suppliers, distributors, competitors), including knowledge about the local business cultures. However, despite calls to flesh out this more complex story of experiential learning, there has been little effort to untangle general strategies of internationalization from those that are specific to a particular country or business/activity (Luo and Peng 1999).

The second key question is: How much learning is necessary? The question of depth of learning has been largely avoided, because with reigning "content-free models" it has been infeasible to compare how entrants face varying local knowledge requirements. The "Y-Axis" on typical learning curve models is denominated in percentage units and it is not clear with such a model what the absolute amount of learning is that constitutes "complete" or "perfect" knowledge. One exception is a study by Petersen and Pedersen (2002), which indicates that across foreign entrants there is significant variation in the depth of the learning engagement – i.e., the effort and ability necessary to learn how to conduct business in a foreign environment. But, in general, there has been a neglect of how different business models lead to variations in local embeddedness, variations in local knowledge requirements, and variations in the depth of learning engagement among firms in the IB literature.

Given the lack of existing theory in this area, this research was designed to generate new theory, not to test existing theory. This chapter takes initial steps toward the construction of a new model, rather than attempting to test an existing model. Thus, in the tradition of inductive research, we do not propose any initial hypotheses, but instead pursue a grounded-theory method in an effort to formulate testable propositions for future researchers.

## Methods

Table 6.1 displays characteristics of the eight firms studied. All of these firms are in the business of providing products and services that contribute to the planning, engineering, and construction of large infrastructure projects. Although not all eight firms would be encountered on any single project, it is conceivable, and even likely, that subgroups of them have collaborated together on past projects in different countries, worldwide.

### Case study design

The study invokes a multiple case study design. The logic underlying the use of multiple cases is replication. To paraphrase Yin (2003), each case must be carefully selected so that it either ... predicts similar results to enhance reliability of the findings (*a literal replication*) or ... produces contrasting results but for predictable reasons (*a theoretical replication*). The eight-firm sample was designed to generate four instances of theoretical replication along the embeddedness dimension (i.e., each of the four types of firm has a different level of local embeddedness); and to generate several literal replications (i.e., there are two instances of each type of firm, and each firm was involved in at least two projects).

### Research setting

Large global infrastructure projects provide a setting where many international firms congregate, each with different roles, responsibilities, and home country affiliations. Literature related to large engineering projects includes studies of temporary organizations that

Table 6.1 *Firm descriptions*

| Firm ID | Firm name | Firm type | Employees | Revenue (m)[a] | Home country | Firm age | Global diversity[b] | Number of interviews |
|---------|-----------|-----------|-----------|----------------|--------------|----------|---------------------|----------------------|
| 1 | Kelso | Systems Contractor | 33,000 | 6,800 | Finland | 90+ | 36/110 | 7 |
| 2 | Archer | Systems Contractor | 76,000 | 21,000 | France | 100+ | 55/150 | 4 |
| 3 | Duke | Developer | 1,800 | 400 | US | 50+ | 5/5 | 5 |
| 4 | Heroic | Developer | 2,800 | 750 | US | 40+ | 12/16 | 13 |
| 5 | Marengo | Project Consultant | 7,000 | 800 | UK | 100+ | 35/120 | 5 |
| 6 | Phantom | Project Consultant | 1,300 | 200 | Japan | 50+ | 17/120 | 11 |
| 7 | Boomerang | General Contractor | 44,000 | 16,000 | US | 100+ | 26/140 | 8 |
| 8 | Forester | General Contractor | 35,000 | 9000 | US | 80+ | 25/95 | 7 |

[a]The revenue and employee figures aggregate international operations, across several corporate divisions, for the calendar year 2003
[b]The left number reflects countries with regional corporate headquarters as of May 2005. The right number reflects countries with project field offices, both past and present.

undergo simultaneous structuring and operations (Thompson 1967); the quasi-firm and the organization of the construction industry (Eccles 1981); mega-projects and the management of uncertainty (Stinchcombe and Heimer 1985); construction projects as hierarchies of contracts (Stinchcombe 1990); and projects as high-stakes, real-options games that involve the shaping of risks, stability, and governability (Miller and Lessard 2000). (See Chapter 1 for a more general discussion.)

Global infrastructure projects provide a unique research setting for two chief reasons. First, most international project participants enter the host market expressly to work on a single project and exit immediately upon completing their work. Thus, they face all of the short-run downside risk that comes with foreign market entry, yet they enjoy little of the long-term advantage that comes with establishing a permanent market presence. Second, different participants face extreme variations in levels of local embeddedness. To execute their work, some players must interact with literally hundreds of local firms and government agencies and maneuver and transact within a gridlock of locally devised rules, requirements, standards, practices, protocols, and assumptions related to the project development and construction industry.

## Data sources

Data collection included open-ended interviews, project visits, structured interviews, meeting observations, and review of project documents.

**Focus on projects**

We interviewed approximately 50 managers who had worked on infrastructure projects with roles and responsibilities in management, engineering, design, and construction. Table 6.2 summarizes the projects that were discussed in the interviews. They ranged in value from $50 million, to $1.7 billion and in scheduled duration from two years to just over five years. Table 6.3 portrays the budget, schedule, staffing, contract, and risk characteristics of the project engagements for each type of firm. At the time of the interviews, all projects were ongoing or had been completed within the prior five years.

Table 6.2 *Project descriptions*

| Project ID | Project description | Firms present | Region | Project duration | Project value | Site visit by 1st author |
|---|---|---|---|---|---|---|
| 1 | Mass Transit System | Kelso, Archer, Boomerang, Phantom | Asia | 61 mo. | $700m | yes |
| 2 | International Airport | Kelso, Phantom | S.E. Asia | 36 mo. | $1.1b | yes |
| 3 | Water Treatment Plant | Archer, Marengo | Asia | 54 mo. | $160m | yes |
| 4 | Rail Transit System | Boomerang | Asia | 78 mo. | $13b | yes |
| 5 | Resort Complex | Duke | Asia | 36 mo. | $1.7b | no |
| 6 | High End Housing Development | Heroic | E. Europe | 24 mo. | $30m | no |
| 7 | High End Housing Development | Heroic | E. Europe | 40 mo. | $45m | no |
| 8 | Commercial Office Development | Heroic | W. Europe | 28 mo. | $100m | no |
| 9 | Commercial Office Development | Heroic | E. Europe | 48 mo. | $50m | no |
| 10 | Motorway | Boomerang | E. Europe | 42 mo. | $260m | no |
| 11 | Petro Chemical Refinery | Forester | Asia | 48 mo. | $1.2b | no |
| 12 | Petro Chemical Refinery | Forester | Middle East | 48 mo. | $900m | no |

Table 6.3 *Project engagement characteristics, by firm, type*[a]

| Activities | Project consultants | Systems contractors | General contractors | Developers |
|---|---|---|---|---|
| Budget | $3m–$24m | $14m–$79m | $50m–$800m | $50m–$1.7b |
| Work Schedule | 2–7 yrs | 1–3 yrs | 2–5 yrs | 2.5–6 yrs |
| Peak Professional Staff | 25–190 | 20–120 | 22–82 | 9–250[b] |
| Peak Labor Force | 0 | 20–120 | 800–3,500 | 0 |
| Type of Contract | Professional Fee | Lump Sum, Fixed Price | Lump Sum, Fixed Price | n/a |
| Profit Terms | Markup on Fee | 5%–40% Contract Value | 1%–5% Contract Value | 12%–25% ROI[c] |
| Primary Project Delivery Risks | Contract termination by a dissatisfied client; liability for professional negligence | Delay caused by other project parties or customs inspection. | Cost or schedule overrun without possibility for claims. | Cost or schedule overrun that impacts ROI profile. |
| Contingency | n/a | 2%–8% | 2%–5% | 5% |

[a]N = 17. Project details are described in Table 6.2. [b]Heroic: 9–31; Duke 30–250. [c]ROI stands for return on investment.

**Open-ended interviews**

The majority of the interviews followed an open-ended protocol, as recommended by Spradley (1979). They lasted between one and two hours, were digitally recorded for subsequent transcription and review, and were conducted during an 18-month period between May, 2003 and November, 2004. Informants also provided more than 200 pages of secondary archival data enriching the contextual background surrounding many of the "critical incidents" that were studied, including newspaper articles, project briefs, internal memos, e-mail, formal organization charts, budgets, schedules, and other project documents. Through the process of conducting and analyzing these interviews, we recognized the critical importance of the local embeddedness concept and subsequently designed structured interviews to deepen the investigation.[2]

## Data analysis

We followed the grounded-theory approach recommended by Glaser and Strauss (1967), Miles and Huberman (1994), and Eisenhardt (1989), analyzing the data in three distinct, yet highly iterative and interrelated phases. As Glaser and Strauss (1967:105) explain, this method entails, "first, coding each incident in the data into as many categories of analysis as possible and comparing incidents [in] each category; second, integrating categories and their properties ... resulting in a unified and ... developing theory; and third, delimiting the theory ... and reformulating it with a smaller set of higher level concepts." Once the categories had emerged and we had developed a coherent and parsimonious conceptual framework to integrate the categories, we selected illustrative quotes and vignettes from the interview transcripts to provide telling examples.

## Challenges when entering foreign markets

### Levels of local embeddedness

As noted, many IB studies suggest a link between the performance of foreign entrants and measures of "cultural distance," "institutional distance," or "psychic distance." Studies that take this perspective make the implicit assumption that cultural, institutional, and psychic distance encumber all global project entrants equally. The data from this research suggests that this assumption is mistaken. Certainly, as these theories well predict, firms that enter foreign markets face unexpected conditions and incur unforeseen costs when they misjudge and misunderstand local culture and institutions. However, these conditions and costs are not *uniformly* distributed across all entrants. Instead, our findings suggest that each type of firm faces a distinct level of *local embeddedness* in the host country context. More formally:

> *Proposition 1: The more deeply an entrant's activities are embedded in the social and institutional environment of an unfamiliar setting, the more local knowledge that entrant needs to achieve its objectives and to avoid unforeseen costs.*

Table 6.4 and Table 6.5 display evidence to show that embeddedness in local relations and institutions varies significantly for different types of global project entrants. Table 6.4 reports our findings regarding the extent of local relational embeddedness, which we define as a measure of the total number of relations between a global project entrant and local organization entities for each category of firm. Relations with local organizations are grouped into four categories:

- *Formal regulatory relations* include interfaces with local arms and agencies of government that grant approvals, permits, and licenses (e.g., transport and highways, fire department, police, building department).
- *Formal market relations* include transactions with local firms in the marketplace that provide products and services (e.g., tool suppliers, materials vendors, subcontractors).
- *Informal community relations* include interactions with community groups and stakeholders that provide legitimacy to a project (e.g., NGOs, school board, shopkeeper's guild).
- *Informal project relations* include noncontractual dealings with other firms on a project that arise by virtue of working side-by-side and sharing limited project resources and physical workspace (e.g., foundation, electrical, or elevator subcontractors).

Table 6.4 reveals that, as a class, general contractors exhibit by far the highest level of local relational embeddedness while systems contractors report the lowest level of local relational embeddedness.

Table 6.4 *Overall local relational embeddedness*[a]

| Type of relation | Project consultants | | | Systems contractors | | | Developers | | | General contractors | | |
|---|---|---|---|---|---|---|---|---|---|---|---|---|
| | Min | Max | Mean | Min | Max | Mean | Min | Max | Mean | Min | Max | Mean |
| Formal regulatory relations | 9 | 24 | 17 | 3 | 5 | 4 | 8 | 29 | 14 | 12 | 21 | 16.75 |
| Formal market relations | 12 | 220 | 78 | 9 | 55 | 36 | 50 | 95 | 64 | 640 | 1600 | 1123 |
| Informal community relations | 3 | 55 | 22 | 0 | 0 | 0 | 5 | 15 | 10 | 5 | 28 | 12 |
| Informal project relations | 12 | 380 | 166 | 6 | 18 | 12 | 0 | 5 | 2 | 12 | 31 | 20.75 |
| **Total number of relations** | **36** | **679** | **282** | **18** | **78** | **52** | **63** | **144** | **90** | **669** | **1680** | **1172** |

[a]N = 17. Project details are described in Table 6.2.

**Table 6.5 *Relative local embeddedness*[a]**

| Activities | Project consultants[b] | Systems contractors[b] | General contractors[b] | Developers[c] |
|---|---|---|---|---|
| Buying land | 0 | 1.3 | 1.3 | 3.0 |
| Handling resettlement issues | 0 | 1.5 | 0.5 | 1.6 |
| Getting goods through customs | 2.0 | 1.0 | 2.5 | 1.6 |
| Applying for permits and entitlements | 0.5 | 1.3 | 1.8 | 3.0 |
| Procuring local labor | 1.3 | 0.5 | 3.0 | 2.0 |
| Procuring local supplies | 3.0 | 1.5 | 1.3 | 1.4 |
| Negotiating with local government | 0 | 3.0 | 2.0 | 2.0 |
| Entering into locally-enforced contracts | 0 | 2.8 | 3.0 | 2.0 |
| **Total relative engagement** | **6.8** | **12.9** | **15.4** | **16.6** |

[a]Values in cells correspond to relative level of engagement in each activity:
$0 =$ None, $1 =$ Low, $2 =$ Medium, $3 =$ High. This scale provides an ordinal indication of a project entrant's level of interaction, negotiation, and coordination with local entities to complete each activity, relative to other project participants.
[b]$N = 4$; [c]$N = 5$. Project details are described in Table 6.2.

Table 6.5 illustrates a measure of *local institutional embeddedness*, which we assess as the relative level of engagement of a global project entrant in eight key project activities typified by high levels of entanglement in local institutions. The evidence indicates considerable variation in local institutional embeddedness across different classes of entrants. For example, as a class, developers face a much higher level of local institutional embeddedness than do systems contractors. This is because developers need to buy land, understand property rights, resettle displaced peoples, and navigate the often political processes of gaining entitlements and building permits, all according to local practices and protocols that vary from country to country and city to city. As one Heroic executive explained, "In Russia, our project was delayed a year and a half because we didn't understand the process of getting all the necessary approvals and permits, and they were a very complex set of requirements we had to comply with." In contrast, systems contractors who supply, install, and maintain building systems such as elevators enter a country, do their work, and then exit without having to undertake many of these locally embedded activities that have a high local knowledge requirement. As one Kelso executive noted, "We have a country manager who sells into each country and once a sale is committed, there really isn't a lot that can go wrong – we pre-fabricate the elevator in our home factory and simply install it upon arrival."

Thus, the level of local embeddedness is not uniform. On the contrary, we found that different types of firms, with different kinds of work and activities, report dramatically different levels of engagement with organizations and institutions in the host country environment.

## Local embeddedness by firm type

Of the four classes of firms we studied, general contractors report the highest levels of local embeddedness and, hence, probably confront the greatest outsider disadvantages when they enter new markets. For example, on a motorway project, Boomerang reported more than 20 relations with regulators, the hiring of more than 200 sub-contractors, and purchases from more than 1,000 vendors and suppliers, connections with more than 20 community groups and more than 30 informal project relations. Ostensibly, outsider disadvantage is magnified when firms confront high levels of formal regulation. As one Forester representative described:

The permit requirements are extremely different in every country. And the branches of government you need to obtain permits from, they differ too. There is no standard government. Some of the agencies that you find – you just shake your head and wonder why they were ever created in the first place ... On this project, we encountered the Executive of Yuan, the Department of Tax, the MRT Company, the Department of Economics, the Department of Labor, the Department of Internal Affairs, the Fire Department, the Police, the Environmental Department, the Road Authorities, the National Water Company, the National Power Company, the City Planning Department, the Department of Construction, the Work and Safety Agency, the Department of Immigration and the Customs & Excise Board and there might be more. And they all require a permit or an approval or an inspection or [who] knows what else.

Outsiders are also challenged by projects requiring high levels of interaction with the local community. As one Boomerang executive noted:

There are a number of groups in the community with whom we coordinate and liaise. The New Delhi Traders Association (who don't want their businesses to be disrupted), the local project directors and investors (who want to be sure contracts are awarded to their FBI clan – friends, buddies, and in-laws), a local environmental conservation group (who is worried about the ecological impacts), the press and media (who claim corruption at every turn), the Imam of local mosques (who dislikes the noise), the schools and shops along the metro corridor (who complain about dust and safety), Members of Parliament and other VIPs (who come to the site for tours and disrupt our work), the squatters (who get into the work area too), and all of the clever locals (who decide to file a lawsuit against you). There can be dozens of them. One by one they take legal action and claim their pound of flesh from the project. They claim for cracks in their walls, differential settlement of their foundations, and whatever else they can dream up to extract a pay-off.

All of these relations bring significant levels of contact with local beliefs, values, conventions, and rules. And, conversely, locals are exposed to international norms and practices. Since general contractors face high levels of formal regulation, informal monitoring, and social scrutiny, they also face greater numbers of obligatory interfaces and a greater necessity, intensity, and complexity of negotiation with local actors. So, the combination of needing to enter large numbers of voluntary relations with local vendors and suppliers and to comply with an assorted variety of social expectations and regulative requirements, prompts a very high level of embeddedness for general contractors.

Developers also face high levels of embeddedness. As Table 6.5 depicts, many activities that developers undertake are in the early "fuzzy front-end" shaping phase of project development. Activities such as buying land, handling resettlement issues, and negotiating with local government officials for entitlements, approvals, and permits all require a deft understanding of local politics, historical precedents, and coalition building with other local actors. In addition, developers usually work at risk, so the consequence of not understanding local facts and trends can be extremely costly. As one Heroic executive noted, "We spent more than $1M on conceptual design for a project in Europe and then we learned that the land title that we thought we had, was in limbo. And we never did build the project."

Project consultants also face high levels of local embeddedness, as indicated in Table 6.4. However, they generally face much less downside risk than general contractors or developers because they have a different risk profile. They tend to be compensated monthly on a reimbursable cost-plus or fixed-fee basis, so they get paid regardless of a particular project outcome. And their product is information – nowadays often delivered in digital form – so they can do much of the work in their home country office and transmit their work product to the local country without having to deal with local customs officials, delivery services, and the like. In contrast, general contractors and developers work primarily at risk – with hard-money, fixed-price contracts and fixed time frames. Moreover, project consultants, especially on civil infrastructure projects such as dams, roads, railroads, or water supply projects, oftentimes work in a supporting role alongside a large international developer or with a local government client. By "drafting in" under the wings of these larger players, they tend to be buffered from the vagaries and hazards of the local market by their "chaperones."

Tables 6.4 and 6.5 indicate that systems contractors face the lowest levels of local embeddedness and that the majority of their relations fall into the "Formal Market Relations" and the "Informal Project Relations" categories. The bulk of the formal market relations are with vendors who supply basic materials, hand tools, and field office supplies. In contrast to developers and general contractors, very few of the formal market relations are with subcontractors, primarily because most of the work associated with installing an elevator in a building or signaling systems along a railroad is of a complex technical nature and thus, not amenable to being outsourced. The large number of informal project relations is explained by the fact that systems contractors provide core systems, such as elevators and escalators in a building, pumps and piping in a water treatment facility, or signals and track in a subway. Thus, they need to coordinate and communicate with other major systems providers and subcontractors to ensure functional integration with other systems and structures.

In general, we observe that the size of an entrant's project team in a country is a useful proxy for the number of linkages with local entities. Large contractors who have hundreds of employees will also tend to have a larger number of local relations than do systems contractors who have only a dozen or so staff members. Of course, this is not a firm and fast rule, and exceptions could be imagined.

## Consequences of local embeddedness

The challenge posed by embeddedness is that for every activity associated with local actors or institutions, an entrant requires a certain basic level of local knowledge about those elements in order to perform well. If the relevant elements are well understood prior to performing the task, much of the activity can be planned in advance and the task is accomplished in the most efficient fashion at a minimum level of effort to the responsible manager (Galbraith 1973). If these elements are not understood, then institutional exceptions – misjudgments, misunderstandings, and conflict – arise that lead to changes in priorities, plans, and strategies. Our evidence suggests that all of these changes require sensemaking, trial-and-error learning, local knowledge search and adaptation, and a high likelihood of relational friction (see Chapter 5). Therefore, the greater an entrant's local knowledge deficit at the outset of a task, the greater the likelihood that sensemaking, trial-and-error learning, rework, and adaptation will occur during task execution to achieve a given level of performance and the greater the probability of unanticipated relational friction with the locals. Thus, the central effect of an actor's local knowledge deficit is a limited ability to anticipate issues, make sense of problems that arise, set priorities, develop strategies, or make decisions about activities in advance of their execution. For example, a knowledge deficit with respect to local contract law can lead to difficulties in relations with local subcontractors. As one Boomerang informant described:

If we don't understand the local law and we muddle the language in the first contract or leave something out, it probably means that we will repeat this mistake in the next 99 contracts, because we use the first as a template for the others. A mistake like that could spell disaster. It could cause lawsuits and months and months of unnecessary claims and counter-claims.

Similarly, lack of understanding of local work practices can lead to relational friction with the craft trades. As one Forester executive explained:

In Hong Kong, it takes a while to figure out all of the trades and their normal working hours. No matter how hard you try, you will never get the electricians to come in before 9am. All of the other trades will come in early, but not the electricians. They feel it is their right to come in at their leisure. And when we first arrived, this caught us by surprise and we spent weeks chasing our tails trying to get them to come in early.

Likewise, lack of knowledge of local political games can lead to confusion about who to believe or trust. For example, one Phantom project executive explained:

In Thailand, the newspaper will print anything if you pay them enough baht. It is common practice for top government officials to buy a nice story about themselves. Or, another common tactic is to call the newspaper if you want to insult an enemy. And I guess it's no different from the political games-manship that you see in other countries. But this makes life miserable when you're trying to run a project, because all of the slanderous stuff that makes its way into the press. And you never know who to believe or trust. So you spend a lot of time tip-toeing around and getting second opinions about everything you hear in the news.

It is evident from the discussion above and the supporting examples, that every interface with a local entity or institutions brings some level of need for local knowledge. This local knowledge is necessary to avoid errors, misunderstandings, and confusion, and to resolve relational friction quickly when it begins to escalate. In general, the greater the number of interfaces with locals, the greater the variety of interfaces, and the greater the intensity of interaction across each linkage, the greater an entrant's aggregate need for local knowledge to perform well.

As entrants become more embedded in the local context, a failure to acquire relevant local knowledge can lead to unforeseen costs. For example, as, one senior VP at Boomerang described:

The four most difficult things to do in a foreign country are buying land, getting things through customs, getting permits and enforcing your contracts. And each country you go it's a different set of hoops you need to figure out and jump through. And if you don't figure it out, these things can add delay to your project and can cost you a whole lot of money. Usually less than 10 percent of your total project costs, but that can be a huge amount if you're operating on a 5 percent contingency and 5 percent profit margin.

Indeed, when an entrant fails to understand local host institutions, then misjudgments, misunderstandings, and conflicts inevitably arise, which translate into unforeseen costs for the entrants: money costs, time delay, relationship damage, and reputation damage (see Chapter 5). One striking example comes from a water treatment facility project in Asia. The Marengo consulting engineer who told the story noted that:

We split the project into two smaller work packages – no difference in scope. We put them out to international tender and two different Chinese firms won the bid. So it was a bit of horse race. Firm One turned around and hired the best local contractor in Pakistan, Habib Rafiq and their name is as good as credit, to manage the project. So it was basically a Habib Rafiq job from day one. Firm Two took a different tack. They sent Chinese managers over, hundreds of them, and tried to self-perform the work. Well, as you might imagine, Firm One finished right on schedule – more than a year ago now – and Firm Two is still goofing around getting materials delivered and finding skilled labor.

Finally, although it is common to assume that embeddedness is a condition imposed on the company, our evidence suggests that it is partially controlled by company decisions. As noted in the story above, Firm One made a strategic decision to outsource the entire project to a local player. Firm Two made the decision to internalize hundreds of local relationships.

As one Heroic informant expressed, "you have to decide how embedded you want to get and that depends on your long term goals." Another Heroic informant noted, "how embedded you get depends on your risk profile – the more embedded, the more risk you take on a big [real estate] development." A senior Boomerang executive explained:

When you win a big project, you can do two [extreme] things. You can farm out the entire job, all kit-and-caboodle, in one big sub-contract package. Or you can try to self-perform the work and hire dozens of sub-contractors, who in turn hire hundreds of sub-subcontractors, until at the bottom of each tentacle you've got five guys and a truck coming in to do some work. But remember, each interface creates some coordination and risk. So, if you adopt this [second] strategy, you really need to be in tune with the local market, means and methods and you need to have an exceptional local staff.

Overall, our evidence suggests that two main factors affect a firm's level of embeddedness in the local context: their role in the global project and the types of activities that they set out to achieve; and the management decisions that are made to allocate responsibility for completing those activities. For example, decisions to execute activities internally versus to outsource activities to a local contractor or consultant can have a big impact on local embeddedness levels.

### Emergent uncertainty

Recently, a number of authors (e.g., Han and Diekmann 2001; Chua, Wang and Tan 2003; Chan and Tse 2003; Wade 2005) have written about political, cultural, and social "risks" in foreign markets in a manner that implies *a priori* predictability. Similarly, many software vendors and consultants[3] suggest in their marketing materials that political instabilities, cultural conflicts, and social uprisings can be assessed and predicted with probabilistic tools and techniques.

Our findings challenge this view. We find that these approaches, which rely on subjective assessment of probabilities (Howard and Matheson 1983), are unreliable unless they are based on significant recent country experience. We also have observed that relational interactions that are characterized by indeterminacy often lead to one-of-a-kind incidents that cannot be predicted in advance, but can only be managed if and as they occur.[4] This suggests:

> *Proposition 2: The more an entrant is embedded in an unfamiliar setting, the more likely that emergent relational dynamics and unanticipated institutional factors will generate unforeseen costs.*
>
> *Proposition 3: The more an entrant is embedded in an unfamiliar setting, the less likely that a priori risk analysis approaches will help to prevent unforeseen costs.*

Table 6.6 illustrates situations where an entrant incurred unforeseen delay as a consequence of an unanticipated event in a foreign host market. The examples illustrate how each situation, from the entrant's perspective, was characterized as unexpected and unforeseen. Such examples highlight the weakness of formal, quantitative methods of risk analysis: without recent country experience and a deep foreknowledge of the pertinent actors, relational dynamics, and historical traditions, an entrant is unable to anticipate many of the main social, political, and institutional risk factors. Thus, while formal risk analysis may be helpful as a proactive exercise to stimulate an entrant

**Table 6.6** *Examples of emergent uncertainty*

| Firm name/informant position | Situation | Unforeseen delay | Quote from interview |
|---|---|---|---|
| Boomerang/Contracts Manager | Local subcontractor incapable to meet delivery schedule | 11 month noncritical-path delay to the completion of several Metro Stations | "Its tough to know who is capable when you enter a new market. One of our sub-contracts was a local firm who we hired based on the recommendation of [one of the key directors]. Probably an FBI connection – friends, buddies and inlaws. They were to provide the roofing for the stations . . . But they were completely incompetent and unable to perform . . . In hindsight, we never should have given them the contract. They are just too small and inexperienced. But you can't ever know that going in." |
| Marengo/Staff Engineer | The project was attacked by armed thieves | Several hour delay each time the project site is attacked | "The project has been attacked three times. The thieves are armed and come to pilfer money, cell-phones and small hand tools. What are you supposed to do when that happens? How can you predict this sort of thing? I guess all you can do is prepare in advance. And we do. That's the reason for the nest of machine guns perched over the gate as we drove in." |
| Heroic/Engineering Executive | Contract was deemed unenforceable under local legal traditions | Six month critical-path delay to project completion | "One of the most unexpected things that happened, was a sub-contractor refused to honor an unforeseen ground conditions clause in our standard form contract. We felt they were contractually responsible to fix a cave-in, but |

they refused and walked off the job. When we talked to a local law consultant, they told us that 'no judge in Spain would enforce such a ridiculously one-sided contract.'"

| | | | |
|---|---|---|---|
| Archer/Project Manager | Customs clearance was delayed for outgoing shipments | Six month critical-path delay to installing water pumps | "The host government created a fast-track program to expedite all of the shipments through customs. But there was no program to get shipments back out of the country; and we needed to send equipment back to the factory for repairs and alteration. And this cost us months of waiting . . . And talking sense into an [Asian] customs agent just isn't even an option. They have their rules to follow." |
| Marengo/Resident Engineer | Equipment was sabotaged by host government to hide corruption | Several week critical-path delay for new equipment | "Officials in the host government dam up the canal and the water runs down the mountain into man made lakes. They pump the water into private water tanker trucks. Then they turn off the water to a part of the city (a desert climate) and run the tankers into town to sell water door to door. Its organized robbery. And they sabotage the water meter in the canal so that no one knows how much they steal. I've already replaced it three times this year and it should have a 20 year life expectancy. And how [on earth] is your risk analysis ever supposed to catch that one?" |

to consider risks and consequences, it is only as informative as the breadth and depth of experience of the analyst. The examples suggest that, when an entrant lacks current local knowledge about factors like the varying capabilities of local actors, incidence of terrorism, legal precedents, customs protocols, or levels and forms of government corruption, then events that are described as unexpected can and do arise.

**Emergent uncertainty, by firm type**
General contractors, with the highest level of local embeddedness, exhibit little faith in formal risk analysis and acknowledge that emergent uncertainty is not an exception, but an everyday business reality. A Forester executive described his view on risk analysis, as follows:

It's like Donald Rumsfeld [then the US Defense Secretary] articulated last week. There are *known knowns*, there are *known unknowns* and there are *unknown unknowns*. And when you're dealing with unknown unknowns, then risk analysis isn't going to do you a damn bit of good. And that's what makes our business so unique. If you want to be a general contractor, you've got to be adaptable. I'd say we have to be a lot more adaptable than the consultant or the systems contractors, because we've got the most exposure to the local dynamics. We're the most connected to the moving cogs and gears that drive the local economy and the project forward.

Reinforcing this point, a second Forester executive noted:

Take for example this project in [the Middle East]. It has just been one firefight after another. And that's how most of our projects go. A lot of this stuff is unpredictable. Its fire fighting. As you get one fire contained, you find the next one you need to fight. And sometimes there are two or three at a time and you have to prioritize. And the faster you get to them, generally the faster you can douse them, but not always. There was a misunderstanding with the Sheik's son last month that is still causing us all kinds of brain damage ... and we got to that one right away.

He went on to explain that high levels of local embeddedness create large numbers of meetings and possibilities for emergent uncertainty:

You can almost characterize the type of work that we do by the number of meetings that we have. Meetings here. Meetings there. It shouldn't be called construction management, it should be called relationship management. And when you go international, every time you need to use a translator, the possibility for miscommunication shoots way up. Our business is all about communication and coordination – thousands of people, systems, and machines have to come together in the proper way – and anytime you're dealing with real people on a deadline, there are going to be disputes to sort through and tough decisions to be made.

Developers, who face relatively high levels of local embeddedness, also tend to face high levels of emergent uncertainty and they also seem to understand intuitively the limits of formal risk analysis. As the CEO of Heroic acknowledged, in response to his own question:

Can we predict the risks in a foreign market – the cultural, political and market risks? Well, hindsight says no. Even if we know what the risks are going to be, we'll never have a clue about what to do about them. There is no formula for it. We don't have any sort of "step-by-step" or "how to" manual ... I think, even if you could figure out what the issues were going in, you couldn't necessarily figure out how to solve them. So, the short answer is no. So what we do instead is we go in and we physically try to find someone who is in the country and who is already effective there to be our guide and mentor.

The same developer also alluded to the fact that the level of local embeddedness faced by his organization is much greater than that faced by other types of internationalizing firms:

We have a lot more to predict going in than a guy who goes in to open up a new coffee shop or a currency exchange booth. I used to subscribe to some of the academic journals on international business, and some of it was good, but so much of it was for the guy that does the fast food restaurant or the currency booth. And we just face so much more complexity than that. So eventually I cancelled the subscriptions because what we do is so much more inherently risky.

Strikingly, project consultants, who are compensated on an hourly basis and whose interests are the least affected by debilitating project risks, were among the strongest advocates of formal risk analysis tools. When we visited one Marengo site office, several of the engineers were proud to show off risk analyses that had been prepared for their project. As one engineer noted:

This is a tool we can offer our clients, to help them plan for the unexpected. Good risk analysis is critical to project success.

Finally, the systems contractors, who reported lower levels of local embeddedness, were also the most likely to use formal risk analysis techniques. For example, at Kelso, conducting a risk analysis is mandatory before every major project, using an MS Excel tool to record the probabilities and consequences of all the uncertain factors. While demonstrating his firm's risk analysis software, one Kelso director of major projects reported:

This is our risk management approach ... Although the tricky part is discerning what to put in here, in our business, most of the factors stay the same from country to country, so the general template and the line items don't tend to change too much from project to project ... And that works pretty well. What's interesting is to go back after we build out a project and check the precision of our numbers. Usually they are right on, except in the impossible case when we don't even know to anticipate a certain cost factor and it jumps out of the bushes like a snake to bite us.

Similarly, at Archer, risk analysis was a deeply engrained aspect of the corporate culture. As one Archer executive explained:

We have had several situations where our risk analysis overlooked the major uncertainties that in the end were the big ticket cost items. But most of the time, our analysis is pretty good. There isn't all that much can go wrong. We have developed our tools and a culture of using the tools to assess most of the factors well before they cause trouble. So, risk analysis is something we're really big on at [Archer].

In summary, our evidence suggests that without knowledge of the local context, an outsider cannot safely rely on formal models of risk analysis tools to predict unforeseeable challenges. Our evidence also indicates that an entrant's level of emergent uncertainty is connected to their level of embeddedness in local relations and institutions – and that the more embedded and dynamic, the less faith tends to be put in risk analysis methods that require foreknowledge of risk factors. In addition, our evidence suggests that social, political, and relational uncertainty is an emergent phenomenon, that is affected by ongoing interactions and events and thus is extremely difficult, if not impossible, to predict *a priori*. For these reasons, among the types of firms we examined, general contractors and developers, who are the most embedded in local institutions, tend to be far less likely to extol the benefits of formal risk analysis processes than project consultants and systems contractors who face much lower levels, and are less vulnerable to the negative consequences of embeddedness in local relations and institutions.

## Firm-specific strategies to cope with challenges in foreign markets

### Firm-specific strategies

Many studies have examined the process of organizations learning to succeed in foreign markets (Johanson and Vahlne 1977; Erramilli 1991; Eriksson et al. 1997; Barkema et al. 1997). Other related studies have focused on one specific aspect of this process, such as, mode of foreign market entry (e.g., Erramilli 1991; Brouthers 2002); sequence of foreign market entry, or staffing policies of new entrant firms (Boyacigiller 1990; Gong 2003).

These studies tend to have two key limitations. First, in the empirical studies, we generally find high levels of aggregation across industry sub-groups (e.g., Erramilli 1991; Brouthers 2002). This approach ensures a statistically significant sample size, but at the cost of ignoring the unique drivers, dynamics, and strategies that characterize different types of firms within the industry. Second, across all of the studies, we find that levels of local embeddedness have not been seriously considered as a determinant of the level of need for organizational learning or the market entry strategies that evolve.

In an attempt to correct these deficiences, our study explores the effects of variance along the embeddedness dimension and finds that degree of local embeddedness plays an important role in how different types of organizations perceive and learn about the challenges in foreign markets. Moreover, our data suggest that degree of local embeddedness is a primary determinant of entry strategy, staffing policy and organization structure. This confirms Melin's (1992) observation, that "when studying internationalization within a strategy process framework, it is crucial to focus on 'organizations in their sectors'" (Child 1988). Our evidence, which is described in detail below by firm type, suggests the following formal proposition:

*Proposition 4: The more an entrant is embedded in an unfamiliar setting, the more it needs local knowledge and hence: 4a) the greater the unforeseen costs associated with a start-up or "green field" investment entry strategy; 4b) the greater the benefit of an acquisition strategy or partnering entry strategy; 4c) the greater*

*the advantages of local staff over expatriate staff; and 4d) the
greater the benefit of decentralizing decision-making and control
to the project site office.*

### Systems contractors

Firms in the systems contractor category fill a specialized technical
role; they manufacture, ship, and install standardized hardware and
equipment systems. They indicate that their international strategy
relies primarily on reducing their level of embeddedness in the foreign
market by pre-fabricating equipment components in their home country or in a third country, where they are already familiar with the local
actors and institutions. An Archer engineer noted, "if the equipment
ships as designed and the design is good, then our job is easy – we
don't have to do workarounds ... and that's important when [we're]
in emerging markets, because the smallest workarounds can be very
costly."[5] By adopting this strategy of prefabrication, shipment, and
assembly, system contractors effectively minimize dependencies on
local organizations, resources, and institutions. In particular, they
avoid the need for local labor, skills, and supplies; and they avoid
having to deal with unfamiliar norms of quality control, standards of
employment, and regulations unique to the local industry. For sales,
both Archer and Kelso employ a single specialist in each country or
region to manage sales and to learn, manage, and navigate the local
interfaces, rules, and requirements. However, dependence on a solitary
sales representative can also create problems, as one Kelso executive
indicated:

Our country managers, with their little black book of contacts, they can be
very secretive about their work and our organization is totally beholden to
them and they can create bottle-necks. But they are hard to replace, because
it takes years to get to know a country like they do.

In addition to selling new equipment systems, Kelso and Archer both
operate a long-term maintenance business in many countries and use
this arm of their business to generate new sales leads and to maintain a
staff of local technicians. However, while Kelso and Archer hire and
prefer to work with locals wherever possible, their performance on
new projects is not strictly tied to the achievements of local staff.
Rather, in a crisis situation where a job falls behind schedule,
both firms quickly revert to sending in highly skilled expatriates to

diagnose, reform, and accelerate project completion. Since their work is mainly of a technical nature, outside expatriates can be a very useful defense against project delay. For example, on the Mass Transit System project, a Kelso senior project manager explained, "After I . . . figured out where things had gone sideways, I sent for 10 or 12 installers from Germany, France and the UK and had them parachuted in to get the job back on track."

As for project entry mode, both Archer and Kelso prefer start-ups. Typically, when they do not already have a local maintenance office, they send in a senior expatriate to rent an office space and to staff-up for an installation. Finally, both firms prefer an organization structure with control centralized to the home office or to the factory. In fact, one senior Kelso project manager reported:

That's the biggest problem with the way Kelso is set-up; every single decision has to go through the factory. If I want to spend $500, I have to call for permission and I've been here almost 25 years. Those guys over there from Boomerang, they can spend up to $50,000 with a field purchase order. Now how do you figure that one out?

### Project consultants

Firms in the project consultant category engage in an advisory capacity to assist a project sponsor in all stages of project implementation, from feasibility, design, and tendering, through construction management, commissioning, and subsequent expansion. Phantom and Marengo indicate that their international strategy relies on a fee and contract structure such that they avoid the consequences of local embeddedness. For example, one Marengo manager explained:

It doesn't much matter how long a project goes or how much it runs over budget, at the end of the day, we get paid. Of course, we have our reputation to protect, but as long as we don't do something stupid, a delay to a project is usually in our favor. So it doesn't matter to us how corrupt or complicated the situation is in whatever country it happens to be – because we always get paid no matter what.

Thus, even though project consultants face medium to high levels of embeddedness in the local context, they are able to avoid the financial consequences that typically come with a lack of knowledge about the local market setting. As for sales and business development, typically a seasoned international executive handles relations with potential leads and with past clients for repeat business. In Phantom's case, the Vice President who fills this sales function speaks five languages and has studied and worked abroad for more than 40 years. As necessary, project developers recruit local professional staff on a project basis, primarily for design and engineering activities.

When entering new projects, the mode of entry that project consultants like Marengo and Phantom adopt is best described as a partnership. But, in some ways, because the partner is with the local government sponsor, it is far more beneficial than a partnership with a private firm. In particular, a government partner is often the author and enforcer of the formal regulations, has access to a large base of tangible and intangible resources, and is a dependable source of payment. In addition, a government sponsor often provides office space and administrative assistance, as was the case for Marengo and Phantom on projects 1 through 4. In a crisis situation, project consultants tend to defer key decisions to their client and thus they avoid primary responsibility for events that arise unexpectedly or for conflicts that escalate beyond a comfortable level. Finally, since most consultants are very experienced and because projects have unique needs, the organization structure that project consultants adopt permits decentralization to the project site office or to a regional office. (For example, in one country, Phantom was managing both a transport project and an airport project, from a single regional office.) In fact, Marengo and Phantom consultants in the individual project site offices enjoy a great deal of autonomy from their head offices in the UK and Japan, respectively. As one consultant bragged, "The best part of my work is my independence. I plan these projects. I build these projects. And I have freedom from headquarters."

### General contractors

General contractors contract for and assume responsibility for completing construction projects and they hire, supervise, and pay all of the subcontractors. In international markets, the primary strategy that Boomerang and Forester employ is to decrease their level of embeddedness and to increase their supply of local knowledge. They do this both by allocating work and responsibility to competent local subcontractors; and by using local staff, agents, partners, and advisors to guide and manage relations with local subcontractors, vendors, regulators, and community stakeholders.

To identify good local suppliers and subcontractors quickly, both Marengo and Forester have formalized a sophisticated "pre-qualification process," so that they can quickly identify which of the local firms are reliable and capable and eliminate those that do not have adequate capacity, skill, or capitalization. They win projects in two main ways: bidding competitively, or negotiating preferred work. On a large infrastructure project, a general contractor often directly employs more than 2,500 laborers, foremen, and field supervisors, and, indirectly, a much larger number. They also hire dozens of local professional staff, including project administrators, translators, procurement managers, engineers, and project managers. In addition, they are especially attuned to enlisting the aid of so-called freelance expatriates, as one Boomerang project executive explained:

The Brits, Aussies, Kiwis, Canucks. You find them all over Asia. They go from project to project ... They can really play an important role because they've already adapted to the local culture and they are versed in the Western management systems.

Research by Mahalingam (2005) confirms and expands on the critical role played by these freelance expatriates from "cricket-playing countries" (see Chapter 4):

In emergency situations, general contractors are conditioned to adapt expediently. They rely both on contingency plans and on the judgments of seasoned expatriates. These expatriates typically have experience on projects in anywhere from 10 to 50 countries and are familiar with managing thorny, unpredictable, high-risk situations. The expatriates usually have very strong personalities, characterized as outgoing, people-friendly, empathetic, curious and resilient. As one Forester informant noted, "Notice all of the top managers in the [general contractors] – they have a high level of emotional intelligence. Notice all of the top managers in the [systems contractors], now they have a more technical persona. It's a different set of skills that you need to handle all of these relationships that we deal with as a [general contractor]."

In addition, general contractors rely on local partners and consultants to provide "localized advice." One Boomerang informant mentioned the value of seeking counsel from local branches of international consultancies, such as Ernst & Young, Price Waterhouse Coopers, and HSBC.

As for project entry mode, general contractors typically implement a single-partner or multi-partner joint venture strategy, usually with at

least one local firm and frequently with other international contractors as well. As a consequence of their large size and temporary nature,
organizational structures of the general contractors are unique and
utilize a complex array of locals to manage local interfaces and freelance expatriates to oversee aspects of the technology and contract.
Although they may vary in terms of details, general contractors'
project organizations tend to include similar elements from project
to project. As one Boomerang executive noted:

> We have the same basic departments on every project. The same template
> organization chart, if you will. And then depending on the size of the
> project, we hire a greater or lesser number of staff to fill each box and to
> balance the workload against the staff that we hire.

Typically, because the pace of change and decision making on a
project is very rapid, project controls are handled directly within the
project site office and thus the home office has little connection with
day-to-day operations.

## Developers

Firms in the developer category sponsor, build, and operate projects with
private funds and specialize in areas such as design, finance, engineering,
construction management, and asset management. A main driver of their
international strategy is the need to localize their operations, because,
after they enter and invest in a new market, they usually intend to stay for
a lengthy period of time – often several decades. Like general contractors, they face high levels of local embeddedness, especially in the front-
end, "shaping" phase of a project, which involves land acquisition,
permitting and seeking government approvals for new development.
When selecting new markets for entry, Duke uses an "income prequali-
fication" process to prioritize market opportunities based on economic
potential. As one Duke vice-president expressed:

> We are by and large indifferent to world location. We have considered
> Europe, Asia, Latin America ... What we care most about is a strong
> customer base with the potential to generate revenues that will pay-back
> the investment in the project and to return a profit that satisfies our execu-
> tives and our shareholders.

Within Heroic, the process of market selection is far less clearly
defined and happens in two main ways. First, because Heroic is a

highly-regarded international developer with the financial capacity to fund projects, many firms from around the world approach them with project opportunities. As one Heroic executive said, "Of the projects that come to us, we pick and choose the ones that are most attractive." Second, Heroic has two senior executives who focus on pro-actively generating new investment opportunities via leads and contacts that come from within their firm and from large personal contact networks that come from a lifetime of experience in the industry. Both Duke and Heroic hire professional local staff, but they avoid hiring labor directly. Once they have a project approved, Heroic prefers to employ a smaller staff of 8 to 13 managers, of which one-half to two-thirds are expatriate, and to divide the overall package of work across 10 to a maximum of 20 local subcontractors. This strategy minimizes the absolute number of interfaces with local firms and institutions, but it also places a greater degree of responsibility and trust with local subcontractors.

Concerning crisis management, in a situation where local contractors were not meeting quality expectations, Duke responded by sending a staff of more than 250 US engineers to micro-manage every aspect of the design and construction integration. Heroic, which is far more experienced internationally, takes a more localized approach to managing crisis situations, which is made possible by their mode of entry approach. As one Duke vice-president explained:

Initially we had a very large expat management group in [the first foreign market that we entered]. There were probably seven expats who were directly involved with [this first] project. Everybody local was middle to lower management. But, we found that was not really the smartest or most effective way of approaching a country. So, we started to move away from creating beachheads in these countries with expat groups, to where we were really finding an established local experienced developer that had been around the block a few times in the country who could partner with us, at first; and if that relationship seemed like it was compatible, then we would either buy out their company or hire the principal away from the company and start a [Heroic] office using experienced local management to really run the office at a very high management level and the expats would be purely resource and support to those people, rather than the main manager or director of those people. And that seemed to be a much more effective way of getting into a country and making fewer mistakes ... And when we did make mistakes, we found that having a committed local partner was the best way to resolve them.

In order to make the acquisition strategy work, Heroic notes a heavy emphasis on so-called "trial partnerships" with potential acquisition targets, education and training to indoctrinate the local acquisitions in the parent firm's practices and protocols, and eventual transfer of operating control to locally acquired partners. While Heroic has evolved to prefer an acquisition entry strategy, Duke, which has far less international experience, has focused more on partnering with local firms and, in one case, on licensing their brand to a local firm to develop and operate a resort. Finally, for both firms, after an investment decision is committed, the structure of local operating units is heavily influenced by the preferences and expectations of local partners and acquisitions, and thus control is highly decentralized down to the level of the country office. However, given the high-profile nature of development and the large sums of money involved, the locus of control is not usually a project field office trailer, but, rather, a regional office established in the central financial district of the nearest major city center.

### *Learning how to match local embeddedness, strategy, and structure*

A prominent business historian has argued that a firm's strategy and structure need to be aligned with the characteristics of its environment if it is to be successful (Chandler 1962), and a great deal of research on US organizations has examined and, generally, verified this proposition (see, e.g., Fligstein 1985; Lawrence and Lorsch 1967; Rumelt 1986). Yet, few studies in the IB literature have built on this classic model despite calls for a more integrated link between the classic management theory and the more recent IB offshoots (Daniels 1991; Melin 1992; Wright 1994).

Although the strategy/structure argument perspective has been overlooked by IB scholars to date, the evidence in Table 6.7 suggests that it may have much to offer scholars of international management. The evidence provides strong indication that firms in different industry subgroups on global projects select their strategies and structures contingent on their level of embeddedness in the foreign market environment. Simultaneously (or alternatively), they select an appropriate level of local embeddedness, given their strategic and structural preferences. For example, systems contractors, with low embeddedness

Table 6.7 *Indicators of local embeddedness and strategy–structure fit*

| | Systems contractors | Developers | Project consultants | General contractors |
|---|---|---|---|---|
| Mean # of embedded relations (see Table 6.4) | 52 | 90 | 282 | 1172 |
| Relative institutional embeddedness score (see Table 6.5) | 6.8 | 16.6 | 12.8 | 15.3 |
| Main entry strategy | Start-Up | License/ Partner/ Acquisition | Partner with project sponsor | Partner/ Multi-Partner JV |
| Main defense against institutional exceptions | Country Manager/ Highly Experienced Expatriates | Partner/ Acquisition/ Highly Experienced Expatriates | Partner | Partners/ Highly Experienced Expatriates |
| Use of local partners or agents/ country/project | 0–2 | 3–12 | 1–7 | 3–14 |
| Ratio of expatriate to total professional staff | 75–90% | 40–70% | 2–45% | 15–40% |
| Centralization of control | Home office | Regional office | Regional office/ Project field office | Project field office |
| # countries with regional office relative to total # countries entered globally | < 20% | > 70% | > 50% | 20–50% |

repeatedly use a start-up mode of entry, whereas general contractors and developers, facing potentially much higher levels of embeddedness learn to use a partnering or acquisition mode of entry.

The evidence from this study indicates a similar trend for staffing policy and organization structure. Systems contractors, with a smaller need for local knowledge, hire very few locals, and control is centralized to the home office or factory. In contrast, general contractors and developers, with a much greater level of embeddedness, hire many locals into key "local interface" positions, and control is decentralized to the project or regional office. Indeed, our evidence indicates that firms adapt their entry strategies, subsidiary staffing plans, and organization structures, whether consciously or otherwise, according to their level of local embeddedness in the unfamiliar project environment. These findings reinforce and extend Chandler's classic theory.

## General strategies to cope with local embeddedness

### When participating in global projects

There have been many fruitful efforts to investigate the linkage between international experience and performance in foreign markets (e.g., Makino and Delios 1996; Barkema et al. 1997; Luo and Peng 1999). Yet, despite these advances, there has been little effort to describe what firms actually learn as they accumulate global experience or to unpack the black box of "general internationalization knowledge" that has been alluded to by many prior scholars (e.g., Benito and Gripsrud 1995; Johanson and Vahlne 1977; Eriksson et al. 1997; Petersen and Pedersen 2002). Specifically, what types of general strategies do firms devise in order to combat the challenges of embeddedness and emergent uncertainty in alien market environments? Our evidence suggests that firms evolve multiple variants of three general strategies: *increasing the supply of local knowledge*; *decreasing the need for local knowledge*; *and reducing potential impacts of a local knowledge deficit*. Instances of these general strategies were observed repeatedly across all eight firms in our sample, across a wide variety of market and global project settings, in a number of world regions. In formal terms:

> *Proposition 5: When firms enter a global project in an unfamiliar setting, they can improve performance by: 5a) increasing the*

*supply of local knowledge; 5b) decreasing the need for local knowledge; and 5c) reducing the consequence of a local knowledge deficit.*

We discuss and provide examples of each of these general strategies below.

## Increase the supply of local knowledge

Table 6.8 provides evidence of at least three tactical strategies that entrant firms use to increase their supply of local institutional and business knowledge: they increase the level of "initial knowledge" contained within the boundary of their firm at the very outset of a new overseas initiative; they accelerate the rate of cognitive learning of their existing members; and they increase the period of cognitive learning, so that their existing members have more time to interpret local realities and align accordingly.

### Increase initial knowledge

In preparation for an overseas assignment, entrants gather intelligence information, prepare executive briefing reports, and investigate key business drivers, economic indicators, and regional trends prior to entering a new market setting. They compile this information from public and proprietary sources such as industry trade associations, market research specialists, and in-country embassies. In addition, several informants report that industry-benchmarking partners can be a key source of unit cost and productivity data for new markets that is recent and reliable.

Entrants also "ingest" locals into their organization. By hiring locally experienced staff and by teaming with local partners, the level of local knowledge accessible within the boundary of the firm is rapidly boosted. Locally recruited personnel, who are hired as individuals or acquired *en masse* through acquisitions, bring a stock of prior accumulated knowledge about local history, patterns of living, politics, and economic trends. Local partners, which can range from individual professionals to formal joint venture partners, bring a similar stock of local knowledge into the firm.

Strikingly, some of the best carriers of local knowledge are not locals per se, but are freelance expatriates – primarily from the UK

Table 6.8 Strategies to increase supply of local knowledge

| Firm name/ informant | Tactical strategy | Example | Quote from interview |
|---|---|---|---|
| Heroic/Vice President | Increase "Start Knowledge" | Procure a "map" of permitting processes prior to entry | "In Poland permitting delayed us a year. So when we went to Czechoslovakia, we paid a local consultant more than US$30,000 to prepare a detailed map of all of the steps to get development approval. Let me show it to you. [Informant rummages in file cabinet and pulls out an 11″ × 17″ flow-chart diagram with dozens of boxes and arrows.] This was a lifesaver. Without it, we wouldn't have known where to begin." |
| Duke/Vice President | Increase "Start Knowledge" | Prepare "executive briefing" reports | "I prepare an executive briefing report before we go into a country. I begin with currency. Bear in mind, these briefs are designed for engineers who one day get a tap on the shoulder and are told, 'you're going to begin to participate on a project in sample market "X"'. So I begin with a basic description of the country, its form of government, its economy from the standpoint of is it free, is it government supported, that kind of stuff. And that's all readily accessible, there's not a whole lot of mystery to finding that kind of stuff. I use both public and private sources and rely on trade-groups like ASEAN, Transparency International, the Economist Intelligence Unit, the ISO site, US government sites [i.e. State Department background notes, CIA fact file], World Bank stuff, newspapers, the library and most importantly our internal benchmarking partners to |

get recent unit costs which are core to competitiveness and you can't just go out and buy."

| Boomerang/ Translator | Increase "Start Knowledge" | Hire locals for "interface roles" and bring in expatriates to form "technical core" | "[Looking at an organization chart together.] See the way it is set up. All of the "interface roles" we call them, they are all filled by locals. The procurement manager, the translator, the assistant project manager who gets the permits. See there, that little box by each person's name, it shows the number of years of local experience on top and number of years of overall experience on bottom. And see, all of the roles in the 'technical core' we call them, they are filled by our expat team." |
|---|---|---|---|
| Boomerang/ Project Executive | Increase "Start Knowledge" | Hire "freelance expatriates" who have two-way cultural knowledge | "You'll notice that we hire a lot of Brits, Aussies, Kiwis, Canucks. You find them all over Asia. They go from project to project. They go from the Hong Kong airport, to the Malaysian monorail, to Singapore and then Bangkok. After a project ends they call their friends and move on to the next one. They often marry Asian women. So they get to the point where they are really good in a culture. So when we start fresh, if we can find a few of them that have just finished a project, they can really play an important role because they've already adapted to the local culture and they also know the Western management systems." |
| Boomerang/ Project Executive | Increase "Start Knowledge" | Hire local media professional to handle the "media spin" | "The guy that sits at the hall. We hired him because most of his experience was in newscasting. He had run hard on his luck and that's why he came to us for a job and we thought we could use him to play the media game. So he actually spends most of his time working the media spin. He knows all of the local reporters and if |

**Table 6.8** (*cont.*)

| Firm name/ informant | Tactical strategy | Example | Quote from interview |
|---|---|---|---|
| | | | they publish something against us he can get a counter story out almost just as fast. And he selectively leaks stories to the press, on the condition they publish his angle. And he's really good. Hard to quantify in numbers just what a guy like him is really worth." |
| Boomerang/ Project Manager | Increase Rate of Learning | Seek advice from local branch offices of global banks & consultancies | "Ernst & Young, Price Waterhouse Coopers and HSBC. They can tell you what to look out for. They will have locals who speak the language of that country. They don't understand your project, but they understand local labor law, contract law and local financial markets. They will keep you legal and give good advice that you can implement and indoctrinate into your system. They are advisors." |
| Forester/Design Engineer | Increase Rate of Learning | Send expatriate staff to cultural "charm school" | "We have used charm school consultants from time to time. They can offer anywhere from a two-day to a two-week seminar on how to nod your head, shake hands, bow . . . say thankyou – argiatou, xie xie, khawp khun khrap – present a business card . . . or send a gift. Especially for new expats going in, this can be a big time-saver as they try and make sense of the new surroundings." |

| | | | |
|---|---|---|---|
| Forester/Vice President | Increase Rate of Learning | Use "spouses" as local guides | "At [Forester], we believe it is important to support the families. And one thing that works really well, is we will pay one of the more outgoing [spouses] who have been there long enough to know the ropes to be a 'friend' to show the new [spouses] around. You know, to help them find the supermarket, show them how to work [air conditioning] and help them to get settled in . . . . This really helps." |
| Boomerang/Business Development Manager | Increase Period of Learning | Build a "doghouse" before you build a factory | "I just built two factories in China. And the key is to build a doghouse first, a small factory, where you work out the kinks, train the locals, build a team and then sink your chest of gold into the big factory that you intended to build all along. You need time to learn . . . . Otherwise, you'll end up with a white elephant, like [Acme Co.] did in [China]." |
| Marengo/Vice President | Increase Period of Learning | Use "trial balloons" | "We like to use trial balloons, scaled-down versions of full projects or partnerships so that we can get up the learning curve before we tackle larger projects. I've done this a number of times now, especially in the US, with a good outcome and avoided a few catastrophes." |
| Heroic/Vice President | Increase Period of Learning | Hold "design competitions" to get acquainted with locals | "One of the things we do now is to hold design competitions. What most of the local developers want is money and that is something that we have. We have a lot of funds that we have access to and can put a lot of money into a project if it makes sense. So, when we hold a competition, we get a lot of interest from the local firms and a lot of local development groups come to [Heroic] with opportunities to develop and that buys us more time and more free help, to learn the 'home court' rules compared to going in all alone." |

**Table 6.8** (*cont.*)

| Firm name/ informant | Tactical strategy | Example | Quote from interview |
|---|---|---|---|
| Heroic/Vice President | Increase Period of Learning | Use "feasibility studies" to avoid committing too early | "It may be that you . . . just look at the feasibility of a project with an individual. You can get a pretty good sense of how somebody approaches a project, what their strategy is with a project, when you just go through the feasibility stage. So, some of these people that we have hired and are working with, came to us because they had what they thought was a good project, what they thought was a good business plan for expanding our company in their country. And we spent a lot of time with those people looking at specific projects, looking at them and their companies and seeing if this is going to be somebody that we want to continue on. That's exactly what happened in Italy . . . and in France." |

and other British Commonwealth countries such as Australia, Canada, India, and New Zealand – who play an important role as cultural intermediaries on many large global projects (Mahalingam 2005 [see Chapter 4]). The freelance expatriates provide technical expertise and act as negotiators, links, and go-betweens to guide relations between culturally diverse project participants. These professionals show little allegiance to a particular firm and rove from project to project through a social network of acquaintances developed on past projects that is maintained and reinforced by social clubs such as the "Hash House Harriers" to which many of them belong. Their unique experience base and skill set enables them to anticipate, assess, and adapt to subtle differences in a new environment; to unify various organizational, professional, and national cultures; and to mediate disputes and standoffs rooted in differing institutional logics. A number of the entrants in our sample routinely hire these freelance expatriates on a project-by-project basis to gain access to their knowledge base, which includes all three types of knowledge: country/institutional, industry/business, and global/internationalization.

### Accelerate learning rate

Entrant firms rely on formal training programs, "executive briefing reports," and other formal intelligence information to train expatriates and their own employees quickly with respect to the local language, history, business practices, economic trends, political influences, and institutions. For example, Duke reported sending expatriates to "charm school" to be trained in the finer nuances of local social niceties and mores. Entrants also accelerate their learning by seeking advice from local consultants who act as mentors and from local guide organizations and agents who provide on-the-job counsel and guidance. For example, one Boomerang executive noted that many global contractors rely extensively on local branches of large global financial advisory firms, such as Ernst & Young, Price Waterhouse Coopers, and HSBC. Law firms also can supply a wealth of local knowledge.

### Increase learning period

Entrants use scaled-down pilot projects and partnerships to immerse themselves in the host market environment and to assess potential partnerships under realistic operating conditions. Experienced managers use this strategy to gain the benefits of trial-and-error learning before they irrevocably commit resources to a high-risk project or partnership. For example, by first building a small factory in China, it is possible to work out the kinks, train the locals, learn the local history, language, and institutions, get a feel for the volatility and dynamics of the marketplace, build a team, and then confidently proceed with building the larger factory.

## Decrease the need for local knowledge

The evidence provided in Table 6.9 is organized into two key tactical strategies that entrant firms use to reduce their level of need for local knowledge when they enter a global project: reducing in-house scope of work, and reducing the number of relationships to be managed locally. In effect, these approaches circumvent the need to learn about local language, history, technologies, and institutions.

### Reduce in-house scope of work

Although it seems obvious, the first question an entrant needs to ask is, "Are we qualified and connected enough to execute our specific scope of work connected with this project?" If not, the best strategy is to avoid internalizing responsibility for the scope of work or to sub-contract all or a substantial portion of the work package to a local firm or another international firm that is more established and connected within the local market. One Boomerang executive confirmed that the "go/no-go decision" – i.e., the decision to take on risk and responsibility or to walk from a specific opportunity – is the most difficult and most important of all strategic decisions in the international contracting business.

### Reduce embeddedness in local context

By outsourcing, subcontracting, and moving key activities offshore, entrants are able to reduce their level of embeddedness and risk in the local context. A simple example of this strategy is a visitor who hires a taxicab to avoid needing to learn the maze of streets, landmarks, and traffic patterns in a new city – as opposed to buying a map, renting a car, asking for directions, and risking "hold-ups" with local law enforcement officers, parking attendants, and the like; the task of getting from point A to B is outsourced to the local taxi driver who

Table 6.9 *Strategies to decrease the need for local knowledge*

| Firm name/informant position | Tactical strategy | Example | Quote from interview |
|---|---|---|---|
| Boomerang/Vice President | Reduce Scope of Work | Avoid taking work that exceeds local knowledge capacity | "You have to begin by asking yourself if you really have the connections and the capacity to pull off a project. And this may sound like a simple enough thing, but it isn't simple. When do you hit that point? Its always going to be a gamble, you'll never know until you're finished. We had an offer to do a project for a client in [Asia] but we just had to say no, we weren't there yet with our team." |
| Boomerang/Vice President | Reduce Embeddedness in Local Context | Hire local agents to handle embedded activities | "For things like buying land, permitting and hiring labor its best to outsource to a local agent . . . or partner, or guide. The key is how we set up the agreements. We pay them a small percent up front, somewhere between 10% and 50% and not another plugged nickel until they perform whatever it is we need. We bind them into integrity. When we need permits along a railroad to install fiber optics, we don't pay them out until they present us with a binder with every single permit in place. If we need a piece of land, we don't pay them out until the title is in our hands and we're sure its not a fake. If we need a labor force, we don't pay them out until the job is moving like clockwork and we're certain that the labor isn't going to [goof] off after they collect a few paychecks." |

**Table 6.9** (*cont.*)

| Firm name/informant position | Tactical strategy | Example | Quote from interview |
|---|---|---|---|
| Heroic/Vice President | " | Outsource to local contractors | "[Heroic] would much rather pay a contractor – with whatever fees he would put on top of vendors and suppliers – so that there is a one-stop shop. If we are in a new country, in a new environment, we are absolutely going to want to push the risk onto another entity. Its best to let that local contractor handle all of the local contracts on your behalf." |
| Heroic/Vice President | " | Push legal risks onto local contractors | "There is a process in Europe called 'novation' where the contractor actually formally becomes the designer on the project. The architect says, I am handing over to you all of my work and you assume all responsibility and liability. So this system makes it a real transfer of liability and risk, as opposed to the US. So in Russia, we hired a local general contractor, gave them all of the design documents and basically said, 'With this certificate of novation you are now responsible to get all the approvals and inspections through the city.'" |
| Forester/Vice President | " | Offshore fabrication to a third country | "We're moving quickly toward a fabricate and assemble approach. If you do the fabrication in a dependable community where you understand the labor situation, the |

| | | |
|---|---|---|
| | | unions and the type of quality you can expect, then you avoid a lot of hassles in the foreign theater. The assembly is easy if all of the components are pre-designed, pre-fabbed and go together like lego, you can do the assembly anywhere, on the moon if you had to." |
| Boomerang/General Counsel | " | Offshore contracts to a third-country legal system |

"One of the key strategies used in the 1990s was to sign contracts under the jurisdiction of a third-country, usually the UK. And that way you can avoid the idiosyncracies of local law and you have a clear picture of the rules. This has been especially useful in countries like Vietnam, where there is a complete absence of a legal framework and what law they do have is published in the newspaper. And it also has the effect of making the locals learn your rules, instead of the other way around."

has the local knowledge in his head. For an entrant organization, the analog is using local agents, guides, partners, and acquisitions to avoid needing to learn to navigate the complex tangle of unfamiliar institutions. This strategy is especially important for activities that are deeply embedded in local institutions, such as filing for incorporation, setting up a new office, obtaining permits, hiring staff, and the like.

Our evidence indicates that entrants use outsourcing and subcontracting as a strategy to contractually assign risk for activities closely intertwined with the local regulatory environment, such as buying land, getting shipments through customs, and seeking regulatory approvals. Heroic, especially, uses this strategy for breaking a project into sub-packages, such as permitting, foundations, buildings, and landscaping, which are procured as complete turnkey packages according to a design specification. Heroic's strategy goes well beyond what typically is known as partnering. A local partnering strategy would merely involve the use of partners to gain access to local knowledge and counsel. In contrast, an outsourcing strategy entails the use of contractors and consultants who are contractually obligated to complete a specific activity or set of activities or to deliver a specified level of service or performance. Thus entrants report that outsourcing can prevent errors and mistakes when they themselves face a shortfall of local knowledge. By using this strategy of shifting the burden of responsibility to local contractors and consultants, entrants report a reduced need to themselves learn or to recruit and manage a staff of locals directly.

Entrants also use the strategy of moving key activities offshore (i.e. off-shoring) to reduce their level of need for local knowledge. By prefabricating and assembling modular system components and sub-components, Kelso and Archer minimize their contacts and interfaces with local actors and institutions. Many equipment and systems providers use this strategy for products such as elevators, pumps, air conditioners, and signaling systems, but this approach is being used for increasingly larger subsystems such as structural steel building frames and bridge decks. Prefabricated members or modules are shipped by barge or inter-modal transport container, and are welded or bolted together with minimal on-site coordination and expertise. This type of strategy reduces reliance on local labor, capabilities, and building technologies – and can be especially effective in countries that are war-torn, conflict-ridden, or otherwise inhospitable. A fully

"off-shored" strategy starts to look a little bit like a military operation, where platoons of troops arrive fully provisioned with little or
no dependence on the local environment for supplies, people, or other
resources.

One specific type of off-shoring that was used extensively by Boomerang and Forester during the 1990s, was the off-shoring of contracts
themselves.[6] By signing contracts under the jurisdiction of international law or under the law of a third country, such as the UK,
rather than under the law in the country where the product or service
is to be provided, there is less need to learn about legal institutions and
protocols in the host country. In addition, there is less dependence on
host country legal professionals. The General Counsel at Boomerang
noted during an interview that this strategy has been especially useful
in weak or failed states where legal institutions are unclear and their
enforcement is unpredictable. However, this strategy also has its problems. Legal decisions reached in offshore courts still generally need to
be enforced in the local courts of the host country. It also reduces
pressures to reform local institutions.

## *Reduce the impact of a local knowledge deficit*

The evidence in Table 6.10 is organized around three tactical strategies that foreign entrants use repeatedly to reduce the consequence of
a local knowledge deficit in a foreign market setting: prepare contingency plans, cultivate adaptability, and insure against uncertainties.

### Prepare contingency plans

Entrants into foreign markets learn, as one Marengo informant noted,
to prepare "mentally and organizationally" for unforeseeable crisis
situations and emergent uncertainties, and to get beyond psychological barriers that create blind spots to unexpected disasters. For
example, at Forester, contingency planning exercises enable executives
to envision a wide range of potential disaster or crisis situations and to
design action plans to cope with them should they occur.

At Boomerang, unexpected situations are sufficiently common that
managers have developed a process-driven approach to systematically
anticipate, assess, monitor, and shape emergent uncertainties as they
arise and unfold. As one executive explained, "Whenever an external
threat arises that could affect our ability to win preferred work or to

**Table 6.10** *Strategies to reduce the impact of a local knowledge deficit*

| Firm name/informant | Tactical strategy | Example | Quote from interview |
| --- | --- | --- | --- |
| Marengo/Project Manager | Prepare Contingency Plans | Imagine crisis situations and prepare to deal with unexpected events | "Last year we had terrorists hit a project in Khazakhstan and having the contingency plan is what saved a number of lives. A lot of what we know about contingency planning comes from Shell, the oil giant. We brainstorm every possible crisis situation that could hit and we develop a compensating plan of action. With a contingency plan, we're ready both mentally and organizationally, to spot smoldering fires and contain them before they spin out of control." |
| Boomerang/Vice President | " | Prepare an "Alignment Paper" to shape emergent uncertainties | "We want to be proactive rather than reactive. The dual nature of our work is anticipating problems and heading them off. Our alignment paper is our most important tool. It has six sections and looks like a balance sheet. (1) Issue: we state the problem; (2) Our Strategic Interests: we make the business case, as affected by the issue; (3) Key Factors: we state the material facts, relationships, or other party interests; (4) Judgments: we go beyond the facts of a professional estimate of likely outcomes; (5) Goals: we describe the goals we should try to achieve, ideally, driven by the facts and judgments; (6) Objectives: we fix concrete |

| Kelso/Senior Project Manager | Cultivate Adaptibility | "Parachute" highly skilled expatriates into a project to accelerate progress | "When things don't go as planned with an installation and we start to fall behind they call me in. That's why I'm here on this [project]. I'm the globe-trotter who orchestrates the turn-arounds. And here we had fallen way back on schedule because we had overestimated the technical capabilities of the locals. So after I came in and figured out where things had gone sideways, I sent for 10 or 12 installers from Germany, France and the UK and had them parachuted in to get the job back on track. This team was excellent and they were here for about three months." |
| Heroic/Vice President | " | Avoid formalizing processes that restrict adaptive thinking | "As we opened up countries, we talked a lot about preparing a manual, or a protocol, that could be used throughout the world. And we were serious, but we decided not to because we are very, very entrepreneurial. And the fear is, once you put something in writing with [the president's name on it] as an edict from the corporate level, people begin to refer to the manual rather than their own gut feeling or intelligence. And we worried that this would be a disadvantage in markets abroad. So we decided not to put a manual together for fear it would really limit people in what they felt was the right response, because they had this manual to follow." |

actions . . . . implementation targets, progress that can be measured."

**Table 6.10** (*cont.*)

| Firm name/informant | Tactical strategy | Example | Quote from interview |
|---|---|---|---|
| Boomerang/General Counsel | Insure Against Uncertainties | Buy political risk insurance to reduce risk of expropriation | "Political risk insurance is purchased for two reasons. From one view, the project sponsor is trying to protect themselves from expropriation risk. At another level, the sponsors are trying to create an incentive for the host government not to expropriate for fear of compromising their relationship with the US government (OPIC) or MIGA who provide the coverage and who bang these countries over the head and threaten to revoke future loans when they [misbehave]." |
| Marengo/Resident Engineer | " | Hold a project "captive" to insure payment | "[The sponsor] is six months in arrears on payment. They're all corrupt, right to the top. But they'll pay. They'll have to pay because we have their project captive. They need two more main lines installed and we won't put in one more pipe until we get paid. In fact, I've drafted a letter and we're halting the works next week until we receive the balance owed." |

perform work as sold, we prepare a document called an Issue Paper to re-visit and re-align our strategy to head-off these threats." The Issue Paper consists of a concise summary of the issue, strategic interests, key facts, judgments, goals, and objectives (see Table 6.10). Within Boomerang, the Issue Paper is viewed as a "living document," one that is continuously revised to match the realities of a dynamic and changing project situation. Such a contingency plan plays a significant role in reducing the impact of breakdown in understanding because it supplies a general framework for organizational action that can significantly accelerate the rate of organizational response and adaptation in the event of an unforeseeable event or outcome.

### Cultivate adaptability

By cultivating an adaptive ability to conflicts, crises, and emergent uncertainties, new entrant firms are able to reduce the unforeseen costs of a lack of local knowledge. In order to endorse and encourage adaptive behaviors, entrants promote adaptable managers into top managerial positions, avoid formalization of "best practices," decentralize control to the front lines, call on highly experienced expatriates to "fight fires," and evolve flexible contract documents.

For example, at Forester, managers who demonstrate an ability to achieve success on difficult international assignments, are rewarded both formally, through promotions and pay increases, and informally, through corporate-wide recognition in a prestigious newsletter. In fact, as one vice-president remarked, "At [Forester], if you don't excel on the tough international assignments and if you can't become a cosmopolitan – you won't move into the upper ranks. It's that simple." In an evolutionary sense, the Forester organization culture and promotion policies serve as a survival-of-the-fittest mechanism to ensure that top managerial and executive positions are filled by individuals with the highest levels of global experience, cross-cultural savvy, and a demonstrated ability to adapt to complex, unfamiliar, and turbulent environments.

At Heroic, executives had discussed the benefits of publishing a corporate manual outlining best practices for foreign market entry. In the end, they dismissed this plan for fear of constraining their innovative and entrepreneurial culture, and for fear that managers would be less apt to "trust their own instincts ... gut-feeling or intelligence."

At all of the firms, with the exception of Kelso and Archer, control was decentralized to the project or regional site office. Local authority to make decisions enables quick, locally informed, proactive decision-making, which is crucial for organizations that face high levels of local embeddedness, allowing local operating units to adapt spontaneously to emergent threats and uncertainties, respond to situational cues, and self-correct when mistakes occur.

At Kelso, Archer, Boomerang, Duke, and Heroic, several situations were observed in which experienced expatriates were called in to troubleshoot or reorganize a project that was facing internal or external barriers to progress. Boomerang has what is known internally as a "SWAT team" – a group of seasoned expatriates who fly from one difficult project to the next, as needed, offering advice and guidance. Kelso also retains a staff of highly experienced managers who perform this function, of "parachuting" in to fix a project that has fallen behind on budget or schedule.

Finally, at Boomerang, a strategy to promote adaptability involves the design of flexible contract documents. Especially for long-term contracts, clauses are intentionally designed to be flexible under conditions of heightened uncertainty and to account for contingencies that cannot possibly be imagined at the time a contract is drawn up.

In addition, special clauses are inserted to provide a framework and process for re-negotiation, should emergent uncertainties – such as fuel prices, labor costs, or interest rates – cross predetermined thresholds.

### Insure against uncertainties

Foreign entrants use various schemes to reduce the consequence of a local knowledge deficit. For example, Duke buys insurance to alleviate political risks, market risks, and currency exchange risks. Kelso and Archer buy insurance to guarantee product shipments and secure inventory against fire, theft, and vandalism. In addition to relying on formal insurance markets, firms use powerful connections or threats (e.g., to withhold resources) to attempt to prevent undesirable events. For example, in a few countries Boomerang relies on top-tier or ex-political and military officials to certify payment and performance of local subcontractors. Similarly, Marengo has threatened to abandon a semi-completed project in order to accelerate intermediate progress payments.

## Towards a model of strategies to succeed in foreign environments

Figure 6.1 pulls together the strategies described above to propose a model of strategies for coping with embeddedness and emergent uncertainty in new market environments. The model displays an array of tactical strategies, all of which converge on the three general strategies that represent different pathways an entrant can take to minimize unforeseen costs and maximize project performance.

While each general strategy offers a theoretically distinct approach to minimizing the likelihood of unforeseen costs in a foreign market, they are not always separable when observed in the field. On the contrary, the general strategies often come bundled together in sets. For example, when an entrant acquires a local firm, the entrant not only increases its stock of local knowledge by ingesting a team of experienced nationals into its organizational boundary, but it also decreases its need for self-learning. Moreover, acquiring a local firm decreases the potential costs associated with resolving emergent uncertainties such as contract disputes or terrorist threats, by virtue of having

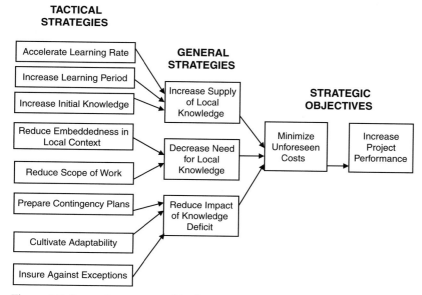

**Figure 6.1** Strategies to succeed in foreign environments

a local team on-call that is well prepared to identify, prioritize, and mitigate emergent uncertainties and their hazardous consequences.

Finally, it is important to point out that none of these strategies is without costs. There are costs of entering into local partnerships, providing training programs, hedging, and moving prefabrication activities offshore. How far do firms want to go in reducing unforeseen transaction costs? Firms do not attempt to drive transaction costs to zero, but rather they seek to minimize the sum of production costs and transaction costs by selecting strategies in order of cost-effectiveness until they reach a point of diminishing marginal returns to additional investment (North 1990).

## *Learning how to circumvent the "country learning curve"*

A number of studies have presented theoretical arguments to suggest a "learning-curve" or "experience curve" relationship between the time spent in a given host country and operational performance (Child and Yan 2003; Isobe, Makino, and Montgomery 2000; Lee 1999; Luo and Peng 1999). Our evidence suggests a more complex story. What we find, in our sample of highly experienced international firms, is that some of the types of strategies available suggest that it is possible to circumvent the learning curve and to avoid cognitive learning, which can be slow, by relying on others. Circumvention strategies enable entrants to succeed rapidly upon arriving in a new host country with only minimal cognitive learning about the local business and institutional environment. Stated more formally:

> *Proposition 6a: As global project participants internationalize, they learn to circumvent the cognitive learning curve in a country by relying heavily on locals, by reducing the need to learn by avoiding deep relational and institutional embeddedness, and by reducing the consequences of not learning.*
> *Proposition 6b: The greater a firm's diversity of international experience, the greater its ability to circumvent the cognitive learning curve for a new country and achieve objectives while avoiding unexpected costs.*

Three main types of "circumvention strategies" were observed. First, purposeful strategies to avoid cognitive learning – e.g., hiring locals into the firm, partnering with local guides and agents, and acquiring local firms – were observed to increase an entrant's access to local knowledge without having to cognitively learn anything themselves (see Table 6.6). As Simon (1991) noted, there are only two ways an organization ever learns anything: by the learning of the firm's existing members or by the ingestion of new members. By incorporating new members, or at least by partnering with them, an entrant organization gains knowledge as an entity and shifts the burden of learning to others. Second, strategies to decrease exposure to local actors and institutions, such as outsourcing and off-shoring, were observed to reduce an entrant's need for local learning too (see Table 6.7). Third, strategies to reduce the severity of unforeseen conditions or events – e.g., planning for contingencies, designing an adaptable organization, and insuring – were observed to dramatically reduce the hazards associated with an entrant's lack of local knowledge (see Table 6.8).

Our findings indicate that as global project participants gain global experience, they enact many variants of these three general strategies, which seem to be applicable across all markets and countries. By using variants of these strategies, global project participants are able to succeed in unfamiliar markets without encountering the steep cognitive learning curve that is so often assumed in the literature. Thus, our findings suggest that rather than investing in the time-consuming processes of educating their own members, firms may instead buy local knowledge, learn to avoid the need for local knowledge, and learn to avoid the impacts of a local knowledge shortfall.

Finally, it is useful to note that each of these general strategies represents an instance of *deutero-learning*, the process of "learning about learning" (Bateson 1972). Our evidence suggests that at its heart, internationalization experience is learning about the process of learning to work in foreign markets. It is learning how to accelerate this process, reduce its complexity, and reduce potential ramifications. As Sinkula (1994) aptly states, "Learning on this level is essential if the organization is to understand its ability to learn, its speed of learning, the correctness and relevance of what it learns, and ultimately the relationship between what it learns and how it performs in relevant markets."

## Conclusion

This chapter has explored the link between the level of local relational and institutional embeddedness an entrant faces when entering a global project, the local knowledge requirement inherent in an entrant's scope of work and execution strategy, and the compensatory strategies used to cope when a local knowledge deficit presents serious risks of missteps and mishaps.

## Contribution to theory

This research proposes a new, grounded-theoretic view of the strategies firms actually develop as they learn to cope with relational and institutional embeddedness and emergent uncertainty in foreign markets, and it entertains the possibility of a linkage between these strategies and firm performance. Table 6.11 lays out six potential contributions of this article to the theory of international business and highlights shortcomings of extant theory that have been identified. For the convenience of readers who wish to refer back to the findings presented in the body of the chapter, Table 6.11 presents a summary organized by article section/subsection.

## Contribution to practice

For international business managers, this chapter identifies three complementary strategies for reducing a firm's exposure to local embeddedness and emergent uncertainty that together provide a set of basic ingredients for strategic planning. The illustrative examples highlight how these strategies are used by successful international firms. Managers can benefit by using these general strategies to craft their own custom-tailored strategies, customized to the specific time, location, and environmental context in which they do business.

## Areas for future research

To advance this line of inquiry, other researchers might use the simple proxy for embeddedness that we have proposed to map out the level of local embeddedness that faces other types of firms in other industry sectors. In addition, it would be beneficial to develop a set of simple measures to measure (1) the pace at which embedded relationships are built up, (2) the "intensity" of interaction, negotiation and coordination across each local linkage, and (3) the level of risk exposure transmitted through each local linkage. Researchers can attempt to

**Table 6.11** *Summary of shortcomings of extant theory and the contribution of this article*

| Inadequacy or inaccuracy of extant theory | Contribution | Article section or subsection |
|---|---|---|
| Inaccurate: Assumes equal embeddedness for all entrants | Show that embeddedness differs by firm type and is linked closely to the size of an entrant's local knowledge deficit and the potential for situations of emergent uncertainty | Embeddedness |
| Inaccurate: Assumes predictability of risks | Show that with increasing embeddedness, risks grow, and become less predictable | Emergent uncertainty |
| Inadequate: Ignores embeddedness, aggregates data across industries | Show that entrant strategies and structures differ across firms, as a function of an entrant's embeddedness | Firm-specific strategies |
| Inadequate: Ignores classic management theory | Show that classic theory is useful, in combination with an embeddedness view, to describe the strategies and structures that entrants adopt | Learning how to match embeddedness, strategy, and structure |
| Inaccurate: Assumes that internationalization knowledge is tacit, a black box that cannot be unpacked | Shows that internationalization knowledge consists of three main strategies: increasing the supply of local knowledge, decreasing the demand for local knowledge, and reducing the consequences of a local knowledge deficit | General strategies |
| Inaccurate: Assumes country learning curves | Show that in addition to learning about the local content in an unfamiliar country, firms learn to "not learn" and learn to reduce the consequence of "not learning" | Learning how to circumvent the "country learning curve" |

replicate or refute our results by adding the dimension of embeddedness into their extant data sets – either using a similar quantitative measure of local embeddedness, if data to do this are available or could be gathered, or simply by categorizing each firm's level of embeddedness qualitatively as "low" or "high" – and reinterpreting previous findings. We would hypothesize the firms that have business models requiring them to become heavily embedded quickly under a business model with fixed-price budgets and tight delivery schedules (i.e., general contractors) would face greater difficulties with internationalization than firms that have a business model requiring them only to be lightly embedded (i.e., software consultants, currency exchange booth operators, or retail distributors). This would also suggest that as a class, general contractors that reduce local embeddedness by taking more of a contract management strategy with heavy reliance on a relatively small number of key local partners and subcontractors would outperform those general contractors that try to do everything in-house and self-perform the work with thousands of local staff. The implication of the evidence presented in this chapter is that general contractors that take the latter strategy tend to get mired inadvertently in local institutions and adverse relational dynamics. Especially if a firm has "no future" in a country beyond a single "hit-and-run" global project, then our research would seem to indicate that employing outsourcing and prefabricate, ship, and install type strategies, as opposed to taking on and trying to manage a large number of embedded relations, would appear to be the more prudent approach to risk management. Further research to test these hypotheses would be worthwhile. Finally, researchers might take steps to test the other propositions we have set out in this chapter using new quantitative data, larger samples, and appropriate statistics.

# *Structured interview protocol*

The structured interviews to measure depth of embeddedness involved two questions:

1. Estimate the number of relations that your firm has with each class of local entities.
   - Vendors and subcontractors (e.g., materials supplier, concrete subcontractor, or any other entity that your firm has paid for products or services in the local market).
   - Formal regulative agencies (e.g., police, building inspection, customs authority, traffic department, etc.).
   - Community organizations (e.g., nongovernmental organizations, community interest groups, school-board, shopkeepers' guild, etc.).
   - Other entities on the project (e.g., architectural designer, power supplier, electrical subcontractor, or any other entity with which you lack a formal contract).

2. For a "typical project," what is your firm's level of engagement in each of the following types of activities, relative to other types of firms on the project?
   - Types of firms: developers, GCs, project consultants, systems contractors.
   - Types of activities: Buying land, handling resettlement issues, getting goods through customs, applying for permits and entitlements, procuring local labor, procuring local supplies, negotiating with local government, entering into locally enforced contracts.

Note on process: This question was presented in accompaniment with a matrix-style visual aid. The matrix displayed "types of firms" across the columns, "types of activities" across the rows.

## Endnotes

1 One key difference is the oscillation between over-socialized and under-socialized views of behavior (Granovetter 1985). Adherents of "cultural distance," "psychic distance," and "institutional distance" typically fall to the side of over-socializing IB theory, claiming that differences in social behavior and relations are central to the success of foreign invested affiliates. By contrast, the proponents of "risk management" generally go towards an under-socialized view, emphasizing the probabilities and consequences of events, with little attention to the nuances and dynamics of social behavior. Those emphasizing a "liability of foreignness" tend to fall somewhere in between these extremes.

2 The structured interview protocol, developed to measure local embeddedness, is available as Appendix 1.

3 For example: Control Risks Group (www.crg.com/), Pegasus Consulting Inc. (www.pegasusconsultinginc.com/), Pertmaster Project Risk (www.pertmaster.com), and Palisade (www.palisade.com/).

4 Miller and Lessard (2000:76) distinguish between weak uncertainty, strong uncertainty and indeterminacy: "*Weak uncertainty* holds when managers have enough information to structure problems, estimate distribution and build decision models. *Strong uncertainty* characterizes situations in which there is such an absence of knowledge and information that decision-making issues are ambiguous. *Indeterminacy* means that future outcomes are not only difficult to assess but depend on exogenous events or endogenous processes that can lead to multiple possible futures. Indeterminacy is thus a risk that can be partly solved by strategic actions." Note that this distinction follows from Knight (1921), who first proposed a difference between insurable risk (i.e. weak uncertainty) and uncertainty/ambiguity (i.e. strong/emergent uncertainty).

5 A "workaround" is a temporary solution used to bypass, mask, or otherwise avoid a bug or design-flaw in some system.

6 Note that these avoidance strategies – outsourcing and deciding which regimes to operate under – can undermine important controls and create unexpected and unpleasant costs and consequences for local host organizations. Nevertheless, from an entrant's self-interested perspective these strategies can be very effective.

# 7 | Who needs to know what? Institutional knowledge and global projects[1]

AMY N. JAVERNICK-WILL
AND W. RICHARD SCOTT

## Introduction

Projections of increased population growth (Sachs 2005), urbanization, and sorely needed civil and social infrastructure worldwide point to increased demand for global projects – even in a time of global economic downturn – and afford attractive opportunities for firms within the Architecture–Engineering–Construction (AEC) sector to expand internationally. According to Morgan Stanley's predictions, emerging market countries will spend US$22 trillion on infrastructure in the next ten years alone (Economist 2008). Many firms are responding to these opportunities and have enjoyed increasing revenues. For example, the revenues of the top 225 international contractors increased 18.5 percent from 2005 to 2006 for projects outside their home markets (Reina and Tulacz 2007).

As exciting as the projections and opportunities appear, international construction projects also involve many uncertainties and risks not found on domestic projects. All projects confront various technical and financial challenges and risks, but international constructions face another special set of problems. These projects involve diverse participants from differing backgrounds and cultures who work together in unfamiliar locations. Projects conducted in countries other than one's own also confront differences in rules and political systems, differences in norms and customs, differences in values and beliefs. We refer to these kinds of challenges as "institutional" differences. Scholars such as Zaheer (1995) label firms who lack knowledge of such differences as suffering from a "liability of foreignness" (Zaheer 1995). This liability of foreignness increases misunderstandings and escalates the risks and costs of doing business in new locations abroad (Flyvbjerg et al. 2003; Orr and Scott 2008; see Chapter 5). Therefore, an entrant firm engaged on an international project faces a knowledge gap – the difference between the institutional knowledge that is needed to work on an international project and the knowledge the entrant firm possesses (Petersen et al. 2008). Firms wishing to reduce these sources of uncertainty and risk can recognize and seek to diminish the knowledge gap by understanding the differences and nuances in the host country where they plan to work, thereby increasing the success of their international projects. As Lord and Ranft (2000) note, acquiring local knowledge is of central importance when planning to enter new countries. Despite the importance of local knowledge for firms entering foreign environments, gaps remain regarding the types of knowledge needed for international infrastructure projects. This paper attempts to fill this void through qualitative case studies of fifteen international firms in the AEC industry, taking a wide-ranging view of the knowledge needed for international projects. Our study aims to: (1) identify the kinds of institutional knowledge that are important for firms working on international projects; (2) analyze and classify these important knowledge types for international projects using a conceptual framework widely employed in institutional theory; and (3) analyze differences in the knowledge needed according to firm type.

In this manner, this study allows managers within AEC firms to identify systematically the important institutional knowledge gaps that exist on international projects to help reduce their "liability of foreignness." In addition, because the important knowledge identified is broad, it is difficult for firms to disseminate these findings easily to various project teams. The categorization of important knowledge therefore provides an initial road map of the local knowledge firms need in order to reduce knowledge gaps and uncertainties. Subsequent papers address (1) the sources and methods firms use to acquire this knowledge initially (Javernick-Will 2009); and (2) the transfer methods firms use to disseminate each of these different kinds of knowledge across their organizations (Javernick-Will and Levitt 2010).

We begin by reviewing and discussing the literature that guides this research before discussing the research methodology. Next, we present the types of knowledge that managers perceive to be important and categorize them into the three pillars of institutional theory – regulative, normative, and cultural-cognitive (Scott1995/2008; see also Chapter 2). Finally, we analyze and discuss differences according to firm type. We contribute to the international project management literature by identifying important knowledge for firms in the AEC industry to collect for their international projects and by applying institutional theory as a framework to recognize and reduce knowledge gaps. By doing this, the research directs new attention to the "normative" and "cultural-cognitive" differences and risks, in addition to "regulative" (political, economic, and legal) differences and risks that others have discussed (Baloi and Price 2003; Bing et al. 1999; Chan and Tse 2003; Gunhan and Arditi 2005; Han and Diekmann 2001; Ofori 2003; Shou Qing et al. 1999). Our final contribution attends to differences in important institutional knowledge based on firm type.

## Points of departure

This study departs from the international business and project management literatures to identify the distinct types of knowledge that different kinds of firms (developers, engineering consultants, and contractors) within the AEC industry consider important when working on projects abroad. We employ institutional theory as a framework to categorize important types of knowledge to acquire. The extant literature on international project management and its relation to institutional theory are discussed below.

### International project management literature

Much of the international business literature focuses on the challenges and risks associated with conducting business abroad. For instance, Pennings (1994) found that differences in economic development, regulatory traditions, and political and social infrastructure all increase the risk involved in foreign expansion. The international project management literature is no different – the majority of international project research in the AEC literature focuses on the additional risks and challenges that affect contractors engaged in international projects. Studies have identified several critical factors and risks in international work. These include: risks associated with projects within a particular country (Bing et al. 1999; Shou Qing et al. 1999); issues and risks in contractual arrangements (Bing et al. 1999; Chan and Tse 2003); opportunities and profit-influencing factors (Gunhan and Arditi 2005; Han and Diekmann 2001); and threats and cross-national challenges (Gunhan and Arditi 2005; Mahalingam and Levitt 2007).

The international factors discussed arise from a variety of differences between the host country and entrant firm. These differences can result in misjudgments, misunderstandings, and conflicts, leading to increased project costs, schedule delays, and damaged reputations (Orr and Scott 2008; see also, Chapter 5). In other words, international differences result in increased risks and costs when conducting work abroad. One of the three strategies that Orr (2005b; see also Chapter 6) identified to decrease misunderstandings and risks abroad is to increase knowledge of the local project area. This strategy is in line with conclusions from prior studies on internationalization and learning (Eriksson et al. 1997; Johanson and Vahlne 1977). However, a firm must first identify the specific kinds of knowledge that are important to acquire for its particular business model. Prior studies within the international business literature tend to generalize and aggregate knowledge and learning across industry groups, making this knowledge less relevant and applicable to firms within a given industry. This study builds upon the theory that local project knowledge is important to reduce knowledge gaps and thus risks, but focuses specifically on the different types of firms conducting international work within the AEC industry.

## Institutional theory

The international project management literature has begun to recognize institutional theory as a useful framework for identifying and analyzing differences encountered on international projects (Mahalingam and Levitt 2007; Orr and Scott 2008). Recognizing the ability of the institutional framework to describe and analyze differences between settings beyond the widely cited differences in beliefs and values espoused by Hofstede (1991) and House (House et al. 2004), we applied institutional theory to categorize the types of knowledge that are important for international projects.

Following Scott, we define institutions broadly as including "regulative, normative, and cultural-cognitive elements that, together with associated activities and resources, provide stability and meaning to social life" (Scott 1995/2008). To elaborate and illustrate these distinctions in the context of international projects:

- *Regulative elements*, stressed particularly by economists, include the formal machinery of governance: laws, rules, surveillance machinery, sanctions, and incentives. These are relatively easily observed and readily manipulated; and hence, they are easier to recognize.
- *Normative elements*, emphasized particularly by sociologists and historical institutionalists, focus primarily on the prescriptive, evaluative, and obligatory dimensions of social life. This category stresses shared values and norms, interpersonal expectations, and valued identities. The corporate culture of participating companies, conventional professional roles and work practices enforced by occupational communities, professional standards, and state-of-the-art practices are salient examples of normative elements at work in international projects.
- *Cultural-cognitive elements*, a focus of cultural anthropologists, cross-cultural psychologists, enthnomethodologists, and organization scholars, tap into a deeper layer that includes widely shared beliefs about the nature of the world (cultural frames and scripts) (Schank and Abelson 1977) and cause-effect relations (institutional logics). The beliefs are "cultural" because they are widely shared, socially constructed symbolic representations; they are "cognitive" because they provide vital templates for framing individual perceptions and decisions. Hofstede (1991) identified a useful set of dimensions for assessing values, one of the key cognitive-cultural elements of institutions (see also, Chapter 2).

It should be noted that the categorization of these elements into regulative, normative, and cultural-cognitive pillars is an analytical distinction. In the real world, these elements overlap and influence each other, providing complex combinations. The cultural-cognitive category is the most basic of the three. It can operate alone, but these elements also underlie, and can motivate the other two categories. For instance, cultural-cognitive elements include widely shared beliefs. These beliefs underpin normative elements specifying how things "should" work and trigger obligations for social life. In turn, beliefs and social obligations can motivate actors to construct laws and regulations to enforce this compliance. We acknowledge the complexity and interdependence of these elements, but nevertheless attempt to identify what appears to be the dominant element at work.

Institutional learning requires obtaining knowledge of the social and cultural frameworks that undergird social life. In a familiar, local context, these frameworks constitute the unnoticed background of social behavior and are already well understood. Institutional frameworks in a single foreign context can include multiple, competing, and conflicting elements with overlapping jurisdictions and can, therefore, be quite challenging to document and understand. Transnational environments involving multiple participants from diverse organizations and cultures working in unfamiliar locales are even more complex, so that institutional differences loom large, and institutional learning becomes of paramount importance. As noted, regulative elements are easier to discern: they are more visible and explicit, and so more easily captured in published information or available from consultants. More difficult are the normative elements, which are encoded into the behavior of individuals and groups in the local context and in the social features of companies and work groups. Cultural-cognitive elements – elements which are more likely to be tacit and taken for granted by all parties – are most difficult to discern. Learning about these elements requires self-conscious and disciplined attention to allow differences in cultural beliefs and mental models to surface.

Most research in the international project literature that attends to institutional differences focuses on the regulative risks (political, economic, and legal) affecting contractors in international work (Baloi and Price 2003; Bing et al. 1999; Chan and Tse 2003; Gunhan and Arditi 2005; Han and Diekmann 2001; Ofori 2003; Shou Qing et al. 1999). "Normative" and "cognitive-cultural" factors, where studied, tend to play a secondary role and are often described in general terms and placed in one category, i.e., "Social, Cultural and Religious beliefs" (Bing et al. 1999) (also see Chan and Tse 2003; Gunhan and Arditi 2005; Han and Diekmann 2001). In addition, research methods that these studies adopted often rely on prior literature reviews and surveys to assess these risks, employing limited choices that restrict the respondent's opportunity to describe novel risks and institutional differences. A notable exception is Mahalingam and Levitt (2007), who used a qualitative case study with a global real estate developer to compare and identify broader risks encountered on international projects, including some of the more normative or social factors (see also, Chapter 4).

Recognizing the important work of these scholars, this study complements prior work by building upon and expanding the focus from regulatory and technical risks to include additional details of the normative and social factors affecting international construction. In addition, it attempts to shift the center of attention from discussing "risks" to focus on identifying important kinds of knowledge needed to reduce these risks. To do this, we employed qualitative methods with open-ended questions to allow managers to describe any type of knowledge they perceived to be important or institutional differences they encountered on international projects in the past. This method did not constrain the interviewee's responses and thus allowed us to expand our understanding of the types of knowledge needed. In addition, we compared responses based on firm type to begin to draw attention to differences in the knowledge required by different firms. The application of institutional theory to the results provides a framework that firms can use to strategically identify important knowledge to collect in order to reduce knowledge gaps and misunderstandings.

## Research methodology

This research uses a qualitative case-based methodology to build theory on important types of knowledge for multinational firms to collect on their international projects. This methodology uses interviewee's responses to open-ended questions, allowing them to respond without constraints and enabling them to provide additional detail and context that standard survey questions do not allow. As a result, it provides a level of in-depth analysis that more general survey methods on larger samples cannot attain, and thus offers the prospect of rich, new insights (Eisenhardt 1989; Yin 2003).

Our data were derived from participant responses to our interview questions and the supplementary materials provided by our informants. Examples of documentation include reports, books, country risk analysis reports, risk checklists, presentations, memos on post-project lessons learned, and other company information. Employing multiple data collection methods increases the validity of the identified constructs (Eisenhardt 1989).

The knowledge constructs from the interviews and documents are embedded in and linked to the type of firm employing the participant that provided the information. We conducted interviews with

**Table 7.1** *Case study information*

|  | Company (coded) | Main office headquarters | # of informants | # countries with offices |
|---|---|---|---|---|
| *Real estate* | A | USA | 6 | 19 |
| *developers* | B | USA | 4 | 16 |
|  | C | UK | 5 | 2 |
|  | D | Norway | 2 | 1 |
| *Contractors* | E | Sweden | 7 | 25 |
|  | F | India | 12 | 18 |
|  | G | Greece | 9 | 32 |
|  | H | Japan | 9 | 12 |
|  | I | Japan | 5 | 21 |
| *Engineering* | J | Canada | 27* | 15 |
| *consultants* | K | USA | 8 | 28 |
|  | L | UK | 8 | 36 |
|  | M | USA | 4 | 26 |
|  | N | Finland | 4 | 11 |
|  | O | Finland | 3 | 29 |

* The five most substantive of these 27 interviews were coded for this analysis

113 informants within 15 companies from 3 types of firms – engineering consultant firms, contractors, and real estate developers/owners – in the AEC sector. The use of multiple case studies addresses internal construct validity concerns by allowing the results to be replicated across cases (Eisenhardt 1991). Varying firm type allowed us to expand on prior literature to include engineering consultants and developers and to build theory on how knowledge importance varies by firm type. To insure that international projects were a significant component of a firm's strategy, we selected for study only those companies that obtained at least 20 percent of their revenue from projects outside their home market. Table 7.1 provides additional details on the case studies (company names are disguised to honor confidentiality agreements).

The first author conducted interviews in company offices from September 2007 through August 2008. She also conducted subsequent phone interviews with informants in other office or project locations during this time. Using ethnographic interviewing techniques proposed by Spradley (1979), she asked descriptive, semi-structured but open-ended questions of the 113 participants within global firms. The selected participants worked at various levels in the project organizations and had past or current experience on international projects. They were involved in shaping the overall strategy of the firm, or had participated in a corporate or project-based knowledge management initiative. We began with general questions to gauge the person's experience, and later progressed to detailed questions that were applicable to their experience and past projects. Some examples of questions included: "Can you tell me some of the challenges you have experienced on international projects?"; "Can you walk me through the process of starting a project in a new region?" More specific detailed questions followed such as: "What kinds of knowledge are most important to understand on your international projects?" By engaging informants and encouraging them to describe their projects, firms, and how they obtained knowledge on a daily basis for their international projects, we gathered information from rich, detailed scenarios based on participants' experience.

We recorded over 100 hours of audiotape which were transcribed and imported (along with other relevant documentation) into a qualitative software coding program, QSR NVivo®. NVivo was selected because it allows researchers to manage and query the data (Bazeley and Richards 2000). We then began a four-month process of "coding" the interviews and documents (Glaser and Strauss 1967; Strauss and Corbin 1998). The first author coded references within the transcripts and documentation to appropriate topics or categories, allowing both expected and unexpected categories to emerge. Throughout this process, she kept detailed records for reliability checks. These records enabled her to go back through the transcripts to verify that added topics were covered. During the analytical coding process, she discussed the features and examples of each of the coded categories with an advisory group to interpret and reflect on the data. After formalizing the categories, she used NVivo queries and checked each category twice to make sure that the references were coded appropriately. This analytical coding process enabled us to draw and verify conclusions from the data. Ultimately, we arrived at the constructs we present in this chapter, reaching the point where we triangulated the findings across the cases to ensure that the results accurately reflected the data. We then used NVivo to calculate the relative frequency of the findings to build theory on the types of institutional knowledge that are important to firms when working internationally.

## Important types of institutional knowledge on international projects

We began with the question, "What types of knowledge gaps exist that are important for firms to understand on international projects?" Although information was collected on the acquisition of other types of knowledge, such as technical and financial matters, and company processes and policies, because of our interest in the distinctive problems confronted by companies working in foreign environments, we restrict attention here to institutional knowledge. To determine important knowledge for international projects, we coded (1) knowledge that managers indicated was important; (2) difficulties that the firm experienced in the past from differences encountered on their international projects; or (3) knowledge that the organization systematically collects through processes and procedures, indicating that it is important to the organization.

Originally, there were 939 total references within the subcategories of institutional knowledge types (references are portions of the original transcribed material); however, after cross-tabulating the results with knowledge categorized as "important," 469 total coded references remained. The results from this analysis indicate that the relative frequency, or percentage of references made to each subcategory of important knowledge, varied between 2 and 10 percent (see Table 7.2).

During the analysis, we wanted to create typologies of knowledge with subcategories that companies can use to collect and disseminate knowledge for their international projects. After analyzing the resulting subcategories, we felt that distinctions developed by institutional theorists would best categorize the important knowledge. We grouped the subcategories or "daughter nodes" into larger "tree nodes" – the three pillars of institutional knowledge: differences in regulations, norms, and cognitive-cultural beliefs, acknowledging, as noted above, that many forms are comprised of multiple elements (Scott 1995/2008). Please refer to Figure 7.1 for the classification of knowledge types into institutional pillars. Using this coding scheme, the relative frequency of important institutional knowledge based on responses from all informants was found to be: (1) Normative (50 percent); (2) Regulative (38 percent); and (3) Cultural-Cognitive (12 percent). We present examples from our data collection and analysis below for each institutional knowledge type.

**Table 7.2** *Relative frequency of important institutional knowledge mentioned by informants for international projects*

| Subcategories of knowledge types | References | | | |
| --- | --- | --- | --- | --- |
| | ALL | | Cross-coded as important | |
| | Number | Relative frequency | Number | Relative frequency |
| Approval processes | 90 | 10% | 45 | 10% |
| Language, concepts, & meanings | 50 | 5% | 37 | 8% |
| Cultural beliefs | 34 | 4% | 21 | 4% |
| Design const. standards & permit | 105 | 11% | 42 | 9% |
| Industry organization | 58 | 6% | 43 | 9% |
| Knowledge of government | 57 | 6% | 30 | 6% |
| Laws & regulations | 70 | 7% | 25 | 5% |
| Logistics | 71 | 8% | 37 | 8% |
| Market knowledge | 41 | 4% | 10 | 2% |
| Mtl & labor avail., prod., qual., $ | 94 | 10% | 45 | 10% |
| Operating laws | 83 | 9% | 37 | 8% |
| Relationships | 34 | 4% | 8 | 2% |
| Social norms, expectations, & preferences | 80 | 9% | 46 | 10% |
| Work practices | 72 | 8% | 43 | 9% |
| *Total references:* | *939* | *100%* | *469* | *100%* |

It should be noted that our methodology allowed us to expand attention to include additional types of important knowledge for international projects, but the knowledge identified is not assumed to be all-inclusive. Specifically, informants may not have recalled or mentioned all knowledge types that are important or needed for international projects. In addition, many types of knowledge, including technical knowledge, are interwoven with institutional knowledge types. For instance, the technical environment in a given area affects design and construction standards, work practices, and the logistics in a given area. These types of knowledge can be classified as both technical and institutional, but have only been analyzed as

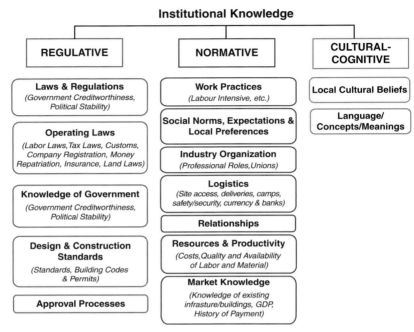

**Figure 7.1** Important types of institutional knowledge

institutional knowledge types for the purposes of this paper. Future work can expand and elaborate on these types of knowledge and their complex relationships with one another.

*Regulative*

Regulative knowledge includes the rules of formal governance structures and legal processes within a given society. Obviously, it is important for companies within the AEC industry to understand the rules and laws, and how they are enforced, within the local project area in order to operate in accordance with these mandates. This knowledge tends to be highly formalized and explicit and thus is more easily learned. As coded, this category also includes knowledge required to secure approvals, which can be much more informal and tacit. Using examples from our interviews, we describe below the subcategories of regulative knowledge: operating laws, other laws and regulations, design and construction standards, knowledge of government, and approval processes.

## Operating laws

The category "Operating laws" consists of multiple daughter codes, including labor laws, customs, company registration, tax laws, money repatriation, insurance policies, land laws, and contractual differences. It is important for the firm to understand these types of laws in order to set up and operate their business during the development, construction, and operation of the project. The most salient of these laws, particularly for contractors, were labor laws. Labor laws focus on the requirements to hire local labor, the ability to mobilize international labor (which often addresses which nationalities are allowed to work in the project location), and the availability of work permits. For example, South Africa's Black Economic Empowerment (BEE) regulation requires sub-contracting a portion of the work to Black South Africans. One contractor described how local labor requirements and immigration restrictions could significantly affect the cost and duration of a project:

The immigration policy for workers [is one of the most important types of knowledge to understand] because construction is still quite people intensive – it has changed some, but people are still required. So we need to determine if the [project and country] will allow a free flow of people to come in and out, or if they require that we use only locals. This makes a big difference. If they insist that you use only local people and the work culture is not conducive to using local labor [due to resource constraints or unskilled manpower], we are in trouble.

In other regions, such as the Persian Gulf, the tremendous amount of ongoing construction projects overwhelms the amount of locally available human resources. Therefore, some of the countries and projects recognize the need to import labor. In many of these cases, however, the governments still impose requirements for diverse labor pools to ensure that contractors are not exploiting only the cheapest labor available in the world. These operating laws require companies to have a disciplined focus on the detailed requirements for the project and country that affect the overall project, often requiring proof that the company complies with these laws.

## Laws and regulations (other)

The category "Laws and regulations" included all other laws or regulations not included in the subcategories of "Operating laws or design" and "Construction standards and permits." Important knowledge in this category primarily revolved around basic country laws, contractual documents, and the dispute system. One developer described the challenge of dealing with the laws and regulations in multiple countries when working internationally. He indicated that these differences constrain the company's ability to share and transfer contractual best practices:

What is challenging internationally is the fact that . . . the legal systems are different, so Southern Europe is under Roman law, Northern Europe is under Anglo-Saxon law, German law is based very heavily on case law, etc. So a loan agreement in Germany might be 8 pages, because so much of it is in case law, whereas that exact same loan agreement in Italy might be 108 pages. Therefore, not only the way deals and contracts are structured but the way they are documented is very different across countries.

Not surprisingly, many of the participants from the USA, UK, or India indicated that it was easier to understand laws in other locations that were former British colonies.

At the same time, many participants indicated the importance in understanding the dispute system and place of arbitration. One participant noted that a major decision factor for the firm when deciding to enter a country or contract for a project was the place of arbitration. Another common discussion regarded the frequency of lawsuits and litigations, a challenge for firms who entered the US.

### Knowledge of government

The "knowledge of government" category includes understanding the local country government's creditworthiness, political stability, and the types of control that public authorities exercise over projects. This type of knowledge is particularly important for projects that are contentious, run the risk of expropriation due to political changes or disputes, or are state run. Project developers, particularly developers of infrastructure projects, talked about this category most frequently. They discussed the importance of understanding the history of payment, supply–demand balance, and management within a country. If these are stable and the government is run predictably, the company has more confidence that they will comply with existing laws and the infrastructure agreement.

Participants also discussed challenges when they entered countries where the government exerts control and ownership through the entire development, construction, and operations process (this was particularly the case in China during the 1980s):

You had to acquire land under a lease agreement which was dictated by the Chinese, the contractor was Chinese, the financing was guaranteed by the Bank of China and to put frosting on the cake, they could determine who would lease the building.

Government controls and stipulations like this can increase project risks and therefore decrease the desire for firms to enter the country. Understanding government operations is therefore critical for firms, particularly when deciding whether to enter a country.

### Design and construction standards

In order to adhere to local requirements, companies need to understand design and construction standards within the area. Since these types of standards are often developed and promulgated by industry bodies and professional associations, they constitute an intermediate category between regulative and normative structures – "soft regulation" (Djelic and Sahlin-Andersson 2006). For instance, professional bodies create standards and accreditation titles that often become requirements that are enforced by the municipality granting building permits. This type of knowledge tends to be most critical for engineers who are designing the project; however, contractors need to understand the standards of practice, and developers are concerned with ensuring that the overall project meets existing guidelines and principles. There was some discussion of the differences and problems resulting from metric versus imperial units in design and construction, but most discussions revolved around regional standards. For instance, one person talked about the different technical standards for concrete in the UK vs. Hong Kong:

The local tweaks on technical requirements [are important to understand]. For instance, for some bizarre reason concrete shrinks more in Hong Kong than it does in UK – No, it doesn't! But [Hong Kong] has within their local codes of practices and regulations a higher value for shrinkage of concrete than the British standards.

Although this type of knowledge is important, it is often explicit and available publicly in codes and standards documents.

### Approval processes

Approval processes are often intertwined with other regulatory processes; however, although the process can be explicitly laid out, gaining approvals and understanding the intimate nuances of systems is often tacit and not available in public documents. For this reason, this type of knowledge spans across regulative and normative knowledge. Often, the actual process of getting approvals for building permits, certificates of occupancy, or land titles is not transparent and requires prior experience or intimate knowledge of the authorities granting approval. Some developers talked about the difficulties of operating in China in the late 1990s because the "rule book" was still being written. During this time, a project could require up to 200 approvals, and the approvals required changed on a day-to-day basis. Others talked about the challenge of acquiring clean land to build property on and the unique processes for acquiring land entitlements in different areas. For instance, in Prague, developers were confronted with claims of land ownership existing prior to the Nazi invasion in World War II. One informant described a similar challenge in India:

In new developments, the biggest challenge has been finding land with clean title. This forced us to partner with locals who own land and who can prove that they have a clean title to a piece of land, have gone through the government approval process and who have been sanctioned for a specific buildable area . . . This is something that we knew was difficult but had no idea how difficult it really was.

Another informant described his frustration in attempting to discern and deal with unfamiliar approval processes – and even the challenge of understanding the meaning of receiving approval. In the example below, he talks about having permission from the planning commission in the UK, but still needing approvals from other city and regional departments that increased the expected cost and complicated the approval process.

Sometimes this leads to frustration . . . clearly, even if you've done some analysis when you are acquiring a site you may not be aware of the different hurdles or requirements for gaining approvals in that country and you can become stuck because it means that the project could be delayed, face additional cost, or create problems to deal with. No one likes surprises.

Understanding the approval processes is therefore critical to the overall cost and duration of the project, but it is often incredibly difficult to anticipate and acquire.

## Normative

Of the three institutional categories, 48 percent of knowledge coded as important pertained to understanding the applicable norms and values. This type of knowledge specifies how things should be done, including adopting socially accepted practices and processes, and fulfilling expectations for roles. Unlike regulative knowledge, which is legally sanctioned, this type of knowledge is morally governed (Scott 1995/2008). As such, this type of knowledge may not be explicit and must often be inferred from observing the behavior of others.

### Work practices

Understanding local work practices is important to be able to create and execute a buildable design. Work practices are heavily dependent on a number of things, including technology, the climate and conditions, and labor within an area. This type of knowledge was particularly important for engineers and contractors. One engineer described how matters such as reinforcement specifications and designs could become an issue on projects. He indicated that relying on typical design practices from a participant's home county, such as optimizing reinforcement by specifying the use of high quality machines for reinforcement bending, are often impossible in areas that do not employ the same work practices (for instance, relying on labor instead of machines).

Another engineer described the need to adjust the design and construction plan for different countries based on differences in the cost of labor:

We tend to design things a little bit more for field installation [in South Africa] because field labor installation is quite cheap. So there is a subtle difference to how we design projects [in South Africa] than how they would design them in Perth where field installation is very expensive.

Creating a buildable design, accurate schedule, and reasonable budget for a project requires knowledge of the work practices typically used in the project location.

### Social norms, expectations, and preferences

Social norms, expectations and preferences guide how one is expected to act in the local context. This can include a host of aspects that range from how to behave in meetings to preferences for office design and layout. Obviously, mindfulness of such expectations can have a tremendous impact on the perception of the company within the local community and the success of the project. This category was particularly important to developers, as their success and financial returns ultimately depend on the local interest and acceptance of the project. For example, this category includes references from informants regarding typical floor plan adjustments (German employees, for example, have a legal right to natural light, which will reduce the typical floor plan), ceiling heights (European ceiling heights are often higher than in the US), operable windows, and toilet partition sizing. One developer with extensive international experience discussed the importance of this category:

> Even though you may have built zillions of buildings when you go to France or to Germany or to Bombay or wherever it is – you will very quickly find out . . . that they don't want a 50-story building because they don't like height or they don't like big floors because, for instance in Europe every secretary . . . has to be right next to a glass window on the outside. So, automatically, social mores start to create a design of a product. So even though you knew what to build in Chicago in New York i.e. big floors or tall buildings, you have to adjust your product to fit what the market wants.

For these reasons, social norms and local preferences greatly influence the perceptions and legitimacy of a project and entrant firm in an area.

### Industry organization

Professional roles and the organization of the industry fall within the normative category but border on the cultural-cognitive category. Different societies establish different norms regarding roles for specified positions – for example, the scope of responsibilities of designers on projects. Roles and relations can also become defined over time through a conflux of interacting parties and systems; for instance, to define how the industry is collectively organized and structured. Work by Taylor and Levitt addresses the latter, describing the ease or lack of diffusion of innovations based upon the division of labor that has evolved in different countries (Taylor and Levitt 2007). Ultimately, we categorized this type of knowledge as normative because it has binding expectations as a basis of order specifying how things should be done in a given location.

References coded to this category ranged from reports about dealing with unions to respondents describing their confusion regarding variations in expectations for role behavior. An example of the latter was a misunderstanding regarding level of work detail required, as exemplified by this response:

> The contractor was expecting a much higher level of drawings than we indicated we would do. And there was a misunderstanding – we said we'd do our normal standard drawings but the [contractor] coming over thought they would receive full shop drawings with minute details of how to form false work, etc.

The different definitions of roles, standard inclusions, and the way that the local industry is organized can cause misunderstandings leading to increased costs and delays. It is therefore important that companies consciously pay attention to these differences and explicitly account for them in their contracts, budgets, and schedules.

### Logistics

Understanding the logistics for a project, including site access, the shipment and transportation of resources, mobilization of labor, payment of subcontractors and employees through the banking system, and the safety, security, and camp set up for workers, is particularly important for contractors. This type of knowledge intertwines country knowledge with project-specific knowledge. Most of the time, this knowledge is collected prior to starting the project or entering the country as this knowledge affects the bid and plan. One contractor described the many logistical factors they need to decide when beginning a project in a new country:

> We need to find a place to live . . . figure out how to set up a camp for workers . . . figure out deals with airlines because we'll have masses of people coming in (we are talking about projects that at peak will have approximately 50% expatriates coming from overseas which can be 1000 or more people) . . . figure out how to bank and deal with money in the country, pay labor, etc.

Logistics significantly affect the schedule, organization, and cost of the project.

### Relationships

Informants also discussed the importance of understanding relationships either between the local host country and their home country, or relationships within the local area. One contractor relied upon their home country embassy to provide information on governmental relationships and their "friendliness" towards business from the country. Another contractor provided a publication on important lessons learned through the years. A common theme within the publication was on the perils of not being local, particularly regarding relationships:

There are many problems if you aren't local . . . Relationships in business are always important . . . The local competitor has a range of advantages: a relationship with the customer, knowledge of and relationships with the local authorities, long relationships with local subcontractors and suppliers, and . . . [relationships with] local labor.

Relationships are still a major influencing factor in the AEC industry. Therefore, understanding the existing relationships and establishing beneficial relationships is critical to gain cooperation on projects. The increasing interest in Social Networking Analysis (Chinowsky et al. 2008) may help companies be able to map and understand these complicated relationships, particularly governmental and regulatory relationships (see Chapter 10).

### Resources and productivity

In any project, it is necessary to understand the cost, quality, and availability of labor, materials, and parts within an area. Operating laws and project requirements will often determine the amount of labor and equipment required from the local area. If the requirement for local sourcing exists, the importance of this category increases. This category is particularly important for contractors who bid, schedule, and execute the work. It includes the availability of equipment and parts, as one informant discussed on a project in Botswana:

We couldn't get our standard construction equipment in the country and operate it efficiently because there was a lack of spare parts. Even though our construction equipment was made by Caterpillar, the equipment is made to different standards in different regions and the spare parts would not fit.

It also includes knowledge of the cost, quality and productivity of local labor, which changes depending on each location:

Productivity norms are very different around the world. If you are accustomed to American welders, you might have a rule of thumb that a welder can do X flanges of 6″ pipes in half an hour. Well, in Azerbaijan, the same scope of work might take an hour and a half. You have to be really careful and understand these differences in productivity norms . . . it affects all parts of your project.

This knowledge changes according to region and over time; however, gaining an understanding of the local resources and productivity is critical to estimate the budget and schedule accurately for the project while ensuring quality and safety requirements.

**Market knowledge**
The final subcategory coded within normative knowledge is market knowledge. This includes knowledge of existing infrastructure and buildings and an understanding of the end user's history of payment (i.e., payment for water or rent) and price point capacity. This category is particularly important for infrastructure and building developers who have a long-term commitment to an area and rely on these payments to fulfill financial expectations for the project. One building developer talked about a formalized benchmarking process they engage in to develop information on the market and opportunities for entrance and growth:

We will literally go to all the offices of our competitors and we'll get as much information as we can about their buildings (specifications, BTU per SF, cooling system, curtain wall, etc.) and the market . . . then, we sit down and start looking at what projects are considered the best in that particular area and decide what we want to do to differentiate ourselves . . . We have a very deep database for the different projects – and it's a different database for each city and market we are in.

Collecting market knowledge influences both the design and the likelihood of reaching financial expectations.

## *Cognitive-cultural*

Cognitive-cultural knowledge includes common beliefs and shared conceptions and meanings. These types of knowledge rely on "preconscious, taken-for-granted understandings" (Scott 1995/2008: 61) that represent the nature of social reality. As a result, this knowledge is often tacit, although some ideas and beliefs can be quite explicit. Whereas normative knowledge is morally governed and regulative knowledge is legally sanctioned, cultural-cognitive behavior occurs because "other types of behavior would be inconceivable and unrecognizable" (Scott 1995/2008). From the interviews, we recognized two subcategories within this type of knowledge: cultural beliefs and language, concepts and meanings.

### Cultural beliefs

The need to understand the local area's culture and beliefs came up in some way in almost every interview. Sometimes differences in cultural beliefs arose between the company and locals from the project area, sometimes within contractual relationships with other international companies, and many times, this category was important when interacting with other employees in the same company. One contractor discussed problems with value engineering due to cognitive-cultural mental models when he worked in Korea:

> In Korea I ran into a problem with saving face. The Koreans believe that once they put something on paper it's sacrosanct. So the concept of value engineering can't exist because nothing could be better than what is on the paper because it's sacrosanct. You can get kind of crazy trying to deal with saving face, particularly if something really won't work.

An engineer discussed the increasing need to understand a local area's culture in order to create a locally accepted and environmentally and socially sustainable project:

> In Australia, our environmental team recently spent a long time trying to locate a route for a new road through Aboriginal land. They spent a lot of time talking to the Aborigines to find out . . . the different meanings and ancient cultural importance of the land . . . in order to come up with a route alignment that avoids all the Aboriginal sites and is therefore acceptable to the local people with minimal objection to the project going forward.

To minimize project objections and decrease misunderstandings between project participants, companies must attempt to identify cultural beliefs in the project area and within the project team. This will play an important role in site selection and project design and aid in meeting project requirements.

### Language, concepts, and meanings

Language, concepts, and meanings are also important to understand to be able to communicate with other project team members and understand the mindset of customers. For instance, developers usually need to develop sales and marketing strategies, and contractors may need to communicate concepts with a local worker who is not familiar with the term. A developer talked about issues trying to lease space in buildings due to a lack of common understanding of what is included in rentable square feet:

The United States has a very sophisticated formula [for determining rentable square footage], so when one building says you have 21,000 sq. ft. of usable space of our building by BOMA (Building Owner's and Manger's Association) standards, you can go to any other building and ask them what their usable square footage on their floor is per BOMA and they'll tell you, and the numbers mean something, you can compare them. In India, that doesn't exist. In India, developers literally just tell you what you're renting, what your rentable area is and you have no idea what that means. There's no transparency as to how they came up with that number, what the number relates to or what's included or not included in that number.

The concept of time also arose frequently in interviews with all types of companies. Frequently, this was an issue within the company or project team. Many participants from the US and UK were particularly frustrated with the concept of time and its relation to risk and risk tolerance on projects. They indicated that certain regions have a much more elastic perception of time than the literal perception of time they are accustomed to.

As already noted, we regard cognitive-cultural elements to be both more fundamental and less recognized than regulative or normative elements. They are fundamental in that they provide the substrata – the concepts, distinctions, assumptions – on which the other elements build. And they are less easily recognized because they are often implicit and taken for granted. Informants underestimate their ubiquity and their importance.

## Differences among types of firms

The AEC industry differs from many other sectors. Infrastructure projects and buildings, in general, are constructed to last for many years. These projects are deeply embedded in the local environment during the development, design, and construction of a project, and need to be locally accepted and valued to achieve use and revenue over the long term. In contrast, products that other industries produce, such as computers, clothing, or coffee, have a short shelf life. These products can be tested and adjusted over time to suit customer tastes. The long-term and embedded nature of infrastructure projects and buildings makes the need for institutional knowledge even greater. However, just as it is a fallacy to assume that all industries are alike in their need for institutional knowledge, it is also misleading to assume that all types of companies within each industry value different types of institutional knowledge equally.

We noted similarities and differences between firm types. According to the larger institutional categories, normative knowledge was the most frequently mentioned type of important institutional knowledge for informants in all types of firms, followed by regulative and then cultural-cognitive knowledge. Nevertheless, each firm type had different levels of importance as measured by relative frequency of responses for each institutional knowledge subcategory. Table 7.3 shows a comparison of the relative frequencies of each knowledge subcategory and overall institutional category for each type of firm.

Many of the differences in levels of importance result from varying time-horizon commitments and sources of revenue for each type of firm. For example, the top three most frequently mentioned types of important knowledge for developers include social norms, expectations, and preferences (18.6 percent), concepts and meanings (12.4 percent), and approval processes (9.3 percent). Developers obtain revenue from rent (or, in the case of infrastructure owners, cost of water, etc.). In order to rent space in a building, local customers have to value the location and features of the building. This requires developers to understand customer preferences as well as to be able to communicate with them in a meaningful way. In addition, developers typically operate in a given area over a long time horizon; thus the perception of the company and its project not only affects current profits but also future opportunities. They are therefore heavily committed to the local area and project and need to understand approval processes and other regulative requirements that extend far beyond the time of initial approval of the project.

Contractors, on the other hand, are committed to fulfilling a specific scope of work that is outlined in a contract with the owner/developer. The contractor typically agrees to complete a particular project for a certain price and within a definitive schedule. To achieve their profit margins, they must accurately estimate and complete the project according to this agreement. The types of knowledge

Table 7.3 *Relative frequency of important knowledge type mentioned by informants for international projects according to company type*

| Knowledge types | | Company types | | | |
| --- | --- | --- | --- | --- | --- |
| | | All | Developers | Contractors | Engineers |
| Regulative | Laws & regulations | 5.3% | 6.2% | 5.3% | 4.8% |
| | Operating laws | 7.9% | 4.1% | 13.0% | 3.6% |
| | Knowledge of government | 6.4% | 7.2% | 9.2% | 2.4% |
| | Design const. standards and permit | 9.0% | 8.2% | 6.3% | 12.7% |
| | Approval processes | 9.6% | 9.3% | 9.2% | 10.3% |
| Normative | Work practices | 9.2% | 3.1% | 7.7% | 14.5% |
| | Social norms, expectations, & preferences | 9.8% | 18.6% | 6.3% | 9.1% |
| | Industry organization | 9.2% | 6.2% | 10.1% | 9.7% |
| | Logistics | 7.9% | 3.1% | 11.1% | 6.7% |
| | Relationships | 1.7% | 5.2% | 1.4% | 0.0% |
| | Mtl & labor avail., prod., qual., $ | 9.6% | 5.2% | 11.1% | 10.3% |
| | Market knowledge | 2.1% | 7.2% | 1.4% | 0.0% |
| Cult.-cog. | Cultural beliefs | 4.5% | 4.1% | 3.4% | 6.1% |
| | Language, concepts, & meanings | 7.9% | 12.4% | 4.3% | 9.7% |
| | *Total:* | *100%* | *100%* | *100%* | *100%* |
| | *Total references:* | *n=485* | *n=97* | *n=207* | *n=165* |
| Regulative | | 38.2% | 35.1% | 43.0% | 33.9% |
| Normative | | 49.5% | 48.5% | 49.3% | 50.3% |
| Cultural-cognitive | | 12.4% | 16.5% | 7.7% | 15.8% |
| *Total:* | | 100.0% | 100.0% | 100.0% | 100.0% |

contractors needed on international projects were more varied; however, the top three most frequently mentioned categories included operating laws (13.0 percent), logistics (11.1 percent), and the cost, quality, availability, and productivity of labor and materials (11.1 percent). These knowledge types relate to everyday working operations, the ability to hire and locate labor and material, and the need to ensure timely delivery of products to the site. All three of these knowledge types affect the cost and duration of a project and therefore affect their profit margins. Their concerns are highly location- and project-specific and are limited to the scope and duration of time set forth in the contract.

Work practices (14.5 percent), design and construction standards (12.7 percent), approval processes (10.3 percent), and the cost, quality, and availability of material and labor (10.3 percent) were the most frequently mentioned types of important institutional knowledge for engineers. Like contractors, engineers achieve revenue for the design of a project according to contract terms. Engineer's contracts can vary significantly based on project type and scope requirements. This variance can also affect the importance level of different types of knowledge. In general, however, engineers need to understand local design standards to ensure their design adheres to local requirements and they need to understand approval processes to receive local approval for their design. Savvy engineers are also interested in understanding work practices and material and labor availability so that they can design a buildable, cost-efficient, and locally legitimate project for the area. This is particularly important for design-build contracts, but less important for engineers who supply designs for specific, and relatively standard equipment, such as boilers.

Differences between AEC companies appear to be rooted primarily in the different sources of revenue and commitment time horizons. However, almost all types of identified institutional knowledge were important to the different firms to some degree. Exceptions included the lack of response from engineers regarding the importance of relationships and market knowledge. However, it is important to emphasize that each company must decide the importance level it places on the types of knowledge according to contract terms and commitments, project type, and other factors.

## Discussion and conclusion

The growth of international construction work, combined with the difficulties firms face when expanding internationally, dictates the need to identify important institutional knowledge to acquire in order to reduce knowledge gaps and decrease a firm's "liability of foreignness." Because international projects bring together participants from multiple societies, participants are exposed to different beliefs, norms, and regulations. AEC scholars have primarily concentrated on the regulatory risks confronting international projects, broadly referencing social and cultural differences. Our research examines a wide range of cross-national differences – and hence, needed knowledge – for international projects. We asked open-ended questions of managers engaged in international work about what knowledge they perceive to be important. We coded knowledge as "important" if: (1) the interviewee experienced difficulties due to the lack of knowledge; (2) the organization strategically collects the knowledge; or (3) the interviewee specifically mentioned it was important. After crosscoding the knowledge types with the attribute of importance, we analyzed the relative frequency of responses to determine knowledge that was most frequently mentioned as being important. This qualitative research method allowed us to broaden our conception of the types of knowledge company participants regarded as important to collect to alleviate risks and knowledge gaps on international projects.

In addition, we employed a framework drawn from institutional theory as a tool to categorize the knowledge identified as important into the three clusters identified by Scott (1995/2008) – regulative, normative, and cultural-cognitive elements. Employing this schema, we identified normative knowledge, a largely understudied area, as the most frequently mentioned type of knowledge participants regarded as important for firms to acquire. We also built on past literature to identify subcategories of regulative and cultural-cognitive knowledge. Finally, recognizing that not all firms are alike, we attended to differences in the level of importance of subcategories of institutional knowledge according to participants within developing companies, contractors, and engineer consulting firms. Differences resulted primarily due to each type of firm's source of revenue and commitment time horizon.

This study endeavors to add to the theoretical knowledge within the international project-based literature, but also refocuses attention from identifying risks to identifying important knowledge to collect for international projects. This allows firms to take a strategic view and actively engage in collecting knowledge to reduce the number and magnitude of critical knowledge gaps encountered. In addition, we employed a research method designed to obtain knowledge that is often implicit and tacit from informants. Analyzing the data through the research process converted the knowledge into an explicit, generalizable form. Categorizing this now explicit knowledge and applying institutional theory provides a framework that firms can use as a tool in order to identify, prioritize, collect, and transfer the knowledge they will need for international projects. Strategically focusing on this knowledge should help firms decrease misunderstandings and thus increase the success rate of international work.

Although our research allowed us to expand types of important knowledge for international projects and propose differences based on company type, the study has several limitations and areas that future work can address. We were limited to the responses provided by the participants and had to rely on their perceptions of important knowledge based on their recollections of past projects. Although written reports and other sources often backed up these statements, perceptions are limited to each individual's experience and are thus necessarily incomplete. Specifically, not all types of important knowledge likely surfaced. In addition, informants may not have realized the importance of certain types of knowledge that are tacit, in particular regarding the deeper cognitive cultural influences on their international projects. We were not surprised that this category was the least often mentioned as it is often the least recognized aspect of institutions. Many of our basic assumptions and beliefs are core to our thought process; as a result, we frequently do not recognize that we even hold them. Consequently, we believe that this category may be more important than the results indicate.

In addition, we used the relative frequency of responses combined with the coding attribute of importance to rank and compare knowledge. Although this serves as a basis to build theory related to the importance of various types of knowledge for firms, future work can validate and refine our findings and propositions by asking participants to rank the level of importance of these identified types of knowledge. In addition, although our sample was relatively large for case study research of this type, the practical limitations of qualitative case studies – the time and resources to travel, interview, collect, transcribe, and analyze our results – restricted the number of participants and firms in the study. Future work can improve our results through additional case studies or surveys to increase the number of participants involved. Future work should also expand differences in company type, project type, scope, project location, and contractual requirements when evaluating important knowledge to collect. Knowledge types can be analyzed according to the project phase in which they are needed. Finally, additional work should focus on the sources, processes, and methods used to acquire this knowledge initially and then transfer the knowledge within the firm.

## Endnote

1 Amy N. Javernick-Will and W. Richard Scott. 2010. "Who needs to know what? Institutional knowledge and global projects," *Journal of Construction Engineering and Management* (136: 546–57). Reprinted with permission from the American Society of Civil Engineers.

# PART III

# Political conflicts and global projects

# 8 | "Site fights": explaining opposition to pipeline projects in the developing world[1]

DOUG McADAM, HILARY SCHAFFER
BOUDET, JENNIFER DAVIS, RYAN J. ORR,
W. RICHARD SCOTT, AND
RAYMOND E. LEVITT

The study of social movements has grown remarkably over the past three decades. From its modest beginnings in sociology in the 1970s, the field has expanded dramatically and become far more interdisciplinary in its focus (see Chapter 3). Yet for all the proliferation of research and new-found intellectual breadth, the field still bears much of the imprint of the period in which it emerged. The field developed apace of the New Left protest cycle of the 1960s and 1970s and in many respects remains oriented toward a 1960s image of contention and, as a number of commentators have noted, biased toward the study of Western-style reform movements (Almeida 2003; Boudreau 1996; Brockett 2005; McAdam, McCarthy, and Zald 1996; Wickham 2002).

This bias persists in the face of two broad trends that appear to be shifting the geographic locus of 1960s-style protest activity away from the democratic West. Starting with Meyer's and Tarrow's (1997) volume entitled, *The Social Movement Society*, the weight of speculative evidence continues to suggest that the social movement "form" has been largely institutionalized across the democratic West (McAdam et al. 2005). Institutionalization has meant an increase in formal social movement organizations (Minkoff 1993, 1995), the development of "hybrid" forms of movement activity (Sampson et al. 2005), and a sharp decline in the kind of disruptive, public protest associated with the 1960s and 1970s (McAdam et al. 2005). By contrast, it seems clear that the last 30 years have witnessed a sharp increase in 1960s-style protest activity outside of the democratic West. This trend was perhaps signaled by the onset of Huntington's Third Wave of democratization in the 1980s (Huntington 1991), but would

279

now seem to be less a trend than an established reality in many corners of the world.

Among the specific types of movements that diffused during this period is the one we take up here: movements designed to delay, block, or permanently disable large infrastructure projects. The spread of this particular category of movement would appear to mirror the general trend noted above. While infrastructure projects were usually completed in the first half of the twentieth century, resistance to such projects increased substantially and has remained high in the developed world since the early 1970s (Rucht 2002). We see the same pattern unfolding in the developing world, only beginning fifteen to twenty years later. Big dams were perhaps the first sector to be impacted by the trend (Khagram 2004), but all large infrastructure projects now appear to be susceptible to mobilized opposition, both from locally affected communities and international nongovernmental organizations (NGOs). And yet, despite the growth in such movements, there has been almost no research by scholars of social movements on opposition to infrastructure projects in the developing world.[2] So what? Why should we care about the Western bias in the study of contention? The answer would seem to be obvious. If our theories of social movements were developed in relation to a geographically and temporally narrow range of cases, how do we know if they apply to episodes of contention in other times, places and regime contexts? As Almeida (2003) noted: "even with the recent gains in explaining social movement emergence and outcomes, we still know relatively little about these same processes in authoritarian states, which tend to be much less homogeneous than core democracies."

To address this gap in the literature, we conducted a comparative case study of 11 different oil and gas pipeline projects, spanning 16 different countries in the developing world. Our goal is to identify combinations of causal factors that are associated with the emergence of legal and political conflict within oil and gas pipeline projects. We differentiate *legal conflict*, or that which occurs within the formal structures provided by the host country, project sponsor, or development agency for voicing concerns or opposition to a project, from *political* conflict, which occurs outside of these structures.

The motivation behind the research reflects practical as well as intellectual concerns. The issue of infrastructure deficits in developing countries is vitally important, but also very complex. The importance of the issue derives from the stark infrastructure deficits projected for the developing world over the next twenty to thirty years. The consensus is that there will be another billion people on earth by 2015. Almost all of that growth will take place within the poorest of the poor countries, and the ones already burdened with inadequate infrastructure (Sachs 2005). Providing these populations with safe drinking water, sewage treatment, sustainable housing, adequate energy, and access to communication, will require an estimated $1 trillion in infrastructure development over the next five years in East Asia alone, and upwards of $5 trillion worldwide (Asian Development Bank, Japan Bank for International Cooperation, and World Bank 2005).

The issue becomes even more complex, however, when we simultaneously recognize the right of local communities to exercise meaningful voice in the siting, construction, and operation of these facilities and the fact that, in the past, a good many of these projects were built to satisfy Western political and financial priorities and with correspondingly little regard for the well-being of either the host country or the people directly affected by the construction (Ferguson 1990; Gary and Karl 2003; Karl 1997). In short, if we are to successfully address the looming infrastructure crisis, we will have to find a way to balance the rights of local communities to protect themselves from legitimate environmental, human rights, and other threats, with the critical infrastructure needs facing the developing world. Understanding the dynamics of reactive resistance to such projects and, eventually, the kind of enlightened governance arrangements that give communities a meaningful say in their design and operation, will be critical, not only to reducing Western exploitation of the developing world, but also to breaking the infrastructure gridlock that has come to characterize much of the globe.

## Searching for insights: four literatures

In the absence of much work on the dynamics of opposition to infrastructure projects in the developing world, we have reviewed four literatures that focus largely on the developed world – social movements, the NIMBY (not-in-my-backyard) phenomenon, public participation, and facility siting – for insights to guide our research. We take up the social movements literature first and then review the other three literatures together.

## Social movements

Though our focus is community response to infrastructure projects, not movements per se, no literature has been as centrally concerned with the dynamics of emergent collective action as the large and rapidly expanding body of work on social movements and contentious politics. We are especially attuned, in this project, to two causal factors – opportunity/threat and resources – that have not only been widely emphasized in studies of social movements, but, as we note below, prominently featured in research on anti-infrastructure movements in developed countries.

We focus first on the longstanding emphasis on "opportunity and threat" in the social movements literature. Underlying this focus is the assumption that movements are very unlikely to develop under stable political conditions. Movements, in this sense, should be seen as responses to disruptive changes that either grant new opportunities/ leverage to potential challengers *or* pose new threats to some segment of the population (Goldstone and Tilly 2001; McAdam 1999[1982]; Tarrow 1998; Tilly 1978). The relevance of this first factor – new political opportunities or threats – to siting decisions should be obvious. The provisional decision to site a facility in a particular location is precisely the kind of "exogenous shock" that has the potential to trigger collective action, as community groups come to define the decision as posing either a significant new threat to, or an opportunity to advance, their interests. But the initial choice of site, is not the only way that threat/opportunity can be manifest in our cases. We also want to pay close attention to two dimensions of threat/opportunity that have been shown in numerous studies to impact the development and/or success of movements. These are: (a) the capacity for repression by social control agents; and (b) the vulnerability of project proponents (public no less than private) to challenge. The latter factor is expected to increase the likelihood of opposition to infrastructure projects while the threat of significant repression should diminish those prospects.

New threats or opportunities may create a motive for collective action, but without sufficient organizational resources – or what

Carmin (2003) calls "community resources" – a sustained opposition movement is unlikely to develop. When it comes to organizational resources, there are two distinct emphases within the social movement literature. Theorists in the "resource mobilization" tradition emphasize the benefits of external resources or elite "sponsorship" in helping to launch and sustain a movement (McCarthy and Zald 1973; Minkoff 1993; Staggenborg 1988).[3] "Political process" theorists, on the other hand, tend to emphasize the critical importance of grassroots community organizations or traditions of struggle to movement emergence. The consistent empirical finding here is that most successful movements are not born de novo, but either piggyback on earlier struggles of the same kind or develop within established social settings – existing organizations, informal networks – largely independent of elite control (Gould 1995; McAdam 1999[1982]; Morris 1984; Osa 2003a; Zhao 1998).

In applying these perspectives to our cases, we want to look closely at the role of NGOs as sponsors of emergent protest (as per resource mobilization) and/or evidence of a sustained tradition of struggle (in keeping with the political process perspective) in helping to explain variation in level of opposition.

Although the study of opposition to infrastructure projects has not drawn as much attention from social movements scholars as some other movements in the developed world (i.e., conventional "rights"-based movements or political movements in general), a handful of important comparative studies have been published on this topic. These studies, which we examine below, highlight the importance of opportunity, threat, and resources in the development of opposition to infrastructure proposals. They also provide more concrete examples of which factors are important and how to measure them.

Walsh et al. (1993, 1997) conducted a comparative study of attempts to site incinerators in eight different communities in the northeastern US. The authors found that opponents were more successful when they sought support outside the immediate community and used political, as opposed to legal, tactics. Grassroots networks were also important for opposition mobilization but seemed to form in response to the proposal, instead of from the pre-existing "mobilizing structures" stressed in the social movement literature (Gould 1995; McAdam 1999[1982]).

Carmin (2003) examined the role of community resources and political opportunities in shaping the responses of more than 200 Czech communities to proposed landfills, incinerators, and highways, among other projects. She found that greater political opportunities – as measured by political access, disagreement among elected officials, presence of elite allies, and political representation – were associated with higher levels of individual participation (i.e., letter writing, etc.), while increased community resources facilitated higher levels of institutional (i.e., town meetings, etc.) and/or collective (i.e., protests, petitions, etc.) action.

In his dissertation, Sherman (2004) sought to explain variation in level of opposition across 21 US counties selected as candidate sites for low-level radioactive waste disposal facilities. He used factors derived from both the "facility siting" and "social movement" literatures to compare his cases. In the end, however, he failed to find support for any single set of static variables across the majority of his cases. Instead, drawing upon recent work by McAdam et al. (2001), he stressed the critical importance of certain key dynamic "mechanisms" – in particular "brokerage" and "certification" – in the mobilization of opposition to these facilities.

In her dissertation research, Boudet (2010) studied community response to the proposed siting of liquefied natural gas (LNG) terminals in two California communities. Findings from the two cases indicated that either a combination of high threat and high political opportunity or a significant endowment of resources is important for mobilization, suggesting the existence of multiple pathways to a similar mobilization outcome.

Finally, Gramling (1995) and Freudenburg and Gramling (1993, 1994) have written extensively about the difference in attitudes and behavior towards offshore oil development in the US. They argue that historical, biophysical, and social factors explain the different responses of these coastal communities and stress the need for "multiple-factor explanations, as opposed to single-factor explanations" of these types of phenomena (Gramling and Freudenburg 1996: 486).

## NIMBY, public participation, and facility siting

Over the last few decades, a growing body of literature has tried to understand the determinants of opposition to locally unwanted land uses in developed countries. Like the social movements literature, this research reinforces the importance of threats (or risks) in mobilizing opponents. However, it also stresses the need for open communication and compensation for locally affected communities as methods for avoiding conflict.

Consistent with the emphasis on "exogenous shocks" in the social movement literature, NIMBY studies also point to the importance of beliefs about the threats (or risks) posed by a facility in mobilizing opposition (Boholm 2004; Dear 1992; Hunter and Leyden 1995; Lesbirel and Shaw 2005; Zeiss 1998). For example, in a survey of almost 250 grassroots organizations involved in environmental health issues (not specifically facility siting), Freudenberg (1984) found that nearly half of the groups were formed ". . . because concerned citizens became alarmed or angry about a suspected health hazard" (p. 445). This work underlines the importance of perceived risks as a motivating factor for action.

Scholars have also examined proponent approaches to siting and how they can be improved to manage conflict. The Decide-Announce-Defend (DAD) strategy, which relies on a technocratic, expert-based approach to determine an appropriate site that is then announced and defended in the public arena, has proven unsuccessful (Beierle and Cayford 2001; Freudenburg 2004; Lesbirel and Shaw 2005). Project proponents have thus been encouraged to move to a more cooperative approach, where communities are consulted and provided with compensation for the impacts associated with construction and operation of the facility (Armour 1991; Dixit, Wagle, and Sant 2001; Freudenburg 2004; Kunreuther, Fitzgerald, and Aarts 1993; Kunreuther, Susskind, and Aarts 1993; Lesbirel and Shaw 2005; O'Hare 1977). This shift in the academic literature to emphasize early communication, consultation and public participation in decision making as a way to avoid conflict in siting processes has been mirrored in regulation. Host country governments and financial institutions actively encourage project sponsors to consult the public, arguing that it ". . . can lead to reduced financial risk (from delays, legal disputes, and negative publicity), direct cost savings, increased market share (through good public image), and enhanced social benefits to local communities" (Environment Division 1998).

While we certainly agree with the normative thrust of the works cited, we are inclined to disagree with the implied empirical prediction. Unless the nature of the consultation is so thorough and proactive as to obviate the need for conflict in the first place, we see consultation as affording opposition groups another opportunity to protest. This is consistent with the general consensus among social movement scholars that open political systems are more prone to protest than closed ones (Eisinger 1973; McAdam 1999[1982]). A real life example of this phenomenon is offered by Espeland (1998). In her detailed case study of a successful effort to block construction of a large dam near Phoenix, Arizona, she saw the opposition of the small, historically powerless Yavapai tribe as especially critical to the success of the movement. She attributes the tribe's decisive effect on the outcome to the legal standing granted them under the terms of the National Environmental Protection Act (NEPA). Consistent with political process theory, the institutional access which NEPA afforded the Yavapai granted them unprecedented leverage with which to press their claims.

Drawing on the insights from these literatures, we will structure the comparative analysis of our cases around the following five causal factors: threat, opportunity, resources, prior conflict, and compensation. Here we simply note the broad categories of "causal conditions" to be employed in the study. Below we detail our methodological approach to each of these factors.

## The study: methodological contributions and procedures

Besides our desire to move outside the democratic West and focus on an increasingly common and consequential form of contention in the developing world, we undertook this research to explore methodological alternatives to traditional social movement scholarship. Our study departs from convention in two ways.

### *"At risk populations" rather than social movements*

The traditional approach to studying social movements would seem to severely truncate the real phenomenon of interest. That is, scholars have tried to infer something about the dynamics of emergent mobilization from instances of successful mobilization. This carries with it all the standard risks associated with "selecting on the dependent variable." It may be that successful movements are so wildly atypical of mobilization attempts generally that our understanding of emergent collective action is critically compromised by focusing only on them. Yet despite some awareness of the issue, movement scholars continue to perpetuate the problem by singling out developed movements for study.

The traditional preoccupation with successful movements as the phenomenon of interest owes as much to practical methodological considerations as conceptual blinders. Successful movements are easy to identify and generate lots of analyzable data. Figuring out how to study non- or possible events isn't easy. That is the practical virtue of focusing not on movements, but on communities targeted for infrastructure projects. In our case, studying variation in community response to pipeline projects allows us to shift the phenomenon of interest from successful social movements to "mobilization attempts" or, more accurately, "communities at risk for mobilization."

## Comparative case analysis

With this research we seek to transcend a second methodological convention in the study of social movements: the dominance of the case study method. Both the virtues and limitations of the case study are well known and fully appreciated. The ideal would be to blend the deeper knowledge one gains from a case study with the inferential power of large "n" data sets. This promise has motivated Charles Ragin to develop and refine a comparative case analytic method that allows researchers to generalize their findings from a relatively limited number of cases. He outlined the first version of his method in his 1987 book, *The Comparative Method*. He followed with *Fuzzy-Set Social Science* (2000) and *Redesigning Social Inquiry* (2008a). Whereas the initial version required researchers to render all causal and outcome conditions in dichotomous terms, the "new and improved" fuzzy set alternative – known as fs/QCA in shorthand – allows researchers to define variables (or "conditions") as continuous fuzzy set values ranging from 0 to 1 (e.g., .25, .40, .65, etc.).

These two innovations define this research as markedly different from the standard approaches to the study of social movements. Rather than studying a single social movement via the case study, we adopt a comparative case approach to explain differences in community opposition to large infrastructure projects. Add to this the choice of cases from all over the globe, and you have an approach to the study of contention that transcends many of the biases inherent in conventional social movement research.

## The method: fuzzy set/Qualitative Comparative Analysis (fs/QCA)

Ragin's fuzzy set/Qualitative Comparative Analysis (fs/QCA) provides a middle road between the rich detail of small-N case study work and the generalizations of large-N statistical analysis. Instead of trying to maximize variation in the independent and dependent variables, fs/QCA scores independent variables, or "causal conditions," and dependent variables, or "outcome conditions," in terms of membership in a set. In developing fs/QCA, Ragin built on previous work that combined methods for comparative case analysis with Boolean algebra, using mainly dichotomous data (Ragin 1987). fs/QCA moves beyond simple dichotomous scoring, allowing for a more nuanced coding of relevant conditions.

A key benefit of using Ragin's method is that it expressly considers how causes combine to create different pathways to similar outcomes. The fs/QCA method is uniquely suited to uncover the causal combinations that are associated with mobilization in infrastructure siting. This method, which combines both in-depth knowledge of a particular case with the ability to scale up to a larger number of cases than qualitative work typically allows, is well matched to our research goals.

## Case selection

Oil and/or gas pipelines provide an ideal sector for this research. Energy provision has gained critical importance in recent years with growing concerns about climate change and national security. Moreover, due to their large size and the visibility of the companies involved, energy projects tend to draw both local and international interest. However, unlike the construction of dams (Khagram 2004) or nuclear power plants (Eckstein 1997), which have been brought to a virtual standstill by public opposition, the construction of oil and/or gas pipelines continues at present. Thus, these projects tend to provoke different levels or degrees of community mobilization.

In addition, several of our authors have experience working in the sector, affording us the "insider's" knowledge so helpful in choosing cases and setting the values of our causal and outcome conditions. Finally, the impact of such projects often spans multiple communities and is thus national, as opposed to local, in scale, thereby justifying the use of national-level data for some of our causal conditions.

Although no definitive list of pipeline projects in the world exists, Simdex maintains a "future pipeline projects worldwide guide."[4] We drew on this database as a starting point for our case selection. Several criteria were used to select pipeline projects for inclusion in the study:

1. All projects had to be located in developing countries to ensure our work would fill a gap in the relevant literatures, which have tended to focus on developed countries.
2. Projects selected had to include a range of funding mechanisms – private, Western commercial bank, export credit agency, multilateral, and/or World Bank involvement.[5] Discussions with experts in the field of oil and gas development convinced us that the sources of funding could be a critical determinant of conflict.
3. Projects selected had to be relatively recent to ensure some data availability.
4. Based on these criteria, a total of 11 projects, spanning 16 countries, were selected. Each project/host country pair became a case in our analysis (n=16). Table 8.1 provides a list of our cases, as well as information on our selection criteria.

## Causal conditions

Our causal conditions were selected based on both theoretical expectations and consultation with experts in the energy sector. We divide them into the five general categories that emerged from our review of the relevant literatures. The five categories are: threat, opportunity, resources, prior conflict, and compensation. We turn now to a discussion of each of our causal conditions, grouped according to the general theoretical category to which they belong.

### Threat

Social movement NIMBY scholars have long regarded perceived threats (and opportunities) as significant catalysts of emergent

**Table 8.1** *List of cases*

| Pipeline project | Funding mechanism | Year of funding commitment | Case |
|---|---|---|---|
| Baku–Tblisi–Ceyhan (BTC) | Private Commercial bank Export credit agency Multilateral World Bank | 1999 | Azerbaijan Georgia Turkey |
| Camisea | Private Multilateral | 2000 | Peru |
| Chad–Cameroon | Private Multilateral World Bank | 2000 | Cameroon Chad |
| Haoud El Hamra to Arzew Oil–OZ2 | Private Export credit agency | 2004 | Algeria |
| Khartoum Refinery to Port Sudan | Private | 2004 | Sudan |
| Manmad to Indore | Private | 2001 | India |
| Nacala to Liwonde | Private | Never funded (discussed 2003–6) | Malawi Mozambique |
| Patagonia | Private | 2004 | Argentina |
| Sakhalin-II | Private Export credit agency Multilateral | 1994 | Russia |
| West African Gas | Private World Bank | 2003 | Ghana Nigeria |
| West–East China | Private | 2000 | China |

collective action. For the purpose of this study, we selected three measures of *threat* associated with pipeline projects: project size, potential environmental impact, and potential impact on local indigenous peoples.

a. The set of large projects – In prior research the overall size of a project has been consistently linked to public opposition (Dear 1992; Haggett 2008). The project's size, measured in terms of the length of the pipeline (in km) in the host country, provided a proxy for the general threat associated with its construction. If the project falls in the set of larger projects, conflict is anticipated.

b.  The set of projects with a significant environmental impact – In formulating our second threat condition, we rely less on theory and more on the insights of industry experts. In their view among the conditions that are most likely to trigger protest are the perceived environmental threats posed by the project. This set was created based on available information regarding the project's potential impact on five environmentally sensitive issues: river crossings, endangered species, park areas, previously inaccessible areas, and whether the pipeline included an offshore portion. If the project falls in the set of projects with a significant environmental impact, conflict is anticipated.

c.  The set of projects that impact indigenous peoples – Industry experts also see impacts to local indigenous groups as another potent trigger of opposition to pipeline projects. Western NGOs, local indigenous groups, and international financial institutions have demonstrated particular concern for the potential impact of infrastructure development on indigenous peoples. Accordingly, we include a dichotomous condition to capture whether indigenous communities had been identified along the pipeline route. We expect the presence of indigenous groups along the route to be associated with conflict.

## Political opportunities

Perhaps no causal factor has received more theoretical attention from movement scholars than political opportunities. In terms of pipeline projects, we see three important sources of political opportunities encouraging opposition: Western funding; stakeholder consultation; and the level of democracy in the host country.

a.  The set of projects with funding from Western sources – Western sources of funding include commercial banks, export credit agencies, and multilateral lenders like the World Bank. The involvement of such institutions in funding projects often leads to another layer of regulation and oversight, as well as another venue for impacted communities to express their concerns, beyond the host country government and sponsoring companies. In addition to the formal procedural mechanisms built into Western funding practices, the presence of these organizations may attract NGOs (and possibly local opposition). By representing both the evils of neoliberalism *and* a certain receptivity or vulnerability to challenge, the involvement of Western funders – especially the World Bank – may encourage opposition to projects they are funding. Thus, if a project falls in the set of those funded by Western sources, we anticipate conflict.

b. The set of projects with little public consultation – As noted in our literature review, the issue of consultation is one that supports opposite predictions by different sets of scholars. Those working in the field of facility siting have argued that consultation reduces conflict by harmonizing the interests of multiple stakeholders at the outset of a project. In contrast, social movement scholars tend to see consultation as a form of political access, granting an incipient opposition the opportunity to mobilize. Insofar as we incline toward the latter point of view, we expect to see projects that feature public consultation as more prone to conflict but allowed for either result in our analysis.

c. The set of projects in a democratic host country was constructed based on the Polity IV dataset (Marshall and Jaggers 2009), with higher Polity IV scores corresponding to higher fuzzy set scores. Given the longstanding stress in the social movement literature on the democratic facilitation of protest, we expect higher scores on this condition to be associated with conflict.

**Resources**

Our third factor again reflects a strong emphasis among social movement scholars. To test the causal importance attributed to resources by proponents of the resource mobilization perspective, we include two specific measures in our analysis: the level of development in the host country and the number of connections to NGOs. We see the former as crudely measuring the "internal" capacity of the population to mobilize on its own behalf and the latter as reflecting the "external" resources available to potential opposition groups.

a. The set of projects in a relatively developed host country was constructed using the United Nations Development Program's Human Development Index (HDI) (Human Development Report Office 2009). This index assigns scores ranging from 0 to 1 to individual countries based on measures of life expectancy, literacy, education, and gross domestic production per capita. A country's score on the index serves as a proxy for the internal resources available for mobilization in a country. Cases based in more developed countries are expected to experience more opposition.

b. The set of projects in a host country with many memberships in NGOs – The World System Integration dataset (Yearbook of International Organizations various years) was used to construct the set of projects in host countries with a large number of memberships in NGOs. Multiple memberships in NGOs indicate a greater connection to organizations that often oppose oil and gas projects and the possibility of additional, external resources for mobilization flowing into a country. In addition, following Meyer and his colleagues (Ramirez and Boli 1987; Boli and Thomas 1997; Meyer 1997; Meyer and Jepperson 2000), membership in many NGOs is likely to signal support for the kinds of normative policies (e.g., women's rights, minority rights, environmental protection) that often encourage protest activity. Thus, we expect membership in this set to be associated with conflict.

## Compensation

In infrastructure siting, the adverse effects of a proposed infrastructure facility are generally concentrated on a small, easily mobilized community, while the benefits accrue to the wider public. Consequently, scholars have argued that special compensation arrangements for the adversely affected community are necessary to even out this mismatched distribution of costs and benefits (Morell and Singer 1980; O'Hare 1977; O'Hare, Sanderson, and Bacow 1983). Although these scholars mainly refer to compensation of an affected community, such information, particularly for private sector projects, is difficult to obtain. As a result, we were forced to rely on two national level measures of compensation from an oil and/or gas pipeline project: host country equity and oil and/or gas provision to the host country.

a. The set of projects with an insignificant role for the host country as an equity partner – Pipeline projects are typically owned by a consortium of equity partners. Projects that fail to offer the host country significant equity participation face heightened risks of local collective action for two reasons. First, local communities that face prospects of social and environmental disruption in the wake of a major project development may be angered by the fact that all of the financial benefits accrue to foreign investors. Second, lacking any real stake in the project, state officials are not likely to play the role of peacemaker should opposition to the project develop.

b. The set of projects with little provision of oil and/or gas to the host country – Another way that a host country can be compensated for the extraction of its resources is in kind, i.e., some or all of the oil and gas remains in the country, as opposed to being transported elsewhere. For this reason, we included this condition as another measure of compensation.

**Previous conflict**

Finally, we wanted to include a measure of prior movement activity in the host country. We created the set of projects in host countries with high levels of previous conflict from the Cross-National Time Series Data Archive's Weighted Conflict Index (Banks and Databanks International 2009). The index weights numbers of assassinations, strikes, guerrilla warfare, government crises, purges, riots, revolutions, and anti-government demonstrations in a given country in a given year. We interpret the condition as a simple reflection of the level of prior contention in the country. Where movement activity has been high in the past, it makes sense to expect conflict in the present.

*Summary of causal conditions*

Table 8.2 summarizes all of our causal conditions, their fuzzy set scoring, and whether the condition's presence or absence is expected to be an important determinant of conflict. Some causal conditions were constructed from larger datasets and then calibrated, as specified by Ragin in a recent article (2008a). This calibration allows the researcher to determine which values in the larger dataset correspond to his or her definition of the threshold for full membership (.95) and the threshold for full nonmembership (.05), as well as the value associated with "maximum ambiguity" as to whether it is in or out of the set (0.5). Once these values are determined, Ragin's calibration method assigns a fuzzy set score to the rest of the values in the larger dataset based on where they fall in relation to the selected values. This calibration method works well when larger datasets are available. However, for some of our causal conditions and both of our outcome conditions, such data were not available. As a result, we created our

Table 8.2 *Causal conditions*

| | Causal condition | Fuzzy set scoring | Presence/absence important for conflict? |
|---|---|---|---|
| Threats | Set of large projects (SIZE) | The length of the pipeline (in km) to be constructed in the host country was calibrated across all cases. | Presence |
| | Set of projects with a significant environmental impact (ENVFOOT) | 0 Pipeline largely follows existing pipeline route<br>0.4 Pipeline only impacts 2 of 5 criteria[a]<br>0.6 Pipeline impacts 3 or 4 of our 5 listed criteria<br>1 Pipeline impacts all 5 listed criteria | Presence |
| | Set of projects that impact indigenous peoples (INDPEOP) | 0 No indigenous peoples[b] have been identified along the pipeline route<br>1 Indigenous peoples have been identified along the pipeline route | Presence |
| Political opportunities | Set of projects with funding from Western sources (WESTFUND) | 0 None<br>0.25 Western bilateral (export credit agency) or commercial bank involvement only, in any capacity<br>0.75 Regional development bank (with or without Western bilateral), in any capacity<br>1 World Bank involvement | Presence |
| | Set of projects with little public consultation (CONSULT) | 0 Evidence of public consultation<br>1 No evidence of public consultation | Presence/Absence |
| | Set of projects located in democratic host country (DEM) | Polity IV data was calibrated across all available countries in the dataset by the average democracy score for the years 1996–2000. The fuzzy set score for an individual project is based on its host country's average democracy score in the dataset over the three years prior to the year of the project's financial closure. | Presence |

**Table 8.2** (cont.)

| | Causal condition | Fuzzy set scoring | Presence/absence important for conflict? |
|---|---|---|---|
| Resources | Set of projects in relatively developed host country (HDI) | The fuzzy set score for an individual project is based on its host country's closest Human Development Index (HDI) score available to the year of the project's financial closure. The fuzzy set was then recalibrated for the countries in our dataset. | Presence |
| | Set of projects in host country with many memberships in nongovernmental organizations (NGO) | World System Integration data was calibrated across all available countries in the dataset for the year 1998. The fuzzy set score for an individual project is based on its host country's score in the dataset in the year of the project's financial closure. | Presence |
| Compensation | Set of projects with an insignificant role for the host country as an equity partner[c] (HCEQUITY) | 0 >50% (i.e., controlling share)<br>0.1 Exactly 50%<br>0.4 20% <= equity < 50%<br>0.8 5% < equity < 20%<br>0.9 0% < equity <= 5% (i.e., token)<br>1 None | Presence |
| | Set of projects with little provision of oil and gas in the host country (OGPROV) | 0 Pipeline has been constructed to provide 100% of oil/ gas transported to host country<br>0.25 More than 50% of oil/gas transported through pipeline earmarked for use in host country<br>0.9 Promise of some small amount of oil/gas transported through pipeline to be sold in host country depending on market<br>1 None of the oil/gas transported through pipeline will be sold in host country | Presence |

| Previous conflict | Set of projects in host country with high levels of previous conflict (WCI) | Presence | The Weighted Conflict Index was calibrated across all available countries in the dataset for the average score across the years 1996–2000. The fuzzy set score for an individual project is based on an average score of its host country in the dataset over the three years prior to the year of the project's financial closure. |
|---|---|---|---|

[a] Criteria include river crossings, endangered species, park areas, previously inaccessible areas, and offshore portion. We realize that whether the pipeline is associated with a larger project that includes oil and gas extraction is also important for potential environmental impact. However, almost all cases that included an extractive component also score high on our environmental impact measure. Exceptions are Azerbaijan and Chad. The Caspian Sea near Azerbaijan had already experienced a significant amount of oil and gas development prior to the BTC project, while Chad scored 0.4 in terms of environmental impact which places it almost in the set of cases with significant environmental impact.

[b] As defined by the World Bank.

[c] Equity stake is included even if it is covered by a loan.

**Table 8.3** *Outcome conditions*

| Outcome condition | | Fuzzy set scoring |
|---|---|---|
| Projects that bring about political conflict (POLCONF) | 0 | No evidence |
| | 0.2 | Evidence of opposition groups |
| | 0.4 | Few peaceful strikes/rallies/demonstrations ($<5$) or damage to project as a result of a separate conflict |
| | 0.6 | Moderate number of peaceful strikes/rallies/demonstrations (5–14) and/or a few arrests, injuries ($<5$) |
| | 0.8 | Moderate number of strikes/rallies/demonstrations (5–14) with more arrests, injuries ($>5$) and damage to project or many peaceful strikes/rallies/demonstrations ($>15$) with significant attendance |
| | 1 | Deaths as a result of activities |
| Projects that bring about legal conflict (LEGCONF) | 0 | No evidence |
| | 0.25 | Petitions, labor disagreements (not involving strikes) |
| | 0.75 | Local permit denied, lender considers project but decides not to invest, official grievances filed with lenders or host country government that launches an official investigation |
| | 1 | National permit denied, lender pulls out of investment after commitment, injunction, lawsuit (national or international) |

own fuzzy set scoring scheme for these conditions, based on our knowledge of the cases.

## Outcome conditions

The outcome condition of interest is the level of opposition in each case. In measuring opposition we differentiate: *legal (institutionalized) conflict*, or that which occurs within the structures provided by the host country, project sponsor or lender for voicing concerns or opposition to a project, and *political (contentious) conflict*, or that which occurs outside of these extant structures. Table 8.3 provides information about the fuzzy set scoring of each of these outcome conditions.[6]

## Results

We present our results for the two outcome conditions: political and legal conflict. For each outcome, fs/QCA provides information about which causal conditions (or combinations of causal conditions) are necessary or sufficient to produce the outcome of interest. Necessary causal conditions are those that must be present but alone are not sufficient to produce the outcome of interest. In other words, fuzzy set scores of a necessary causal condition (X) are consistently greater than or equal to fuzzy set scores of the outcome condition (Y) for most cases, or $X_i \geq Y_i$.[7] Sufficient causal conditions (or combinations of causal conditions) are those that are sufficient but not necessary (because of multiple causal pathways) to produce the outcome of interest. In other words, fuzzy set scores of a sufficient causal condition (X) are consistently less than or equal to fuzzy set scores of the outcome condition (Y) for most cases, or $X_i \leq Y_i$.

In addition, fs/QCA provides information about the *consistency* and *coverage* of both individual causal recipes and the combination of causal recipes produced in an analysis. Consistency, the more important calculation, measures the degree to which one condition is a subset of the other. A consistency score of greater than 0.8 for sufficient conditions (or causal combinations) and 0.9 for necessary conditions are commonly used as guidelines by scholars of fs/QCA to establish the relevant set-theoretic relationship between the causal and outcome conditions (Ragin 2008b). Once this relationship is established, coverage becomes important. Coverage assesses relevance. For example, if X is determined to be a consistent subset of Y (or a sufficient condition of Y), then its coverage score reveals how important the combination of conditions represented in X is in accounting for Y.

## *Political conflict*[8]

Our analysis showed that the following conditions were generally necessary for political conflict in oil and gas pipeline projects:

- little provision of oil and/or gas to the host country (0.97);
- an insignificant role for the host country as an equity partner (0.90); and
- a significant amount of public consultation (0.93).

Thus, each of these conditions is relevant to the sufficiency recipes provided below and is generally shared by instances of the outcome. Consistency scores for these supersets are provided in Figure 8.1. Both the level of oil and/or gas provision to the host country and the role of the host country as an equity partner are *compensation* conditions and occur in the anticipated direction, i.e., little compensation is associated with conflict. Consultation, an *opportunity* condition, acts as expected as a precursor to conflict.

Our analysis finds four different causal pathways sufficient for political conflict. Figure 8.1 provides a mathematical and graphical representation of these causal recipes.[9] The *consistency* of this set of sufficient causal recipes in producing political conflict is 0.88 – meaning that cases with these causal configurations are 88 percent consistent in exhibiting political conflict. The *coverage* is 0.65 – meaning that 65 percent of the sum of the membership scores in the outcome can be explained using these causal recipes. All four pathways required a combination of some environmental impact and Western funding. With these conditions met, the paths split by projects located in more or less developed and democratic host countries. Projects in more developed and more democratic host countries, like Georgia and Turkey, experienced political conflict despite low levels of prior conflict. Or, like Russia and Peru, these projects in more developed and more democratic host countries were moderately large in size and impacted indigenous peoples. For projects located in less developed and less democratic host countries, political conflict was associated with either little connection to the NGO community, as in Chad, or a moderately large project with impact on indigenous peoples, as in Cameroon.

The project in Azerbaijan does not fit into any of these four causal pathways, yet it experienced political conflict. There are several possible explanations as to why Azerbaijan does not fit into one of the recipes but still experienced conflict. First, according to our informants, the conflict in Azerbaijan was primarily local and related to construction impacts and worker relations. In most of our other cases, political conflict was more global in scope and aided by international NGOs. Perhaps our causal conditions are more related to this latter type of political conflict than that which occurred in Azerbaijan. There is another possibility. The pipeline in Azerbaijan was just part of a larger BTC project that drew much critical attention, especially in

Sufficient causal recipes (mathematically):

~LOW_ENVFOOT*WESTFUND*HDI*DEM*~WCI +

~LOW_ENVFOOT*WESTFUND*HDI*DEM*~LOW_SIZE*INDPEOP +

~LOW_ENVFOOT*WESTFUND*~HDI*~DEM*LOW_NGO +

~LOW_ENVFOOT*WESTFUND*~HDI*~DEM*~LOW_SIZE*INDPEOP

Sufficient causal recipes (graphically):

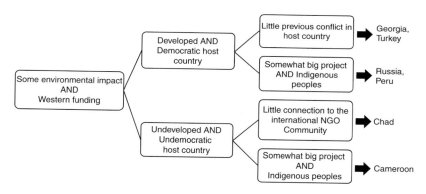

Solution coverage: 0.65

Solution consistency: 0.88

Azerbaijan not explained by these recipes.

**Figure 8.1** Causal recipes for political conflict

Europe. It may well be that the causal dynamics of this case reflect the broader project and not the specific segment in Azerbaijan.

## Legal conflict

Our analysis showed that the following conditions were usually necessary for legal conflict in oil and gas pipeline projects:

• little provision of oil and/or gas to the host country (0.90);

- Western funding (0.88); and
- a significant amount of public consultation (1.00).

Thus, each of these conditions is relevant to the sufficiency recipe provided below and is generally shared by instances of the outcome. Consistency scores for these supersets are provided in Figure 8.2. Like political conflict, we find a combination of *compensation* and *political opportunity* conditions as almost always necessary for legal conflict in oil and gas pipeline projects.

Our analysis finds one causal pathway sufficient for legal conflict: the combination of some environmental impact *and* the provision of almost no equity to the host country. Thus, the sufficiency recipe for legal conflict is a combination of *threat* and *compensation* conditions. Figure 8.2 provides a mathematical representation of this causal recipe. The *consistency* of this sufficient causal recipe in producing political conflict is 0.92 – meaning that cases with this causal configuration are 92 percent consistent in exhibiting legal conflict. Its *coverage* is 0.58 – meaning that 58 percent of the sum of the membership scores in the outcome can be explained by this causal recipe. Quintessential examples of this recipe are Peru (Camisea) and Russia (Sakhalin-II). Both projects scored high on all three necessary conditions, generated a moderate level of environmental impact, and, at least initially, provided no equity to the host country.

The projects in Azerbaijan, Nigeria, and China are not well explained by this causal recipe. As discussed above, Azerbaijan was part of the larger BTC pipeline, which drew a lot of attention from Europe. And, although it received a high ranking in terms of legal conflict on our scale because of the activities of some international NGOs and activists from Georgia, no formal complaints were submitted from Azerbaijan as part of the International Finance Corporation's Compliance Advisor Ombudsman Office. Moreover, the BTC project in Azerbaijan was quite similar to the West African Gas Pipeline Project in Nigeria. Both projects were high profile projects, funded by the World Bank, and spanning multiple countries. In addition, when compared with other projects that generated legal conflict, neither the pipeline in Azerbaijan nor Nigeria had a particularly significant environmental impact. In fact, the West African Gas Pipeline was touted for its environmental benefits because it would limit

Sufficient causal recipes (mathematically):

~LOW_ENVFOOT*HIGH_HCEQUITY

Sufficient causal recipes (graphically):

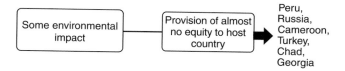

Solution coverage: 0.58

Solution consistency: 0.92

Azerbaijan, Nigeria, China not explained by this recipe.

**Figure 8.2** Causal recipes for legal conflict

the flaring of natural gas that had been associated with oil production in Nigeria. In addition, both offered some compensation to the host country in the form of a 25 percent equity stake to the state-owned oil company.

Similarly, the West–East China pipeline was fully owned and developed by a Chinese company to produce oil and gas that would be used within China. According to newspaper reports, legal conflict in the West–East China pipeline was driven mainly by disagreements on the rate of return required for investment by foreign companies, as well as pressure by Tibetan activists at the shareholder meetings of potential foreign investors. This legal conflict is substantially different in nature from that experienced by other projects, where legal conflict was more directly related to project impacts on the environment and the surrounding population. China and Nigeria are also the only two cases in our study that experienced legal conflict without political conflict. The fact that a host country company had at least some stake in these projects may have increased their legitimacy in the eyes of both the locally affected population and international

NGOs. Thus, opponents may have felt that complaints against the project could be resolved within existing institutions, as opposed to outside of them.

## Discussion and conclusion

In closing, we want to highlight what we see as the four most interesting theoretical implications of our findings. The first is really a nonfinding. That is, we were surprised that the general level of prior social movement activity in the country contributed little to the causal recipes that explained most cases. Perhaps the reactive form of opposition we are studying is different from the generally proactive types of collective action that comprise the Cross-National Time Series Data Archive's Weighted Conflict Index data set. This finding is consistent with the conclusions of Walsh, Warland, and Smith (1997). They argue that "technology movements" – movements characterized by the "quick response" of "local residents" to a "perceived environmental threat" – are fundamentally different from "equity movements" – movements characterized by "gradual mobilization around long-standing grievances among members of a culturally identifiable collectivity."

We were also surprised by the relatively marginal contribution made by our two resource measures to the various causal recipes. In terms of external resources, ties to NGOs did figure in the mix of factors that explained particular cases (e.g., Chad) but not in the hypothesized direction. In general, this causal condition was absent from most of our recipes. It could be that our measure of NGO presence is too broad to pick up any role of external allies in these cases or that these alliances form as a reactive response to a specific proposal, but for now we are left to conclude that other factors matter more to the mobilization of contention around infrastructure projects. In terms of internal resources, the level of the host country's development only figures marginally into our recipes for political conflict. Pending further research, these findings prompt us to conclude that for this type of reactive mobilization, determined individuals and groups seem to be able to find a way to express opposition to oil and gas pipeline projects without significant external or internal resources.

Third, our results imply that project-specific characteristics (e.g., project size, impact, funding structure, compensation mechanisms) are more important in determining conflict than contextual factors specific to the host country (e.g., development, democracy, NGO connections). It is possible that our contextual conditions, measured as they are at the national level, are simply too broad to capture the localized nature of these conflicts. If, however, the lack of contextual effects is real, it would be good news for project sponsors and proponents, suggesting that the responses to such proposals are not context-specific but result from more easily manipulated aspects of the project.

The strongest and most theoretically compelling set of findings, however, involves our *threat* and *opportunity* conditions. *Threat* figures into our account of conflict mainly as a sufficient condition, i.e., it serves as the spark that ignites conflict. Thus, at a very general level, all of the conflicts we observe can be seen as responses to some kind of threat posed by the project. But what can we say about the causal importance of the different threat conditions? Perhaps reflecting the contemporary global salience of environmental and human rights issues, one or more of our *threat* conditions appeared in most of our causal recipes. It is also worth noting that the objective level of threat associated with these conditions did not have to be particularly high to figure in the recipes.

But as central as *threat* is to the analysis, we are struck nonetheless by just how much the expression of this shared sense of threat is mediated by *opportunity*. In essence, no matter what the level of threat, it is difficult for opponents to mobilize if not given an opportunity to do so. Indeed "Western funding" and "consultation" figure more prominently in the causal recipes than any other causal conditions in the study. Consultation emerged as a necessary condition in both recipes for conflict, while Western funding achieved this same status for legal conflict. A point we made above regarding the especially prominent role of consultation in our results bears repeating. While the facility-siting literature embraces public consultation as a way to reduce or eliminate conflict, our results support a very different view of the phenomenon. Whatever its normative virtues, in the real world consultation grants opponents entrée to the project, thereby encouraging mobilization. Indeed, one could argue that the mediating factor of opportunity is missing in the multitude of projects now being built in Africa by Chinese contractors. These deals, generally made between heads of authoritarian states and with no Western funding or provision for consultation, effectively fore-close any meaningful opportunity for local groups or Western NGOs to mobilize.

We close with one final observation regarding threat and opportun-ity. Social movement scholars have tended to represent *threat* and *opportunity* as "either/or" features of contention, as if movements were catalyzed by one or the other. Theoretically, we have long been skeptical of this view (McAdam 1996), but here we are afforded empirical support for the skepticism. We are struck, instead, by just how consistently *threat* and *opportunity* appear to work jointly to shape opposition to these projects. Perceived *threats* may be sufficient for opposition to arise, but it is the *opportunities* afforded opponents by consultation and/or Western funding that appear to be necessary for high levels of conflict to eventuate.

Finally, we offer two methodological notes, the first programmatic, the second cautionary. The programmatic note is straightforward. We undertook this research in an exploratory fashion. While persuaded in the abstract by the argument underlying Ragin's comparative case method, we were novices at the technique and somewhat skeptical about the open-ended nature of the process by which the researcher conceives and assigns values to their fuzzy set conditions. We are novices no more and convinced that the approach does, indeed, offer researchers a valuable alternative to the well-known limits of both the case study and "large *N*" analysis.

That brings us to the caution. For all the virtues of the comparative case approach – virtues which we hope our results have served to underscore – the limits should be apparent as well. We note only one. It is incompatible with recent calls, by scholars of contention (Campbell 2005; Hedstrom and Swedberg 1998; Mayntz 2004; McAdam, Tarrow, and Tilly 2001; Tilly 2001), for more attention to the dynamic *mechanisms* that actually account for the causal force of static variables. As deployed here, the comparative case method leaves the actual mechanisms of contention unexplored. We cannot, for instance, say what processes actually account for the apparently strong relationship between legal and political conflict. Did project opponents turn to political conflict only after becoming frustrated with legal avenues of redress? Or was the issue turned over to the courts following an initial period of political contention? We can't say, any more than we can tell, from our results, exactly how threat and opportunity appear to work in combination to shape opposition to pipeline projects. For that one would need to invest in other methods, ones more attuned to the actual mechanisms of struggle (McAdam, Tarrow, and Tilly 2008).

## Endnotes

1 Reprinted from *Sociological Forum* (2010). Reproduced by permission of the Eastern Sociological Society. We owe the clever phrase, "site fights," to Daniel P. Aldrich, who recently published a book entitled *Site Fights: Divisive Facilities and Civil Society in Japan and the West* (2008, Cornell University Press).

No piece of published scholarship ever depends on the authors alone, but in this case, our debt to others is much greater than normal. This paper is only a small part of a much larger, ongoing project that has drawn on the labors of a large number of faculty and graduate students at Stanford University. Our first and largest debt of gratitude goes to all the graduate students (and a few courageous undergraduates) who have participated in the project. These include: Henry Chan, Cheryl Chi, Mo Peng, Andrew Peterman, Linh Pham, Amanda Sharkey, Meg Waltner and Amy Javernick-Will. But no graduate student deserves more thanks for their help on the project than Dilanka Clinthana "D.C." Jayasundera. Not only has D.C. been involved in the project from the outset, but he has also served as one of two principal coders and data analysts on this particular piece of research. Stanford was the source, not only for faculty and graduate student collaborators, but for critical funding support as well. Without a seed grant from the Freeman Spogli Institute for International Studies, we would never have been able to undertake the research in the first place. In collecting data on our 16 cases, we benefited enormously from information given to us by informants affiliated with a number of NGOs and lenders with personal knowledge of the projects we were seeking to understand. We also owe a great deal to the late Richard Burt, who advised on the project up until his untimely death in 2007. From Rick, we learned a great deal about the dynamics of infrastructure projects from the firm point of view. Finally, we cannot say enough about the help, advice, and patient counsel we received from Charles Ragin as we sought to employ his comparative case method as the analytic basis for our research.

2 Anthropologists have, however, covered this subject, looking extensively
at the effects of neoliberal development policy and displacement of locally
affected populations (Conway 2004; Fox and Starn 1997; Kirsch 2007;
Shultz et al. 2009).

3 The "world society" perspective also emphasizes external resources –
normative as well as organizational – in accounting for increasing movement activity by environmentalists, feminists and human rights activists
in the contemporary world (Brysk 2000; Frank, Hironaka, and Schofer
2000; Keck and Sikkink 1998; Paxton, Hughes, and Green 2006; Tsutsui
2004). The argument is straightforward. As women's rights, environmentalism, and human rights have attained normative "standing" in the
international community, we should expect to see "local" activism
around these issues in those countries that are most integrated into the
world system.

4 See/www.simdex.com/future_pipeline_projects/index.htm for more information.

5 World Bank involvement includes funding from any of the members of
the World Bank Group or its affiliates: International Bank for Reconstruction and Development (IBRD), International Development Assistance (IDA), International Finance Corporation (IFC), Multilateral
Investment Guarantee Agency (MIGA).

6 Data on each case was collected using information available from a
variety of sources, including academic literature, official project websites,
opposition websites, and newspaper accounts. In addition to this Stan-
ford-based data collection, a legal librarian from Akin Gump Strauss
Hauer & Feld LLP also completed a desktop study of all cases, helping
us to differentiate levels of legal and political conflict. Information was
limited for some cases; however, cost considerations prohibited travel to
each project location to collect additional data. We also felt that library
and archival research was most appropriate at this exploratory stage of
the project. In the future, we hope to conduct several in-depth field
studies on location as an extension of this first phase of the study. To
check the validity of our findings from the desktop study and to further
delineate levels of conflict, we also electronically surveyed individuals in
lender organizations and nongovernmental organizations (NGOs) who
were familiar with each project. Most of the survey questions were related
to outcome conditions; however, respondents from the lenders also
reviewed a brief summary of our findings for the causal conditions. In
all, 17 surveys (9 with lenders; 8 with NGOs) were conducted, covering 9
of our 16 cases.

7 This relation implies that the causal condition is a superset of the outcome. Similar to statistical analysis, it is important to remember that this

mathematical relationship does not imply necessity without concrete causal evidence from our individual, real-world cases. Absent this concrete linkage, such a condition could simply be an attribute that is shared by instances of the outcome, and may not be causal. The condition could be constitutive – essential in some definitional way to the outcome – or merely descriptive – something that the cases displaying the outcome just happen to share.

8 We find an interesting association between our two outcome conditions. None of our cases have political conflict without legal conflict. This finding could indicate either that opposition groups tend toward legal avenues first and resort to political avenues only when legal channels fail or are not available *or* that political conflict motivates later legal efforts to adjudicate the conflict. Additional case study work would be required to tease out the mechanisms behind this relationship.

9 In this and subsequent fs/QCA results, the notation is as follows: shorthand representations of the causal and outcome conditions correspond to those provided in Tables 8.2 and 8.4. "LOW_" or "HIGH_" in front of a causal condition corresponds to a recoding of the causal condition for a sensitivity analysis. For example, LOW_ENVFOOT is the set of cases with a low environmental impact when compared with our original conception of the set of projects with environmental impact (ENVFOOT). The "~" symbol is used to indicate negation or "not." Multiplication (*) signals combined conditions (set intersection); addition (+) signals alternate combinations of conditions (set union).

# 9 To talk or to fight? Effects of strategic, cultural, and institutional factors on renegotiation approaches in public–private concessions

HENRY CHAN AND RAYMOND E. LEVITT

## Introduction

### Public–private partnership overview

Many developing and developed countries around the world face the challenge of meeting their growing infrastructure needs with limited fiscal resources. It is estimated that worldwide population will increase by approximately one billion between 2005 and 2015 (Sachs 2005). Large-scale development and maintenance of infrastructure will be needed to accommodate the basic needs of these new inhabitants, as well as those of the existing population. However, many developing countries receive less financial support from the World Bank in recent years than they did during the 1960s and 1970s for infrastructure development as a result of the multilateral agencies' shift in focus from infrastructure development to social program development during the 1980s (Harris 2003). At the same time, developed nations such as the United States have found it difficult to raise taxes to maintain their existing infrastructure systems, especially amid the economic crisis of the recent 2000s. Years of delayed or cancelled infrastructure maintenance projects led the American Society of Civil Engineers (ASCE) to give a grade "D" to America's existing infrastructure in 2009 (ASCE 2009). It is estimated that $2.2 trillion of investment will be needed for the next 5 years to fix America's infrastructure (ASCE 2009).

In response to these challenges, some governments have invited private investors to participate in infrastructure development through schemes such as Public–Private Partnership (PPPs), Private Finance Initiative (PFI), and Build–Operate–Transfer (BOT) (Clarke 2000;

Gerrard 2001; Lonsdale 2005). Readers interested in an introduction to public–private development can consult Miller (2000), which discusses in detail the differences among various public–private development models and their applications to infrastructure delivery (see also, Chapter 11). For simplicity, different schemes of public–private collaboration will be generally referred to as PPP in this section.

Typically in a PPP project, the host government invites a private investor to finance the construction cost of an infrastructure project such as a road, power plant, or sewer system that has been traditionally financed by the government through sales of bonds or from current funds. In return, investors are granted a period of time, called the "concession period" that typically runs for 15 to 30 years, to operate and collect revenue from the government and/or end users to recoup their investment. The long concession periods, political sensitivity, and technical challenges of PPP projects create a high level of uncertainty over a long period of time for all stakeholders involved.

## High renegotiation rate in PPP projects

Although PPP may provide a means for governments with limited fiscal resources to bring bridges and electricity to citizens, private participation in infrastructure development presents numerous governance challenges. International infrastructure developments often experience renegotiations during the concession period, adding uncertainties to both governments and investors. A study by the World Bank found that 40 percent of Latin American infrastructure concessions during the 1990s were renegotiated at some point (Guasch and Straub 2006). Another report on energy concessions in developing countries found that 21 of the 34 cases studied (62 percent) underwent either mutual or unilateral renegotiations (Woodhouse 2006). Harris (2003) warns that renegotiation concerns and other political risks could lead to lower levels of private investment in infrastructure. A better understanding of PPP renegotiations enables private investors and governments to better manage PPP projects, and thus deserves the attention of both researchers and practitioners.

## Studies of PPP renegotiations

The development of infrastructure and the renegotiation of concession agreements have attracted academic interest from multiple disciplines, including economics, management, and law. Scholars from these disciplines have offered different explanations for the high renegotiation rate in infrastructure concessions, including incomplete contracts (Hart and Moore 1999), the "obsolescing bargain" (Ramamurti and Doh 2004; Vernon 1971), and opportunistic bidding (Ho and Liu 2004).

In his study of independent power projects (IPPs), Woodhouse (2006) suggests that risks associated with infrastructure concessions can be managed by two different approaches: (1) *risk engineering* – identifying and allocating risks in order to minimize their potential detrimental effects; and (2) *strategic management* – anticipating key vulnerabilities and actively managing them during the course of a long-lived asset. He further concludes that risk engineering is insufficient by itself to effectively manage infrastructure projects. Strategic management, though the term is "somewhat amorphous, has often been a more important determinant of outcomes for IPPs." (Woodhouse 2006: 172). That view is shared by Miller and Olleros, who use the phrase *project shaping* to refer to the investors' continued, flexible effort to guide a project to viability along the entire development process (Miller and Olleros 2000). As they cogently put it:

. . . successful projects are not selected but shaped. Rather than evaluating projects at the outset based on projections of the full sets of benefits and costs over their lifetime, successful sponsors start with project ideas that have the possibility of becoming viable. They then embark on shaping efforts that are most likely to unleash this value during a long front-end process. (Miller and Olleros 2000: 93)

While many scholars have conducted studies identifying renegotiation risk factors, relatively few have written on the renegotiation process itself. In other words, existing literature tends to focus on risk engineering and underemphasize strategic management (Woodhouse 2006). The study described in this chapter is one that adopts the strategic management perspective. Specifically, it aims to help practitioners to better manage the renegotiation process by providing new insights to our understanding of PPP renegotiations.

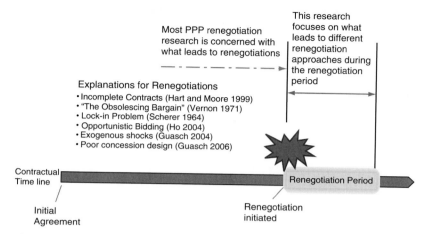

Figure 9.1 Positioning of current research with respect to the existing literature

## Research design and methods

### Research focus

This study has the goal of deepening our understanding of the PPP renegotiation process. In order to achieve this objective, it moves beyond analysis of renegotiation causes and instead focuses on the renegotiation process that follows (Figure 9.1). Specifically, it focuses on the investor's choice between legal actions and relational bargaining as a response to government-initiated renegotiations. Government-initiated renegotiation is defined in this study as a dispute between the host government and the investor over the potentially detrimental effects to the viability of an active concession agreement due to government actions. For instance, if a new government enters office and wants to challenge the investor's right to increase tolls at a rate specified in the original contract, it is considered a government-initiated renegotiation, even if the terms of the contract may not undergo official modifications.

### Research questions

Confronted with government-initiated renegotiations, investors generally can choose to respond with legal actions – seeking arbitration or litigation, or they can give up the right to seek legal actions and choose to renegotiate a new agreement. A natural question that arises out of this observation is "What motivates investors to choose one approach over another?" Previous studies on renegotiations have generally adopted a rational, calculating, economic perspective in their analyses. Albeit important, strategic reasons are only one of the kinds of factors actors consider as they make decisions. Cultural and institutional effects can also come into play as investors weigh different options. The objective of this study is to investigate how strategic factors, cultural dimensions, and institutional environments collectively and interactively affect investors' choice between legal and relational responses to government-initiated renegotiations. This raises the following research questions:

- Which factors contribute to leading investors to choose the relational bargaining approach over legal actions in government-initiated renegotiations?
- What combinations of strategic, cultural, and institutional factors affect investors' preference for arbitration or renegotiation bargaining?
- Is there one factor that can dominate the effect of others and be sufficient by itself to predict investor's renegotiation approach?

The remaining topics in this section are devoted to the design of the research study set up to answer the above research questions.

## Research design

In order to answer the research questions raised, propositions relating to investors' renegotiation approaches (dependent variable) to their strategic, cultural, and institutional attributes (independent variables) are presented.[1] The conceptual model of the analysis is illustrated by Figure 9.2, which also shows each of the independent variables and its proposed effect on the renegotiation approach. The independent and dependent variables are discussed in detail below.

### Dependent variable: renegotiation approach

An important part of the renegotiation process is the negotiation approach taken by the stakeholders. In a strategic alliance,

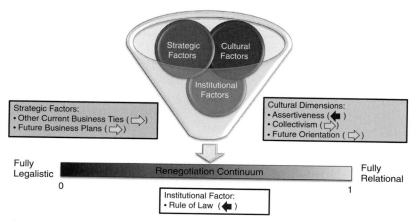

**Figure 9.2** Conceptual model of analysis

partnering companies can choose between two approaches – the structural/legal approach vs. the relational approach – as the basis of governance for the collaboration (Faems et al. 2008). The structural/legal approach emphasizes the enforcement of the legally binding contract; whereas the relational approach focuses on the ongoing relationship with the business partner and "emphasizes the importance of trust for safeguarding and coordinating alliances." (Faems et al. 2008: 1053). In the context of PPP projects, these two approaches have been associated with arbitration and relational renegotiation (Wells and Ahmed 2006). Investors who want to challenge a host government's renegotiation request (or actions that lead to a dispute) legally often choose to file a claim to initiate the arbitration or litigation process; whereas those who want to resolve differences relationally often set aside the right to legal actions and opt instead for renegotiation bargaining. It is important to note that the line between the two approaches is often not clear in practice, and they can be used in tandem as a deliberate strategy. For instance, an investor who prefers relational renegotiation may file a claim to fulfill its legal responsibility and use arbitration as a fallback plan should the negotiation break down. Edkins and Smyth (2006) developed a relational-legal continuum (Figure 9.3) to illustrate that the two approaches vary by degree, rather than differ by type.

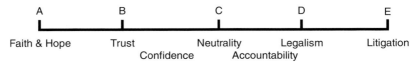

**Figure 9.3** Relational-legal contract performance continuum (Edkins and Smyth 2006)

## Independent variables
### Strategic factors

Many of the strategic motivations for an investor's renegotiation approach fall under the influence of what Heide and Miner (1992) refer to as the "shadow of the future." As game theorists would put it, in a repeated game a player's current strategy is affected by the future consequences due to today's action. Thus, investors who hope to maximize long-term gain may take actions that do not necessarily maximize immediate reward but are expected to lead to cumulatively more favorable scenarios in the future.

Based on their involvement as consultants in several concession renegotiations, Wells and Ahmed (2006) observed that investors are much more willing to renegotiate relationally when they either have other current business ties in the host country, or when they want to continue doing business with the host government in the future. Legal actions such as arbitration often damage business relationships and thus investors who have ongoing or future business presence in the host country will tend to favor renegotiation over legal means of dispute resolution. Although this argument is consistent with game theory, the extent of their observation was limited to a handful of cases in one country (Indonesia). In our research, Wells and Ahmed's suggested causal relationship between level of current/future business ties in the host country and preferred renegotiation approach is tested in a broader sample. The following two propositions are presented:

> *Proposition 1: The higher the level of current investment an investor has in the host country besides the project in dispute, the more likely it will employ a relational renegotiation approach.*
>
> *Proposition 2: The higher the level of future business activities an investor has in the host country beyond the project in dispute, the more likely it will employ a relational renegotiation approach.*

## Cultural dimensions

In addition to his observations on how business ties to the host country may influence an investor's renegotiation approach, Wells also mentions that Japanese investors tend to engage in renegotiation bargaining and attempt to reach compromise when confronted with renegotiation requests initiated by the Indonesian government, whereas Americans tend to seek remedies to renegotiation disputes through legal means. While his comment marks an important awareness of the potential impact culture has on the renegotiation process, it shares a common shortcoming with many early applied psychology studies of intercultural negotiations: namely it uses "geographical location as a surrogate for culture, and consequently, it is often not possible to specify the aspects of culture that account for observed differences" (Gelfand and Dyer 2000: 63).

One way to conceptualize cultural differences beyond labeling them as "Japanese" or "American" is the dimensional approach. Markus and Hamedani (2007) explain that the concept behind the dimensional approach is that:

> Cultural differences may reflect underlying basic value orientations, beliefs, and worldviews prevalent in a context; however, these differences can be best and most parsimoniously captured by identifying and describing cultures according to where they fall along a series of dimensions (Markus and Hamedani 2007: 14)

Research by Hofstede (1984, 1991), Schwartz (1992, 1994, 1999), Inglehart (1997), Inglehart et al. (1998), and Inglehart and Welzel (2005), and the GLOBE project group (House et al. 2004) helped operationalize the abstract idea of culture into different cultural dimensions. A detailed comparison of the four research projects is beyond the scope of this chapter and readers can consult Terlutter, Diehl, and Mueller (2006) for a comprehensive review. For this study, the GLOBE study cultural dimension values are used to represent the cultural attributes of the investor. The decision to use the GLOBE study values over the widely used Hofstede dimensions is based on a number of considerations.

First, the GLOBE study clearly distinguishes between cultural values (desired behaviors) and practices (frequently observed behaviors). The two are often different, or even in conflict, as demonstrated by Den Hartog's finding of slightly negative correlation between societal values and societal practices for the cultural dimension of assertiveness (Den Hartog 2004; Terlutter, Diehl, and Mueller 2006). In other words, the GLOBE study pointed out the fact that members of a society do not generally engage in assertive behaviors (practice) but admire the assertive quality (value). The fact that Hofstede's studies make no such distinction presents a major limitation of his research findings (Terlutter, Diehl, and Mueller 2006). Another advantage of the GLOBE study is that the results are based on a survey of 17,300 middle managers in 951 organizations conducted after 1994 from three industries: financial services, food processing, and telecommunications. Hofstede's data collection took place between 1968 and 1972 and involved IT workers in only one firm (IBM). The more current data from a broader spectrum of businesses, when compared to Hofstede's study, makes the GLOBE scores a timelier and more comprehensive tool to study national cultural differences (Terlutter, Diehl, and Mueller 2006).

The nine cultural dimensions from the GLOBE study are:

1. *assertiveness*, the degree to which members in societies are confrontational and straightforward;
2. *uncertainty avoidance*, the degree to which individuals rely on established social norms and practices to avoid uncertainty;
3. *power distance*, the degree to which members accept and expect power to be distributed unevenly;
4. *collectivism I* (institutionalism), the degree to which collective distribution of resources and collective action is upheld;
5. *collectivism II* (in-group collectivism), the extent to which individuals express loyalty and cohesiveness to their in-groups, organizations, or families;
6. *gender egalitarianism*, the degree to which gender role differences are de-emphasized in a society;
7. *future orientation*, the degree to which individuals engage in future-oriented activities such as planning, investing in the future, and delaying gratification;
8. *performance orientation*, the degree to which society rewards group members for performance improvement or excellence;
9. *humane orientation*, the degree to which individuals are rewarded for being fair, altruistic, generous, and kind to others.

In this research, the national culture of the lead investor in a project is used as the independent variable based on culture. As such, one of the case selection criteria is that the case project needed to have a lead sponsor that has significantly more equity ownership than all other investor partners. The lead sponsor of each project is assumed to have the greatest influence over the major decisions pertaining to the project. This assumption was cross-checked during the review of the project renegotiation history as recorded by various sources. The identification of a clear lead investor also makes it possible to assign the cultural attribute to the lead investor based on the cultural dimension score of the lead investor's country of origin.

Although the GLOBE study captures cultural values and practices at a societal level instead of an individual level, individuals share values and adopt practices through interactions with other members of their society. Thus, average or typical values and practices of a society are reasonable proxies for the values and practices of its individual members (Terlutter, Diehl, and Mueller 2006). Since this research involves observing and coding investor renegotiation *behaviors*, the GLOBE study's *cultural practice* scores, as opposed to the *cultural value* scores, are used as the inputs for the investor's cultural dimensions. The GLOBE cultural dimensions believed to relate to the investor's preferred renegotiation approach are discussed below, followed by corresponding propositions.

Assertiveness
Members of a society with a high degree of *assertiveness* tend to be confrontational and straightforward (House et al. 2004). They are encouraged by the society to be tough and competitive (Javidan et al. 2006). People high in assertiveness often use inflexible tactics to force concessions from the other side; they are also found to employ more competitive strategies in simulated buyer–seller negotiations (Ma and Jaeger 2005). In Japan, where the GLOBE assertiveness cultural score is low, the lawyer-to-population ratio is low (Kawashima 2001), reflecting the "embed[ded] cultural preference for harmonious reconciliation and disapproval of the assertiveness and contentiousness that are associated with litigation" (Galanter 1983: 30). Since relational renegotiations require cooperative discussions and often lead to compromises, assertive members are expected to

prefer going straight to their legal remedies to resolve disputes in concession agreements.

> *Proposition 3: A higher assertiveness score of the lead investor will lead to a more legalistic renegotiation approach.*

Collectivism

Members of a society with a high level of *collectivism-I* expect collective distribution of resources and uphold collective actions (House et al. 2004). Members of individualistic cultures uphold individual rights while those of collectivistic cultures are more concerned with preserving relationships (Markus and Lin 1998). Thus, members from individualist cultures are more likely to attempt to resolve conflicts through competition and problem solving; whereas those from collectivist cultures tend to handle conflicts without direct confrontation in order to preserve the relationship (Leung 1998). These investors' preferences of conflict resolution approaches can be expected to be similar over concession renegotiation strategies.

In many cases, unforeseen events trigger the need to adjust an ongoing agreement and test the willingness of stakeholders to redistribute the benefits. For example, during the current global economic crisis that began in the late 2000s, the demand for many natural resources and types of infrastructure has declined significantly. At the same time, the financing costs of many loans have greatly increased. These new conditions often require major adjustments to the original contracts of ongoing projects from both the government and investors to keep the deal viable. Facing the new economic conditions, individualistic investors are expected to be more likely to be concerned with protecting their rights and ensuring that their profit margins remain intact, through legal means if necessary. On the other hand, since group goals and interests are considered more important than individual goals and interests in collective societies (Javidan et al. 2006), investors with a high level of *collectivism-I* are expected to be more likely to engage in relational renegotiations to keep the project going forward and preserve the business relationship.

> *Proposition 4: A higher collectivism-I score of the lead investor will lead to a more relational renegotiation approach.*

Future orientation

Members of a society with a high degree of *future orientation* have a higher capacity to take on delayed gratification and are more willing to invest for the future (House et al. 2004). Negotiators with a long-term orientation favor integrative negotiating strategies as opposed to competitive strategies (Usunier 2003). Since legal actions such as arbitration and litigation often lead to damaged relationships and hinder future collaborations (Wells and Ahmed 2006), it is expected that investors high on future orientation will be more willing to avoid resolving matters through legal means if possible, in order to preserve the business relationship for potential future collaborations.

Proposition 5: *A higher future orientation score of the lead investor will lead to a more relational renegotiation approach.*

*Institutional effects*

One of the institutional measures that has been found relevant to renegotiations of infrastructure concession agreement is the *rule of law* of the host country. Using indices from Political Risk Service and International Country Risk Guide as proxies for the rule of law of a host country, Guasch et al. (2006) and Guasch and Straub (2006) found that rule of law is negatively correlated with the occurrence of renegotiation in Latin American concessions. In other words, the stronger the rule of law a host country has, the less likely a project would be renegotiated and cause modifications to the original contract. To extend on the study by Guash and colleagues, this research project investigates how rule of law may affect the renegotiation process – i.e., the investor's renegotiation approach – once the dispute takes place.

It is reasonable to expect that weak rule of law undermines the investor's confidence in getting a fair trial once legal action is sought. If an investor is not protected by strong rule of law, either from the host country's strong judicial system or through a predetermined arbitration procedure in a country with strong rule of law, he/she may have no choice but to renegotiate if a dispute arises.

Proposition 7: *Weak rule of law will lead to a more relational renegotiation approach.*

A recent attempt to codify the many facets of rule of law was carried out by the scholars from the World Justice Project (Agrast et al. 2009), who presented their rule of law index in the World Justice Forum in November of 2009. Consisting of 16 factors and 68 subfactors under four principles (Table 9.1), this rule of law index offers a comprehensive measure of a country's rule of law – from checks and balances within the government to protection of personal security.

The World Justice Project report separates the scores for each of the 16 factors as well as the 68 subfactors, allowing for the utilization of their findings for specific (sub)factors that are of interest to the researcher. Three of the 16 factors are particularly relevant to this study:

- 9.0 – Laws protecting security of property
- 11.0 – Fair and efficient administration
- 15.0 – Fair and efficient alternative dispute resolution

When a contract does not have any predetermined Alternative Dispute Resolution (ADR) clause, which would allow the investor to bypass the court system and seek ADR methods such as arbitration to settle the dispute, the investor will have to rely on the host country's judicial system as the primary means to resolve the difference between the host government and investors. Whether the investor can get a fair trial depends on the sophistication and independence of the country's judicial system. Two factors of the World Justice Project are particularly relevant to PPP cases that would be litigated under the host country's judicial system – Factor 9 deals with the judicial system upholding and protecting the property and right of private investors; whereas Factor 11 measures the degree to which the court system in the host country can effectively and independently administer their judicial duties.

Factor 9:

9.  The laws protect the security of property and the rights to engage in private economic activity.
9.1. The laws protect the right to hold, transfer, lease or license property (including real property, personal and intellectual property).
9.2. The laws prohibit arbitary deprivations of property, including the taking of property by the government without just compensation.

Table 9.1 *Rule of law index by subfactors (Source: Agrast et al. 2009) rule of law index 2.0 – Table by subfactors*

| Band | Factor | Subfactor | Abbreviated description |
|---|---|---|---|
| 1. Accountable government | 1. Government powers limited by constitution | 1.1 | Government powers defined and limited |
| | | 1.2 | Constitution amended only according to law |
| | | 1.3 | Rights suspended only as constitution permits |
| | 2. Governmental and nongovernmental checks | 2.1 | Powers distributed to keep government in check |
| | | 2.2 | Government subject to independent audits |
| | | 2.3 | Executive shares information with other branches |
| | | 2.4 | Government information publicly disclosed |
| | | 2.5 | Reporters and whistleblowers free from retaliation |
| | 3. Accountable government officials and agents | 3.1 | Government officials accountable for misconduct |
| | | 3.2 | Government officials subject to law |
| | | 3.3 | Government officials sanctioned for misconduct |

**Table 9.1** (*cont.*)

| Band | Factor | Subfactor | Abbreviated description |
|---|---|---|---|
| | 4. Accountable military, police, and prison officials | 4.1 | Civilian control over police and the military |
| | | 4.2 | Police and military accountable for misconduct |
| | | 4.3 | Police and military subject to law |
| | | 4.4 | Police and military sanctioned for misconduct |
| | 5. Compliance with international law | 5.1 | Persons treated according to international law |
| | | 5.2 | International relations according to law |
| 2. Publicized and stable laws that protect fundamental rights | 6. Laws are clear, publicized, and stable | 6.1 | Comprehensible laws |
| | | 6.2 | Accessible laws |
| | | 6.3 | Stable laws that are not changed in secret |
| | 7. Laws protect fundamental rights | 7.1 | Discrimination prohibited by law |
| | | 7.2 | Rights of speech and association protected |
| | | 7.3 | Freedom of thought and religion protected |
| | | 7.4 | Forced labor and child labor prohibited |

| | | |
|---|---|---|
| | 7.5 | Rights of the accused protected |
| | 7.6 | Access to remedies for violations of rights |
| 8. Laws protect security of the person | 8.1 | Unjust treatment or punishment prohibited |
| | 8.2 | Crimes against persons prohibited and punished |
| 9. Laws protect security of property | 9.1 | Right to hold and transfer property protected |
| | 9.2 | Arbitrary deprivations of property prohibited |
| | 9.3 | Crimes against property prohibited and punished |
| | 9.4 | Private economic activity protected |
| 10. Accessible process | 10.1 | Government proceedings open to the public |
| | 10.2 | Legislative process open to diverse views |
| | 10.3 | Administrative process open to interested parties |
| | 10.4 | Proposed rules available to the public |
| | 10.5 | Timely access to rules and decisions |
| | 10.6 | Police accessible to public |

3. Accessible, fair, and efficient process

**Table 9.1** (*cont.*)

| Band | Factor | Subfactor | Abbreviated description |
|---|---|---|---|
| | 11. Fair and efficient administration | 11.1 | Laws effectively enforced |
| | | 11.2 | Laws not applied on an arbitrary or selective basis |
| | | 11.3 | Laws enforced without improper influence |
| | | 11.4 | Laws enforced without bribery or excessive fees |
| | | 11.5 | Proceedings conducted without unreasonable delay |
| | | 11.6 | Police given adequate training and resources |
| | | 11.7 | Correctional facilities maintained in proper condition |
| 4. Access to justice | 12. Impartial and accountable judicial system | 12.1 | Judicial process free of bias or improper influence |
| | | 12.2 | Judicial officers accountable |
| | | 12.3 | Judiciary independent of government control |
| | 13. Efficient, accessible, and effective judicial system | 13.1 | Judicial officers competent and of sufficient number |
| | | 13.2 | Judicial proceedings without unreasonable delay |

13.3 Effective remedies for violations of law

13.4 Safe and accessible courts

13.5 Court access without bribery or excessive fees

13.6 Court access without undue procedural hurdles

13.7 Court access for defendants with disabilities

13.8 Court access for defendants with language barriers

14. Competent and independent attorneys or representatives

14.1 Right to legal representation in criminal cases

14.2 Access to competent legal services for the poor

14.3 Attorneys independent and accountable

14.4 Attorneys competent and of sufficient number

15. Fair and efficient alternative dispute resolution

15.1 ADR providers impartial and independent

15.2 ADR providers accountable for misconduct

15.3 ADR providers competent and of sufficient number

Table 9.1 (cont.)

| Band | Factor | Subfactor | Abbreviated description |
|------|--------|-----------|------------------------|
| | | 15.4 | ADR affords efficient access to justice |
| | | 15.5 | ADR not binding without consent |
| | 16. Fair and efficient traditional justice | 16.1 | Traditional justice independent and impartial |
| | | 16.2 | Traditional justice respects fundamental rights |
| | | 16.3 | Traditional justice not binding without consent |

9.3. The laws protect against and punish crimes against property.

9.4. The laws protect the right to engage in private economic activity subject to reasonable regulation.

Agrast et al. 2009

Factor 11:

11.  The laws are fairly and efficiently administered and enforced.

11.1. The laws are effectively enforced.

11.2. The laws are not applied or enforced on an arbitrary or selective basis, for political advantage or in retaliation for lawful activities or expression.

11.3. The laws are administered and enforced without the exercise of improper influence by public officials or private interests.

11.4. Persons and entities are not subjected to excessive or unreasonable fees, or required to provide payments or other inducements to officials or their agents who administer or enforce the law in exchange for the timely discharge of their official duties other than as required by law.

11.5. Administrative proceedings are conducted without unreasonable delay and administrative decisions are enforced in a timely fashion.

11.6. Police are adequately trained, are of sufficient number, have adequate resources and broadly reflect the makeup of the communities they serve.

11.7. Correctional facilities are maintained in proper condition.

Agrast et al. 2009

In contrast, if a contract has a predetermined ADR clause in the contract, the effectiveness of the ADR measure will hinge on access to a fair and efficient ADR process involving competent and independent arbitrators. The World Justice Project analyzes the quality of the ADR process in a country by probing five subfactors:

Factor 15:

15.  Alternative dispute resolution mechanisms provide independent, impartial, fair and efficient access to justice.

15.1. Mediators and arbitrators are impartial and independent of government control.

15.2. Mediators and arbitrators adhere to high standards of conduct and are subject to effective sanctions for misconduct.

15.3. Mediators and arbitrators are competent, adequately trained, and of sufficient number.

15.4. Alternative dispute resolution mechanisms provide efficient access to justice.
15.5. Alternative dispute resolution mechanisms provide procedures to ensure that they are not binding on persons who have not consented to be bound, except as required by the law or a court of law.

Agrast et al. 2009

## Analytical approach

In his review of infrastructure investment literature, Woodhouse (2006) states that most studies on PPP are either reviews of large statistical samples or specific case studies. Research using statistical quantitative analysis (Guasch 2004; Sirtaine et al. 2005) "offers the rigor of systematic analysis and large data sets, but suffers where key variables that relate to plant operations have been difficult to quantify and measure" (Woodhouse 2006: 124). Taylor and colleagues echo this view by stating "Many construction industry phenomena of interest are often too large or too expensive to test in a more traditional experimental fashion and the variables in play can be too numerous for a meaningful quantitative analysis." (Taylor et al., forthcoming). On the other hand, specific case studies allow researchers to capture project phenomena that may be overlooked in a statistical analysis, but they cannot be used to make generalized statements beyond the limited number of observed cases (Yin 2003; Flyvbjerg 2006; Taylor, et al., forthcoming).

In order to answer the research questions of how strategic, cultural, and institutional factors interactively and collectively affect investors' renegotiation approach, an alternative analysis method is needed.

### Qualitative Comparative Analysis (QCA)

A recently developed research tool that enables scholars to find combinations of causal factors based on a modest number of cases is the Qualitative Comparative Analysis (QCA), developed by Charles Ragin in the late 1980s (see also Chapter 8). Unlike traditional quantitative statistical analysis, QCA uses Boolean logic to determine the necessity and sufficiency of conditions (independent variables) to cause the observed outcomes (dependent variables). Based on a thorough understanding of the cases he/she is coding, the researcher assigns value of 0 (nonmembership) or 1 (full-membership) to each of the variables in the analysis. Next, a truth table analysis is performed, where all possible combinations of values are listed in a table and, based on the assigned value of the dependent variable, the researcher can observe which combination of independent variables (referred to as causal factors in QCA analysis) would lead to the observed outcome. While statistical analysis shows the net effect that independent variables have on the direction of the dependent variable (Ragin 2008b), QCA allows the user to define meaningful thresholds and combinations of conditions that will lead to the observed outcome. QCA also allows researchers to investigate the integrative and conditional effects of multiple independent variables. This helps achieve the research objective of finding the conditions under which strategic and cultural factors affect investors' renegotiation approach.

Another advantage of the QCA method over traditional statistical/quantitative method is that QCA allows researchers to identify multiple pathways to the same outcome. In social science, it is often true that different combinations of various factors can create observed effects and there can be more than one way to lead to the outcome of interest (Ragin 2008b). Ragin refers these different pathways as "recipes" for creating the observed outcome.

*Fuzzy set Qualitative Comparative Analysis (fsQCA)*
One of the limitations of the original QCA (later differentiated as crisp-set QCA or csQCA) is that the variables are restricted to binary memberships. As a result, csQCA is effective in coding definitive conditions such as gender (male/female) and home ownership (rent/own) but is less effective in handling continuous variables such as preferences or strengths of cultural beliefs. Ragin overcame this shortcoming by introducing the fuzzy set QCA (fsQCA) method (Ragin 2000). Instead of force-fitting data for each case into one of the two memberships, fsQCA "permit[s] the scaling of membership scores and thus allows partial membership [in multiple categories]" (Rihoux and Ragin 2009: 89). The assignment of fuzzy membership scores for multiple categories requires researchers to combine qualitative and quantitative assessment of the cases (Rihoux and Ragin 2009). With its flexible membership scoring, fsQCA is especially applicable to this research since it allows researchers to capture some

of the qualitative detail behind many conditions, such as the degree of willingness to bargain in a renegotiation situation, before subjecting the data from the cases to QCA analysis. Under this methodology, qualitative details of the projects are captured and can be analyzed to generalize results beyond the cases being studied. The operations and mechanics of the fsQCA analysis are further discussed in our section on results.

### Case selection
In this research, empirical renegotiation behaviors of infrastructure investment firms were collected and analyzed. Cases are referred to as projects in dispute instead of renegotiation incidents. In other words, a single project undergoing multiple rounds of renegotiation, as they often do, is treated as one case in this study. This definition is primarily a pragmatic decision – it is almost impossible to delineate definitive start and end points for multiple rounds of renegotiation in the same project. Moreover, any subsequent renegotiations are inevitably affected by previous renegotiations. As such, it is more appropriate to treat the entire renegotiation process as one case study instead of multiple incidents.

In total, 14 cases – 6 transportation projects and 8 power plants – were identified and public records of these projects were thoroughly studied. We selected transportation and power subsectors as the sample for various reasons. First, these two sectors have been found to have significant rates of renegotiations in two separate studies. Guasch et al. (2006) found that close to half of the Latin American transport projects built in the 1990s were renegotiated. Another report on power plant concessions in developing countries found that 21 of the 34 cases studied (62 percent) underwent renegotiations (Woodhouse 2006). Second, PPP transport and power projects somewhat resemble true private operations as they do not deal with the livelihood of the host country's citizens. If the government and the investor do not have an agreement over toll rates or electricity tariffs, it may bring inconvenience to the citizens. However, if the dispute involves a project that is more closely tied to health and livelihood of the general public – such as water supply project – the government and the private investor may have different negotiation practices given the criticality of the project. Finally, the project data for transport and power plant projects are often readily available since they are well covered by the news media and scholars, given their high profiles, and the enormous impact they can have on large populations. Different perspectives of the project history by different sources also help to verify the project history and ensure the accuracy of the coding.

In order to identify renegotiated PPP projects and obtain their project data, various PPP databases and news record databases were extensively searched, including World Bank's Private Participation in Infrastructure (PPI) project database, Public Works Financing (PWF) database, and Factiva.

Before an identified renegotiated project was included as a case project, a few criteria had to be met. First, the project must have been extensively documented with information that is accessible. The available project information ideally came from multiple sources, including news reports, commentaries, and scholarly works from different organizations to increase its reliability. Second, the collective sample of projects should include cases with different values on both dependent and independent variables. In other words, the sample should include projects that are sponsored by investors from countries that are high on the *long-term orientation* cultural dimension as well as some by those who are low on the same dimension. Finally, the case projects needed to take place in different regions of the world to improve the external validity of the research findings. Geographically, the 14 case projects took place in host countries in North America, South America, Asia, Africa, and Europe. Main investors of these projects included companies from Spain (5 cases); the US (4); Malaysia (3); China (1); and Brazil (1).

In addition to relying on the aforementioned news record database for data collection, the first author had the opportunity to interact with the project executives from two of the cases. The managers from both projects had intimate knowledge of the project and generously shared their experience on their respective projects. Their recollections of the project events were consistent with the news reports and were incorporated in the analyses.

## Coding/scoring/calibration

Calibration is the process of assigning numerical value to an abstract concept (Ragin 2008b). For the causal factors (independent variables) that are derived from other established studies, i.e., GLOBE cultural dimensions scores and Rule of Law index, the calibration

Table 9.2 *Coding scheme for the relational–legalistic renegotiation approach continuum*

---

Relational–legalistic renegotiation approach continuum

| Coded value | Variable description and threshold criteria |
|---|---|
| 0 | **Fully legalistic** Investor initiates litigation or arbitration without any recorded attempted negotiation with the government. The outcome of the dispute is determined by the court/arbitrator ruling. |
| 0.33 | **Mostly legalistic** Investor takes legal actions, by initiating litigation or arbitration, and also engages in some extent of bargaining with the government. However, the two sides fail to reach a settlement before the court or arbitrator provides a ruling. After the ruling, the government and the investor may or may not have an ultimate settlement. |
| 0.66 | **Mostly relational** Investor takes legal actions, by initiating litigation or arbitration, and also engages in some extent of bargaining with the government. Prior to any court or arbitrator ruling, the two sides manage to agree on an out-of-court settlement. |
| 1 | **Fully relational** Investor engages in relational bargaining with the government during the dispute between the two parties. No documentation of legal action being filed. The two sides reach agreement without the court or arbitrator being involved. |

---

was performed using the software developed by Ragin based on the values from the corresponding datasets according to the recommendations by Ragin (2008b). For the remaining variables that were defined for this study, i.e. both strategic factors and Legalistic/Relational Index, four-value fuzzy set scoring values (0, .33, .66, and 1) were developed based on my observations of the cases. The coding schemes for all variables are discussed in detail in the following sections.

*Coding scheme for dependent variable – renegotiation approach*
Building on the relational–legal continuum developed by Edkins and Smyth (2006), Table 9.2 shows the fuzzy set coding scheme we developed to codify the legalistic–relational response from the investor.

Table 9.3 *Coding scheme for future business index (FBI)*

| FBI fs-QCA Score | During the 5 years since the beginning of the dispute, the main investor has |
|---|---|
| 0 | *sold or attempted to sell* infrastructure business in the host country; may or may not have maintained other businesses |
| 0.33 | *retained ownership* of case project, but no new infrastructure business |
| 0.66 | introduced new project(s) and/or *moderately increased* ($< 2x$) its infrastructure investment in the country |
| 1 | *substantially increased* ($>2x$) its infrastructure investment in the country |

*Coding scheme for independent variables – strategic factors*
In order to analyze the influence of strategic factors on an investor's behavior, we introduce two indices – the *Future Business Index* (FBI) and *Current Integrated Activity* (CIA) – to measure the extent to which future and current business ties with the host government might impact the investor's renegotiation approach. For the FBI, an investor's investment activity in the host country during the five years following the government action that leads to the dispute is used as the basis for the coding scheme. Assuming the investor takes into account the amount of future business he/she plans to invest going forward as he/she chooses the renegotiation approach, the suggested measure is designed to capture the level of actual future business dealings the investor commits to amid the ongoing dispute with the host country. Specifically, the coding scheme for the FBI is shown in Table 9.3.

As for the CIA, we use the ratio of the combined value of the investor's other current business to the case project value as the benchmark for level of current investment an investor has. Other current business is defined as any commercial operation the investor, including the parent company of any subsidiary, has in the host country at the time the dispute arose. Both values are for the year the dispute first arose. Public documents, including annual reports and news records provided most of the information on project value. The thresholds for the different CIA scores are listed in Table 9.4.

**Table 9.4** *Coding scheme for current investment activity (CIA)*

| CIA fs-QCA Score | combined value of other businesses / case project value |
|---|---|
| 0 | 0–0.10 |
| 0.33 | 0.11–1.00 |
| 0.66 | 1.01–3.00 |
| 1 | 3+ |

*Coding scheme for independent variables – cultural factors*
Using the findings from the GLOBE (House et al. 2004) study, the cultural dimension scores of the three relevant cultural dimensions – assertiveness, collectivism, and future orientation – were translated from their original seven-point scale to the 0 to 1 fuzzy set scores using the software developed by Ragin.

*Coding scheme for independent variables – institutional effects*
As discussed above, the World Justice Index is broken into sub-category scores for individual issues such as arbitration and judicial independence. In turn, the scores from these categories are used to derive the rule of law score for the case projects, depending on the dispute resolution mechanism of the projects. The case study projects in this research can be classified into one of the following three categories:

- Does not have predetermined ADP clauses and dispute between the investor and the host government will be resolved in the local court.
- Contains predetermined ADP clauses and the venue of arbitration is within the host country.
- Contains predetermined ADP clauses and the venue of arbitration is set at a location outside of the host country, such as London or Geneva.

For projects that do not have predetermined ADP clauses, the judicial system of the host country would generally have jurisdiction over the project should disputes arise. In those cases, Factor 9 – protection of private property – and Factor 11 – fairly administered judicial process – will both be applicable. For investors to have a fair trial in a legal dispute with the host government, the judicial system of the host country must uphold and protect the ownership of private property, including privatized infrastructure. Equally important, the judicial system must have enough independence from the ruling government's influence such that the court can provide impartial rulings. Thus, for projects that do not have predetermined ADP clauses in their contracts, the average score of Factor 9 and Factor 11 was used as the score for the institutional factor.

For projects that have predetermined ADP process administered in the host country, Factor 15 – fair and efficient use of ADP process – of the host country was used as the score for the institutional factor of each project. It measures important ADR factors such as availability of a competent arbitrator. If a third-party location away from the host county is chosen as arbitration venue, the Factor 15 score of the arbitration country was assigned as the value of the institutional factor. If the arbitration country is not included in the World Justice Project study (neither the UK nor Switzerland are included in the study, yet the UK and Geneva are both frequently chosen locations for arbitration), the highest score of Factor 15 obtained by other countries, (i.e., Singapore = 1.0) was assigned. The rationale is that the investor must believe the independent venue would give them a fair arbitration process, otherwise they would not have chosen it in the first place. Thus, it warrants the highest score to reflect the investor's confidence in the legitimacy of the arbitration process. The scores of the applicable subcategories are converted to a continuous-value fuzzy set score following the guideline of Ragin (2008b).

## Results

The 14 case projects were coded according to the coding scheme discussed above. Table 9.5 summarizes the scoring summary of both the dependent and independent variables for each of the projects.

For the three variables that are created for this study (i.e. FBI, CIA, and Legalistic/Relational Index) and thus take on a 4-value fuzzy set scale, all possible values (0, .33, .66, and 1) are represented in each variable. For the remaining four variables that are translated into continuous fuzzy sets (any value between 0 and 1, inclusive) using results from other studies, the distribution of the coding assignment spans the two ends of the scale. The broad distribution of the coding

Table 9.5 Coding summary

| Case | Project name | Lead investor country | FBI | CIA | Assertiveness | Collectivism | Future orient | Legal support | Rel/legal index |
|---|---|---|---|---|---|---|---|---|---|
| 1 | US CA SR-91 | USA | 1 | 1 | 0.98 | 0.78 | 0.85 | 0.95 | 0.33 |
| 2 | Canada ETR 407 | Spain | 0.33 | 0 | 0.94 | 0.36 | 0.2 | 0.97 | 0.33 |
| 3 | India Enron Dabhol Power | USA | 1 | 0.33 | 0.98 | 0.78 | 0.85 | 1 | 0.33 |
| 4 | Chile R. 78 | Spain | 0 | 1 | 0.94 | 0.36 | 0.2 | 0.4 | 1 |
| 5 | Hong Kong EHC | China | 0.33 | 1 | 0.01 | 0.98 | 0.44 | 0.95 | 0 |
| 6 | Indo-Karaha Bodas Power | USA | 0 | 0 | 0.98 | 0.78 | 0.85 | 1 | 0 |
| 7 | Arg. Autopista del Oeste | Spain | 0.33 | 0 | 0.94 | 0.36 | 0.2 | 0.92 | 1 |
| 8 | Malay Tanjong Power | Malaysia | 0.33 | 0.66 | 0.05 | 0.96 | 0.98 | 0.89 | 1 |
| 9 | Malay Genting Sanyen | Malaysia | 0 | 1 | 0.05 | 0.96 | 0.98 | 0.89 | 1 |
| 10 | Brazil Termoceará Power | Brazil | 1 | 0.66 | 0.67 | 0.33 | 0.51 | 0.4 | 0.66 |
| 11 | Kenya Iberafrica Power | Spain | 1 | 0.33 | 0.94 | 0.36 | 0.2 | 0.01 | 1 |
| 12 | Tanzania IPTL Power | Malaysia | 0 | 0.33 | 0.05 | 0.96 | 0.98 | 1 | 0.33 |
| 13 | Poland Elcho Power | USA | 0 | 0.33 | 0.98 | 0.78 | 0.85 | 0.71 | 0.66 |
| 14 | Portugal Norte Litoral | Spain | 0.66 | 0.66 | 0.94 | 0.36 | 0.2 | 0.9 | 0 |

results satisfies the goal of finding cases that contain combinations of factors with different values.

Of the 14 cases, sponsors on three of them are considered to have pursued wholly legalistic responses to government-initiated renegotiation. Sponsors on six projects employed both legalistic and relational responses: sponsors on four of these projects are judged to have pursued more legalistic responses, while the other two are considered to have pursued more relational responses. Sponsors on the remaining five projects pursued a fully relational response and did not respond with any legal action.

This section begins with the discussion of some key concepts in the fsQCA analysis that are pertinent to the discussion of the results, including consistency, coverage, and different types of solutions. The focus then shifts to the discussion of the research results.

## fsQCA primer – consistency and coverage in sufficiency and necessity analyses

In order to determine the necessity and sufficiency of causal conditions leading to observed outcomes, researchers need to calculate the consistency and coverage of their solutions. As Ragin explains, these measures have similarities to their counterparts in quantitative research:

Consistency, like significance, signals whether an empirical connection merits the close attention of the investigator. If a hypothesized subset relation is not consistent, then the researcher's theory or conjecture is not supported. Coverage, like strength, indicates the empirical relevance or importance of a set-theoretic connection. (Ragin 2008b: 45)

Specifically, consistency is the degree to which one condition (or combination of conditions) is a subset of another. The relative position of the causal factors and the outcome vary depending on which analysis is being performed. In the sufficiency analysis, the consistency measures the degree to which the causal factor(s) is a subset of the outcome. The relationship is reversed in the necessity analysis, as consistency measures the level to which an outcome is a subset of the causal factor. Ragin (2008b) recommends a threshold consistency score of at least 0.8 as justification for asserting that the causal variable or recipe is a *sufficient condition* for the outcome; and a

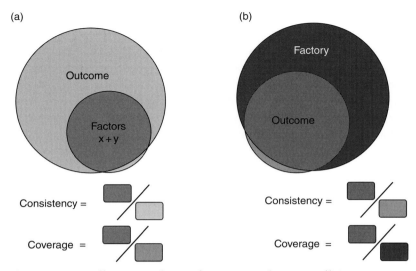

**Figure 9.4**(a) Sufficient condition (factors X and Y are sufficient to cause the outcomes) (b) Necessary condition (factor Y is necessary to cause the outcome)

threshold of at least 0.9 for asserting that it is a necessary condition. Figure 9.4 illustrates the difference between the two analyses.

If, and only if, a solution passes the consistency test, coverage analysis can be performed to verify the solutions' relevance. Simply put, the coverage is the measure of the proportion of the outcome explained by the solution. A solution can be highly consistent but if only a small number of cases from the outcome are tied to this solution, the coverage will be low and the solution will be considered irrelevant or empirically insignificant, despite its high consistency.

## *Necessary conditions to predict a relational bargaining approach*

The necessity of each of the independent variables was individually tested using the software developed by Ragin. The result of the consistency analysis is shown in Table 9.6.

Since none of the factors had a consistency level exceeding 0.9, the threshold for necessary condition as recommended by Ragin (2008b),

Table 9.6 *Consistency analysis for necessity*

| Independent variable | Consistency |
|---|---|
| Future business index | 0.433 |
| Current investment activities | 0.681 |
| LOW assertiveness | 0.440 |
| Collectivism | 0.694 |
| Humanity | 0.478 |
| Future orientation | 0.737 |
| LOW rule of law | 0.390 |

it implies there is no single factor among the variables measured that is deemed necessary for investors to favor the relational bargaining approach over legalistic actions. For this reason, there was no need to check any combination of factors for potential necessary conditions.

Multiple factors affect the investors' decision on the renegotiation approach and the finding is based on a medium-size sample, so it is not useful to compare which factors may have more association with either renegotiation approach based on the above result. In order to do that, researchers will either need to control for other variables or use a large-size sample to offset the effects of other variables.

An implication from the research finding that no necessary condition existed for the relational approach is that one cannot expect an investor to opt for relational bargaining based on the value of any one independent variable. In order to do so, researchers must take into account the value of other variables and understand the interactive effect of these variables on the investor's decision about a renegotiation approach to pursue. This leads to the next topic of discussion – sufficient conditions for the relational renegotiation approach.

## Sufficient conditions to predict a relational bargaining approach

As discussed above, a major strength of the QCA method is that it helps identify multiple causal pathways to the outcome of interests. In this study, three intermediate solutions involving four different factors were found to be *sufficient conditions* for investors to choose a relational approach over legalistic actions in government-initiated renegotiations.

They are:

1. High *future business index with* low *legal support*

   Consistency = 0.925; Coverage = 0.243

2. High *current investment activities with* low *legal support*

   Consistency = 0.933; Coverage = 0.274

3. High *current investment activities* with high *humane index* and high *future orientation* and high *collectivism* and low *assertiveness*

   Consistency = 0.821; Coverage = 0.271

A careful examination of the three solutions reveals that no single factor was present in all three sufficient conditions. This confirms the previous finding that no single factor is a necessary condition for investors to opt for one renegotiation approach over another. The consistency levels of these three solutions all exceed the 0.8 threshold recommended by Ragin for necessary conditions. The aggregate coverage of the solution (sufficiency conditions) for this study was 0.602. In other words, slightly more than 60 percent of the relational bargaining cases are attributed to one of the three solutions presented above.

## Conditions for legalistic approach

Necessary and sufficient conditions analyses were also performed for the legalistic approach. Unlike the relational approach, there was one necessary condition for legalistic renegotiation actions from investors – High Rule of Law (Consistency = 0.976; Coverage = 0.565). The finding indicates investors will not seek legal actions to resolve disputes with the government if they are not supported by a strong rule of law either from the host government's judicial system or the arbitration process. While strong rule of law is a necessary condition for legal responses, it is important to note that the presence of strong rule of law does not necessarily lead to a legalistic approach from investors. Under the influence of strategic and cultural factors, an investor can still choose relational response under a strong rule of law. The sole necessary condition merely means that legal actions were generally taken under a strong rule of law.

The sufficient condition analysis for legalistic response yielded no combination that suffices the 0.8 consistency threshold suggested by Ragin. This implies that it is harder to predict when investors will choose legal actions over relational bargaining, although the necessary condition analysis suggests legal actions cannot happen in the absence of a strong rule of law.

## Discussion

This section will begin by describing how our empirical results address our initial research questions. Then we discuss the implications of our findings for the management of public–private infrastructure projects.

### Answers to research questions

Three research questions were raised in this study.

Question 1: Which factors conduce leading investors to choose the relational bargaining approach over legal actions in government-initiated renegotiations?

All seven independent variables were involved in the solution set of sufficient conditions for the relational bargaining approach. Among the three sufficient conditions, i.e., "recipes," for the relational bargaining approach, high scores for strategic factors appear in all three solutions. Weak rule of law appears twice, and favorable cultural factors appear once.

Both strategic factors were included as aspects of different sufficient conditions to prompt investors to choose the relational approach in government-initiated renegotiations. A high level of current investment (high CIA score) or increasing future business presence (high FBI score) in the host country were found to be factors that favor the relational approach. This finding is consistent with the observations made by Wells (Wells and Ahmed 2006), who linked strategic factors to renegotiation approach based on the handful of cases in Indonesia power plant. The results from this study show Wells' suggested relationship to be empirically valid in a broader sample in terms of both scope and location, as the relationship was observed in transportation and power projects located in different regions of the world.

Similar to strategic factors, the institutional factor – *rule of law* – also had a broad impact on investor's renegotiation approach, as it was included in two of the three sufficient conditions. This finding confirms the proposition that weak rule of law leads investors to pursue a relational response to government-initiated renegotiation. The combination of cultural dimensions also forms a part of a sufficient condition to encourage the pursuit of relational bargaining by sponsors, and thus confirms the prediction of their effect on the sponsor's renegotiation approach.

Question 2: What combinations of strategic, cultural, and institutional factors affect investors' preference for arbitration or renegotiation bargaining?

While the first research question aims to identify factors relevant to the relational renegotiation strategy, the second question investigates the collective and interactive effects these factors have on the renegotiation approach. Two of the sufficient conditions for relational bargaining were composed of weak rule of law and a high score on one of the two strategic factors (i.e., either high future business or high current investment). However, the third condition did not involve the rule of law factor. When high current business activities combine with favorable cultural dimensions, investors tended to favor the relational approach regardless of strength of the host country's rule of law. This empirical finding suggests that favorable cultural factors can substitute for favorable institutional conditions in predicting relational renegotiation. In other words, even with the support of a strong rule of law for legal remedies, an investor may still opt for a relational approach if the investor has both strong current business ties and cultural dimensions that favor relational approaches.

In the Malaysia Genting Sanyen power plant case, the investor, a Malaysian conglomerate that has many current business activities in the country, was supported by a strong rule of law offered by the Malaysian judicial system. Unlike the investor of the CA SR-91 case presented above, who chose legal actions when presented with these similar attributes, the Malaysian investor chose a fully relational approach to resolve the dispute. The sharp differences between these two investors were caused by their different cultural dimension values. While the US investor had very high assertiveness (0.98) and low humane orientation (0.49) scores, the Malaysian investor had very low assertiveness (0.05) and high humane orientation (0.98) scores.

The fact that cultural dimensions combine with current business connections, in contrast to future business projects, to form a sufficient set of conditions for a relational response to government-initiated renegotiations also provides some insights on the relative importance of the two strategic factors when investors consider their renegotiation approaches. While both strategic factors can lead to the relational approach when combined with weak rule of law, only strong current business connection is included in the solution that includes cultural dimension scores to favor the relational approach. It is quite possible that investors consider current investment to be a more important factor than future business as they select a response to government-initiated renegotiations. Since an investor's other current business activities are currently under the influence of various government agencies (in the form of regulations, inspections, licensing, etc.), they can raise greater concerns about government retaliation than future business, which may or may not materialize.

Question 3: Is there one factor that can dominate the effect of others and be sufficient by itself to predict investors' renegotiation approach?

It is important to observe that all three sufficient conditions for the relational bargaining approach consisted of more than one factor. In other words, weak rule of law, strong business ties with the host country (present or future), and favorable cultural dimensions each encouraged the investor to take on a relational approach in government-initiated renegotiations, but they must be combined with at least one other favorable factor to prompt an investor to choose bargaining strategies over legal actions. This implies that no causal factor had a dominant effect on investors' renegotiation approach, and the effects of any one variable could be offset by combinations of other factors. For example, as a component in each of the three sufficient conditions, high values of strategic factors (i.e., CIA and FBI) are important considerations in the investor response analysis. Yet, even a high CIA or high FBI score is not enough by itself to conclusively predict the renegotiation approach.

Take the California SR-91 case as an example. The project's lead investor, Kiewit, had a very strong business tie with the California department of transportation as it had built many projects for the agency and would likely continue to do business with the California state agency, not to mention with the many transportation departments from other states and the US federal government. If one looks at this strong business tie and concludes the investor will choose to bargain relationally, one will be surprised to learn that Kiewit in fact chose a mostly legalistic approach.

A careful examination of the other attributes of the investor would reveal that the cultural dimensions of the US, where Kiewit is based, involves high assertiveness, a cultural attribute positively related to legalistic action. More importantly, the rule of law in the host country (US) is very strong. Unlike many countries in the world, whether an investor can secure future business from the federal and state government agencies in the US has relatively little to do with the relationship between the government and the firm on ongoing or past projects. In order to promote open competition and uphold transparency, the US government and state governments in the US are typically required to award infrastructure contracts to the lowest qualified bidder. The absence of interference from government officials in the contract award process provides a transparent bidding process – and thus the high rule of law score in the US.

In this environment, Kiewit's legal action against the government was unlikely to undermine its prospects for securing future projects in the US, as long as its bids remained competitive with other bidders. This helps explain why Kiewit ended up with a legalistic response to the dispute with the government.

In addition to the answers to the research questions posed for this study, another observation was made during the analysis of the sample cases. There were a total of 5 case projects that had low strategic scores. Interestingly, all five projects had very high legal support scores, averaging 0.92, as opposed to the overall average of 0.785 (See Table 9.7).

A closer review of the project details shows that the connection between low strategic scores and high legal support exhibited by these five cases is unlikely to be coincidental. In two projects – Indonesia Karaha Bodas Power and Tanzania IPTL Power – the investors deliberately set up ADR clauses in the contract that allowed for offshore arbitration, to Geneva and World Bank's ICSID respectively, should future disputes arise.

Table 9.7 *Cases with low strategic scores*

| Project | FBI score | CIA score | Legal support |
|---|---|---|---|
| Canada Ontario ETR 407 | 0.33 | 0 | 0.97 |
| Indonesia Karaha Bodas Power | 0 | 0 | 1 |
| Argentina Autopista del Oeste | 0.33 | 0 | 0.92 |
| Tanzania IPTL Power | 0 | 0.33 | 1 |
| Poland Elcho Power | 0 | 0.33 | 0.71 |

If these clauses had been absent from the contract, the investors would have had to count on the local court system, so the legal support score for these projects would have been much lower. Indonesia would have received a legal support score of 0.29 based on the finding from the World Justice Index. While Tanzania was not included in the World Justice Index, the World Bank's Worldwide Governance Indicators rank the country's rule of law to be between the 25th and 50th percentile between 1998 and 2008. For the other three projects, the investors enjoyed the stronger rule of law from a more effective and fair judicial system in the host country, and did not introduce ADR clauses in the contract.

From these five cases, it is apparent that when investors enter into a new market (indicated by low CIA) or recognize they may not be able to influence the government through future business investments (indicated by low FBI), they tend to ensure the current project will be supported by a strong legal system. If the host country's judicial system does not give the investor adequate confidence of receiving a fair and efficient judicial review process, the investor can enhance its legal protection by seeking ADR coverage in a third country with strong rule of law, bypassing the local court system.

## Implications for management of infrastructure concessions

The findings of this study confirm the proposition that strategic, cultural, and institutional factors interact in nuanced ways to influence investor behavior. When a stakeholder wants to anticipate how another stakeholder may react in a dispute, it is pertinent to understand each of these attributes and how they may impact one's decision.

The fact that all three categories of variables were present in the solution set underlines the importance of including each of these variables in the analysis of dispute resolution. We found that none of the variables (or categories of variables) was sufficient by itself to form a necessary condition. This suggests that the effect of any one factor could be offset by the effect of another variable or combination. The findings from this study provide some insights as to which variables may interact with others to bring predictable outcomes, and at what level.

As Miller and Olleros (2000) and Woodhouse (2006) point out, risk engineering by itself has been found insufficient to guarantee desirable outcomes in infrastructure investments. Strategic management often plays a more significant role in the success of projects. With its strategic management perspective, this research helps practitioners to manage the renegotiation process of infrastructure concession agreements more effectively by understanding what conditions drive different renegotiation approaches of counterparties. A host government can use the finding from this study to analyze the likely behavior of the investor should a renegotiation situation arise in the future. To the extent allowed by the law and applicable procurement rules, the government may even have the liberty to introduce specific requirements to qualify bidders so that it can increase the likelihood of partnering with an investor who will be more likely to use a preferred renegotiation approach. For instance, if the government wants to avoid being sued by the investor for publicity and marketing reasons, it can require bidders to have a certain level of current business involvement in the local economy (although governments often tend to do the opposite in order to "spread the wealth"). In addition, it can give favorable considerations to bidders who are from countries that are low on assertiveness and high on collectivism, as these cultural attributes become a sufficient condition for a relational approach when combined with a high current investment level.

Even in situations when the government may not have the liberty to prequalify bidders in the ways suggested above, the research findings can still help the government anticipate the likely response from the investor in a renegotiation situation. The government can then use this knowledge to find alternative measures to manage the renegotiation process before and during the renegotiation process.

Host governments are not the only stakeholders who can benefit from this research project's findings. Investors who are seeking other business partners can also use the findings to evaluate the likely renegotiation approach of their partner candidates. This increases the likelihood that the partners will share a similar renegotiation approach preference and avoid internal dispute over what actions to take in response to a government-initiated renegotiation.

By applying the research findings in this study, both governments and investors can better manage the renegotiation process by anticipating likely response from business counterparties or partners. While the occurrence of renegotiation is considered a major risk, what to expect during the renegotiation process is also a great unknown. This study helps further understand the latter and better manage one of the major risks associated with infrastructure concessions between governments and private investors.

## Conclusions

High renegotiation rates have been observed in infrastructure concession agreements. Two recent studies found close to half of infrastructure concessions were renegotiated (Guasch and Straub 2006, Woodhouse 2006). While previous studies have offered different explanations for the occurrence of renegotiations, relatively few have written on the renegotiation process itself. Moreover, most infrastructure investment research has studied renegotiations from a rational "calculating" perspective, but has generally overlooked other nonstrategic factors that may influence stakeholder decisions. This study addressed these issues by investigating the integrative and collective effects of three sets of variables – *strategic factors, cultural dimensions,* and *institutional environment* – on the renegotiation process. Specifically, the study investigated how these three sets of variables affect investors' renegotiation strategy, ranging from relational bargaining to legalistic arbitration or litigation, in responding to government-initiated renegotiations. Data assembled through archival research on project histories of 14 privatized transportation and power projects are analyzed using the fuzzy set Qualitative Comparative Analysis (fsQCA). The fsQCA analysis finds that combinations of *strategic, cultural,* and *institutional* variables interact in three different ways that cause investors to adopt a *relational renegotiation* versus a *legalistic* response. Furthermore, the net effect of any one variable can be offset by a combination of other factors that influence investors' renegotiation approach. The goal of this interdisciplinary research is to help balance the prevalent risk engineering approach to renegotiation management with a study adopting the strategic management perspective. While other studies offer comprehensive causes for renegotiations and ways to mitigate them, this study provides readers with insights on how investors choose to respond to government-initiated renegotiations. Analyses incorporating a balanced viewpoint between the risk engineering and strategic management approaches offers practitioners a more holistic perspective as they continue to find effective measures to set up and manage public–private partnership infrastructure projects.

## Endnote

1 Note that our approach distinguishes between institutional and cultural factors whereas most of the other chapters in this volume treat cultural factors as a subset of institutional characteristics (see Chapter 2). In our approach, the institutional characteristics examined – the rule of law – relate primarily to Scott's "regulative" and "normative" pillars (see Scott 1995/2008), while the cultural factors are considered separately.

# PART IV

# Governance strategies and structures

# 10 | Network-based strategies and competencies for political and social risk management in global projects[1]

WITOLD J. HENISZ

## Introduction

The incorporation of information on the structure of political and social networks for global projects into data acquisition and analysis, as well as strategy implementation, is accelerating the transformation of political and social risk management from art to quasi-formal science. Sophisticated project managers grappling with conflicting pressures from multiple social and political actors abroad and at home have for some time relied upon a broad set of informants as sources of information for as well as myriad agents for the collection and analysis of this externally sourced information, and the design and implementation of an influence strategy. While those sources of information and agents of implementation have long formed a network structure in which the project is embedded, the analysis of the incoming information and design of an influence strategy has too often occurred without reference to that structure neglecting important information and insight. Each piece of information is viewed independently and equally or its importance is determined by a process that neglects its position of origin in the network of informants. Similarly, agents of influence are employed in an uncoordinated manner, or the form of that coordination fails to fully incorporate their position in the network of policymaking. Perhaps most critically, this process of political and social risk mitigation is isolated from broader financial, economic, and engineering planning functions. This chapter outlines the past, present, and future frontier of political and social risk management for global projects with particular attention to the importance of perceiving, analyzing, and acting upon the political and social environment with reference to the network structure of that environment.

Political and social risk management comprises the set of activities undertaken within a global project to influence political or social policy outcomes that have the effect of impinging upon or facilitating the ability of the project to realize its own stated objectives. Classes of examples include global project managers who seek to:

- reduce the likelihood of expropriations or renegotiations of contract terms by governments of countries in which they operate;
- implement strategies that raise short-term economic costs but increase political or social support thereby generating medium- to long-term economic benefits in the form of increased willingness of consumers to pay, members of the value chain to share rents, or policymakers to desist from interventions; and
- defuse an activist campaign that seeks to generate a consumer boycott, a reluctance by suppliers to provide crucial inputs (e.g., capital), an increase in media criticism, or government intervention.

In each of these cases while technical, marketing, financial, and operational efficiency and capability are clearly important, a substantial driver of value creation and appropriation for the global project will be the actions and reactions of political and social actors that influence the ability of the project to realize its financial and operational goals.

Despite the clear and widespread acceptance that political and social risks are of large and growing importance for global projects, the political and social risk management capabilities are not that different in many corporations than they were four decades ago when Franklin Root wrote based on his survey of large US firms that "no executive offered any evidence of a systematic evaluation of political risks, involving their identification, their likely incidence, and their specific consequences for company operation" (Root 1968). Kobrin (1979) surveyed the literature and similarly concluded that "rigorous and systematic assessment and evaluation of the political environment is exceptional. Most political analysis is superficial and subjective, not integrated formally into the decision-making process." A recent PriceWaterhouseCoopers-Eurasia report based upon a 2005 survey echoes this conclusion. Of the firms surveyed, 73 percent were dissatisfied with the effectiveness of the political and social risk management processes:

Risk managers, chief financial officers, and international division heads contacted for our survey said frequently that the complex web of information that would enable them to assess political risk was difficult to obtain and evaluate. Many expressed frustration that when they were able to glean information from local sources, the information was inevitably biased. Moreover, funding for specific risk management techniques (e.g., risk mapping) was often lacking within their organizations, because the benefits were not well understood. As a result, CEOs and boards of directors were not getting the timely, accurate information they needed to make good decisions about international exposures – or, conversely, information was not effectively communicated and utilized to manage risk in the field. (PwC Advisory and Eurasia Group, 2006)

The scope and magnitude of the resulting financial losses can be acute. Merchant International Group reported that from 1995 to 1998, 84 percent of operations in emerging markets failed to reach their earnings targets resulting in an 8–10 percent diminution of total corporate returns or a loss of $24 billion in 1998 alone (Poole-Rob and Bailey 2003). In an earlier survey, PwC reported that a one standard deviation in a country's "opacity" was equivalent in its predicted financial impact to raising taxation rates by between 33 and 46 percent or borrowing costs by 9 to 13 percent on the operations of an otherwise identical country with mean levels of opacity (Kurtzman, Yago, and Phumiwasana, 2004).

Given the high political salience of many global projects and the cross-border nature of the project teams, the incidence and magnitude of financial losses in global projects are even larger than these aggregate figures. A World Bank study in 2004 revealed that 15 to 30 percent of the contracts covering $371 billion of private infrastructure investment in the 1990s were subject to government-initiated renegotiations or disputes. Zelner et al. (2009) report a rate of public disputes or renegotiations of 20.1 percent in their population of 974 independent power projects. While there exist no firm estimates of the financial losses to global projects resulting from political and social risk management, given the $5.6 trillion size of the market for global construction estimated by McGraw Hill, and assuming 20 percent of global projects encounter a renegotiation or dispute whose average cost is 5 percent of the value of the project, leads to a back-of-the-envelope estimate of annual losses of $56 billion. Even lowering the estimated average cost of a renegotiation or dispute to 1 percent of the project value leads to an estimate of $11 billion per annum.

The crucial pieces of data needed to formulate an influence strategy to alter policy outcomes to avoid these losses and, more importantly, continue to expand the market for global projects, are the identity, preferences, and power of various political and social actors as well as the formal and informal process of their interaction that generate that policy outcome. A simple example of such data needed for the analysis in the case of a committee vote in a legislative chamber would include information on committee members, their constituents, and fundraising sources. The preferences of each of these actors, their power (one vote for each committee member but a more complex function of votes, jobs, status, and dollars for constituents and fundraising sources), and the strength of each actor's preferences (i.e., the extent to which they are willing to use their power on this issue) could be analyzed to assess the likely outcome of the committee vote. In countries with strong party systems, perhaps the analysis could be reduced to a consideration of the partisan affiliation of each committee member and the preferences and salience of the issue to each party. More complex issues would require consideration of a multistage policymaking processes that might include committee votes, full chamber votes, presidential authorizations, regulatory enactments, legal rulings, and media campaigns by various interest groups to feed back into future policymaking or the enforcement of current policy.

Turning from the political to the social arena, the crucial actors expand to include the nongovernmental, interest group, media, and other opinion leader space. The policy outcome is a project's reputation, which can be attacked or devalued by any number of actions with substantial financial consequences. Consumers may switch to competitors or demand lower prices to maintain their purchases of what they now perceive as an inferior good. Suppliers may restrict the availability of capital or other key resources or charge more for those inputs to offset their risk of becoming a target of the activists. Employees may seek to depart the project, demand higher wages for staying, or become less productive. Governments may also intervene to regulate or otherwise alter the operations that are the focus of the activist campaign. The managers of the project seek to protect its reputation and thus need to follow the sentiment expressed towards it by each of its stakeholders. The relative power of these stakeholders can be a function of an objective indicator such as their number of press mentions or a subjective judgment of their importance for the intangible "reputation."

In the remainder of this chapter, I outline the tools used within global projects to gather information on the identity, preferences, and power of the relevant political and social actors, analyze that information to identify an influence strategy, and implement that strategy. In each section, I note how over time a network methodology or perspective has enhanced a more traditional conception of the political and social environment. I close with a detailed caselet of a current $10 billion megaproject by ChevronTexaco to build a liquid natural gas facility in poverty-stricken, corrupt, and war-torn Angola that has followed the framework identified here and, remarkably, encountered little formal or informal opposition while meeting its internal financial and operational performance targets.

## Sources of information on political and social risks

### Traditional

Because the decision makers at headquarters tasked with making major strategic decisions affected by the political or social environment information often lack information on the political and social context of host countries, such information must be obtained from sources with more context-specific knowledge (see Chapters 6, 7). In contrast to many external sources of uncertainty (e.g., exchange rates, interest rates, and input prices), however, political and social risks cannot easily be priced and hedged via financial market instruments. The likelihood that a political or social actor will seek to alter the revenue stream of a corporation in a manner inimical to shareholders is typically neither a country- nor industry-specific risk. Rather, the largest determinant of the risk of an adverse event is often the strategy of the investor. How do they enter? With whom do they ally? Who do they hire and from whom do they source materials and credit? On what terms? Where do they sell? What do they do with their returns? What are their future investment or expansion plans? What sort of public relations, corporate social responsibility, and government affairs strategy do they pursue? Absent a sophisticated understanding of both the specific risks that the investor faces and the strategies that they pursue to mitigate these risks by insurers or traders, the market for cover or hedging instruments collapses.[2] In this manner, political and social risk management bears greater similarity to the management of uncertainty over technology, market demand forecasts, or competitor strategies than it does to more exogenous financial risks. In short, it lies in the domain of management not finance.

Information on such risks should be drawn from as wide an array of sources as possible to avoid the insular focus of many homogenous deliberative bodies. The obvious sources include the managers responsible for the geographic region or country together with relevant functional managers such as those responsible for government, public, and media affairs. A recent PriceWaterHouseCoopers-Eurasia Group survey found 70 percent of the largest multinational corporations rely most heavily upon this source of information. This result echoes those of Kobrin (1979), who found a figure of 74.6 percent for subsidiary managers and 68.9 percent for regional managers.

These internal sources of information should, however, be supplemented by an equally frequent and institutionalized process of consultation with stakeholders across the project's value chain. Any local partners (e.g., joint venture partners, licensees, or franchise owners) should be given a central role in deliberations as the navigation of the local political and social environment may well be one of their distinct competitive advantages. Suppliers of labor, capital, goods, and services – particularly those that are local or have longer experience in the host country – may provide a richer or more independent analysis of the local context.

Analogous to Clay Christensen's pioneering work on technological uncertainty, managers of political and social risks should also speak to their consumers. Just as consumers are at the frontier of new technology and the demands that give rise to it, so too may they be at the frontier of new political demands particularly those with a strong social dimension. Campaigns against the private provision of infrastructure services are often organized around consumer opposition to rate rebalancing or rates aligned with the cost of service provision as opposed to the political benefits that consumers can provide. Similarly, campaigns for improved environmental compliance can gain momentum when consumers are coopted by nongovernmental organizations (NGOs) to mobilize and pressure supplying companies to alter their production processes. By listening carefully to the demands of sensitive classes of consumers at an early stage in the design of global projects, managers may have been better able to manage or get out in front of these challenges to their business model.

In some cases, the activist groups themselves may be a powerful source of information. Yaziji (2004) argued that multinational corporations should transform their perspective of NGOs from that of gadflies to allies. He provides several examples in which such partnerships have avoided strategic surprise or have been designed to preempt attacks. A prominent example of just such a strategy can be found in the case of Royal Dutch Shell Petroleum's inclusion of Greenpeace in any substantive environmental discussions after the conflict between the two organizations over the disposal of the Brent Spar North Sea oil platform.

Another class of actors that can provide useful information, for a fee, is specialized lawyers or consultancies. In fact, the aforementioned PwC-Eurasia Group report found that these are the most common sources of information after internal resources. Political risk consultancies range in form from well positioned ex-government officials operating on retainer, to the stringers who write for the Economist Intelligence Unit, Stratfor, or Oxford Analytica, to global specialized political consultancies such as Political Risk Services or the Eurasia Group. While suppliers, consumers, and activists may each have better information or better incentives to gather and filter information, they may lack the formal and specialized training in the art of politics that such specialists bring to the table. By focusing on the political incentives and constraints generally neglected by financial markets or other analysts, Eurasia Group was able to make predictions that contradicted the conventional wisdom. Two prominent examples were the early expression of concern that policy incoherence in Russia in 1998 could trigger a financial crisis and an early and sustained confidence in Brazilian President Lula's commitment to fiscal discipline in the run-up to his 2002 election (Bremmer 2006).

The most distant set of actors from the project – but still potentially valuable sources of information – are independent third-party monitors such as bankers, the media, or foreign governments. While the information that they provide may not be sufficiently tailored to the needs of the project, they do have substantial resources, in-country knowledge and expertise, and strong incentives to follow developments that may have a substantial macroeconomic, political, or social impact.

## Network

A crucial determinant of the quality of this information-gathering process is the means of information acquisition and aggregation of multiple elements of data from multiple sources. At one extreme, information can be sourced as needed or in response to a crisis-generated request, and then averaged or reduced to a point estimate with a distribution that treats each source of information equally. A more sophisticated, network-based approach would seek to transform the various internal and external sources into an active scanning network that would report in real time any relevant changes in the political and social environment. The importance of reported changes would be assessed taking into account the structural position of the information source and the consistency of the information that they are providing with that of other sources.

For example, PwC-Eurasia note that one of their survey respondents had established such a network to monitor political events that could disrupt their supply chain in any one of 120 countries. Companies that develop such scanning networks for clients include Strategic Radar and the Probity Group, who offer engagements involving the monitoring of strategically important shifts in the competitive, market, social, and government landscapes. Companies offering a similar scanning network with a focus on the management of corporate reputation risk include Attensity, Evolve24, Strategic Radar, and the Probity Group. Evolve24 and Attensity each add to the insight provided by sources within the value chain with information drawn from media and other third-party sources. These reports on the actions of members in the value chain or expressions of their sentiment provide both a denser and, more important, realtime information flow for the purpose of subsequent analysis.

An extension of these outsourced scanning capabilities is the development of a network risk scanning capability. Instead of merely listening for problems or negative reactions to strategic decisions and reacting to them, managers of global projects can engage stakeholders more deeply. They can listen before decisions are made, alter decisions based on that *ex ante* feedback, and agree which decisions should be made in cooperation or partnership with a network of actors (Kytle and Ruggie, 2005).

Relatedly, as opposed to simple aggregation rules that treat each source of information independently or weight them according to some predetermined quality or reliability metric, the consistency of the information across the network, particularly across sources whose own preferences may differ substantively, can be used to improve upon aggregation rules that ignore this structure. At least two dimensions of the structure should be factored into the aggregation process.

The first is geography. PwC-Eurasia highlight that "long-term expatriates and local employees rarely provide an objective view of the political environment. These biases are largely unintentional but are inherent to their roles within the company." Given the trade-off between the greater quantity of information and the inherent bias in the provision of such information, disparities between the information provided by more proximate and distant sources should be evaluated with particular care.

A second dimension of structure extends the logic of geography to the geography of the network. Actors may well perceive allied actors to have more closely aligned preferences than they actually do whereas they may perceive opponents to be more extreme. Proximity of preferences thus plays an analogous role to geographic proximity in that it increases the quantity of information but also the need to filter that information and to pay special attention to disparities between reports from proximate and distant sources of information.

A network approach offers relative benefits both by exploiting multiple ties among stakeholders to enhance realtime information flow across the value chain and by providing analytical guidance as to the marginal value of new information based upon its structural location within that network.

## Developing a strategy to manage political and social risks

### Traditional

While many organizations have adopted formal structures or appointed C-level executives with responsibility for political and social risks (e.g., Corporate Risk Officers or Corporate Responsibility Officers), the tools employed have evolved less quickly than the organizational structures within which they are employed. Furthermore, in comparison to the modeling of financial and economic risks in which Corporate Risk Officers are typically expertly trained, the modeling of political and social risks is more complex due to the need to incorporate and indeed focus upon individual and group beliefs, actions, and interactions that explicitly respond to stimuli other than the price mechanisms (e.g., perceptions of fairness, identity, or legitimacy). The lack of analytical tools to generate indicators of policy risk from these massively complex systems limits the ability to extend enterprise risk modeling frameworks to cover political and social risks.

Similarly, in contrast to the emphasis on compliance with a code of conduct or agreed principles of behavior with which Corporate Responsibility Officers are well-versed, the management of political and social risks requires an emphasis on the assessment of stakeholder preferences on a wide range of issues, the design of a set of practices and influence strategies to alter preferences towards the project and the implementation and communication of those practices and strategies. While a growing number of companies, particularly those with a history of being the targets of a negative stakeholder campaign, are realizing the benefits of such a proactive and sophisticated stakeholder relations strategy, it remains far from the norm even in many of the largest global projects. The next step of linking stakeholder relations to the value of an asset or the size of a net revenue stream associated with an asset represents a level of financial sophistication beyond the level of most corporate responsibility staff (though we discuss an important exception in Anglo-American Corporation in more detail below).

Regardless of the structure within which the analysis takes place, the prevailing mechanisms for that analysis range from the informal to the formal. At one extreme is the gut instinct of the decision maker who has spoken with the relevant sources or been briefed on their views, and draws upon her own experience in knowledge of similar cases to reach a decision based upon what informally in the industry is known as the "tummy test." In this case, nothing more than accumulated experiential knowledge and sensemaking capability drives the final decision. The likely accuracy of such judgments can clearly vary enormously according to the skill set and biases of the decision maker, and the comparability and relevance of his or her past experience to the situation at hand. One means of improving the accuracy of such judgments is to rely on specialized consultancies, which can draw upon a more diverse set of analogies and experiences from multiple firms and industries in the target country or a comparable one, before reaching a final recommendation as to how to reduce the impact of a risk.

A more sophisticated extension of the "tummy test" can be the development of a "war room," in which relevant project staff come together for a one-off meeting or series of brainstorming sessions on how best to proceed. Such sessions may be scheduled regularly or triggered by a shock or event that requires a strategic response. Such discussions are often guided by visual representations of the "battle field" in which the positions and power of various players are captured graphically through the use of "influence maps." These visual diagrams depict each politically relevant actor as a bubble arrayed in space according to the player's position on a given issue, with the size of the bubble proportional to the player's power. Linkages across actors or clusters of actors can be depicted by either location or dyadic ties. While no formal analytic tools are deployed on the resulting visualization, influence maps do help guide "what-if" discussions regarding various strategies that could be expected to improve the policy outcome. The insights into strategy are only as good as the information brought into the room and the quality of the team assembled to transform that information into actionable insight. Once again specialized consultancies such as Hill and Knowlton's Commetric and Alan Kelly's Plays2run (Kelly 2006) can augment an internal capability, provide rich visuals, and consider substantially more complex "plays."

Where the scope and range of uncertainty is high and the time horizon sufficiently long, depictions of the current battlefield, the movement of its players, and the plays they are making may not offer sufficient insight into key long-term strategies. Players may be too focused on today's battle and paying insufficient attention to sea changes over the horizon. Scenario planning exercises are a strategic tool that forces managers to consider the implications of combining known trends with a series of uncertainties to generate internally consistent narratives of future scenarios with vastly different strategic implications (Schoemaker 2002; Day, Schoemaker, and Snyder 2008). Like influence maps, such narratives are most useful for the questions that they trigger here regarding preparedness for a radically different environment.

The most analytically rigorous process involves the incorporation of the individual actors' preferences, power, and issue salience (i.e., the extent to which they are willing to deploy their power on this issue) to develop a dynamic expected utility-based model of the policymaking environment. In such models (Bueno de Mesquita 1992), each actor makes a decision in each time period whether to propose a policy, oppose a policy, or do nothing. The decision is made with the knowledge that proposals and opposition are costly and that the preferences, power, and salience of other actors on this issue are public information, though potentially measured with error or bias by some actors. Each actor therefore undertakes an exercise in expected utility maximization (i.e., will I be better off if I propose, oppose, or do nothing given my expected utility from each choice, and the probability distribution across the outcomes based upon my choice) and chooses accordingly. Each actor proceeds in a similar manner, generating a prediction of the likely policy outcome. The sensitivity of this outcome to various parameter estimates can then be calculated, giving guidance about the identity of the pivotal actor(s) in the policymaking process (i.e., the actors for whom a change in preferences, power, or salience would have the largest impact on the predicted policy outcome), who can subsequently be made the focus of an influence strategy.

These models are widely used within the intelligence community, as well as by a growing number of multinational corporations. Engagements by Sentia Group (previously Decision Insights Inc.) spanned international security (the stability of the Soviet Union, Russia, Saudi Arabia, Iraq, Korea, Yugoslavia, and Northern Ireland); privatization and regulation (Poland, Czechoslovakia, and Italy); legislative reform of health care (US), trade (US), or investment liberalization (Sri Lanka); earmarking and other funding authorizations within the US, EU, and China; regulatory rulings on rates of return in the US and EU; and government approvals of mergers in the US and EU.[3]

An example of a company at the frontier of current practice is AngloAmerican Corporation whose SEAT (Socio-Economic Assessment Toolbox) is a new standard against which many multinational corporations are measuring their political and social risk management practices. This toolbox offers a comprehensive system for continuously improving and managing stakeholder relations based on frequent communications, formal data gathering and analysis, informal consultation, tracking and quantification of activities, impact, monitoring, and stakeholder reactions. Importantly, the process begins at the onset of any project and continues through its termination, involves a locally determined set of relevant stakeholders who are given voice and power, and incorporates transparent and credible monitoring and feedback loops. SEAT constitutes an actionable plan as opposed to a high-level checklist.[4]

## Network

Each of these analytical methods omits crucial elements of the network structure of policymaking, and may therefore lead to suboptimal recommendations with regard to the design of an influence strategy. However, modeling the interdependence among the reactions of each actor to each possible influence strategy will likely strain the capabilities of any informal process. It might be obvious that two actors will tend to move in tandem or that the efforts to sway one actor will have a negative impact on another, but capturing the full set of such interdependencies across political and social actors with different objective functions and ideological beliefs or world views residing in different cities, states/provinces, and nations will prove extremely difficult, particularly across time. The quasi-formal scenario planning exercise, by contrast, is a powerful means to model such interdependencies and the future states of the world that they may generate, as well as to focus attention on an organization's preparedness for that future. Unfortunately, these benefits come at the cost of sacrificing insight into the identification, design, and implementation of strategies that can alter the evolution of the future.

Expected utility models explicitly assume that each actor makes a decision about how to proceed based on an analysis of their own utility, which is a function of similar decisions by other strategic actors. While the analysis formally incorporates the interdependence of the decisions of multiple actors, it typically views the objective of each actor as structure-free (i.e., each actor seeks to maximize utility over some policy outcome but does not care about the proximity of their final position to the position of any other actor). This assumption can be relaxed by allowing utility to vary not only with regard to the policy outcome, but also with reference to the positions of other actors. For example, it may be the case that environmental groups and anti-Russian lobbies both prefer the development of oil and gas pipeline routes from the Caspian Sea to Europe that avoid Russian territory and the Black Sea. Environmental groups favor such routes because they avoid the risk of underwater contamination, particularly in the environmentally fragile and strained Bosphorus, whereas anti-Russian groups favor this routing because it avoids or minimizes Russian control. Absent a recognition that environmentalists and anti-Russian interests often oppose each other in the policymaking arena, an expected utility analysis might view them as close allies. While they are likely to cooperate on certain issues or elements of the campaign, incorporating their typically divergent positions into the analysis would more likely capture the inherent suspicion, tensions, or friction that would make such a coalition more difficult to maintain. In other words, not only must information on preferences be adjusted to reflect the current network structure of the policymaking environment, but the analysis of how those preferences are likely to or could evolve must incorporate the network structure of the other policymaking environments in which the same political and social actors interact.

Finally, and perhaps most importantly, analysis of the external political and social network has to be connected to the internal drivers of value creation. How does a given change in the political and social environment impact the value of an asset and/or the net revenue stream generated by that asset? Absent the connection to observable consequences, the exercise stumbles in its efforts to provide guidance as to the allocation of scarce resources. The decision-making body ultimately must perceive not only the most efficient mechanism to influence policy outcomes, but also the value proposition in doing so. Here, building on well-established tools in enterprise risk management, specific policy outcomes need to be linked to assets (e.g., capital equipment, reputation, intellectual property), and the impact of changes in the external environment need to be quantified in terms of potential costs or revenues. All too often, analysis stops at the point of increasing the threshold return for a project as opposed to actually modeling the implications of political and social risk for revenues and costs under various scenarios.

Network approaches to political and social risk management strategies offer greater potential to incorporate information on relationships between various trends or uncertainties, stakeholder preferences or actions, and their combined impact on multiple asset values or net revenue streams than traditional analytical models. These advantages are increasingly important as international economic, political, and social interdependence expand.

## Implementing political and social risk management strategies

### Traditional

Once these mechanisms have been used to identify a strategic goal, the next step is strategic implementation: the transformation of that strategic objective into a realized outcome. In contrast to typical discussions of implementation, however, the challenge in political and social risk management is heightened by the need to influence behavior and actions by nonemployees who often operate in response to a motive other than profit maximization. Influencing behavior among a diverse group of managers or workers spanning functions, divisions, and/or nations is already an extremely challenging task. Extending the focus of that effort to politicians, regulators, bureaucrats, activists, lobbyists, and other politically relevant groups spread across multiple organizations in multiple countries clearly magnifies the difficulty of the exercise.

As compared to profit-maximizing entities, political and social actors possess a far wider range of objectives, typically including re-election/reappointment or maintenance of status, social welfare maximization, and, in some instances, personal wealth or reputation maximization. They are often agents of or otherwise dependent upon the favor of other political and social actors ranging from voters to interest groups to individual enterprises, each with their own blend of political, social, and economic objectives. How can one best influence such a heterogeneous playing field?

As the target is both more remote and the objectives of that target more disparate, the leverage applied to influence that target must be substantial. A small number of large entrenched organizations may possess enough leverage to affect such a complex playing field. For the vast majority, however, action requires assembling a coalition of actors and convincing them of a shared interest and a need to act to achieve that shared interest. The coalition may include other economic organizations, trade associations, consultants, lawyers, and lobbyists, as well as allied political and social actors. Relevant political or social actors include representatives of the home country embassy or government, host country politicians at the federal, sub-federal, or local levels, political actors of powerful third countries, or multilateral organizations or nongovernmental actors from the home, host, or third countries. Ideally, the focal organization can coordinate both the message and the target of that message for all actors in this coalition. Great skill is required in orchestrating such an outcome due to the need to understand the particular interests and capabilities of each member of the coalition, the direct and indirect ties that they have to the target, and the most effective means for the coalition members to present their case to the target, particularly with regard to the manner in which that communication may be portrayed by the media.

One key trade-off in the implementation of influence is that between a reliance upon agents from the home country (e.g., the government of the home country, international financial institutions including private and multilateral lenders, a chamber of commerce or other international trade association, management at headquarters, affiliated foreign firms, international NGOs) versus the host country (e.g., local government officials, a local trade association, local financial institutions, the host country management team, affiliated local firms, and local NGOs). On the one hand, foreign influence channels are relatively low-cost and expedient. In addition, particularly for large or otherwise more powerful home countries, they offer the focal organization an ability to use the leverage of linkage to other issues between the two countries. On the other hand, foreign influence can generate a perception of meddling, stoke fears of nationalism, and may lack sufficient leverage to generate deep-seated structural reforms. There is also always the risk that the foreign actor will sacrifice the needs of the focal organization for another more salient issue. In contrast, local influence channels require much up-front investment in political capital and even more careful ongoing management of the alignment of interests. In return for these higher fixed and ongoing costs, such coalitions have a greater likelihood of effecting deep-seated change that persists over the medium to long term.

A second key trade-off within the subset of local influence coalitions is that between envelopment of and partnership with the focal organization's competitors or direct opponents. In some instances it may be feasible to form alliances with members of the value chain in a country without going so far as to strike a deal with your local competitor. In other instances, where the battle is more over the size of the pie or where the local competitor has such power in the policymaking structure, sharing the spoils and investing in maintaining an alignment of interests over the medium to long term may be necessary.

## Network

Similar to the extensions to the information sourcing and analysis processes, a network approach to implementation incorporates information on network structure and feedbacks more comprehensively and systematically to improve the efficacy of influence strategies. Just as the network position of information sources should influence the aggregation of that information, the network position of potential allies should influence the design and implementation of an influence strategy. Rather than focus solely on the relationship between a potential ally and the target of an influence strategy, consider as well their structural position in the policymaking network, particularly as it is perceived by third-party actors. These actors will seek to interpret the behavior of your coalition allies and infer whether they are acting as proxies or as allies. Interventions by coalition partners that are dependent upon the focal actor or otherwise always support the preferences of the focal actor will be discounted as compared to interventions by structurally independent actors (i.e., those that are perceived to have come to their own conclusion on the issue). Particularly where the coalition members themselves are not traditional allies, the credibility of the influence strategy is further enhanced. The design of an influence strategy should thus incorporate not only information on the power and preferences of each individual actor, but the structural position of that actor as perceived by others. This additional information can augment traditional analysis focused on power and alignment of preferences by identifying untraditional or credible organizations that play a prominent role in implementation. Examples of such an approach include efforts to have NGOs certify or monitor compliance with agreed standards in global projects. As compared to self-monitoring or consultancy-based certification, the oversight of a presumably skeptical third party adds credibility to reports of compliance.

In addition, a network approach aspires to go beyond partial analysis of individual interventions and consider seriously how various interventions will interact. Strategies designed to meet individual objectives (e.g., the severing of a tie between two actors or the development of greater local support among undecided constituencies) may undermine each other when implemented together. Viewing influence strategies in isolation, as opposed to as part of an interconnected policymaking network, can undermine their efficacy or even generate negative feedbacks. One needs to look ahead and see not only the likely reaction of the target(s), but also the reactions of parties to whom the target is tied. It is possible that the indirect effect of strong negative reactions from tied actors can overwhelm any beneficial direct effect of an influence strategy. Coordinated and coherent strategies therefore need to be deployed. Furthermore, in the connection of the external political and social network structure to the internal structure of assets of the corporation, this need for coordination and coherence requires linking an organization's influence strategy to its technological, financial, marketing and competitive strategy as well.

## Best practice: ChevronTexaco in Angola

As ChevronTexaco planned for the development of a $10 billion onshore liquid natural gas processing and shipping facility, they initiated an extensive stakeholder consultation effort, which worked synchronously with the engineering and financial planning teams and led to substantive adaptation of project design and implementation. As illustrated in Figure 10.1, first, key stakeholders were identified, including the project management team and its workers, community leaders, vulnerable groups of the local community, actual and potential suppliers and contractors, local businesses and cooperatives, local churches, and civic organizations and the local governments. Secondary stakeholders included the Angolan national government, the provincial government, ministries, NGOs, academia, customers, industry associations, labor associations, political parties, financiers, and the media. Key performance criteria in the environmental and socioeconomic dimensions were identified, and monitoring and tracking of quantifiable indicators of performance in these domains were initiated.

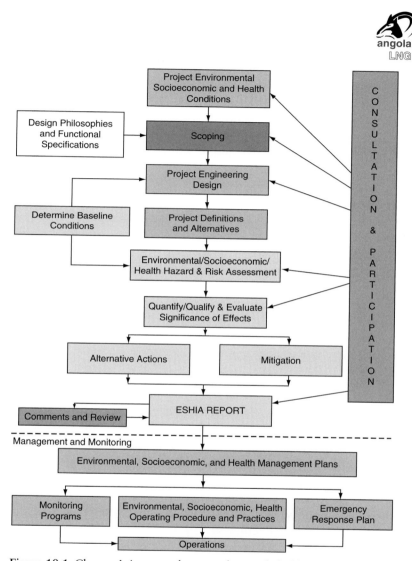

**Figure 10.1** Chevron's integrated approach to stakeholder consultation

As a result of this consultation, ChevronTexaco:

- relocated the onshore site to minimize the perceived impact on mangroves;
- rescheduled offshore work to minimize the perceived risk to turtle nesting, whale calving, and fish spawning;
- built a wave barrier and imposed a speed restriction on boards to minimize erosion and siltation;
- placed greater emphasis on the elimination of gas flaring; created a fishermen-based monitoring system for any negative impact of the project on local fisheries;
- reduced the capital intensity of the construction process so as to increase local employment;
- provided subsidized cooking fuel to the local population;
- took responsibility for physical and social infrastructure for migrant workers;
- conducted blessing ceremonies to comply with religious custom;
- sold shares of the liquid natural gas onshoring facility in Florida to the Angolan state-owned enterprise; and
- supported Angolan government efforts to distribute offshore rights to Norwegian, Chinese, and Russian interests instead of concentrating them in a smaller number of investors.

These decisions had a material impact on the costs and timing of the project. The impact was so large in fact that ExxonMobil walked away from the investment claiming that ChevronTexaco was throwing money away. A lack of internal documentation and the early stage nature of the project preclude an analysis of the efficacy of the stakeholder engagement strategy. It is notable, however, that operating in one of the most corrupt, impoverished, and war-ravaged nations, ChevronTexaco has successfully executed a $4 billion investment without any reported opposition from the NGO community or the various levels of local government.

While the public documentation does not provide sufficient information to conclude whether the cost-benefit analysis followed all of the guidelines outlined in this chapter, several aspects of ChevronTexaco's strategy do stand out and are broadly consistent with the themes stressed here. As highlighted in Figure 10.2, ChevronTexaco's process incorporated stakeholder feedback into every element of engineering and financial design. Social and political considerations were not

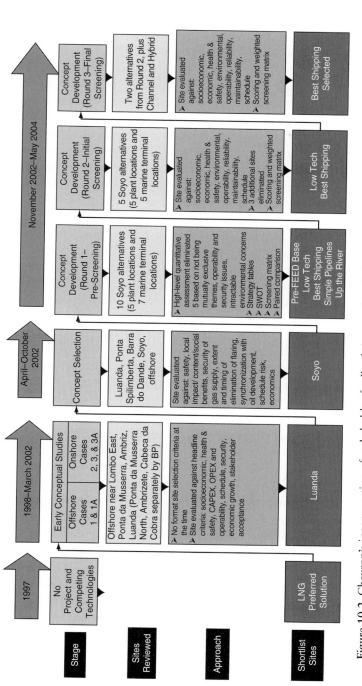

**Figure 10.2** Chevron's incorporation of stakeholder feedback into project design

addressed at the end of the process with the objective of defending key decisions that had already been publicly announced, but rather each decision was assessed holistically combining economic, social, and political considerations. Not every stakeholder demand was met. Some stakeholder demands were perceived as self-serving or otherwise not warranting the demanded action. The active and synchronous stakeholder feedback mechanism constructed helped to identify key stakeholders, their preferences, and a means to address them as well as monitor compliance with those commitments. The analysis incorporated dozens of stakeholders, multiple issues of concern, variation in the salience of issues across stakeholders, as well as potential coalitions of stakeholders that might form around distinct issues.

A key unobserved element of the process, however, was the precise means by which this information was aggregated, used to alter the ongoing engineering and financial plan, and used to influence the preferences of key political and social stakeholders. How did Chevron build and maintain its political and social coalition? What direct and indirect channels of communication and influence did they employ? What was the structure of their stakeholder network in Angola and globally, and how did they choose which actions to take to shape it? Providing corroborating evidence of the centrality of these points to successful political and social risk management was Chevron's response when asked to cooperate in the development of a best practice teaching case study: they claimed that this process was a source of competitive advantage that they preferred not to have publicized.

## Conclusion: from information overload to actionable insight

Whereas political and social risk management has typically been viewed as more art than science, a set of analytic capabilities developed independently across various social science disciplines offers the potential for substantive improvements to the aggregation of sourced information, the analysis of influence maps, the development of comparative scenarios, and, most importantly, the design of influence strategies to alter those scenario outcomes. Due to the inherent complexity of the system of interactions among corporations, governments, NGOs, and each of their respective stakeholders, political and social risk monitoring will never approach the level of refinement and sophistication of financial modeling of exchange rate or credit risk. Global project managers are, however, in the midst of a radical transformation of their processes in this area moving far beyond the "tummy test" to a much more scientific model of external stakeholder relations. Enacting such change involves increasing the sophistication of data acquisition and analysis, as well as the implementation of influence strategies. In each of these endeavors, applying insights developed within the modeling of networks offers substantial benefits.

Information sources exist within a structure that influences their perspective and the accuracy of reporting of that perspective. Dynamic political models designed to forecast policy outcomes and identify pivotal actors toward which to target influence strategies should similarly incorporate information on that structure. Each actor proceeds not independently or merely with reference to the likely reactions of other actors, but also cognizant of the broader political and social structure in which they are embedded, and in which they will interact with these same actors in the future. As a result, their objective is not just to maximize utility on the issue at hand, but to consider how their position today will influence their ability to achieve their objectives on this and other issues in the future. Once again, the network structure of policymaking provides useful insight into the analysis. Finally, in the implementation of influence strategies, the choice of a messenger and message, as well as the incorporation of feedback effects over time, are both enhanced by viewing the policymaking structure as an interconnected network.

## Endnotes

1 Witold J. Henisz, "Network-based strategies and competences for political and social risk management," in *Network-based strategies and competencies*. Upper Saddle River, NJ: Wharton School Publishing. Revised version of original article reprinted by permission of Wharton School Publishing. Thanks to Dick Scott, Stephen Kobrin, Bennett Zelner, and Paul Kleindorfer for their comments on previous drafts.

2 A growing quantity of political and social risk coverage is available but such coverage is typically limited to the value of the investment, not the revenue stream it is meant to generate, and costs frequently amount to 10 percent of the asset at risk with coverage rarely available for more than 10 years. Given the 20- or 30-year exposure an investor is taking on and the gap between the cost of the investment and the revenue stream it is meant

to generate in such a risky market, even investors who purchase such coverage are internalizing a substantial portion of residual risk management.

3 See www.diiusa.com/experience.html.

4 For a more detailed overview of SEAT see www.angloamerican.com/aal/development/social/community-engagement/seat/.

# 11 Organizations enabling public–private partnerships: an organization field approach

STEPHAN F. JOOSTE AND W. RICHARD SCOTT

## Introduction: increasing the sustainability of public–private partnership projects

The pivotal role of civil infrastructure in enhancing public health and accelerating economic growth has been widely acknowledged in the literature (Estache 2004). It thus remains a central part of improvement initiatives in both developed and developing countries. Although responsibility for infrastructure development has alternated between private and public provision over the past century, in recent times it has largely been the responsibility of the public sector.

The last two decades have seen significant changes in the modes of government intervention in many developed countries. Reforms in countries like Great Britain and New Zealand have been at the forefront of this movement, largely driven by two broad factors: perceived public sector inefficiencies, and the ascendance of liberal economic ideology (Salamon 2002). Changes have broadly involved a reduction in the role of government or, more accurately, a change in the functions it performs, and greater private sector involvement (Hood 1991; Kaul 1997; Osborne and Gaebler 1992; Peters and Pierre 2002; Rhodes 1996; Salamon 2002). For infrastructure development this has meant a move toward increased reliance on public–private partnerships (PPPs) that involve private companies in the financing and provision of infrastructure. In most countries these PPP arrangements have been aimed at overcoming two broad public sector constraints: (1) a lack of public capital; and (2) a lack of public sector capacity – the resources and specialized expertise to develop, manage, and operate infrastructure assets (Bovaird 2004; Kumaraswamy and Zhang 2001).

The 1990s saw proliferation of PPPs in both developed and developing countries, totaling almost $755 billion in private investment across nearly 2,500 private infrastructure projects globally in developing countries alone (Harris 2003), an amount estimated to account for more than 20 percent of all infrastructure investment during this period (Izaruirre 2004). However, after peaking in 1999, private investment in infrastructure fell off dramatically at the beginning of the first decade of the twenty-first century, only recently returning to its former level. A number of reasons have been proposed for this downturn, including highly publicized cases of public opposition to private provision, and large numbers of contract renegotiations and cancellations (Guasch, Laffont, and Straub 2002).

These pervasive failures of infrastructure PPPs in recent years (Guasch, Laffont, and Straub 2002) illustrate the need to address four challenges:

1. market failures associated with private infrastructure provision (rooted in the natural monopoly characteristics and externalities of infrastructure) (Goldberg 1976; Mody 1996; Savas 2000);
2. agency failures relating to the limited capacity of public entities;
3. perceived legitimacy issues surrounding private provision of public infrastructure; and
4. government opportunism stemming from the fact that infrastructure is plagued by what has been called the "obsolescing bargain" – once the facility is completed and in operation, the private developer loses much of its bargaining power in subsequent negotiations over tariffs or other matters (Ramamurti and Doh 2004; Woodhouse 2005).

Because of these and related problems, current levels of private investment in infrastructure are insufficient to address the growing global needs (Gil and Beckman 2008). This shortfall has been exacerbated by the recent global financial crisis, which has seriously curtailed the availability of private financing.[1] If PPPs are to play a part in the global infrastructure solution, the sustainability of PPP arrangements clearly needs to be addressed.

A significant amount of work on increasing PPP effectiveness and sustainability has focused on the constraints from the private perspective, stressing the limits of employing private incentives to overcome public problems. A number of scholars, however, have recently highlighted the critical role that the public sector plays in ensuring PPP success (Estache and Serebrisky 2004; Van Slyke 2003). For instance, based on a review of the World Bank's experience with infrastructure PPPs, Harris proposes that:

. . . if private provision is to be sustainable and to benefit consumers of infrastructure services, governments will have to address many of the problems overlooked in the initial rush towards private participation (Harris 2003: vii).

Rather than alleviating a deficit in the institutional capacity of the public sector, the use of PPPs actually depends for its success on the development of a variety of new types of capacity from governments. As Dutz et al. (2006) propose:

This shift from traditional public sector methods places new demands on government agencies. They need the capacity to design projects with a package of risks and incentives that makes them attractive to the private sector. They need to be able to assess the cost to taxpayers, often harder than for traditional projects because of the long-term and often uncertain nature of government commitments. They need contract management skills to oversee these arrangements over the life of the contract. And they need advocacy and outreach skills to build consensus on the role of PPPs and to develop a broad program across different sectors and levels of government. (Dutz et al. 2006: 1)

This assertion makes it clear that ensuring the success of PPP projects goes beyond successfully governing the projects that have been developed; indeed, the recent history of PPPs seems to suggest that some projects are flawed from the outset (Klijn and Teisman 2000). Of critical importance are the choices made in deciding which projects to pursue, and developing these projects in a way that makes them attractive to private investors while still protecting the interest of users and taxpayers in general, including securing legitimacy and curtailing corruption. Moreover, actions are required that not only focus on the success of single PPP *projects* in isolation, but rather aim to sustain the wider portfolio of PPP projects, the PPP *program*.

The global recognition of these challenges presented in both developing and governing infrastructure PPPs has led to the emergence of a variety of new organizational forms internationally. These organizations, in varying ways, attempt to enable the development and continued operation of PPPs, for the benefit of public, private, and civic actors. Moreover, to be successful, these organizations need to be combined in varying constellations of field configurations. The remainder of this paper describes this collection of new forms and illustrates some of the combinations which have been assembled in varying international contexts.

## Identifying typical types of public–private partnership enabling organizations

The first to emerge were *Public Regulators*, organizations focused on regulating the performance of the private providers after the contracts were awarded. These agencies have often been set up to be independent from the executive branch, thereby seeking autonomy, transparency, and accountability (Andres, Gausch, Diop, and Azumendi 2007). Their optimal structuring has been widely debated in the literature, specifically the trade-off between centralized versus decentralized agencies, and sector-specific versus multi-sector agencies (see for instance Laffont 2005). For contemporary PPPs the form of regulator is highly dependent on the type of arrangement regulated. The formal independent regulator model was developed specifically to address sectors that faced large-scale privatizations (such as energy and telecoms). More recent Greenfield PPP projects have seen the regulatory function residing within the line agency which "owns" the project, rather than in a separate entity. To achieve independence in regulation, many governments have made use of an auditor (such as the Auditor General in Australia and South Africa) or nonpublic regulators in addition to the line-agency regulatory body. In general, the public regulatory bodies address the issue of agency failure and the need for improved legitimacy.

*Nonpublic Regulators* emerged in support of public regulators. This group of actors includes private consultants, technical specialists, such as academic institutions or experts, and nongovernmental organizations (NGOs). Tremolet (2007) has divided this type of service into two broad groups: (1) "advisory outsourcing" bodies are external advisors providing input to regulatory decision makers which they are not obliged to follow,[2] in contrast to (2) "binding outsourcing" groups whose recommendations must be heeded. Clearly, the motive underlying the latter is curbing the discretion of public regulators, or increasing their legitimacy, while the former is more generally aimed at providing specialist input to decision makers. A number of advantages have been proposed in support of the use of nonpublic regulators. Since regulatory workflow can be very cyclical in nature (Eberhard 2007), with major regulatory reviews occurring only every few years, it is difficult for public agencies to retain qualified staff throughout. Regulatory outsourcing therefore provides regulating agencies with highly skilled resources at a lower cost (due to economies of scale for service providers),[3] while increasing organizational flexibility. In addition, it also improves the legitimacy of regulatory bodies by fostering regulatory independence (Trémolet 2007). Contemporary examples of nonpublic regulators include the "probity auditor" in use in Australia, and the "fairness advisor" which is used in British Columbia (Canada).

The use of nonpublic service providers has been expanded by the introduction of *transaction advisors*.[4] These organizations are private service providers who assist public agencies in the formulation and negotiation of PPP arrangements. In general they play a strictly advisory role, assisting governments to overcome technical capacity shortfalls when developing PPPs. Their focus is specifically on setting up the initial "transaction" by developing the project concept, managing the tender process, and guiding the contract formation. These types of organizations operate primarily to increase the capacity of the public agencies to manage PPP programs.

*PPP Units* (sometimes referred to as "PPP Coordination Agencies") are a more recent addition to the PPP enablement spectrum. Although the concept of PPP Unit is not new, research into these public sector organizations has only recently emerged. These agencies have been established as governments realized the difficulty of consistently identifying, setting up, and managing PPP relationships. Generally the units aim to improve the sustainability of PPP arrangements by:

1. undertaking research and disseminating PPP information and best practices;
2. setting policy and proposing legislation on PPPs;
3. proactively identifying projects and developing them;
4. providing a consulting service to other public agencies when engaging in PPPs;
5. funding PPP studies or project development;
6. playing a role in the monitoring (regulation) of PPP contracts; and
7. approving which projects are undertaken or, secondarily, giving advice to decision makers in the approval process.

In their study of eight PPP Units, Farrugia et al. (2008) identified two broad types of agencies: (1) "Review Bodies" are primarily responsible for reviewing project business plans and providing recommendations to decision makers; (2) "Full Service Agencies" perform review services but, in addition, take on proactive roles to develop the PPP market, providing consulting services to service agencies and, in some cases, supplying capital for proposed projects. PPP Units are an attempt to address virtually all of the challenges confronting PPP projects, including market and agency failures, legitimacy, and attempt to increase the stability of governments allowing them to serve as reliable partners.

An interesting recent trend is the creation of private and nonprofit *Advocacy Associations* that emerge as private infrastructure providers and other proponents of PPPs band together to form organizations for collective action. These associations specifically aim to develop the local PPP market, and can take both informal and more formal (and permanent) forms. The development of the Tirurpur water supply project in India is an example of a temporary advocacy organization, where a group of textile manufacturers came together to present an unsolicited bid to the state government. The project was aimed at implementing a PPP to develop a water system that would solve the water supply problems of the specific textile factories involved. More formal associations focus on local advocacy, as is the case of the Slovak PPP association. This association represented the interests of more than forty private companies, and was tasked with creating favorable conditions for the development and implementation of PPP projects in Slovakia. In general, Advocacy Associations focus primarily on the problems of increasing stakeholder participation and transparency, thus enhancing legitimacy.

A final, but significant type of PPP enabling organization consists of a variety of *local, regional,* and *multinational development agencies* that assist public sectors in emerging markets. These include transnational actors such as the Bretton-Woods organizations (World Bank, IMF, ADB, IADB, etc.) who have been at the forefront of promoting private participation in developing countries. These regional and multinational agencies have taken leading roles in supporting governments in initiating – often choosing which projects to pursue – developing, and sustaining PPP infrastructure projects, through varying levels of direct involvement (advice, funding, or even taking on some of these roles themselves). Not only have they provided invaluable assistance to governments lacking the necessary expertise and experience in contracting private providers, but in addition they have attempted to constrain opportunistic behavior of both private and public actors by bringing international influence networks to bear. Another mode of intervention is the involvement of local development agencies. Often a product of multinational development assistance, local development agencies are governmental organizations mandated to initiate and develop major infrastructure projects on behalf of the government. With the growth in popularity of PPPs, many local development agencies have responded by including PPP project development as part of their mandates both locally and regionally (Viljoen 2006). The development agencies address issues of both market and agency failures.

## Assessing the combined use of public–private partnership enabling organizations

While it is clear that a variety of enabling organizations have emerged in the last two decades to assist organizations to address the challenges faced by infrastructure PPPs, as noted, most of them address only a subset of the problems confronted. Thus, it appears that these organizations do not ordinarily confront these challenges in isolation, but rather work together to collectively enable and sustain PPP projects. For this reason, we think understanding will be advanced by considering how these organizations function in combination, including exploring how these combinations are shaped by their institutional environments. By "institutional" we mean the elements that create shared meanings and controls, thereby providing order to social action. These elements include regulatory and legal frameworks, norms and value systems, and cultural elements and beliefs (Scott 1995/2008).

## Organizational fields as a theoretical lens

The remainder of this paper seeks to develop this approach by drawing on the notion of organizational fields, as developed within institutional theory (see Chapter 2). DiMaggio and Powell (1983: 148) define an organizational field as "those organizations that, in the aggregate constitute a recognized area of institutional life: key suppliers, resource and product consumers, regulatory agencies, and other organizations that produce similar services and products." This is very congenial to Scott and Meyer's (1983, 1991) concept of a "societal sector," which includes both organizations in a given domain delivering similar service or products, as well as the other organizations that "critically influence their performance," stressing functional interrelation over geographical proximity. While DiMaggio and Powell focus on the ties (reflected in aspects of "connectedness" and structural equivalence) and mechanisms of influence operating between the organizations in a field, Scott and Meyer focus attention on the structural characteristics of the field itself and their impact on organization characteristics.

Scott et al. (2000) identify three salient components that undergird organizational fields: *actors*, including both types of roles for individuals and types of organizations; *logics*; and *governance arrangements*. More recently Hoffmann and Ventresca (2002) have expanded this by identifying two additional field elements: *intermediary institutions*; and *local sensemaking activities*.

Together these components both constrain and enable action within fields, and thereby shape the behavior and characteristics of organizational participants (Campbell 2004; DiMaggio and Powell 1983; Meyer and Rowan 1977; Scott and Meyer 1983, 1991). The concept of a field points to an "empirical trace" (Hoffman and Ventresca 2002) that is helpful because it defines the boundaries within which these shaping processes (such as competition, influence, coordination, and innovation) take place (DiMaggio 1991).

The use of the field concept is of specific relevance to the present examination of PPP enabling organizations, because it provides a way of considering these organizations in combination and in interaction with their institutional contexts. We build on the five components identified above as a foundation for exploring the fields in which these organizations are located.

## Three levels of public–private partnership fields

Although enabling organizations participate in a number of organizational fields, we believe fields operating at three levels are of particular significance: (1) the local field within which specific PPP projects are carried out; (2) the state or federal field within which the enabling organizations operate; and (3) the wider transnational PPP field that spans national contexts (see also, Chapter 2).[5]

## Local project field

At the most basic level, PPP enabling organizations are involved in developing and sustaining specific PPP projects in their project locale. At this level the interests of local participants and affected parties are more visible, and therefore the local field is dominated by this broad group of actors, which, in addition to the types of PPP enabling organizations described above, include the following.

- *End users* are all the local citizens that will make use of the PPP assets once they are constructed, whether they pay for the privilege or not (e.g., in projects based on shadow tolls or direct subsidies).
- *Local stakeholders* consist of actors that are in any way affected (both positively and negatively) by the PPP project under concern. This would include local landowners, residents, and local tax payers, where impacts range from environmental and social effects, to employment opportunities, and even tax implications (where projects might be funded through local tax measures).
- Stakeholder interests will often be represented by *nongovernmental organizations* (NGOs) or groups mobilized through *local social movement organizations* (see also, Chapter 3).
- *Local governmental organizations* include all subnational/state governmental organizations that affect the work of the public regulatory agencies having specific jurisdiction over the project implementation. In many cases PPP projects will not be subject to local regulatory approvals because they will fall under the jurisdiction of national or state line agencies (such as ministries of transportation, health, or education) as described in the following section. However, most PPP projects are implemented in coordination with local government agencies including local municipalities, water boards, and health agencies. Obviously these organizations are even more salient in projects that are implemented solely at a local level (such as municipal PPPs).
- *Local trade unions* are often important players in the local PPP field. Such organizations have historically been quite vocal in the

PPP debate on both sides of the spectrum: on the one hand public sector unions have argued against private involvement in infrastructure, while private sector unions have seen PPPs as a way to increase employment opportunities for their members.

## National/state level field

PPP enabling organizations generally operate at a national level in most countries, although this is sometimes narrowed to states in a federalized system. Although organizations occasionally focus on a single infrastructure sector (transportation, water, etc.), the organizational field spans all these sectors at the nation/state level. At this level PPP enabling organizations are joined by the following diverse group of salient actors/organizations:

- *Governmental agencies* include all bodies within the nation state that play a role, have a stake, or are impacted by the PPP projects under concern, in addition to the PPP enabling organizations. Most important, this includes the line agencies or departments that initiate and take responsibility for these projects. In addition, various other departments are involved in providing project approvals, including cases where overall project approval is centralized under departments such as the ministry of finance.
- *Private for-profit firms* include those having influence on the PPP projects themselves (including developers, lenders, financiers, designers, contractors, and operators), and those that are indirectly involved with current projects (such as various service providers) or hope to participate in future projects.
- *Local normative organizations* provide input to PPP projects based on concern for values such as environmental protection, health standards, and equity considerations. These include research and academic organizations and professional associations.
- *National NGOs* include advocacy (nonprofit) organizations who seek to stimulate the PPP market and increase deal flow, such as those found in Canada, the US, and Australia. To a lesser extent, various other national NGOs play a part in shaping the national PPP field on issues such as employment, fairness, and sustainability.
- *National trade unions* are the higher level equivalents of the local unions discussed above.

## Transnational public–private partnership governance field

In addition to the local and national fields that PPP enabling organizations operate in, they also form part of a wider transnational field of organizations that together form the global infrastructure PPP market. We prefer the term transnational rather than global to indicate that this field does not necessarily include all nations, but rather those that have an active PPP market.

In addition to the enabling organizations themselves, the primary actors in this field are:

- *International consulting firms* supply international experts who work at multiple levels, including the local level, and serve to convey information and best practices through professional networks.
- *International infrastructure design, construction, and development firms* (often connected to the for-profit firms in the local PPP field) work on PPP projects in a variety of different countries, and bring with them the technical, financial, and negotiating skills and experience needed to execute the PPP assignment. Ironically enough, these actors use their specialized skills and experience both to benefit governments (ensuring they get a first-class development) and to exploit them (through aggressive contract negotiations and renegotiations).
- *International NGOs* are very active at the transnational level, applying normative controls through mechanisms such as "naming and shaming" campaigns via the media, voluntary audits, and peer controls (Djelic and Sahlin-Andersson 2006). They are often activated by their local counterparts to participate in PPP developments.
- *Professional associations and research and academic institutions* also apply cognitive frameworks and normative controls through standard setting, educational programs, and professional forums for information sharing.

## Other field components

The above discussion highlights the primary types of *actors* (or organization archetypes) that are found in the three fields within which PPP enabling organizations are located. However, our examination of these fields can also be elaborated by utilizing the four other field elements identified earlier: governance arrangements, institutional logics, intermediaries, and local sensemaking activities.

*Governance arrangements* may be subdivided into those relying primarily on (1) regulatory controls, based on the use of formal authority backed by sanctions; and (2) normative controls, based on the exercise of influence stemming from shared values and actors who elicit compliance based on moral, obligatory, and prescriptive arguments (Scott 1995/2008). No fully legitimate regulatory organizations operate at the transnational level, but the multinational and regional development agencies, such as the World Bank described above, do control important financial sanctions and exercise some suasion based on normative claims. International NGOs and transnational professional associations employ primarily normative influence, as they attempt to set standards and promulgate best practices related to their areas of expertise.

Organizations operating at the national and state levels, by contrast, include governmental actors – political leaders and agency executives – who employ regulatory powers based on occupancy in positions of authority backed by the legitimate exercise of coercive power. These organizations are joined by – often, opposed by – a variety of NGOs who challenge and attempt to influence their exercise of control. And, at the local level, we find the same types of actors, local governance organizations and NGOs, and, in addition, social movements that arise in reaction to the project – some in support, others in opposition.

Projects operating under PPP arrangements entail an effort to create a partnership among types of organizations operating with quite dissimilar *institutional logics* (Friedland and Alford 1991). Institutional logics "are the cognitive maps, the belief systems carried by participants in the field to guide and give meaning to their activities" (Scott et al. 2000: 20). Public leaders are highly sensitive to the election cycle and often concentrate on short-term objectives. They attend to shared beliefs and public sentiments, and most attempt to comply with widely shared norms regarding their legitimate role. Government agency officials stress conformity to rules and procedures and often emphasize transparency and the use of structures fostering wide information sharing and participation from affected parties. These agencies typically are highly specialized, so that officials are likely to concentrate on a relatively narrow set of concerns to the exclusion of broader performance objectives. This narrowness of focus is also likely to occur among NGOs and professional associations. By contrast, for-profit firms are likely to embrace market-efficiency logics and to be guided by the standards and operating procedures largely drawn from professional and craft sources. Developers must attend closely to cost-containment measures, protecting the financial interests of owners and shareholders. Clearly, PPP structures are complex coalitions of partners with divergent identities guided by diverse interests following varying and often contradictory institutional logics.

A majority of the new types of actors in the PPP field act as *intermediaries* among the main players. Between the primary organizations – government agencies, project firms, local stakeholders, and end users – a growing collection of information brokers, advisors, consultants, and watchdog organizations have arisen. The most prominent intermediaries at the transnational level are the regional and multilateral development agencies. These organizations affect diffusion of practice within PPP fields in a number of ways: using normative influence to shape player decisions; employing coercive pressure by threatening to withhold development assistance; and sponsoring advisory projects to foster capacity building in local areas. When we talk about the changing "structure" of a field, we refer not only to more regularized patterns of interaction among the main players, but also to growth in the number and importance of organizations whose principal function is to oversee, steer, and mediate the transactions among the primary players.

Finally, *local sensemaking activities* arise in the local project field as the diverse players converge around the focal project and begin to interact, often for the first time. Some of the players have come from distant locations and bring with them beliefs and practices shared from earlier projects. Others, at the national and the local level, may be involved in such international construction projects for the first time, and must find ways to interpret unfamiliar demands and events and develop modes of reacting to them. All groups must adapt their expectations and behavior to accommodate these varying interests. Each type of organization confronts novel situations and unknown types of actors. Hence, sensemaking is the order of the day as organizations in these novel fields strive to understand the situation they are in and what course of action to pursue (Weick 1995; Weick, Sutcliffe, and Obstfeld 2005). The confluence and interaction of these diverse players results in, at best, a pragmatic fusion of institutional logics as organizations adapt to their new partners and novel circumstances. At its worst, serious misunderstandings, disappointment, and conflicts may arise among the host government, the private provider and the end users, as illustrated by the failure of the Cochabamba water concession in Bolivia. Such public failures can have transnational repercussions, shaping user resistance to private water supply projects globally (Davis 2005).

## Comparing public–private partnership enabling fields

The preceding discussion presents the kinds of actors and processes that may characterize the organizational fields that surround PPP enabling organizations. In surveying the current scene, however, we can identify significant differences internationally in the composition of, in particular, the national/state level field. For this reason we present three contemporary examples of state level fields in this section. In addition, we attempt to make preliminary sense of the variety of present-day field compositions by drawing on previous work by Scott and others (Scott and Meyer 1991; Scott et al. 2000; Wooten and Hoffman 2008) on organizational field characteristics.

## Selected examples of public–private partnership enabling fields

To illuminate the divergence of PPP enabling fields, we present three contemporary examples: South Africa; the Province of British Columbia in Canada; and the Republic of Korea. Although they are not archetypes of typical field compositions, these cases provide a useful indication of variations in the types of players and configurations to be found in diverse regions.

### South Africa

The South African context has seven principal types of organizational actors in the national PPP enablement field. The first can be referred to as the *sponsoring agency,* and is the government department or agency that contracts for the private infrastructure provision. The sponsoring agency is responsible for identifying and developing the project concept, carrying out the feasibility study, conducting the procurement phase, and obtaining Treasury approval after each step. After contract signature the sponsoring agency is also responsible for monitoring and regulating performance, dispute resolution, and reporting to the Auditor-General. In this way they act as the public regulator of the PPP project.

Due to the complexity of the project development process, sponsoring agencies generally appoint *transaction advisors* to carry out the project preparation and approval process on their behalf. These advisors most often comprise a team of private consultants that include legal, financial, and technical experts. Many of these consultants have direct (in the case of an international consulting firm) or indirect (by way of personal or professional ties with consultants in other countries) links with international consultancy organizations, thereby enabling them to draw in best practices from abroad.

Less common than the use of transaction advisors, sponsoring agencies can also make use of *regulatory consultants* in performing their functions during the project term (after contract award). The aim of using these consultants is almost exclusively aimed at overcoming skill and capacity shortages that the line agency might face in executing their regulatory functions.

A fourth actor is the *PPP Unit* located within National Treasury, responsible for controlling progress of the PPP project development through four distinct approval steps (Levinsohn and Reardon 2007). In this way the unit is focused on ensuring the quality of PPPs and protecting the larger government against imprudent commitments made by sponsoring agencies. In addition it provides advice to agencies interested in PPPs, mostly through periodic publications and their internationally commended PPP guides. The PPP Unit is focused exclusively on the pre-award process. Final approval of all PPP transactions is conferred by *National Treasury*, based on the recommendation provided by the PPP Unit.

External auditing of the sponsoring agency's oversight activities during the project term falls to the *Auditor-General* of South Africa. The Auditor-General is an independent government entity focused on safeguarding the public interest in governmental expenses. It can therefore be viewed as "an independent auditor acting on behalf of taxpayers, and auditing and reporting on the activities of all government institutions" (Treasury 2004). The Auditor-General reviews the PPP project's annual progress reports, and conducts various audits as required.

Finally, local *development agencies* play a role in helping sponsoring agencies to identify and develop possible infrastructure projects. The two most prominent of these public players are the Development Bank of South Africa (DBSA) and the Industrial Development Corporation (IDC). These agencies, however, have played a decreasing role in PPP projects since PPP authority was centralized in the PPP Unit. Multinational development agencies (such as USAID) were instrumental in the initial surge of PPPs during the late 1990s, but are no longer active in this field.

The above description does not hold for sectors that have been fully privatized, most notably the communications and energy sectors. Private participation in these sectors is regulated by dedicated public regulatory agencies, such as the National Energy Regulator (NERSA) and the Independent Communication Authority (ICASA). In addition, the South Africa National Road Agency (SANRAL) and TRANSNET handle all transactions that involve road, commercial rail, port, and pipeline infrastructure, without the oversight of the PPP Unit (Farrugia et al. 2008).

A graphic representation of the South African field is presented in Figure 11.1.

## British Columbia, Canada

In comparison with the South African case, PPPs are viewed as much more central to infrastructure delivery in the Canadian province of British Columbia. All public infrastructure investment initiatives with an estimated project value over $50 million are required to pass through a PPP qualification review, with normal procurement only followed if there is a compelling reason not to undertake the project as a PPP. In addition, projects between $20 million and $50 million are generally also evaluated for PPP appropriateness. Again, we can identify six main actors in this field.

Project concepts are developed by various governmental *sponsoring agencies*. These agencies are the governmental agents who ultimately sign the PPP contract, and they therefore retain the main responsibility for project oversight and regulation throughout the life of the project.

Sponsoring agencies are at liberty to appoint any private consultants for the PPP qualification process (or business case development), but generally they make use of the provincial PPP Unit, Partnerships BC (PBC), for this task. The reason for preferring PBC over private

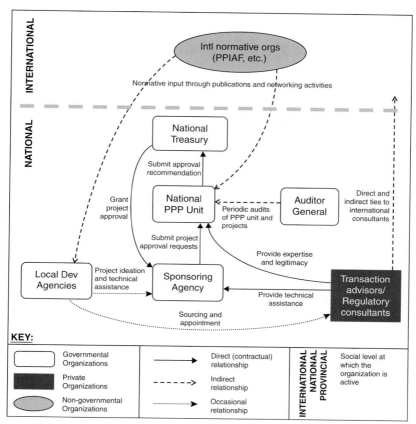

**Figure 11.1** Graphic representation of South African PPP enabling field

consultants is that PBC is responsible for assessing all business case evaluations and making a recommendation (based on value for money and affordability assessments) to the *Ministry of Finance* for final approval. Involving PBC early on in the process improves the chances of eventual project approval. Sponsoring agencies also often retain PBC during the options analysis phase and subsequent competitive procurement processes. However, the extent of PBC services utilized depends greatly on the expertise and experience of the sponsoring agency: their role can range from completely managing the PPP development process to taking only an advisory role.[6] PBC sometimes provides input to sponsoring agencies during the construction phase as well, but is generally not involved during the operational period.

It should be emphasized that PBC, a fully publicly owned crown corporation, takes on a much more proactive role in developing the local PPP market than is the case with the South African PPP unit. They actively identify possible PPP projects, as well as serve as a center of PPP excellence, distributing best-practice information to governmental departments through positional papers, recommended procedures, and policy input. PBC's forward-leaning stance to PPP development is partially motivated by the organization being financed through a fee for service funding structure. Some critics have suggested that this incentive, coupled with significant influence on the PPP approval process, might lead to more PPPs being approved than is optimal. The government of British Columbia has attempted to combat this possible agency dilemma by providing strict oversight by the Ministry of Finance. In addition, PBC contracts with independent *private consultants* on most projects to ensure impartiality: each project includes a "conflict of interest consultant" and a "fairness advisor." PBC also employs legal, financial, or technical consultants to supplement their in-house expertise where needed. Private consultants can therefore either be employed by the sponsoring agencies directly (where PBC has not been appointed for management of advisory services) or (more commonly) as consultants to PBC.

Two players at a national level complement these provincial actors. First, the Canadian federal government has also been involved in developing the PPP market through the establishment of a *federal PPP Unit*, known as "PPP Canada Incorporated" (GoC 2009). The office is primarily tasked with managing and investing Canada's $1.25 billion Public–Private Partnerships Fund that supports "innovative projects that provide an alternative to traditional government infrastructure procurement" (Building-Canada 2009). In addition, the office advises the government of Canada on the execution of PPP projects, and requires that PPPs be considered in connection with other federal infrastructure programs. The focus of the Federal PPP office is therefore exclusively on federal PPP projects.

Second, the *Canadian Council for Public–Private Partnerships* (CCPPP) also operates at a national level in Canada. The council primarily focuses on promoting and increasing the success of PPPs through industry-wide research and information disseminating via various publications.[7] In addition it facilitates knowledge

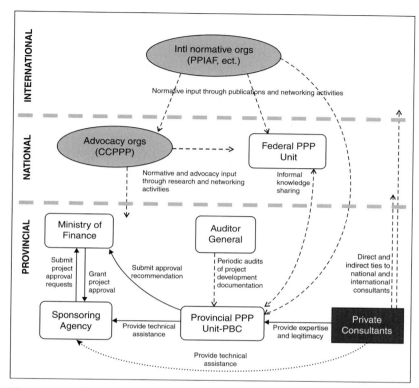

**Figure 11.2** Graphic representation of British Columbian (Canada) PPP enabling field

sharing and networking by way of annual conferences, regional PPP events, and focused workshops. Lastly the CCPPP acts as a normative force by recognizing leading projects through their Canadian Council National Awards for Public–Private Partnerships (CCPPP 2009).

A graphic representation of the British Columbia field is presented in Figure 11.2.

## Republic of Korea

A final case for consideration is the Republic of Korea (or South Korea) where extensive PPP activity has taken place since 1994 (most recently under the Build-Transfer-Lease program) (Nam 2009). Korea presents an interesting alternative to the other two cases because its public PPP enabling organizations are highly centralized and insulated, with little involvement of private or nongovernmental agents. We can identify five main players in this field, all governmental agencies.

The responsibility for overseeing Korea's PPP program is concentrated in the *Ministry of Strategy and Finance* (MOSF). The MOSF is responsible for developing PPP policy and establishing the Korean government's comprehensive PPP investment plans, through the creation of an annual PPP plan and guidelines document.[8] The MOSF controls the quality of projects delivered by Line Agencies through the review of quarterly PPP implementation status reports. Most of the decisions on large PPP deals are delegated to a specialized entity within the MOSF, the Project Review Committee (Kim 2009). This Committee generally is staffed by high-ranking governmental officials, but may also include private consultants as "technical experts" (ibid).

The primary work of PPP project implementation is undertaken by various Korean *Sponsoring Agencies* (such as the Ministry of Land, Transportation and Maritime Affairs in the case of a national transport infrastructure project). The relevant agency undertakes the necessary work to develop the project, including conducting a project feasibility study and value-for-money appraisal, undertaking the procurement process, identifying the preferred bidder, approving the engineering plan, and confirming project completion. Although private consultants are sometimes employed by line agencies, their use is much less prevalent than in the other two cases.[9]

Instead of using consultants, line agencies often request technical assistance from the *Public and Private Infrastructure Investment Management Center* (PIMAC) during the execution of their project development tasks. The general reluctance to involve private consultants in the project development process means that PIMAC plays a much larger supporting and execution role on specific projects than in the other cases discussed. PIMAC is the "central government's primary administrative entity for interfacing with the private sector on infrastructure investment projects" (Nam 2009). The role of PIMAC includes reviewing project proposals, helping to negotiate concession contracts, and mediating disputes. In addition, PIMAC offers educational workshops to increase private sector interest in infrastructure finance and conducts research on the infrastructure market (Kim 2009). To assist under-skilled local governmental authorities, PIMAC specifically works to protect the interests of government in their dealings with private sector concessionaires (Nam 2009).

The *public auditor* of Korea is known as the "Board of Audit and Inspection" (BAI). This agency works to make "sure that administrative practices and services of government and public bodies are fair, reasonable and appropriate" (BAI 2009). The BAI provides independent oversight of the PPP process, auditing the practices (specifically in terms of procurement) of the line agency.

A final player in the Korean PPP enabling field is the *Korean Infrastructure Credit Guarantee Fund* (KICGF), which provides funding guarantees to private providers. Guarantees can take the form of a term loan structured to protect the project's senior debt service (available upon demand), or a revenue guarantee loan. These guarantees serve to minimize the risks borne by the concessionaire, thereby developing the local PPP market by making investment more attractive to private providers (BAI 2009). The KICGF partly matches our definition of a local development agency, but their program development activities are limited to these financial measures.

A graphic representation of the Korean field is presented in Figure 11.3.

## *Other examples*

Four other cases can help us further distinguish differences between national fields, and are therefore worth mentioning here:

- As mentioned earlier, in many developing countries the development of PPP projects is heavily dominated by multinational development agencies. The formation of the Maputo Water Concession in Mozambique is a case in point. Not only was the project concept proposed by the World Bank, the subsequent procurement and appointment process was dominated by Bank employees and selected private consultants (Zandamela 2001). In addition, the Bank executed the restructuring of the governmental organizations that oversaw the PPP, creating the public asset holder and the public regulator. Consultants (mostly employed directly by the World

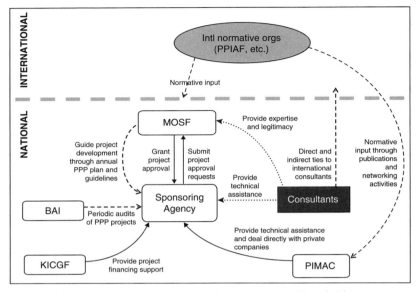

**Figure 11.3** Graphic representation of Korean PPP enabling field

Bank) were heavily relied upon to assist these public organizations in managing the PPP contract.

- The Chilean case is also of interest due to the centrality of decision making and strong political commitment for pursuing PPPs. The Minister of Public Works has historically taken responsibility for the implementation of the program, with only partial scrutiny by the Minister of Finance and the public auditor ("Contraloría General"). The result has been a rapid, but somewhat controversial history of PPP development (culminating in a series of corruption and irregularity trials). Other features of the program are a substantial reliance on international consultants in project development, and low accountability and transparency of PPP policy formulation and project selection.
- The Indian case is of interest due to the highly fragmented and decentralized nature of the program. Reflective of Indian bureaucracy in general, a multitude of governmental organizations provide alternative routes for project implementation in an uncoordinated manner. These organizations include PPP Units at the national and state level, as well as within some sector-specific bodies. In addition,

a variety of local development agencies (most remnants of earlier project financing initiatives) litter the landscape of project identification and development.

- A final example is the Chinese PPP field, where two broad tiers of projects can be identified: (1) interprovincial projects or projects that are of national significance, requiring major financial investments; and (2) provincial or local projects that are of much more modest scale (generally involving urban infrastructure). Approval of both types of projects is centralized under the National Development and Reform Commission (NDRC),[10] but nationally significant projects require approval at the State Council level as well (GoPRC 1995). The responsibility for project development and procurement falls to the applicable authority (local, provincial, or department within the central government) for both types of projects (GoPRC 2004, 2005). Consultants are more prevalent than in the Korean case, but are afforded limited responsibility, mostly acting in a supporting role.

## Towards a classification of public–private partnership field characteristics

The examples presented above illustrate the diversity of application in contemporary PPP enabling fields. Although an in-depth classification of present-day examples is beyond the scope of this chapter, we can identify several broad dimensions along which the case examples (and selected others) vary.

Scott and Meyer (1983, 1991) were among the first to identify some of the ways in which one field differs from another, and these efforts have multiplied over time (e.g., Campbell, Hollingsworth, and Lindberg 1991; Scott et al. 2000; Whitley 1999). A number of broad dimensions along which fields vary have been identified, including the extent of centralization of decision making, the mixture of public and private sector players, and the number of levels (e.g., local, state, national, transnational) at which actors operate. Reflecting on the case of PPP, we propose that fields appear to vary on at least five salient dimensions:

- *Centralization of governance* entails whether the responsibility for project enablement and governance is located within a central agency, or duplicated within various line agencies. The Korean and British Columbia cases present examples of highly centralized enablement, while the Indian case is much more decentralized.

- *Sectoral consistency* represents the extent to which PPP enablement is consistent across different infrastructure sectors (transportation, energy, telecoms, and water and sewerage). In many countries (South Africa and India for example) the transportation sector has taken the lead in developing PPPs (due to the ease of applying direct user-fees), leading to a separate PPP program in these sectors. In other countries (such as British Columbia and Korea in our sample) PPP programs have been developed as a single coherent initiative across all sectors.
- *Involvement of private enablers* signifies the extent to which governmental agents make use of private consultants for the PPP enablement process. Extreme cases in our sample are Korea on the one hand (where there is very limited use of private consultants), and India on the other (where governmental agents are very reliant on private consultants).
- *Influence of multinational development agencies* entails the extent to which multinational development agencies like the World Bank and IFC have an influence on both the choice of PPP projects, and the way they are developed. A higher level of influence (such as Mozambique in our sample and to a lesser extent India) generally signifies a lower level of governmental capacity within the host government, with the multinational development agencies often stepping in to ensure project success and protect both local and private interests.
- *Dominant logics* refer to the types of institutional logics which guide the emergence and use of enabling organizations. They appear to vary from an emphasis on control to a concern for empowerment. The "logic of control" stresses the need for central government control of private service provision, specifically to limit market failures associated with infrastructure provision – natural monopoly characteristics and significant externalities (Goldberg 1976; Mody 1996; Savas 2000). This logic has also been the driving force behind measures to ensure control of governmental discretion, both the discretion of local government (applied through central government) and central government (applied through independent auditors and measures of transparency and accountability). In the spectrum of enabling organizations, this "logic of control" has led to the emergence of public regulators, private consultants that provide

"binding outsourcing" services (Trémolet 2007), and PPP Units that function as "review bodies" (Farrugia et al. 2008). A contrary "logic of empowerment" views the challenge of PPP sustainability as a process of increasing the ability of the players involved in the service delivery relationship. Most notably this logic has been the driving force behind initiatives aimed at empowering public actors, but it has also led to governmental programs focused on developing the environment for private participation.

## Concluding statement

In this study we have investigated the emergence of a collection of diverse organizations designed to enable and govern public–private partnership projects for infrastructure development. We have observed that these enablement and governing responsibilities are not restricted to a single governmental body, but rather are shared between networks of public and nonpublic organizations. These organizational networks are being used in varying combinations in efforts to address multiple challenges that PPPs face internationally. We utilize the concept of organizational fields as a theoretical lens to help us investigate these combinations of organizations in a comparative way. Based on a review of a small number of cases, we identified five dimensions that can be used to distinguish field-level differences between cases.

The work to date is no more than an initial step towards a more complete understanding of these networks of enabling organizations. More work is needed to better document the range of networks that have developed, unearth the reasons why these fields differ along the dimensions identified (see Jooste, Levitt, and Scott, forthcoming), and, more importantly, to assess what the impacts of these differences might be on PPP success at both a project and a program level.

## Endnotes

1 The recent inability of concessionaires to raise sufficient private financing has led to a number of contentious governmental "bailouts" of PPP projects. Examples include the Port Mann bridge and highway project now being undertaken as a Design-Build arrangement (rather than the originally planned Design-Build-Operate-Maintain arrangement), and a number of controversial cases of governmental assistance to distressed PFI projects in the UK (Milmo et al. 2009).

2 It should be noted that even in cases where recommendations are strictly advisory, public disclosure of such information will pressurize decision makers into compliance.

3 In many cases, however, highly skilled consultants might come at such a premium that their cost offsets the gains from economies of scale. This is specifically the case where the consultants are not local to the developing country.

4 We employ the term "transaction advisors" to collectively represent all the advisors that support government in the development and execution of PPP projects, including financial, legal, and technical advisors. This would include private organizations that play a project management type role on behalf of government, which are sometimes exclusively referred to as "transaction advisors."

5 See Scott, Levitt, and Orr (2008) for a related discussion of fields operating at varying levels on global infrastructure projects. Defining field boundaries is a heuristic exercise in which boundaries vary depending on the problems of interest to the analyst.

6 Agencies that have had more experience with PPPs (such as in transportation) mostly only require advisory services, while agencies that are newer to PPPs (such as in healthcare) would employ PBC to manage the whole process.

7 Publications sponsored by CCPPP include informative newsletters, research papers, case studies, guidelines, opinion surveys, and national inventories on key public–private partnership subjects (CCPPP 2009).

8 "The purpose of this plan and guidelines is to weigh national and regional infrastructure priorities, provide administrative rules governing the PFI program, and announce any adjustments in public support to be provided for new projects under the program. Although it does not carry the enforceability of law, the annual plan provides guidelines to which all levels of government have shown commitment when implementing their relevant PPP project" (Nam 2009).

9 Two reasons are mentioned for the small role that private consultants play: (i) the high levels of technical competence within the public organizations we mention here; and (ii) a general resistance within the Korean government to involve private entities in public decision making.

10 The NDRC approval ensures that "the project complies with the maintenance of economic security and rational exploitation of resources, protection of the ecological environment, optimization of the layout of industry, protection of the public interest and prevention of monopoly" (GoPRC 2005).

# References

Abbott, A. 1992. "What do cases do?" in *What is a case? exploring the foundations of social inquiry*, ed. Ragin, C. and Becker, H., 53–82. New York: Cambridge University Press.

Abbott, Kenneth W., and Snidal, Duncan. 2001. "Hard and soft law in international governance," in *Legalization and world politics*, ed. Goldstein, Judith L., Kahler, Miles, Keohane, Robert O., and Slaughter, Anne-Marie, 37–72. Cambridge, MA: MIT Press.

Abbott, Kenneth W., Keohane, Robert O., Moravcsik, Andrew, Slaughter, Anne-Marie, and Snidal, Duncan. 2001. "The concept of legalization," in *Legalization and world politics*, ed. Goldstein, Judith L., Kahler, Miles, Keohane, Robert O., and Slaughter, Anne-Marie, 17–35. Cambridge, MA: MIT Press.

Abernathy, W. and Wayne, K. 1974. "Limits to the learning curve," *Harvard Business Review* 52(8):109–19.

Abernethy, David B. 2000. *The dynamics of global dominance: European overseas empires, 1415–1980*. New Haven: Yale University Press.

Adler, Paul S. ed. 2009. *Sociology and organization studies: classical foundations*. Oxford University Press.

Agarwal, S. and Ramaswami, S. N. 1992. "Choice of foreign market entry mode: Impact of ownership, location, and internationalization factors," *Journal of International Business Studies* 23:1–28.

Agrast, M., Botero, J. C., Ponce, A. 2009. *The rule of law index*. Washington, DC: The World Justice Project.

Ajuha, M. K. and Carley, K. M. 1999. "Network structure in virtual organizations," *Organization Science* 10:741–57.

Alberts, D. S. and Hayes, R. E. 2005. *Power to the edge: command and control in the information age*. Washington, DC: Department of Defense Command and Control Research Program.

Aldrich, Howard E. 1979. *Organizations and environments*. Englewood Cliffs, NJ: Prentice Hall.

2005. "Entrepreneurship" in *The handbook of economic sociology*, 2nd edn., ed. Smelser, N. J., and Swedberg, R., 451–77. Princeton, NJ and New York: Princeton University Press and Russell Sage Foundation.

Aldrich, Howard E. and Fiol, Marlene C. 1994. "Fools rush in? The institutional context of industry creation," *Academy of Management Review* **19**:645–70.

Aldrich, Howard E. and Ruef, M. 2006. *Organizations evolving*, 2nd edn. Thousand Oaks, CA: Sage.

Almeida, P. D. 2003. "Opportunity organizations and threat-induced contention: Protest waves in authoritarian settings," *The American Journal of Sociology* **109** (2):345–400.

American Society for Civil Engineers (ASCE). 2009. "*Report card of America's infrastructure,*" www.asce.org/reportcard/2009/index.cfm.

Aminzade, Ronald R. and McAdam, Doug. 2001. "Emotions and contentious politics," in *Silence and voice in the study of contentious politics*, ed. Aminzade, Ronald R., Goldstone, Jack A., McAdam, Doug, Perry, Elizabeth J., Sewell, Jr., William H., Tarrow, Sidney, and Tilly, Charles, 14–50. New York: Cambridge University Press.

Andersen, O. 1993. "On the internationalization process of firms: a critical analysis," *Journal of International Business Studies* **24**:209–32.

Andres, L., Gausch, J. L., Diop, M., and Azumendi, S. L. 2007. "Assessing the governance of electricity regulatory agencies in the Latin American and the Caribbean region: A benchmarking analysis," World Bank.

Anheier, Helmut. 2003. "Movement development and organizational networks: the role of 'single members' in the German Nazi Party, 1925–30," in *Social movements and networks*, ed. Diani, Mario and McAdam, Doug, 49–74. Oxford University Press.

Aoki, M. 2001. *Toward a comparative institutional analysis*. Cambridge, MA: MIT Press.

Appadurai, Arjun. 1996. *Modernity at large: Cultural dimensions of globalization*. Minneapolis: University of Minnesota Press.

Armour, A. M. 1991. "The siting of locally unwanted land uses: Towards a co-operative approach," *Progress in Planning* **35** (1):1–74.

Armstrong, Elizabeth A. 2005. "From struggle to settlement: The crystallization of a field of lesbian/gay organizations in San Francisco, 1969–1973," in *Social movements and organization theory*, ed. Davis, Gerald F., McAdam, Doug, Scott, W. Richard, and Zald, Mayer N., 161–87. Cambridge University Press.

Arnold, D. J. and Quelch, J. A. 1998. "New strategies in emerging markets," *Sloan Management Review* **40**:7–21.

Artto, K., Davies, A., and Prencipe, A. 2011. "The project business: analytical framework and research opportunities," in *The Oxford handbook of project management*, ed. Morris, P. W. G., Pinto, J., and Söderlund, J., 133–53. New York: Oxford University Press.

Artto K., Heinonen, R., Arenius, M., Kovanen, V., and Nyberg, T. 1998. *Global project business and the dynamics of change*. Helsinki, Finland: Technology Development Centre Finland and Project Management Association Finland.

Artto, K. A. and Wikström, K. 2005. "What is project business?" *International Journal of Project Management* 23:343–53.

Asian Development Bank, Japan Bank for International Cooperation, et al. 2005. *Connecting East Asia: a new framework for infrastructure*. A Joint Study by ADB, JBIC, and World Bank.

Autio, E., Sapienza, H. J., and Almeida, J. G. 2000. "Effects of age at entry, knowledge intensity, and imitability on international growth," *Academy of Management Journal* 43:909–25.

Babb, Sarah. 1996. "'A true American system of finance': Frame resonance in the U.S. Labor Movement, 1866 to 1886" *American Sociological Review* 61(6):1033–52.

Baccarini, D. 1996. "The concept of project complexity – a review," *International Journal of Project Management* 14:201–04.

BAI. 2009. "The board of audit and inspection of the Republic of Korea," Retrieved 07–09–2009, from http://park.org/Korea/BAI/home-e.html

Bair, J. ed. 2009. *Frontiers of commodity chain research*. Stanford, CA: Stanford University Press.

Baldassarri, Delia and Diani, Mario. 2007. "The integrative power of civil networks," *American Journal of Sociology* 113:735–80.

Baloi, D., and Price, A. D. F. 2003. "Modeling global risk factors affecting construction cost performance," *International Journal of Project Management* 21(4):261–69.

Banks, A. S., and Databanks International. 2009. *Cross-National Time-Series Data Archive*.

Barkema, Harry G. and Nadolska, Anna. 2003. "How internationalizing firms develop their absorptive capacity over time: The case of acquisitions," Academy of Management Proceedings.

Barkema, Harry G. and Vermeulen, F. 1998. "International expansion through start-up or acquisition: A learning perspective," *Academy of Management Journal* 41:7–27.

Barkema, Harry G., Shenkar, O., Vermeulen, F., and Bell, J. H. J. 1997. "Working abroad, working with others: How firms learn to operate international joint ventures," *The Academy of Management Journal* 40:426–42.

Barley, Stephen R., and Tolbert, Pamela S.. 1997. "Institutionalization and structuration: Studying the links between action and institution," *Organization Studies* 18:93–117.

Bartlett, C. and Ghoshal, S. 1987. "Managing across borders," *Sloan Management Review* 29(1):43–53.

Bartlett, C. and Ghoshal, S. 1992. "What is a global manager," *Harvard Business Review* 70(5):124–32.

Bateson, G. 1972. *Steps to an ecology of mind*. New York: Ballantine Books.

Baum, J. A. C. ed. 2002. *The Blackwell companion to organizations*. Oxford: Blackwell Publishing.

Baviskar, A. 1996. *In the belly of the river: Tribal conflicts over development in the Narmada Valley, studies in social ecology and environmental history*. New York: Oxford University Press.

Bazeley, P., and Richards, L. 2000. *The NVivo qualitative project book*, Sage.

Bazerman, M. H., and Neale, M. A. 1992. *Negotiating rationally*. New York: Free Press.

Beamish, P. W. and Kachira, A. 2004. "Number of partners and JV performance," *Journal of World Business* 39:107–20.

Beierle, T. C., and Cayford, J. 2001. *Evaluating dispute resolution as an approach to public participation*. Washington, DC: Resources for the Future.

Bell, Daniel. 1973. *The coming of post-industrial society*. New York: Basic Books.

Benito, G. R. G. and Gripsrud, G. 1995. "The internationalization process approach to the location of foreign direct investments: An empirical analysis," in *The location of foreign direct investment*, ed. Green, M. B. and McNaughton, R. B. London: Avebury.

Bennis, Warren G., and Slater, Philip E. 1968. *The temporary society*. New York: Harper and Row.

Berger, Peter L. 2002. "The cultural dynamics of globalization," in *Many globalizations: Cultural diversity in the contemporary world*, ed., Berger, Peter L. and Huntington, Samuel P., 1–16. New York: Oxford University Press.

Berger, Peter L., and Luckmann, Thomas. 1967. *The social construction of reality*. New York: Doubleday Anchor.

Berger, Suzanne, and Dore, Ronald, eds. 1996. *National diversity and global capitalism*. Ithaca, NY: Cornell University Press.

Berkovitch, Nitza. 1999. *From motherhood to citizenship: Women's rights and international organizations*. Baltimore: Johns Hopkins University Press.

Bertalanffy, Ludwig von. 1956. "General system theory," in *General systems: Yearbook of the Society for General Systems Theory*, ed. Bertalanffy, Ludwig von and Rapoport, Anatol. Ann Arbor, MI: The Society. 1:1–10.

Biggart, Nicole Woolsey, and Guillén, Mauro F. 1999. "Developing difference: Social organization and the rise of the auto industries of South Korea, Taiwan, Spain, and Argentina," *American Sociological Review* 64:722–47.

Bijker, W. E., Hughes, T., and Pinch, T. 1987. *The social construction of technological systems: New directions in the sociology and history of technology*. Cambridge, MA: MIT Press.

Binder, Jean. 2007. *Global project management*. Aldershot: Gower.

Bing, L., Tiong, R. L. K., Fan, W. W., and Chew, D. A. S. 1999. "Risk management in international construction joint ventures," *Journal of Construction Engineering and Management* **125**(4): 277–84.

Blau, P. M. 1970. "A formal theory of differentiation in organizations," *American Sociological Review* 35:201–18.

Boh, W. F., Ren, Y., Kiesler, S., and Bussjaeger, R. 2007. "Expertise and collaboration in the geographically dispersed organization," *Organization Science* **18**:595–612.

Boholm, A., ed. 2004. *Facility siting: Risk, power and identity in land use planning*. Toronto, CA: Earthscan Canada.

Boli, John and Thomas, George M., eds. 1999. *Constructing world culture: International nongovernmental organizations since 1875*. Stanford, CA: Stanford University Press.

Boli, John and Thomas, George M. 1997. "World culture in the world polity: A century of international non-governmental organization," *American Sociological Review* **62**:171–90.

Boudet, H. S. 2010. *Contentious politics in liquefied natural gas facility siting*. Ph.D. Dissertation, Emmett Interdisciplinary Program in Environment and Resources, Stanford University, Stanford, CA.

Boudreau, V. 1996. "Northern theory, southern protest: Opportunity structure analysis in cross-national perspective," *Mobilization* 1(2):175–89.

Bovaird, T. 2004. "Public–private partnerships: from contested concepts to prevalent practice," *International Review of Administrative Sciences* 70(2):199.

Boyacigiller, N. 1990. "The role of expatriates in the management of interdependence, complexity, and risk in multinational corporations," *Journal of International Business Studies* 21:357–81.

Brannen, M. Y. 2004. "When Mickey loses face: Recontextualization, semantic fit, and the semiotics of foreignness," *Academy of Management Review* 29:583–607.

Bremmer, Ian. 2006. *The J Curve: A new way to understand why nations rise and fall*. New York: Simon & Schuster.

Broadbent, Jeffrey. 1998. *Environmental politics in Japan: Networks of power and protest*. Cambridge University Press.

Brockett, C. D. 2005. *Political movements and violence in Central America*. New York: Cambridge University Press.

Brouthers, K. D. 2002. "Institutional, cultural and transaction cost influences on entry mode choice and performance," *Journal of International Business Studies* 33:203–22.

Brown, L. David, and Fox, Jonathan A. 1998. "Accountability within transnational coalitions," in *The struggle for accountability: The World Bank, NGOs, and grassroots movements*, ed. Fox, Jonathan A. and Brown, David L., 439–84. Cambridge, MA: MIT Press.

Brunsson, Nils, and Jacobsson, Bengt, eds. 2000. *A world of standards*. Oxford: Oxford University Press.

Brysk, A. 2000. *From tribal village to global village: Indian rights and international relations in Latin America*. Palo Alto: Stanford University Press.

Bueno de Mesquita, Bruce. 1992. *Predicting politics*. Columbus, OH: Ohio State University Press.

Building-Canada. 2009. "Public–private partnership fund," Retrieved 2 March 2008, from www.buildingcanada-chantierscanada.gc.ca/funprog-progfin/target-viser/pppf-fppp/pppf-fppp-eng.html

Burns, Tom and Stalker, George M. 1961. *The management of innovation*. London: Tavistock.

Busenitz, L., Gomez, C., and Spencer, J. W. 2000. "Country institutional profiles: Unlocking entrepreneurial phenomena," *Academy of Management Journal* 43:994–1003.

Busenitz, L., Gomez, C., and Spencer, J. W. 2009. "Public–private partnership fund," Retrieved 2 March 2008, from www.buildingcanada-chantierscanada.gc.ca/funprog-progfin/target-viser/pppf-fppp/pppf-fppp-eng.html

Campbell, D. 1988. "Task complexity: A review and analysis," *Academy of Management Review* 13:40–52.

Campbell, John L. 2004. *Institutional change and globalization*. Princeton, NJ: Princeton University Press.

2005. "'Where do we stand?': Common mechanisms in organizations and social movements research," in *Social movements and organization theory*, ed. Davis, G. F., McAdam, D., Scott, W. R., and Zald, M. N., 41–68. New York: Cambridge University Press.

Campbell, John L., Hollingsworth, J.Rogers, and Lindberg, Leon N., eds. 1991. *Governance of the American economy*. Cambridge University Press.

Campbell, John L. and Lindberg, Leon N. 1990. "Property rights and the organization of economic activity by the state," *American Sociological Review* 55:634–47.

Carmel, E. and Agarwal, R. 2001. "Tactical approaches for alleviating distance in global software development," *IEEE Software* (March/ April), 22–29.

Carmin, J. 2003. "Resources, opportunities and local environmental action in the democratic transition and early consolidation periods of the Czech Republic," *Environmental Politics* 12(3):42–64.

Carroll, T. N., Burton, R. M., and Levitt, R. E. 2004. "Fallacies of fast track tactics: Implications for organization theory and project management," *CRGP Working Paper Series #005*

CCPPP. 2009. *The Canadian Council for Public–Private Partnerships.* Retrieved 28 February 2009, from www.pppcouncil.ca/

Cebrowski, A. K. 2003 "Network-centric warfare: An emerging military response to the information age," *Military Technology* 27:16–22.

Chan, E. H. W., and Tse, R. Y. C. 2003. "Cultural considerations in international construction contracts," *Journal of Construction, Engineering and Management* 129(4):375–81.

Chandler, A. 1962. *Strategy and structure.* Cambridge, MA: MIT Press.

Chiesa, V. 1995. "Globalizing R&D around centers of excellence," *Long-Range Planning* 28:19–28.

Child, John. 1988. "On organizations in their sectors," *Organization Studies* 9:13–19.

2000. "Theorizing about organization cross-nationally," in *Advances in International Comparative Management*, ed. Cheng, Joseph L.C. and Peterson, Richard B. 13:27–75. Stamford, CT: JAI Press.

2005. *Organization: Contemporary principles and practice.* Oxford: Blackwell Publishing Press.

Child, John and Yan, Y. 2003. Predicting the performance of international joint ventures: An investigation in China," *Journal of Management Studies* 40:283–321.

Chinowsky, P., Diekmann, J., and Galotti, V. 2008. "Social network model of construction," *Journal of Construction Engineering and Management* 134(10): 804–12.

Chua, D. K. H., Wang, Y., and Tan, W. T. 2003. "Impacts and obstacles in East Asian cross-border construction," *Journal of Construction Engineering and Management* 129:131–41.

Clark, G. L. and Wójcik, D. 2007. *The geography of finance: Corporate governance in the global marketplace.* Oxford: Oxford University Press.

Clarke, G. 2000. "The decline of Leviathan state, market and civil society in South-East Asia 1986–1998," in *Public–private partnerships: Theory and practice in international perspective*, ed. Osborne, S. 149–62. London: Routledge.

Clemens, Elisabeth S. 1996. "Organizational form as frame: Collective identity and political strategy in the American labor movement," in *Comparative perspectives on social movements*, ed. McAdam, Doug, McCarthy, John D., and Zald, Mayer N., 205–26. New York: Cambridge University Press.

    1997. *The people's lobby: Organizational innovation and the rise of interest group politics in the United States, 1890–1925*. Chicago: University of Chicago Press.

Cohen, Michael D. and Sproull, Lee S., eds. 1991, "Organizational learning: Papers in honor of (and by) James G. March," *Organization Science* 2:1–145.

Cohen, Robin and Rai, Shirin M., eds. 2000. *Global social movements*. London: Athlone Press.

Conway, J. M. 2004. *Identity, place, knowledge: Social movements contesting globalization*. Chicago: Fernwood Publishing Company.

Corley, E., Boardman, C., and Bozeman, B. 2006. "Design and the management of multi-institutional research collaborations: Theoretical implications from two case studies," *Research Policy* 35:975–93.

Costain, Anne W. 1992. *Inviting women's rebellion: A political process interpretation of the women's movement*. Baltimore: Johns Hopkins University Press.

Cova, B., Ghauri, P., and Salle, R. 2002. *Project marketing: Beyond competitive bidding*. Chichester: John Wiley & Sons Ltd.

Craig, C. S. and Douglas, S. P. 1996. "Developing strategies for global markets: An evolutionary perspective," *Columbia Journal of World Business* 31:70–82.

Cramton, C. D. and Hinds, P. L. 2005. "Subgroup dynamics in internationally distributed teams: Ethnocentrism or cross-cultural learning?" *Research in Organization Behavior* 26:231–63.

Cress, Daniel M. and Snow, David A. 2000. "The outcomes of homeless mobilization: The influence of organization, disruption, political mediation and framing," *American Journal of Sociology* 105:1063–104.

Cummings, J. L. and Doh, J. P. 2000. "Identifying who matters: Mapping key players in multiple environments," *California Management Review* 42:83–105.

Cummings, J. N. and Kiesler, S. 2007. "Coordination costs and project outcomes in multi-university collaborations," *Research Policy* 36:138–52.

Cyert, R. M. and March, J. G. 1963. *A behavioral theory of the firm*, 2nd edn. Cambridge, MA: Blackwell Business.

Czarniawska, Barbara and Joerges, Berward. 1996. "Travels of ideas," in *Translating organizational change*, ed. Czarniawska, Barbara and Sevón, Guji, 13–48. Berlin: Walter de Gruyter.

Dalton, B. M. 2005. "Corruption in cultural context: Contradictions within the Korean tradition," *Crime, Law and Social Change* 43:237–62.

Damian, D. and Zowghi, D. 2002. "An insight into the interplay between culture, conflict and distance in globally distributed requirements negotiations," in *Proceedings of the 36th Hawaii International Conference on System Sciences*, Hawaii.

Daniels, J. D. 1991. "Relevance in international business research: A need for more linkages," *Journal of International Business Studies* 22:177–86.

Das, S. K. 2000. *Public office, private interest: Bureaucracy and corruption in India*. Delhi: Oxford University Press.

Davies, Andrew and Hobday, Michael. 2005. *The business of projects: Managing innovation in complex products and systems*, Cambridge University Press.

Davis, Gerald F. 2000. "Corporations, classes, and social movements," in *Research in organizational behavior*, ed. Straw, Barry and Sutton, Robert I., 22:195–238. Oxford: Elsevier Science.

Davis, Gerald F. and McAdam Doug. 2000. "Corporations, classes, and social movements," in *Research in Organization Behaviour*, ed. Staw, Barry and Sutton, Robert I. 22:195–238. Oxford: Elsevier Science.

Davis, Gerald F. and Zald, Mayer N. 2005. "Social change, social theory, and the convergence of movements and organizations," in *Social movements and organization theory*, ed. Davis, Gerald F., McAdam, Doug, Scott, W. Richard, and Zald, Mayer N., 335–50. Cambridge: Cambridge University Press.

Davis, Gerald F., McAdam, Doug, Scott, W. Richard, and Zald, Mayer N., eds. 2005. *Social movements and organization theory*. Cambridge University Press.

Davis, Jennifer. 2005. "Private-sector participation in the water and sanitation sector," *Annual Review of Environment and Resources* 30: 145–83.

Davis, Jennifer, Boudet, Hilary Schaffer, and Jaya, D. C. In press. "Drivers of conflict in global infrastructure projects: Experience from the water and pipeline sectors," *Journal of Construction Engineering Management*.

Day, G. S., Schoemaker, P. J. H., Snyder, S. A. 2009. "Extended intelligence networks: Minding and mining the periphery," in *The network challenge: Strategy, profit and risk in an interlinked world*, ed. Kleindorfer, Paul and Wind, Jerry. 277–95. Upper Saddle River, NJ: Wharton School of Publishing.

Dear, M. 1992. "Understanding and overcoming the NIMBY syndrome," *Journal of the American Planning Association* 58(3):288.

Delios, A. and Beamish, P. W. 2001. "Survival and profitability: The roles of experience and intangible assets in foreign subsidiary performance," *Academy of Management Journal* 44:1028–39.

Delios, A. and Henisz, W. J. 2003. "Policy uncertainty and the sequence of entry by Japanese firms, 1980–1998," *Journal of International Business Studies* 34:227–41.

Den Hartog, D. N. 2004. "Assertiveness," in *Culture, leadership, and organizations: The GLOBE study of 62 societies*, ed. House, R., Hanges, P., Javidan, M., Dorfman, P., and Gupta, V. 395–436. Thousand Oaks, CA, Sage Publications, Inc.

Denzau, A. and North, D. C. 1994. "Shared mental models: Ideologies and institutions," *Kyklos*. Blackwell Publishing 47:3–31.

Dezalay, Yves and Garth, Bryant G. 1996. *Dealing in virtue: International commercial arbitration and the construction of a transnational level order*. University of Chicago Press.

Diani, Mario. 1995. *Green networks: A structural analysis of the Italian environmental movement*. Edinburgh: Edinburgh University Press.

1996. "Linking mobilization frames and political opportunities: Insights from regional populism in Italy," *American Sociological Review* 61: 1053–69.

Diani, Mario and Bison, Ivano. 2004. "Organization, coalitions and movements," *Theory and Society* 33:281–309.

DiMaggio, Paul J. 1988. "Interest and agency in institutional theory," in *Institutional patterns and organizations: Culture and environment*, ed. Lynne G. Zucker, 3–21. Cambridge, MA: Ballinger.

1991. "Constructing an organizational field as a professional project: U.S. art museums, 1920–1940," in *The New Institutionalism in Organizational Analysis*, ed. Powell, W. W. and DiMaggio, P. J., 267–92. Chicago: University of Chicago Press.

DiMaggio, Paul J. ed. 2001. *The twenty-first-century firm: Changing economic organization in international perspective*. Princeton, NJ: Princeton University Press.

DiMaggio, Paul J. and Powell, Walter W. 1983. "The iron cage revisited: Institutional isomorphism and collective rationality in organizational fields," *American Sociological Review* 48:147–60.

Dixit, S., Wagle, S., and Sant, G. 2001. "The real challenge in power sector restructuring: Instilling public control through transparency, accountability and public participation (TAP)," *Energy for Sustainable Development* 5(3):95–102.

Djankov, S., La Porta, R., Lopez-De-Silanes, F., and Shleifer, A. 2002. "The regulation of entry," *The Quarterly Journal of Economics* 117:1–37.

Djelic, Marie-Laure, and Quack, Sigrid. 2003. "Introduction: Governing globalization – bringing institutions back in," in *Globalization and institutions: Redefining the rules of the economic game,* ed., Djelic, Marie-Laure and Quack, Sigrid, 1–14. Cheltenham: Edward Elgar.

Djelic, Marie-Loure, and Quack, Sigrid, eds. 2003. *Globalization and institutions: Redefining the rules of the economic game.* Cheltenham: Edward Elgar.

Djelic, Marie-Laure, and Sahlin-Andersson, Kerstin, eds. 2006. *Transnational governance: Institutional dynamics of regulation.* Cambridge: Cambridge University Press.

Dobbin, Frank R. 1994. "Cultural models of organization: The social construction of rational organizing principles," in *The sociology of culture: Emerging theoretical perspectives,* ed. Crane, D., 117–41. Oxford: Blackwell.

Dobbin, Frank R., and Sutton, John R. 1998. "The strength of a weak state: The rights revolution and the rise of human resources management divisions," *American Journal of Sociology* 104:441–76.

Doh, J., Rodriguez, P., Uhlenbruck, K., Collins, J., and Eden, L. 2003. "Coping with corruption in foreign markets," *Academy of Management Executive* 17:114–127.

Doig, A. and Theobald, R. 2000. *Corruption and democratization.* London: Frank Cass.

Douglas, Mary. 1986. *How institutions think.* Syracuse University Press.

Doz, Y. L. 1996. "The evolution of cooperation in strategic alliances: Initial conditions or learning processes?" *Strategic Management Journal* 17:55–83.

Doz, Y. L., Bartlett, C., and Prahaldad, C. K. 1981. "Global competitive pressures vs. host country demands: Managing tensions in MNCs," *California Management Review* 23:63–74.

Drori, Gili S., Meyer, John W., and Hwang, Hokyu, eds. 2006. *Globalization and organization: World society and organizational change.* Oxford University Press.

Dudziak, Mary L. 2000. *Cold War civil rights.* Princeton University Press.

Dunning, J. H. 1988. *Explaining international production.* London: Unwin Hyman Ltd.

1993. *Multinational enterprises and the global economy.* Reading, MA: Addison-Wesley.

Dutz, M., Harris, C., Dhingra, I., and Shugart, C. 2006. "Public private partnership units: what are they and what do they do," *Public Policy for the Private Sector.* Washington, DC: World Bank Group.

Duyvendak, Jan Willem. 1995. *The power of politics: New social movements in France.* Boulder, CO: Westview Press.

Eberhard, A. 2006. "Infrastructure regulation in developing countries: An exploration of hybrid and transitional models," African Forum of Utitlity Regulators, 3rd Annual Conference, Windhoek, Namibia.

Eccles, R. 1981. "The quasi-firm in the construction industry," *Journal of Economic Behavior and Organization* 2:335–57.

Eccles, R. and Crane, D. B. 1988. *Doing deals: Investment banks at work.* Boston, MA: Harvard Business School Press.

Eckstein, R. 1997. *Nuclear power and social power.* Philadelphia: Temple University Press.

Economist, (Anonymous). Editors 2008. "Economics focus: Building BRICs of growth," *The Economist* 387:92.

Edelman, Lauren B. and Suchman, Mark C. 1997. "The legal environments of organizations," *Annual Review of Sociology* 23:479–515.

Eden, L. and Miller, S. 2004. "Distance matters: Liability of foreignness, institutional distance, and ownership strategy," in *Advances in institutional management*, 187–221, ed. Hitt, Michael and Cheng, J., 187–221. New York: Elsevier.

Edkins, A. J. and Smyth, H. J. 2006. "Contractual management in PPP projects: Evaluation of legal versus relational contracting for service delivery," *Journal of professional issues in engineering education and practice* 132: 82–93.

Eisenhardt, Kathleen M. 1989. "Building theories from case study research," *Academy of Management Review* 14:532–50.

Eisenhardt, Kathleen M. 1991. "Better stories and better constructs: The case for rigor and comparative logic," *Academy of Management Review* 16(3):620–27.

Eisinger, P. K. 1973. "The conditions of protest behavior in American cities," *American Political Science Review* 67:11–28.

Emery, Fred E. 1959. *Characteristics of socio-technical systems.* Tavistock Document 527. London: Tavistock.

Emirbayer, Mustafa and Mische, Ann. 1998. "What is agency?" *American Journal of Sociology* 103:962–1023.

Environment Division. 1998. *Doing better business through effective public consultation and disclosure: A good practice manual.* Washington DC: International Finance Corporation.

Epple, D., Argote, L., and Devedas, R. 1991. "Organizational learning curves: A method for investigating intra-plant transfer of knowledge acquired through learning by doing," *Organization Science* 2:58–70.

Eriksson, K., Johanson, J., Majkgard, A., and Sharma, D. 1997. "Experiential knowledge and cost in the internationalization process," *Journal of International Business Studies* 28:337–60.

Erramilli, M. K. 1991. "The experience factor in foreign market entry behavior of service firms," *Journal of International Business Studies* 22:479–501.

Espeland, W. N. 1998. *The struggle for water: Politics, rationality, and identity in the American Southwest, Chicago Series in Law and Society*. University of Chicago Press.

Estache, A. 2004. "Emerging infrastructure policy issues in developing countries: A survey of the recent economic literature," *World Bank Policy Research Working Paper No. 3442*.

Estache, A., and Serebrisky, T. 2004. "Where do we stand on transport infrastructure deregulation and public–private partnerships?" *Policy Research Working Paper Series No. 3356*. Washington, DC: World Bank.

Evan, William M. 1966. "The organization set: Toward a theory of inter-organizational relations," in *Approaches to organizational design*, ed. Thompson, James D., 173–88. University of Pittsburgh Press.

Evans, P. 2004. "Development as institutional change: The pitfalls of mono-cropping and the potentials of deliberation," *Studies in Comparative International Development* 38:30–52.

Evans, Sarah. 1980. *Personal politics*. New York: Vintage Books.

Facione, P. A., Sanchez, C. A., Facione, N. C., and Gainen, J. 1995. "The disposition toward critical thinking." *The Journal of General Education* 44:125.

Faems, D., Janssens, M., Madhok, A., and Van Looy, B. 2008. "Toward an integrative perspective on alliance governance: Connecting contract design, trust dynamics, and contract application," *Academy of Management Journal* 51:1053–78.

Farrugia, C., Reynolds, T., and Orr, R. J. 2008. "Public–private partnership coordination agencies: A global perspective," *CRGP Working Paper*. Stanford: Collaboratory for Research on Global Projects.

Ferguson, J. 1990. *The anti-politics machine: "development," depoliticization, and bureaucratic power in Lesotho*. New York: Cambridge University Press.

Flacks, Richard. 1988. *Making history*. New York: Columbia University Press.

Fligstein, Neil. 1985. "The spread of the multidivisional form among large firms, 1919–1979," *American Sociological Review* 50:377–91.

    2001a. *The architecture of markets: An economic sociology of twentieth-century capitalist societies*. Princeton, NJ: Princeton University Press.

    2001b. "Social skill and the theory of fields," *Sociological Theory* 19:105–25.

Flyvbjerg, B. 2006. "Five misunderstandings about case-study research," *Qualitative Inquiry* 12:219–45.

Flyvbjerg, B., Bruzelius, N., and Rothengatter, W. 2003. *Megaprojects and risk: An anatomy of ambition*. Cambridge University Press.

Fox, Jonathan A., and Brown, David L., eds. 1998. *The struggle for accountability: The World Bank, NGOs, and grassroots movements*. Cambridge, MA: MIT Press.

Fox, R. G. and Starn. O. 1997. *Between resistance and revolution: Cultural politics and social protest*. Piscataway: Rutgers University Press.

Frank, David J., Hironaka, Ann, and Schofer, Evan. 2000. "The nation-state and the natural environment over the twentieth century," *American Sociological Review* 65:96–110.

Freudenburg, N. 1984. "Citizen action for environmental health: Report on a survey of community organizations," *American Journal of Public Health* 74(5):444–48.

Freudenburg, W. R. 2004. "Can we learn from failure? Examining U.S. experiences with nuclear repository siting," *Journal of Risk Research* 7(2):153–69.

Freudenburg, W. R. and Gramling, R. 1993. "Socioenvironmental factors and development policy: Understanding opposition and support for offshore oil," *Sociological Forum* 8(3):341–64.

   1994. *Oil in troubled waters: Perceptions, politics, and the battle over offshore drilling, SUNY Series in Environmental Public Policy*. Albany: State University of New York Press.

Friedland, Roger, and Alford, Robert R. 1991. "Bringing society back in: Symbols, practices and institutional contradictions," in *The New Institutionalism in Organizational Analysis*, ed. Powell, Walter W. and DiMaggio, Paul J., 232–63. University of Chicago Press.

Friedman, Thomas L. 2005. *The world is flat: A brief history of the twenty-first century*. New York: Farrar, Straus and Giroux.

Galanter, M. 1983. "Reading the landscape of disputes: What we know and don't know (and think we know) about our allegedly contentious and litigious society," *UCLA Law Review* 31:4–69.

Galbraith, Jay R. 1973. *Designing complex organizations*. Reading, MA: Addison-Wesley.

   1974. "Organization design: An information processing view," *Interfaces* 4:22–36.

   1977. *Organization design*. Reading, MA: Addison-Wesley.

Gamson, William A. 1990. *The strategy of social protest*. Belmont, CA: Wadsworth.

Gary, I. and Karl, T. L. 2003. *Bottom of the barrel: Africa's oil boom and the poor*. Catholic Relief Services.

Gatignon, H. and Anderson, E. 1988. "The multinational corporation's degree of control over foreign subsidiaries," *Journal of Law, Economics and Organization* 4:305–36.

Gay, John. 2005. "The world is round," *New York Review of Books* 52(13).

Geertz, Clifford. 1973. *The interpretation of cultures*. New York: Basic Books.

1983. *Local knowledge: Further essays in interpretive anthropology*. New York: Basic Books.

Gelfand, M. and Dyer, N. 2000. "A cultural perspective on negotiation: Progress, pitfalls, and prospects," *An International Review* 49:62–99.

Gereffi, G. and Korzeniewicz, M. 1994. *Commodity chains and global capitalism*. Greenwich, CT: Greenwood Press.

Gerrard, M. B. 2001. "Public–private partnerships," *Finance and Development* 38(3):44.

Ghemawat, Pankaj. 1985. "Building strategy on the experience curve," *Harvard Business Review* 42. 63(2): 143–49.

2001. "Distance still matters: The hard reality of global expansion," *Harvard Business Review* 79:137–47.

2007. "Managing differences: The central challenge of global strategy," *Harvard Business Review* 85:58–68.

2007. *Redefining global strategy: Cross borders in a world where differences still matter*. Boston: Harvard Business School Press.

Ghoshal, Samatra and Nohria, N. 1989. "Internal differentiation within multinational corporations," *Strategic Management Journal* 10:323–37.

Ghoshal, Samatra and Westney, D. Eleanor, eds. 1993. *Organization theory and the multinational corporation*. New York: St. Martin's Press.

Giddens, Anthony. 1979. *Central problems in social theory: Action, structure and contradiction in social analysis*. Berkeley: University of California Press.

1984. *The constitution of society*. Berkeley: University of California Press.

Gil, N., and Beckman, S. 2008. "Infrastructure meets business: Building new bridges, mending old ones," *California Management Review* 51:6–29.

Giugni, Marco G. 2002. "Explaining cross-national similarities among social movements," in *Globalization and resistance: Transnational dimensions of social movements*, ed. Smith, Jackie, and Johnston, Hank, 13–29. Lanhamm MD: Rowman & Littlefield Publishers.

Glaser, B. M. and Strauss, A. L. 1967. *The discovery of grounded theory: Strategies for qualitative research*. Hawthorne, NY: Aldine de Gruyter.

GoC. 2009. *Canada Gazette*, 142(26):1954. Government of Canada, Ottawa.

Goffman, Erving. 1974. *Frame analysis*. New York: Harper Colophon.

Goldberg, C. V. P. 1976. "Regulation and administered contract," *Bell Journal of Economics* 7(2):431.

Goldstein, Judith, Kahler, Miles, Keohane, Robert O., and Slaughter, Anne-Marie. 2001. *Legalization and world politics*. Cambridge, MA: MIT Press.

Goldstone, Jack A. and Tilly, Charles. 2001. "Threat (and opportunity): Popular action and state response in the dynamics of contentious action," in *Silence and voice in the study of contentious politics*. Aminzade, Ronald R., Goldstone, Jack A., McAdam, Doug, Perry, Elizabeth J., Sewell, Jr., William H., Tarrow, Sidney, and Tilly, Charles, 179–94. New York: Cambridge University Press.

Gong, Y. 2003. "Subsidiary staffing in multinational enterprises: Agency, resources and performance," *The Academy of Management Journal* 46:728–39.

Goodnow, J. D. and Hansz, J. E. 1972. "Environmental determinants of overseas market entry strategies," *Journal of International Business Studies* 3:33–51.

Goodwin, Jeff and Jasper, James M. 1999. "Caught in a winding, snarling vine: The structural bias of political process theory," *Sociological Forum* 14:7–54.

Goodwin, Jeff, Jasper, James M. and Polletta, Francesca, eds. 2001. *Passionate politics: Emotions and social movements*. Chicago: University of Chicago Press.

GoPRC. 1995. "Ministry of Foreign Trade and Economic Corporation's announcement on absorbing foreign investment in the form of BOT (in Chinese)," Beijing: Former Ministry of Foreign Trade and Economic Corporation of the People's Republic of China.

2004. "The State Council's decision on the investment system reform (in Chinese)," Beijing: The State Council of the People's Republic of China.

2005. "The State Council's views on encouraging, supporting and guiding individual, private and the other non-public sectors of the economy (in Chinese)," Beijing: The State Council of the People's Republic of China.

Gordon, S. L. 1990. "Social structural effects on emotions," in *Research agendas in the sociology of emotions*, ed. Kemper, T. D., 1–335. American Psychological Association.

Gould, Debbie. 2002. "Life during wartime: emotions and the development of ACT UP," *Mobilization* 7:177–200.

2009. *Moving politics: Emotion and ACT UP's fight against AIDS*. University of Chicago Press.

Gould, Roger. 1991. *Multiple networks and mobilization in the Paris Commune, 1848 to the Commune*. University of Chicago Press.

1995. "Insurgent identities: Class, community, and protest in Paris from 1871," *American Sociological Review* 56:716–29.

Gramling, R. 1995. *Oil on the edge: Offshore development, conflict, gridlock*. Albany: State University of New York Press.

Gramling, R. and Freudenburg, W. R. 1996. "Crude, coppertone, and the coast: Developmental channelization and constraint of alternative development opportunities," *Society & Natural Resources* **9** (5):483.

Gramling, R. and Freudenburg, W. R. 2006. "Attitudes toward offshore oil development: A summary of current evidence," *Ocean & Coastal Management* **49**(7):20.

Granovetter, Mark. 1973. "The strength of weak ties," *American Journal of Sociology* **78**:1360–80.

1985. "Economic action and social structure: The problem of embeddedness," *American Journal of Sociology* **91**:481–510.

Greenwood, Royston and Hinings, C. R. 1993. "Understanding strategic change: the contribution of archetypes," *Academy of Management Journal* **36**:1052–81.

Greif, Avner. 1994. "Cultural beliefs and the organization of society: A historical and theoretical reflection on collectivist and individualist societies," *Journal of Political Economy* **102**:912–50.

2000. "The fundamental problem of exchange: A research agenda in historical institutional analysis," *Review of European Economic History* **4**: 251–4

2006. *Institutions and the path to the modern economy: Lessons from Medieval trade.* Cambridge University Press.

Grün, O. 2004. *Taming giant projects: Management of multi-organization enterprises.* Berlin: Springer.

Guasch, J. L. 2004. *Granting and renegotiating infrastructure concessions: Doing it right.* Washington, DC: World Bank Publications.

Guasch, J. L. and Straub, S. 2006. "Renegotiation of infrastructure concessions: An overview," *Annals of Public and Cooperative Economics* **77**:479–93.

Guasch, J. L., Laffont, J. J. et al. 2006. "Renegotiation of concession contracts: a theoretical approach," *Review of Industrial Organization* **29**:5–73.

Guasch, J. L., Laffont, J. J., and Straub, S. 2002. "Renegotiation of concession contracts in Latin America," USC Law School, *Olin Research Paper No. 02–7 and World Bank Policy Research Working Paper No. 3011.*

Guillén, Mauro F. 2001a. "Is globalization civilizing, destructive or feeble?" *Annual Review of Sociology* **27**:235–60.

2001b. *The limits of convergence: Globalization and organizational change in Argentina, South Korea, and Spain.* Princeton University Press.

2002. "Structural inertia, imitation, and foreign expansion: South Korean firms and business groups in China, 1987–95," *Academy of Management Journal* **45**:509–26.

Gunhan, S., and Arditi, D. 2005. "Factors affecting international construction," *Journal of Construction Engineering and Management* **131**:273.

Haggett, C. 2008. "Over sea and far away? A consideration of the planning, politics, and public perception of offshore wind farms," *Journal of Environmental Policy and Planning* 10(3):289–306.

Hall, E. T. 1966. *The hidden dimension*. New York: Doubleday.

1976. *Beyond culture*. New York: Anchor/Doubleday.

Hall, Peter A. and Soskice, David, eds. 2001. *Varieties of capitalism: The institutional foundation of comparative advantage*. Oxford University Press.

Hall, Peter A. and Taylor, Rosemary C.R. 1996. "Political science and the three new institutionalisms," *Political Studies* 44:936–57.

Hallett, Tim and Ventresca, Marc J. 2006. "Inhabited institutions: Social interactions and organizational forms in Gouldner's Patterns of Industrial Bureaucracy," *Theory and Society* 35:213–36.

Hamel, G. and Prahalad, C. K. 1994. *Competing for the future: Breakthrough strategies for seizing control of industry and creating markets of tomorrow*. Boston, MA: Harvard Business School Press.

Hameri, A. P. 1997. "Project management in a long-term and global one-of-a-kind project," *International Journal of Project Management* 15:151–57.

Han, S. H. and Diekmann, J. E. 2001a. "Approaches for making risk-based go/no-go decisions for international projects," *Journal of Construction Engineering and Management* 127(4):300–08.

Han, S. H. and Diekmann, J. E. 2001b. "Making a risk-based bid decision for overseas construction projects," *Construction Management and Economics* 19:765–77.

Hancké, Bob, Thodes, Martin, and Thatcher, Mark, eds. 2008. *Beyond varieties of capitalism*. Oxford University Press.

Hannerz, U. 1996. *Transnational connections*. London: Routledge.

Hardy, C. and Maguire, S. 2008. "Institutional entrepreneurship," in *The Sage handbook of organizational institutionalism*, ed. Greenwood, R., Oliver, C., Sahlin, K., and Suddaby, R., 198–217. Los Angeles: Sage.

Harris, C. 2003. *Private participation in infrastructure in developing countries: Trends, impacts, and policy lessons*. Washington DC: World Bank Publications.

Harrison, B. 1994. *Lean and mean: The changing landscape of corporate power in the age of flexibility*. New York: Basic Books.

Hart, O. and Moore, J. 1999. "Foundations of incomplete contracts," *Review of Economic Studies* 66:115–38.

Hedberg, Bo L.T., Nystrom, Paul G., and Starbuck, William H. 1976. "Camping on seesaws: Prescriptions for a self-designing organization," *Administrative Science Quarterly* 21:41–65.

Hedstrom, P. and Swedberg, R., eds. 1998. *Social mechanisms: An analytical approach to social theory.* Cambridge University Press.

Heide, J. B. and Miner, A. S. 1992. "The shadow of the future: Effects of anticipated interaction and frequency of contact on buyer-seller cooperation," *Academy of Management Journal* 35:265–91.

Heimer, C. 1999. "Competing institutions: Law, medicine, and family in neonatal intensive care," *Law and Society Review* 33:17–66.

Henisz, Withold J. 2000. "The institutional environment for multinational investment," *Journal of Law, Economics and Organization* 16:334–64.

2003. "The power of the Buckley and Casson thesis: The ability to manage institutional idiosyncrasies," *Journal of International Business Studies* 34:173–84.

2009. "Network-based strategies and competencies for political and social risk management," in *Network-based strategies and competencies,* ed. Kleindorfer, Paul R. and Wind, Yoram. Upper Saddle River, NJ: Wharton School of Publishing.

Henisz, Withold J. and Delios, A. 2001. "Uncertainty, imitation, and plant location: Japanese multinational corporations 1990–1996," *Administrative Science Quarterly* 46:443–75.

Henisz, Withold J. and Williamson, O. E. 1999. "Comparative economic organization within and between countries," *Business and Politics* 1:261–77.

Henisz, Withold J., Zelner, B. A., and Guillén, M. F. 2005. "The worldwide diffusion of market-oriented infrastructure reform, 1977–1999," *American Sociological Review* 70:871–97.

Hennart, J-F. 1982. *A theory of the multinational enterprise.* Ann Arbor: University of Michigan Press.

Hennart, J-F., Roehl, T., and Zeng, M. 2002. "Do exits proxy a liability of foreignness?: The case of Japanese exits from the U.S.," *Journal of International Management* 8:241–65.

Hennart, J-F. and Zeng, M. 2002. "Cross-cultural differences and joint venture longevity," *Journal of International Business Studies* 33:699–717.

Herbsleb, J. D., Mockus, A., Finholt, T. A., and Grinter, R.E, 2000. "Distance, dependencies, and delay in a global collaboration," Proceedings of the 2000 ACM Conference on Computer Supported Cooperative Work, 319–28, December, Philadelphia, PA.

Hinds, P. and Kiesler, S. 2002. *Distributed work.* Cambridge, MA: MIT Press.

Hinds, P. and Mortensen, M. 2005 "Understanding conflict in geographically distributed teams: The moderating effects of shared identity, shared context, and spontaneous communication," *Organization Science* 16:290–307.

Hines, J. R. 1995. "Forbidden payment: Foreign bribery and American business after 1977," *National Bureau of Economic Research Working Paper, No. 5266*, Cambridge, MA.

Hirsch, P. M. 1997. "Review essay: Sociology without social structure: Neoinstitutional theory meets Brave New World," *American Journal of Sociology* 102:1702–23.

Hirschmann W. 1964. "Profit from the learning curve," *Harvard Business Review* 42(1):135–39.

Ho, S. P. and Liu, L. Y. 2004. "Analytical model for analyzing construction claims and opportunistic bidding," *Journal of Construction Engineering and Management* 130:94–104.

Hodgson, Geoffrey M. 1996. "Institutional economic theory: The old versus the new," in *After Marx and Straffa: Essays in Political Economy*, ed. Hodgson, Geoffrey M., 193–213. New York: St. Martin's Press.

Hoegl, M., Weinkauf, K., and Gemuenden, H. G. 2004. "Interteam coordination, project commitment, and teamwork in multiteam R&D projects: A longitudinal study," *Organization Science* 15:38–55.

Hoffman, A. J. and Ventresca, M. J. 2002. "Introduction," in *Organizations, policy, and the natural environment: Institutional and strategic perspectives*, ed. Hoffman, A. J. and Ventresca, M. J. Stanford, California: Stanford University Press.

Hofstede, Geert. 1984. *Culture's consequences: International differences in work-related values*. Beverly Hills, CA: Sage.

   1991. *Cultures and organizations: Software of the mind*. New York: McGraw-Hill.

Hofstede, Geert. 1993. "Cultural constraints in management theories," *Academy of Management Executive* 7:81–94.

Hollingworth, J. R. and Boyer, R. 1997. *Contemporary capitalism: The embeddedness of institutions*. Cambridge University Press.

Homans, George C. 1950. *The human group*. New York: Harcourt.

Hood, C. 1991. "A public management for all seasons," *Public Administration* 69(1):3–19.

Horii, T., Jin, Y., and Levitt, R. 2005. "Modeling and analyzing cultural influences on project team performance," *Computational and Mathematical Organization Theory* 10:305–21.

House, Robert J., Javidan, Mansour, Hanges, Paul, and Dorfman, Peter. 2002. "Understanding cultures and implicit leadership theories across the globe: An introduction to project GLOBE, *Journal of World Business* 37:3–10.

House, Robert J., Hanges, P. J., Javidan, M., Dorfman, P. W., and Gupta, V. 2004. *Culture, leadership & organization: The GLOBE study of 62 societies.* Thousand Oaks, CA: Sage.

Howard, R. A. and Matheson, J. 1983. *The principles and applications of decision analysis* (2 vols.). Palo Alto, CA: Strategic Decisions Group.

Huberman, B. A. 2001. "The dynamics of organization learning," *Computational and Mathematical Organization Theory* 7:147–53.

Hughes, Thomas P. 1998. *Rescuing Prometheus.* New York: Pantheon.

2004. *Human-built world: How to think about technology and culture.* University of Chicago Press.

Hult, Karen M. and Walcott, Charles. 1990. *Governing public organizations: Politics, structures and institutional design.* Pacific Grove, CA: Brooks/Cole Publishing.

Human Development Report Office. 2009. *Human Development Index.* United Nations Development Program.

Hunter, S. and Leyden, K. M. 1995. "Beyond NIMBY: Explaining opposition to hazardous waste facilities," *Policy Studies Journal* 23 (4):601–04.

Huntington, Samuel P. 1991. *The third wave: Democratization in the late twentieth century, Julian J. Rothbaum distinguished lectures.* Norman: University of Oklahoma Press.

1996. *The clash of civilizations and the remaking of world order.* New York: Simon & Schuster.

Hymer, S. H. 1976. *The international operations of national firms: A study of direct investment.* Cambridge, MA: MIT Press.

Inglehart, R. 1997. *Modernization and postmodernization: Cultural, economic, and political change in forty-three societies.* Princeton University Press.

Inglehart, R. and Welzel, C. 2005. *Modernization, cultural change, and democracy: The human development sequence.* Cambridge University Press.

Inglehart, R., Moreno, A., and Basanez, M. 1998. *Human values and beliefs: A cross-cultural sourcebook.* Ann Arbor, MI: University of Michigan Press.

Ionascu, D., Meyer, K., and Erstin, W. 2004. "Institutional distance and international business strategies in emerging markets," *The William Davidson Institute Working Paper No. 728.*

Isobe, T., Makino, S., and Montgomery, D. B. 2000. "Resource commitment, entry timing, and market performance of foreign direct investments in emerging economies: The case of Japanese international joint ventures in China," *Academy of Management Journal*, **43**:468–85.

Izaruirre, A. K. 2004. "Private infrastructure: Activity down by thirteen percent in 2003," in *Public policy for the private sector*. Washington DC: World Bank, note 274.

Jacobsson, Bengt and Sahlin-Andersson, Kerstin. 2006. "Dynamics of soft regulation," in *Transnational governance: Institutional dynamics of regulation*, ed. Djelic, Marie-Laure and Sahlin-Andersson, Kerstin, 247–65. Cambridge: Cambridge University Press.

Javernick-Will, Amy N. 2009. "Organizational learning during internationalization: Acquiring local institutional knowledge," *Construction Management and Economics* **27**:783–97.

Javernick-Will, Amy, N. and Levitt, Raymond E. 2010. "Mobilizing institutional knowledge for international projects," *Journal of Construction Engineering and Management* **136**:430–41.

Javernick-Will, Amy, N. and Scott, W. Richard. 2010. "Who needs to know what? Institutional knowledge and global projects," *Journal of Construction Engineering and Management* **136**:546–7.

Javidan, M., and House, Robert. 2002. "Leadership and cultures from around the world: Findings from GLOBE," *Journal of World Business* **37**:1–2.

Javidan, M., House, R. J., Dorfman, P., Hanges, P., and de Luque, M. 2006. "Conceptualizing and measuring cultures and their consequences: a comparative review of GLOBE's and Hofstede's approaches," *Journal of International Business Studies* **37**:897–914.

Jelinek, Mariann and Wilson, Jeanne. 2005. "Macro influences on multicultural teams: A multi-level view," in *Managing multinational teams: Global perspectives, advances in international management*, vol. ed. Shapiro, Debra L., Von Glinow, Mary Ann, and Cheng, Joseph L.C., **18**:209–31. Amsterdam: Elsevier.

Jennings, E. T. 1994. "Building bridges in the intergovernmental arena: Coordinating employment and training programs in the American States," *Public Administration Review* **54**:52–60.

Jepperson, Ronald L. 1991. "Institutions, institutional effects, and institutionalization," in *The new institutionalization in organizational analysis*, ed. Powell, Walter W. and DiMaggio, Paul J., 143–63. University of Chicago Press.

Jin, Y. and Levitt, R. E. 1996. "The virtual design team: A computational model of project organizations," *Journal of Computational and Mathematical Organizational Theory* **2**:171–95.

Johanson, J. and Vahlne, J. E. 1977. "The internationalization process of the firm: A model of knowledge development and increasing foreign market commitments," *Journal of International Business Studies* **8**:23–32.

Johnson, S., McMillan, J., Kaufmann, D., and Woodruff, C. 2000. "Why do firms hide? Bribes and unofficial activity after communism," *Journal of Public Economics* 76:495–520.

Jones, M. 1992. "Mainstream and radical theories of the multinational enterprise: Toward a synthesis." Paper presented at the Annual Meetings of the Academy of Management, Los Vegas, NV.

1993. "Mainstream and radical theories of the multinational enterprise: Complementary approaches?" *International Executive* 35(4): 339–56.

Jonsson, N., Novosel, D., Lillieskold, J., and Eriksson, M. "Successful management of complex, multinational R&D projects," 34th Annual Hawaii International Conference on System Sciences. HICSS-34 ed. 2001.

Jooste, Stephan F., Levitt, Raymond E., and Scott, W. Richard. Forthcoming. "Beyond 'one size fits all': How local conditions shape PPP-enabling field development," *Engineering Project Organization.*

Kahneman, D. 2003. "Maps of bounded rationality: A perspective on intuitive judgment and choice," in *Les Prix Nobel, The Nobel Prizes 2002,* ed. Frängsmyr, Tore, 1–41. Stockholm: Nobel Foundation.

Kano, M., Sriram, D., and Gupta, A. 2003. "International multi-company collaborative engineering: a study of Japanese engineering and construction firms." *Working papers* No. 94–17, Massachusetts Institute of Technology (MIT), Sloan School of Management

Karl, Terry L. 1997. *The paradox of plenty: Oil booms and petro states.* Berkeley: University of California Press.

Katz, Daniel and Kahn, Robert L. 1966. *The social psychology of organizations.* New York: John Wiley.

Katzenstein, Peter J. and Keohane, Robert O. eds. 2007. *Anti-Americanisms in world politics.* Ithaca, NY: Cornell University Press.

Kaul, M. 1997. "The new public administration: Management innovations in government," *Public Administration and Development* 17(1):13–26.

Kawashima, T. 2001. "Dispute resolution in contemporary Japan," *Harvard East Asian Monographs* 198:115–17.

Keck, Margaret E. and Sikkink, Kathryn. 1998. *Activists beyond borders: Advocacy networks in international politics.* Ithaca, NY: Cornell University Press.

Kelly, Alan. 2006. *The elements of influence.* New York: Penguin Group.

Kerney, S. 2005. Special Issue: "Globalizations from 'above' and 'below' the future of world society," *Journal of World-Systems Research* 11:263–86.

Khagram, Sanjeev. 2004. *Dams and development: Transnational struggles for water and power.* Ithaca, NY: Cornell University Press.

Khanna, T. and Palepu, K. G. 2000. "Is group affiliation profitable in emerging markets? An analysis of diversified Indian business groups," *Journal of Finance* 55:867–91.

Khanna, T., Palepu, K. G., and Sinha, J. 2005. "Strategies that fit emerging markets," *Harvard Business Review* 83(6):63–76.

Kharbanda, O. P. and Pinto, J. K. 1996. *What made Gertie gallop? Lessons from project failures.* New York, USA: Van Nostrand Reinhold.

Kharbanda, O. P. 1983. *How to learn from project disasters – true life stories with a moral for management.* Hampshire: Gower Publishing Co.

Kim, J.-H. 2009. Managing PPP in Korea through a think tank institution," *OECD Second Annual Meeting on Public Private Partnerships.* OECD Conference Center, Paris: OECD.

King, B. G., Felin, T., and Whetten, D. A., eds. 2009. *Studying differences between organizations: Comparative approaches to organizational research,* vol. 26, *Research in the sociology of organizations.* Bingley: Emerald, JAI.

Kirsch, S. 2007. "Indigenous movements and the risks of counterglobalization: Tracking the campaign against Papua New Guinea's Ok Tedi mine," *American Ethnologist* 34(2):303–21.

Kitschelt, Herbert P. 1986. "Political opportunity structures and political protest: Anti-nuclear movements in four democracies," *British Journal of Political Science* 16:57–85.

Klijn, E. H., and Teisman, G. R. 2000. "Governing public–private partnerships: Analyzing and managing the processes and institutional characteristics of public–private partnerships," in *Public–private partnerships: Theory and practice in international perspective,* ed. Osborne, S. P., 84. London: Routledge.

Kline, J. M. 2005. *Ethics for international business.* New York: Routledge.

Kluckhohn, F. and Strodtbeck, F. 1961. *Variations in value orientations.* Evanston, IL: Row Paterson.

Knight, G. A. and Cavusgil, S. T. 2004. "Innovation, organizational capabilities, and the born-global firm," *Journal of International Business Studies* 35:124–46.

Knorr-Certina, K. 1999. *Epistemic cultures: How the sciences make knowledge.* Cambridge, MA: Harvard University Press.

Kobrin, S. J. 1976. "The environmental determinants of foreign direct manufacturing investment: An ex-post empirical analysis," *Journal of International Business Studies* 7:29–42.

1979. "Political risk: A review and reconsideration," *Journal of International Business Studies* 10:67–81.

Kogut, B. and Singh, H. 1988. "The effect of national culture on the choice of entry mode," *Journal of International Business Studies* 19:411–32.

Koopmans, Ruud. 1995. *Democracy from below: New social movements and the political system in West Germany.* Boulder, CO: Westview.

Koopmans, Ruud and Olzak, Susan. 2004. "Discursive opportunities and the evolution of right-wing violence in Germany," *American Journal of Sociology* 110:198–230.

Kornhauser, William. 1959. *The politics of mass society.* Glencoe, IL: The Free Press.

Kostova, Tatiana. 1999. Transnational transfer of strategic organizational practices: A contextual perspective," *Academy of Management Review* 24:308–24.

Kostova, Tatiana and Zaheer, Shilata. 1999. "Organizational legitimacy under conditions of complexity: The case of the multinational enterprise," *Academy of Management Review* 24:64–81.

Krasner, Stephen. 1993. "Westphalia," in *Ideas and Foreign Policy*, ed. Goldstein, Judith and Keohane, Robert. Ithaca, NY: Cornell University Press.

Kriesi, Hanspeter. 1988. "Local mobilization for the people's petition of the Dutch peace movement," in *From structure to action*, ed. Klandermans, Bert, Kriesi, Hanspeter, and Tarrow, Sidney, 41–81. Greenwich, CT: JAI Press.

1989a. "The political opportunity structure of the Dutch peace movement," *West European Politics* 12: 295–312.

1989b. "New social movements and the new class in the Netherlands," *American Journal of Sociology* 94:1078–116.

Krücken, Georg and Drori, Gili S., eds. 2009. *World society: The writings of John Meyer.* Oxford University Press.

Kumaraswamy, M. M. and Zhang, X. Q. 2001. "Governmental role in BOT-led infrastructure development," *International Journal of Project Management* 19(4):195–205.

Kunreuther, H., Fitzgerald, K., and Aarts, T. 1993. "Siting noxious facilities: A test of the facility siting credo," *Risk Analysis* 13 (3):301–18.

Kunreuther, H., Susskind, L. E., and Aarts, T. 1993. *The facility siting credo: Guidelines for an effective facility siting process.* University of Pennsylvania, Wharton School, Risk and Decision Processes Center.

Kurtzman, Joel, Yago, Glenn, and Phumiwasana, Triphon. 2004. "The global costs of opacity," *Sloan Management Review* 46(1):38–44.

Kytle, Beth and Ruggie, John Gerard. 2005. "Corporate social responsibility as risk management: A model for multinationals," *Harvard University's*

*John F. Kennedy School of Government's Corporate Social Responsibility Working Paper,* 10.

Laffont, J.-J. 2005. *Regulation and development.* Cambridge University Press.

Lave, C. A. and March, J. G. 1975. *An introduction to models in the social sciences.* Lanham, MD: University Press of America.

Lawrence, P. R. and Lorsch, J.W 1967. *Organization and environment; Managing differentiation and integration.* Boston: Graduate School of Business Administration, Harvard University.

Layton, Azza Salama. 2000. *International politics and civil rights policies in the United States, 1941–1960.* New York: Cambridge University Press.

Lee, J. S. Y. 1999. "Organizational learning in China," *Business Horizons* 42:37–45.

Lee, J.-Y. and Mansfield, E. 1996. "Intellectual property protection and U.S. FDI," *Review of Economics and Statistics* 78:181–86.

Lesbirel, S. H. and D. Shaw, eds. 2005. *Managing conflict in facility siting: An international comparison.* Cheltenham: Edward Elgar Publishing.

Leung, K. 1998. "Negotiation and reward allocations across cultures," in *New perspectives on international industrial/organizational psychology,* ed. Earley, P. C. and Erez, M., 640–75. San Francisco, Lexington.

Levin, D. Z. 2000. Organizational learning and the transfer of knowledge: An investigation of quality improvement," *Organization Science* 11:630–47.

Levinsohn, D. and Reardon, D. 2007. "Municipal PPP project in South Africa: Obstacles and opportunities," *IP3's Public–Private Partnership Information Series.* Washington, DC: Institute for Public–Private Partnerships, Inc.

Levitt, Barbara, and March, James G. 1988. "Organizational learning," *Annual Review of Sociology* 14:319–40.

Levitt, R. E., Thompsen, J., Christiansen, T. R., Kuntz, J. D., Jin, Y., and Nass, C. I. 1999. "Simulating project work processes and organizations: Toward a micro-contingency theory of organizational design," *Management Science* 45:1479–95.

Levitt, T. 1983. "The globalization of markets," *Harvard Business Review.* 61:92–102.

Li, J. and Guisinger, S. 1991. "Comparative business failures of foreign-controlled firms in the United States," *Journal of International Business Studies* 22:209–25.

Lincoln, Y. and Guba, E. 1985. *Naturalistic inquiry.* Beverly Hills, CA: Sage.

Lindblom, Charles E. 1959. "The science of muddling through," *Public Administration Review* 19:79–88.

Lindesmith, A. R. 1947. *Opiate addiction*. Bloomington, IN: Principia Press.

Loch, C. H. and Terwiesch, C. 1998. "Communication and uncertainty in concurrent engineering," *Management Science* 44:1032–48.

Lonsdale, C. 2005. "Contractual uncertainty, power and public contracting," *Journal of Public Policy* 25:219–40.

Lord, M. D. and Ranft, A. L. 2000. "Organizational learning about new international markets: Exploring the internal transfer of local market knowledge," *Journal of International Business Studies* 31:573–90.

Louis, M. R. 1980. "Surprise and sense making: What newcomers experience in entering unfamiliar organizational settings," *Administrative Science Quarterly* 25:226–51.

Lu, J. W. and Beamish, P. W. 2004. "International diversification and firm performance: The S-curve hypothesis," *Academy of Management Journal* 47:598–610.

Luo, Y. and Mezias, J. 2002. "Liabilities of foreignness: Concepts, constructs, and consequences," *Journal of International Management* 8:217–221.

Luo, Y. and Peng, M. 1999. "Learning to compete in a transition economy: Experience, environment, and performance," *Journal of International Business Studies* 30:269–96.

Ma, Z. and Jaeger, A. 2005. "Getting to yes in China: Exploring personality effects in Chinese negotiation styles," *Group Decision and Negotiation* 14: 415–37.

Mahalingam, Ashwin. 2005. *Understanding and mitigating institutional costs on global projects*. A doctoral dissertation submitted to the Department of Civil and Environmental Engineering, Stanford University: CA.

Mahalingam, Ashwin and Levitt, Raymond E. 2007. "Institutional theory as a framework for analyzing conflicts on global projects," *Journal of Construction Engineering and Management* 133(7):517.

Mahmood, I. P. and Rufin, C. 2005. "Government's dilemma: The role of government in imitation and innovation," *Academy of Management Review* 30:338–60.

Makino, S. and Delios, A. 1996. "Local knowledge transfer and performance implications for alliance formation in Asia," *Journal of International Business Studies* 27:905–28.

Malone, T., Yates, J., and Benjamin, R. 1987. "Electronic markets and electronic hierarchies," *Communications of the ACM* 30:484–97.

Manheim, M. 1993. "Integrating global organizations through task/team support systems," in *Global networks: Computers and international communication*, ed. Harasim, L. M. Cambridge, MA: The MIT Press.

March, James G. 1990. "Exploration and exploitation in organizational learning," *Organization Science* 2: 71–87.

March, James G. 1991. "Exploration and exploitation in organization learning," *Organization Science* 2:71–87.

1994. *A primer on decision making: How decisions happen.* NY: Free Press.

March, James G. and Olsen, Johan P. 1989. *Rediscovering institutions: The organizational basis of politics.* New York: The Free Press.

March, James G. and Simon, Herbert A. 1958. *Organizations.* New York: John Wiley.

Markus, H. R. and Hamedani, M. G. 2007. "Sociocultural psychology: The dynamic interdependence among self systems and social systems," in *Handbook of cultural psychology,* ed. Kitayama, S. and Cohen, D., 3–39. New York: The Gilford Press.

Markus, H. R. and Lin, L. R. 1998. "Conflict ways: Cultural diversity in the meanings and practices of conflict," in *Cultural divides: Understanding and overcoming group conflict,* ed. Prentice, D. and Miller, D., 302–33. New York: Russell Sage Foundation.

Marshall, M. G. and Jaggers, K. 2009. *Polity IV project.* Center for Systemic Peace, George Mason University.

Martin, L. L. 2005. *International institutions in the new global economy.* Northhampton, MA: Edward Elgar.

Mayntz, R. 2004. "Mechanisms in the analysis of social macro-phenomena," *Philosophy of the Social Sciences* 34:237–59.

McAdam, Doug. 1986. "Recruitment of high-risk activism: The case of freedom summer," *American Journal of Sociology* 92:64–90.

1996. "Conceptual origins, current problems, future directions," in *Comparative perspectives on social movements,* ed. McAdam, D., McCarthy, J. D., and Zald, M. N. New York: Cambridge University Press.

1999[1982]. *Political process and the development of black insurgency, 1930–1970.* University of Chicago Press.

McAdam, Doug and Paulsen, Ronnelle. 1993. "Specifying the relationship between social ties and activism," *American Journal of Sociology* 98:640–67.

McAdam, Doug and Scott, W. Richard. 2005. "Organizations and movements," in *Social movements and organization theory,* ed. Davis, Gerald F., McAdam, Doug, Scott, W. Richard, and Zald, Mayer N., 4–40. Cambridge University Press.

McAdam, Doug, McCarthy, J. D., and Zald, M. N., eds. 1996. *Comparative perspectives on social movements.* Cambridge and New York: Cambridge University Press.

McAdam, Doug., Sampson, R. J., Weffer. S., and MacIndoe, H. 2005. "'There will be fighting in the streets': The distorting lens of social movement theory," *Mobilization* 10 (1):1–18.

McAdam, Doug, Tarrow, Sidney and Tilly, Charles. 2001. *Dynamics of contention*. New York: Cambridge University Press.

McAdam, Doug, Tarrow, Sidney and Tilly, Charles. 2008. "Methods for measuring mechanisms of contention," *Qualitative Sociology* 31:307–31.

McCarthy, John D. and Zald, Mayer N. 1973. *The trend of social movements in America: Professionalization and resource mobilization*. Morristown, NJ: General Learning Press.

1977. "Resource mobilization and social movements: A partial theory," *American Journal of Sociology* 82:1212–41.

McLaughlin, Milbrey, Scott, W. Richard, Deschenes, Sarah, Hopkins, Kathryn, and Newman, Anne. 2009. *Between movement and establishment: Organizations advocating for youth*. Stanford University Press.

McMillan, J. and Woodruff, C. 1999. "Interfirm relationships and informal credit in Vietnam," *Quarterly Journal of Economics* 114:1285–320.

McMillan, J., Johnson, S., and Woodruff, C. 2002. "Courts and relational contracts," *Journal of Law, Economics, and Organization* 18:221–77.

Mehta, L. 2009. *Displaced by development: Confronting marginalisation and gender injustice*. Thousand Oaks, CA: SAGE Publications.

Melin, L. 1992. "Internationalization as a strategy process," *Strategic Management Journal* 13:99–118.

Melucci, Alberto. 1980. "The new social movements: A theoretical approach," *Social Science Information* 19:199–226.

1985. "The symbolic challenge of contemporary movements," *Social Research* 52:789–815.

1989. *Nomads of the present*. Philadelphia: Temple University Press.

Mendez, A. 2003. "The coordination of globalized R&D activities through project teams organization: An exploratory empirical study," *Journal of World Business* 38:96–109.

Meyer, A., Loch, C., and Pich, M. T. 2002. "Managing project uncertainty: From variation to chaos," *MIT Sloan Management Review* 43:60–67.

Meyer, D. and Tarrow, S. 1997. *The social movement society: Contentious politics for a new century, people, passions, and power series*. Lanham: Rowman & Littlefield Publishers.

Meyer, J. W. and Rowan, B. 1977. "Institutionalized organizations: Formal structure as myth and ceremony," *American Journal of Sociology* 83:340–63.

Meyer, J. W., Boli, J., Thomas, G. M., and Ramirez, F. O. 1997. "World society and the nation state," *American Journal of Sociology* 103:144–81.

Meyer, J. W., Frank, David John, Hironaka, Ann, Schofer, Evan, and Tuma, Nancy. 1997 "The structuring of a world environmental regime," *International Organization* 51:623–51.

Meyer, J. W. and Jepperson, Ronald L. 2000. "The 'actors' of modern society: The cultural construction of social agency," *Sociological Theory* 18: 100–20.

Meyer, J. W., Kamens, Davis S., and Benavot, Aaron. 1992. *School knowledge for the masses: World models and national primary curricular categories in the twentieth century.* Washington, DC: Falmer Press.

MIGA. 2006. *The impact of Intel on Costa Rica: Nine years after the decision to invest*, Washington, DC: The World Bank Group/MIGA.

Miles, M. B. and Huberman, A. M. 1994. *Qualitative data analysis: An expanded sourcebook*, 2nd edn. Thousand Oaks, CA: Sage.

Miles, Raymond E. and Snow, Charles C. 1992. "Causes of failure in network organizations," *California Management Review* 34:53–72.

Miller, J. B. 2000. *Principles of public and private infrastructure delivery.* Netherlands: Springer.

Miller, Roger and Lessard, Donald. 2000. *The strategic management of large engineering projects: Shaping institutions, risks and governance.* Cambridge, MA: MIT Press.

Miller, Roger and Lessard, Donald. 2001. "Understanding and managing risks in large engineering projects," *International Journal of Project Management* 19:437–43.

Miller, Roger and Olleros, Xavier. 2000. "Project shaping as a competitive advantage," in *The strategic management of large engineering projects: Shaping institutions, risks, and governance* (pp. 93–112), eds. Miller, Roger and Lessard, Donald R. Cambridge, MA: MIT.

Milmo, D., Inman, P., and Durrani, A. 2009. "A bridge too far for PFI schemes," *The Guardian.*

Minkoff, Debra C. 1993. "The organization of survival: Women's and racial-ethnic voluntarist and activist organizations, 1955–1985," *Social Forces* 71:887–908.

1995. *Organizing for equality: The evolution of women's and racial-ethnic organizations in America, 1955–1985.* New Brunswick, NJ: Rutgers University Press.

Mintzberg, Henry. 1979. *The structuring of organizations.* Englewood Cliffs, NJ: Prentice-Hall.

Misra, B. B. 1986. *Government and bureaucracy in India, 1947–76.* Delhi: Oxford University Press.

Mody, A. 1996. *Infrastructure delivery: Private initiative and the public good.* Washington, DC: World Bank, EDI Development Series.

Moe, Terry M. 1984. "The new economics of organization," *American Journal of Political Science* 28:729–77.

Mol, A. P. 2003. "Global institutional clashes: Economic vs. environmental regimes," *International Journal of Sustainable Development and World Ecology* 10:303–18.

Morell, D., and Singer, G., eds. 1980. *Refining the waterfront: Alternative energy facility siting policies for urban coastal areas.* Cambridge: Oelgeschlager, Gunn and Hain.

Morris, Aldon D. 1984. *The origins of the civil rights movement: Black communities organizing for change.* New York: Free Press.

Morris, P. W. G. and Hough, G. H. 1987. *The anatomy of major projects – a study of the reality of project management.* Chichester: John Wiley & Sons.

Mörth, Ulrika. 2006. "Soft regulation and global democracy," in *Transnational governance: Institutional dynamics of regulation,* eds. Djelic, Marie-Laure and Sahlin-Andersson, Kerstin, 119–35. Cambridge University Press.

Nachum, L. and Zaheer, S. 2005. "The persistence of distance? The impact of technology on MNE motivations for foreign investment," *Strategic Management Journal* 26:747–67.

Nair, Jeevan and Jain, U. C. 2000. *The Indian bureaucratic system.* Jaipur, India: Pointer Publishers.

Nam, K. 2009. *The PFI governance of public sectors in Korea.* Seoul, Korea: Ministry of Strategy & Finance.

Nelson, Richard R. and Winter, Sidney G. 1982. *An evolutionary theory of economic change.* Cambridge, MA: Belknap Press of Harvard University Press.

Nissen, M. E. 2006. *Harnessing knowledge dynamics: Principles of organizational knowing and learning.* Hershey, PA: IRM Press.

Nohria, N. and Eccles, R. G., eds. 1992. *Networks and organizations: Structure, form, and action.* Boston: Harvard Business School Press.

Nohria, Nitin and Ghoshal, Sumantra. 1997. *The differentiated network: Organizing multinational corporations for value creation.* San Francisco: Jossey-Bass.

Nonaka, I. and Takeuchi, H.. 1995. *The knowledge-creating company: How Japanese companies create the dynamics of innovation.* New York: Oxford University Press.

Noonan, Rita K. 1995. "Women against the state: Political opportunities and collective action frames in Chile's transition to democracy," *Sociological Forum* 19:81–111.

Nordic Project Management Terminology (NPMT). 1985. *NORDNET.* Oslo: Reistad Offset.

North, Douglass C. 1990. *Institutions, institutional change, and economic performance*. Cambridge University Press.

North, Douglass C. 2005. *Understanding the process of economic change*. Princeton University Press.

Ofori, G. 2003. "Frameworks for analysing international construction," *Construction Management and Economics* 21(4):379–91.

O'Grady, S. and Lane, H. W. 1996. "The psychic distance paradox," *Journal of International Business Studies* 27:309–33.

O'Hare, M. 1977. "Not on my block you don't . . . Facility siting and the strategic importance of compensation," *Public Policy* 24(4):407–58.

O'Hare, M., Sanderson, D., and Bacow, L. 1983. *Facility siting and public opposition*. New York: Van Nostrand-Reinhold.

Oliver, C. 1991. "Strategic responses to institutional processes," *Academy of Management Review* 16:145–59.

Orlikowski, W. J. 1992. "The duality of technology: Rethinking the concept of technology in organizations," *Organization Science* 3:398–427.

Orr, R.J. 2005a. "General counsels' roundtable: The legacy of failed projects," *The Collaboratory for Research on Global Projects, Working Paper Series* 1–49. Available at: http://crgp.stanford.edu/news/gcr.html

2005b. *Unforeseen conditions and costs on global projects: learning to cope with unfamiliar institutions, embeddedness and emergent uncertainty*. Doctoral dissertation submitted to the Department of Civil and Environmental Engineering, Stanford University: CA, 1–205.

Orr, R. J. and Scott, W. R. 2008. "Institutional exceptions on global projects: A process model," *Journal of International Business Studies* 39:562–88.

Osa, Maryjane. 2003a. *Solidarity and contention: The networks of Polish opposition, 1954–1981*. Minneapolis: University of Minnesota Press.

2003b. "Networks in opposition: Linking organizations through activists in the Polish People's Republic," in *Social Movements and Networks*, ed. Diani, Mario and McAdam, Doug, 77–104. Oxford University Press.

Osborne, D. and Gaebler, T. 1992. *Reinventing government: how the entrepreneurial spirit is transforming the public sector*. Reading, MA: Addison-Wesley.

Oviatt, B. M. and McDougall, P. P. 1994. "Toward a theory of international new ventures," *Journal of International Business Studies* 25:45–64.

Oxley, J. E. 1999. "Institutional environment and the mechanisms of governance: the impact of intellectual property protection on the structure of inter-firm alliances," *Journal of Economic Behavior & Organization* 38:283–309.

Park, S. H. and Ungson, G. R. 1997. "The effect of national culture, organizational complementarity, and economic motivation on joint venture dissolution," *Academy of Management Journal* 40:279–307.

Parkhe, A. 1993. "'Messy' research, methodological predispositions, and theory development in international joint ventures," *Academy of Management Review* 18:227–68.

Parkhe, A. and Shin, R. 1991. "The case study method in international joint ventures research: A critical assessment and a program of application," Paper presented at the Academy of International Business Meetings, Miami, FL.

Parsons, Talcott. 1956. "Suggestions for a sociological approach to the theory of organizations," parts 1 and 2, *Administrative Science Quarterly* 1:63–85; 225–39.

Passy, Florence. 2003. "Social networks matter. But how?" in *Social movements and networks*, ed. Diani, Mario and McAdam, Doug, 21–48. Oxford University Press.

Paxton, P., Hughes, M. M., and Green, J. L. 2006. "The international women's movement and women's political representation, 1893–2003," *American Sociological Review* 71(6):23.

Peng, Mike W. 2002. "Toward an institution-based view of business strategy," *Asia Pacific Journal of Management* 19: 251–67.

   2003. "Institutional transitions and strategic choices," *Academy of Management Review* 28:275–96.

   2004. "Identifying the big question in international business research," *Journal of International Business Studies* 35:99–109.

Peng, Mike W., Wang, Denis Y.L., and Jiang, Yi. 2008. "An institution-based view of international business strategy: A focus on emerging economies," *Journal of International Business Studies* 39:920–36.

Peng, Mike W., LiSun, Sunny, Pinkham, Brian, and Chen, Hoo. 2009: "The institution-based view as a third leg for a strategy tripod," *Academy of Management Perspective* 23: 63–81.

Pennings, J. M. 1994. "Organizational learning and diversification," *Academy of Management journal*, 37(3):608.

Penrose, Edith. 1959/1995. *The theory of the growth of the firm.* Oxford University Press.

Peters, B. Guy. 1999. *Institutional theory in political science: The "new institutionalism."* London: Pinter.

Peters, B. Guy, and Pierre, J. 2002. "Governance without government? Rethinking public administration," *Journal of Public Administration Research and Theory* 8(2):223–43.

Petersen, B. and Pedersen, T. 2002. "Coping with liability of foreignness: Different learning engagements of entrant firms," *Journal of International Management* 8:339–50.

Petersen, B., Pedersen, T., and Lyles, M. A. 2008. "Closing knowledge gaps in foreign markets," *Journal of International Business Studies* **39** (7):1097–113.

Pfeffer, J. and Salancik, G. R. 1978. *The external control of organizations: a resource dependence perspective.* New York: Harper & Row.

Pierson, Paul. 2004. *Politics in time: History, institutions, and social analysis.* Princeton, NJ: Princeton University Press.

Pinch, M. T., Loch, C. H., and Meyer, A. 2002. "On uncertainty, ambiguity, and complexity in project management," *Management Science* **48**:1008–23.

Polanyi, K. 1944. *The great transformation: The political and economic origins of our time.* Boston: Beacon Press.

Poole-Rob, Stuart and Bailey, Alan. 2003. *Risky business: Corruption, fraud, terrorism and other threats to global business.* London: Kogan Page Ltd.

Powell, W. W. 1990. "Neither market nor hierarchy: Network forms of organization," in *Research in organizational behavior,* ed. Staw, B. and Cummings, L. L., **12**:295–336. Greenwich, CT: JAI Press.

Powell, W. W. and DiMaggio, P. J., eds. 1991. *The new institutionalism in organizational analysis.* University of Chicago Press.

Prahaldad, C. K. and Doz, Y. 1987. *The multinational mission: Balancing local demands and global vision.* New York: The Free Press.

Przeworski, A. and Teune, H. 1970. *The logic of comparative social inquiry.* New York: John Wiley.

PwC Advisory and Eurasia Group. 2006. *How managing political risk improves global business performance.*

Ragin, Charles C. 1987. *The comparative method: Moving beyond qualitative and quantitative strategies.* Berkeley, CA: The University of California Press.

   2000. *Fuzzy-set social science.* University of Chicago Press.

   2008a. *Redesigning social inquiry: fuzzy sets and beyond.* University of Chicago Press.

   2008b. "Qualitative Comparative Analysis using fuzzy sets (fsQCA)," in *Configurational comparative analysis,* eds. Rihoux, B. and Ragin, C.. Thousand Oaks, CA and London: Sage Publications.

Ramamurti, R. and Doh, J. P. 2004. "Rethinking foreign infrastructure investment in developing countries," *Journal of World Business* **39**:151–67.

Ramirez, Francisco O. and Boli, John. 1987. "Global patterns of educational institutionalization," in *Institutional structures: Constructing state, society, and the individual* (150–72), eds. Thomas, George et al. Newbury Park: Sage.

Rao, Hayagreeva, Monin, Philippe, and Durand, Rodolphe. 2003. "Institutional change in Toque Ville: Nouvelle cuisine as an identity movement in French gastronomy." *American Journal of Sociology* **108**:795–843.

Reina, P. and Tulacz, G. 2007. "The top 225 international contractors: firms are now more selective," *Engineering News Record* **255**:30–53.

Reuber, A. R. and Fischer, E. 1997. "The influence of the management team's experience on the internationalization behaviors of SME's," *Journal of International Business Studies* **28**:807–25.

Reuer, J. J., Shenkar, O., and Ragozzino, R. 2004. "Mitigating risk in international mergers and acquisitions: The role of contingent payouts," *Journal of International Business Studies* **35**:19–33.

Rhodes, R. A. W. 1996. "The new governance: Governing without government," *Political Studies* **44**(4):652–67.

Richards, D. P. 1999. "Engineering overseas," *Journal of Management in Engineering* **15**:24–29.

Rihoux, B. and Ragin, C., eds. 2009. *Configurational comparative methods.* Thousand Oaks, CA: Sage.

Robinson, W. S. 1951. "The logical structure of analytic induction," *American Sociological Review* **16**:812–18.

Robson, M. J., Leonidou, L. C., and Katsikeas, C. S. 2002. "Factors influencing international joint venture performance: Theoretical perspectives, assessment, and future directions," *Management International Review* **42**:385–418.

Rohlinger, Deana. 2002. "Framing the abortion debate: Organizational resources, media strategies, and movement-countermovement dynamics," *Sociological Quarterly* **43**:479–507.

Roland, Gérard. 2004. "Understanding institutional change: Fast-moving and slow-moving institutions," *Studies in Comparative International Development* **4**:109–31.

Romano, Roberta. 1985. "Law as product: Some pieces of the incorporation puzzle," *Journal of Law, Economics, and Organization* **1**:225–83.

Root, Franklin R. 1968. "Attitudes of American executives towards foreign governments and investment opportunities," *Economics and Business Bulletin* **20**:14–23.

Rose-Ackerman, S. 1999. *Corruption and government: Causes, consequences and reform.* Cambridge University Press.

Rucht, D. 2002. "Mobilization against large techno-industrial projects: A comparative perspective," *Mobilization* **7**(1):79–95.

Ruef, Martin and Scott, W. Richard. 1998. "A multidimensional model of organizational legitimacy: Hospital survival in changing institutional environments," *Administrative Science Quarterly* **43**:877–904.

Rumelt, R. 1986. *Strategy, structure, and economic performance.* Boston: Harvard Business School Press (first published in 1974).

Saastamoinen, H. 1995. "Case study on exceptions," *Information Technology & People* 8:48–78.

Sachs Jeffrey. 2005. *The end of poverty: Economic possibilities for our time.* New York: The Penguin Press.

Salamon, L. M. 2002. *The tools of government: A guide to the new governance.* Oxford University Press.

Salk, J. E. 1996. "Partners and other strangers: Cultural boundaries and cross-cultural encounters in international joint venture teams," *International Studies in Management Organization* 26:48–72.

Sampson, R. J., MacIndoe, H., McAdam, D., and Weffer-Elizondo, S. 2005. "Civil society reconsidered: The durable nature and community structure of collective civic action," *American Journal of Sociology* 111 (3):673–714.

Sassen, Saskia. 1996. *Losing Control? Sovereignty in an Age of Globalization.* New York: Columbia University Press.

Savas, E. 2000. *Privatization and public–private partnerships.* Chatham, NJ: Chatham House.

Schank, Roger C. and Abelson, Robert P. 1977. *Scripts, plans, goals, and understanding: An inquiry into human knowledge structures.* Hillsdale, NJ: L. Erlbaum Associates.

Schmitter, Philippe. 1990. "Sectors in modern capitalism: Models of governance and variations in performance," in *Labour Relations and Economic Performance,* eds. Brunetta, Renato and Dell-Aringa, Carlo, 3–39. Houndmills: Macmillan Press.

Schneiberg, Marc. 2002. "Organizational heterogeneity and the production of new forms: Politics, social movements and mutual companies in American fire insurance, 1900–1930," *Research in the Sociology of Organizations* 19:39–89.

Schoemaker, Paul J. H. 2002. *Profiting from uncertainty: Strategies for succeeding no matter what the future brings.* New York, The Free Press.

Schwartz, S. H. 1992. "Universals in the content and structure of values: theoretical advances and empirical tests in twenty countries," *Advances in Experimental Social Psychology* 25:1–65.

   1994. "Beyond individualism/collectivism: New cultural dimensions of values," *Cross Cultural Research and Methodology Series* 18:85.

   1999. "A theory of cultural values and some implications for work," *Values and Work: A Special Issue of the Journal of Applied Psychology* 48:23–47.

Scott, James C. 1998. *Seeing like a state.* New Haven, CT: Yale University Press.

Scott, W. Richard. 1965. "Field methods in the study of organizations," *Handbook of Organizations*, ed. March, James G., 261–304. Chicago: Rand-McNally.

1994. "Institutions and organizations: Toward a theoretical synthesis," in *Institutional environments and organizations: Structural complexity and individualism*, eds. Scott, W. R. and Meyer J. W., 55–80. Thousand Oaks, CA: Sage.

1994. "Conceptualizing organizational fields: Linking organizations and societal systems," in *Systemrationalitat und Partialinteresse*, ed. Derlien, Hans-Ulrich, Gerhardt, Uta, and Scharpf, Fritz W., 203–23. Baden-Baden, Germany: Nomos Verlagsgellschaft.

1995/2001/2008. *Institutions and organizations: Ideas and interests.* 1st, 2nd, and 3rd edn. Thousand Oaks, CA: Sage.

2003a. "Institutional carriers: Reviewing modes of transporting ideas over time and space and considering their consequences," *Industrial and Corporate Change* 12:879–94.

2003b. *Organizations: Rational, natural and open systems.* Englewood Cliffs, NJ: Prentice Hall.

2004. "Reflections on a half-century of organizational sociology," *Annual Review of Sociology* 39:1–20.

Scott, W. Richard and Davis, Gerard F. 2007. *Organizations and organizing: Rational, natural, and open system perspectives.* Thousand Oaks, CA: Sage Publications.

Scott, W. Richard and Meyer, John W. 1983. "The organization of societal sectors," in *Organizational environments: Ritual and rationality*, 155–75, ed. Meyer, John W. and Scott, W.Richard. Newbury Park, CA: Sage.

Scott, W. Richard and Meyer, John W. 1991. "The organization of societal sectors: Propositions and early evidence," in *The New Institutionalism in Organizational Analysis*, ed. Powell, Walter W. and DiMaggio, Paul J., 108–40. University of Chicago Press.

Scott, W. Richard, Levitt, R. E., and Orr, R. J. 2008. "Infrastructure construction projects in transnational contexts," Paper presented at SCANCOR 20th Anniversary Conference. Stanford University.

Scott, W. Richard, Ruef, Martin, Mendel, Peter J., and Caronna, Carol A. 2000. *Institutional change and healthcare organizations: From professional dominance to managed care.* University of Chicago Press.

Searle, John R. 1995. *The construction of social reality.* New York: Free Press.

Selznick, Philip. 1949. *TVA and the grass roots.* Berkeley: University of California Press.

Sen, A. 2004 "How does culture matter?" in *Culture and public action*, eds. Rao, V. and Walton, M., 37–58. Stanford University Press.

Seward, J. P. 1949. "An experimental analysis of latent learning," *Journal of Experimental Psychology* **39**: 177–86.

Shenhar, Aaron J. and Dvir, Dov. 2007. *Reinventing project management: The diamond approach to successful growth and innovation.* Boston: Harvard Business School Press.

Shenhav, Y. A. 1999. *Manufacturing rationality: The engineering foundations of the managerial revolution.* New York: Oxford University Press.

Shenkar, O. 2001. "Cultural distance revisited: Toward a more rigorous conceptualization and measurement of cultural differences," *Journal of International Business Studies* **32**:519–35.

Shenkar, O. and Seira, Y. 1992. "Role conflict and role ambiguity of chief executive officers in international joint ventures," *Journal of International Business Studies* **23**:55–75.

Shenkar, O., Luo, Y., and Yeheskel, O. 2008. "From 'distance' to 'friction': Substituting metaphors and redirecting intercultural research," *Academy of Management Review* **33**:905–23.

Sherman, D. J. 2004. *Not here, not there, not anywhere: The federal, state and local politics of low-level radioactive waste disposal in the United States, 1979–1999.* Unpublished dissertation, Department of Government, Cornell University, Ithaca, NY.

Shore, B. and Cross, B. 2005. "Exploring the role of national culture in the management of large-scale international science projects," *International Journal of Project Management* **23**:55–64.

Shou Qing, W., Robert, L. K. T., Seng Kiong, T., and David, A. 1999. "Political risks: Analysis of key contract clauses in China's BOT Project," *Journal of Construction Engineering and Management*, **125** (3):190–97.

Shultz, J. and Draper, M. C. 2009. *Dignity and defiance: Stories from Bolivia's challenge to globalization.* Berkeley: University of California Press.

Sim, A. B. and Ali, Y. 1998. "Performance of international joint ventures from developing and developed countries: An empirical study in a developing country context," *Journal of World Business* **33**:357–77.

Simon, Herbert A. 1945/1997. *Administrative behavior: A study of decision-making processes in administrative organizations.* New York: The Macmillan Company. 4th edn. New York: Free Press.

1969. *The sciences of the artificial.* Cambridge, MA: MIT Press.

1991. "Organisations and markets," *Journal of Economic Perspectives* **5**:25–44.

Sinkula, J. 1994. "Market information processing and organizational learning," *Journal of Marketing* **58**:35–45.

Sirtaine, S., Pinglo, M. E., Guasch, J. L., and Foster, V.. 2005. *How profitable are infrastructure concessions in Latin America? Empirical evidence and regulatory implications.* International Bank for Reconstruction and Development. Washington, DC: The World Bank Publishers.

Skrentny, John David. 1998. "The effect of the Cold War on African-American civil rights: America and the world audience, 1945–1968," *Theory and Society* 27:237–85.

Smelser, Neil J. 1962. *Theory of collective behavior.* New York: Free Press.
1973. "Social and psychological dimensions of collective behaviour," in *The sociology of revolution* (pp. 314–18), ed. Cheng, Ronald Ye-Lin. Chicago: Henry Regnery.

Smith, Jackie. 1998. "Global civil society: Transnational social movement organizations and social capital." *American Behavioral Scientist* 42:93–107.
2005. "Globalization and transnational social movement organizations," in *Social movements and organization theory*, eds. Davis, Gerald F., McAdam, Doug, Scott, W. Richard, and Zald, Mayer N. 226–48. New York: Cambridge University Press.

Smith, Jackie, Chatfild, C., and Pagnucco, Ron, eds. 1997. *Transnational social movements and global politics.* Syracuse University Press.

Smith, Jackie and Johnston, Hank, eds. 2002. *Globalization and resistance: Transnational dimensions of social movements.* Lanham, MD: Rowman & Littlefield Publishers.

Smith, V. 2003. "Constructivist and economic rationality in economics," in *Les Prix Nobel, The Nobel Prizes 2002*, ed. Frängsmyr, Tore, 1–60. Stockholm: Nobel Foundation.

Snow, David A., Burke Rochford Jr., E., Worden, Stephen K., and Benford, Robert D. 1986. "Frame alignments processes, micromobilization, and movement participation," *American Sociological Review* 51: 464–81.

Snow, David A., Zurcher Jr., Louis A., and Ekland-Olson, Sheldon. 1980. "Social networks and social movements: A microstructural approach to differential recruitment," *American Sociological Review* 45:787–801.

Solomon, C. M. 1995. "Global teams: The ultimate collaboration," *Personnel Journal* 74:49–58.

Sorokin, P. A. 1964. *Sociocultural causality, space and time.* New York: Russell & Russell.

Soysal, Y. N. 1995. *Limits of citizenship: Migrants and postnational membership in Europe.* Chicago: University of Chicago Press.

Spradley, J. P. 1979. *The ethnographic interview.* New York: Holt, Rinehart and Winston.

Staddon, J. E. R. 1983. *Adaptive behavior and learning.* Internet edition. Cambridge, MA: 1st edn. published by Cambridge University Press. Available at: http://psychweb.psych.duke.edu/department/jers/abl/

Staggenborg, S. 1988. "The consequences of professionalization and formalization in the pro-choice movement," *American Sociological Review* 53:585–606.

Stanat, R., West, C., and West, C. 2000. *Global jumpstart: The complete resource for expanding small and midsize businesses.* Reading, MA: Perseus Books.

Starbuck, W. H. and Milliken, F. J. 1988. "Challenger: Fine-tuning the odds until something breaks," *Journal of Management Studies* 25:319–40.

Stigler, George J. 1971. "The theory of economic regulation," *Bell Journal of Economics and Management Science* 2:3–21.

Stinchcombe, Arthur L. 1959. "Bureaucratic and craft administration of production: A comparative study," *Administrative Science Quarterly* 4:168–87.

   1985. "Contracts as hierarchical documents," in *Organization theory and project management: Administering uncertainty in Norwegian offshore oil*, 121–71. Bergen: Universitetsforlaget.

   1990. "Organizing information outside the firm: Contracts as hierarchical documents," in *Information and organizations*, ed. Stinchcombe, A., 194–239. Berkeley: University of California Press.

Stinchcombe, Arthur L. and Heimer, Carol. 1985. *Organizational theory and project management: Administering uncertainty in Norwegian offshore oil.* Oslo: Norwegian University Press.

Strang, David and Soule, Sarah A. 1998. "Diffusion in organizations and social movements: From hybrid corn to poison pills," *Annual Review of Sociology* 24:265–90.

Strang, David and Sine, Wesley D. 2002. "Interorganizational institutions," in *The Blackwell companion to organizations*, ed. Baum, Joel A.C., 497–519. Oxford: Blackwell.

Strauss, Anselm and Corbin, Juliet. 1998. *Basics of qualitative research.* 2nd edn. Thousand Oaks, Sage

Streeck, Wolfgang and Thelen, Kathleen, eds. 2005a. *Beyond continuity: Institutional change in advanced political economies.* Oxford University Press.

Streeck, Wolfgang and Thelen, Kathleen 2005b. "Introduction: Institutional change in advanced political economies," in *Beyond continuity: Institutional change in advanced political economies*, ed. Streeck, Wolfgang and Thelen, Kathleen, 1–39. Oxford University Press.

Streeck, Wolfgang and Schmitter, Philippe C. 1985. "Community, market, state – and associations? The prospective contribution of interest governance to social order," in *Private interest government: Beyond market and state*. Beverly Hills, CA: Sage.

Suchman, Mark C. 1995. "Managing legitimacy: Strategic and institutional approaches," *Academy of Management Review* 20:571–610.

Sumner, William Graham. 1906. *Folkways*. Boston: Ginn & Co.

Surabhi. 2007. "Private consultants to help government on PPP projects," *Financial Express*.

Tarrow, Sidney. 1983. *Struggling to reform: Social movements and policy change during cycles of protest*. Western Societies Program Occasional Paper No. 15. New York Center for International Studies, Cornell University, Ithaca, NY.

1989. *Democracy and disorder: Protest and politics in Italy, 1965–1975*. Oxford University Press.

1998. *Power in movement: Social movements and contentious politics*. Cambridge University Press.

Tate, J. 2001. "National varieties of standardization," in *Varieties of capitalism*, ed. Hall, P. A., and Soskice, D., 442–73. Oxford University Press.

Taylor, John E., Dossick, C. S., and Garvin, M. Forthcoming 2009. "Constructing research with case studies," *CRC Conference 2009*, Seattle, WA.

Taylor, John E. and Levitt, R. 2007. "Innovation alignment and project network dynamics: An integrative model for change," *Project Management Journal*, 38(3):22–35.

Teasley, S. and Wolinsky, S. 2001. "Scientific collaborations at a distance," *Science* 292: 2254–55.

Teece, David J. 2009. *Dynamic capabilities & strategic management: Organizing for innovation and growth*. Oxford University Press.

Teece, David J. and Pasano, G. 1994. "The dynamic capabilities of firms: An introduction," *Industrial and corporate change* 3:537–56.

Terlutter, R., Diehl S., and Mueller, B. 2006. "The GLOBE study–applicability of a new typology of cultural dimensions for cross-cultural marketing and advertising research," in *International Advertising and Communication: New Insights and Empirical Findings*, ed. Terlutter, R., Diehl, S., and Mueller, B., 419–38. Gabler DUV, Wiesbaden.

Thagard, P. and Kroon, F. W. 2006. "Emotional consensus in group decision making," *Mind & Society* 5:85–104.

Thelen, Kathleen. 1999. "Historical institutionalism in comparative politics," *Annual Review of Political Science* 2:369–404.

Thibaut, J. W. and Kelley, H. H. 1969. *The social psychology of groups*. New York: Wiley.

Thompson, J. D. 1967. *Organizations in action*. New York: McGraw-Hill.

Tilly, Charles. 1978. *From mobilization to revolution*. Reading, MA: Addison-Wesley.

———. 2001. "Mechanisms in political processes," *Annual Review of Political Science* 4:21–41.

Tilly, Charles, Tilly, Louise, and Tilly, Richard. 1975. *The rebellious century, 1830–1930*. Cambridge, MA: Harvard University Press.

Tjosvold, D., Andrews, J. R., and Struthers, J. T. 1991. "Power and interdependence in work groups: Views of managers and employees," *Group and Organization Studies* 16:285–99.

Tjosvold, D., Cho, Y.-H., Park, H.-H., and Liu, C. 2001. "Interdependence and managing conflict with sub-contractors in the construction industry in East Asia," *Asia Pacific Journal of Management* 18:295–313.

Toffler, Alvin. 1970. *Future shock*. New York: Random House.

Tolbert, Pamela S. and Zucker, Lynne G. 1996. "The institutionalization of institutional theory," in *Handbook of organization studies*, eds. Clegg, Stewart R., Hardy, Cynthic, and Nord, Walter R., 175–90. London: Sage.

Tolman, E. C. and Honzik, C. H. 1930. "Introduction and removal of reward, and maze performance in rats," *University of California Publications in Psychology* 4:257–75.

Tosini, Domenico. 2008. "A sociological understanding of suicide attacks." Unpublished paper. Department of Sociology and Social Research. University of Trento, Italy.

Touraine, Alain. 1981. *The voice and the eye: An analysis of social movements*. Cambridge University Press.

Treasury, S. 2004. *Public–private partnership manual*. ed. South African National Treasury. Pretoria.

Trémolet, S. 2007. "Outsourcing regulation: When does it make sense and how do we best manage it?" PPIAF Working Paper No. 5. Washington, DC: World Bank.

Trémolet, S. and Shah, N. 2005. *Wanted! Good regulators for good regulation: An evaluation of human and financial resource constraints for utility regulation*. Washington, DC: Environmental Resources Management and Tremolet Consulting for the World Bank.

Trist, Eric L. 1981. "The evolution of sociotechnical systems as a conceptual framework and as an action research program," in *Perspectives on organization design and behavior*, 19–75, eds. Van de Ven, Andrew H. and Joyce, William F.. New York: John Wiley, Wiley-Interscience.

Trompenaars, Fons. 1993. *Riding the waves of culture*. New York: McGraw-Hill.

Trompenaars, Fons and Hampden-Turner, Charles. 1998. *Riding the waves of culture: Understanding cultural diversity in global business*. New York: McGraw-Hill.

Tse, D. K., Pan, Y., and Au, K. Y. 1997. "How MNCs choose entry modes and form alliances: The China experience," *Journal of International Business Studies* 28:779–806.

Tsutsui, K. 2004. "Global civil society and ethnic social movements in the contemporary world," *Sociological Forum* 19(1):25.

Tversky, A. and Kahneman, D. 1974. "Judgment under uncertainty: Heuristics and biases," *Science* 185:1124–31.

Union of International Organizations. [various years]. *Yearbook of International Associations*. Munich, Germany: K.G. Saur.

Ursic, M.L.C.M.R. 1984. "An experience curve explanation of export expansion," *Journal of Business Research* 12:159–68.

Usunier, J.-C. 2003. "Cultural aspects of international business negotiations," in *International Business Negotiations*, eds. Ghauri, P. and Usunier, J.-C., 97–137. Oxford: Elsevier Ltd.

Van de Ven, A. H., Delbecq, A. H., and Koening, R. Jr. 1976. "Determinants of coordination modes within organizations," *American Sociological Review* 41:322–38.

Van Dijek, Jules J.J. and Groenewegen, John P.M. 1994. "An institutional framework for studying international(izing) business systems," in *Changing business systems in Europe: An institutional approach*, eds. van Dijek, Jules J.J. and Groenewegen, John P.M., 13–40. Brussels: VUBPRESS.

Van Fenema, P. C. and Kumar, K. 2000. "Coupling, interdependence, and control in global projects," in *Projects as business constituents and guiding motives*, eds. Lundin, R. A. and Hartman, F. Boston, MA: Kluwer Academic Publishers.

Van Maanen, John and Barley, Stephen R. 1984. "Occupational communities: Culture and control in organizations," in *Research in Organization Behavior*, eds. Staw, Barry M. and Cummings, L. L., 6:287–365. Greenwich, CT: JAI Press.

Van Slyke, D. M. 2003. "The mythology of privatization in contracting for social services," *Public Administration Review* 63(3):296–315.

Vernon, R. 1971. *Sovereignty at bay: the multinational spread of US enterprises*. New York: Basic Books.

Viljoen, P. 2006. "Regional integration through infrastructure development," *Third regional consultation on "rethinking the role of national development banks in Africa."* Johannesburg, South Africa.

Vives, A., Paris, A., and Benavides, J.. 2006. *Financial structuring of infrastructure projects in public–private partnerships: An application to water projects*. Washington, DC: Inter-American Development Bank.

Vogus, Timothy J. and Davis, Gerald F. 2005. "Elite mobilizations for anti-takeover legislation, 1982–1990," in *Social movements and organization theory*, eds. Davis, Gerald F., McAdam, Doug, Scott, W. Richard, and Zald, Mayer N., 96–121. New York: Cambridge University Press.

Voropajev, V. 1998. "Change management. A key integrative function of PM in transition economies," *International Journal of Project Management* 16:15–19.

Wade, J. 2005. "Political risk in Eastern Europe," *Risk Management* 52:24–30.

Wageman, R. 1995. "Interdependence and group effectiveness," *Administrative Science Quarterly* 40:145–80.

Walsh, Edward J. and Warland, Rex H. 1983. "Social movement involvement in the wake of a nuclear accident: Activists and free riders in the Three Mile Island area," *American Sociological Review* 48:764–81.

Walsh, Edward. J., Warland, R. H., and Smith, D. C. 1993. "Backyards, NIMBY's, and incinerator sitings: Implications for social movement theory," *Social Problems* 40(1):25–38. 1997.

1997. *Don't burn it here: Grassroots challenges to trash incinerators.* University of Pennsylvania Press.

Walsh, J. P., Meyer, A. D., and Schoonhoven, C. B. 2006. "Future of organization theory: Living in and living with changing organizations," *Organization Science* 17: 657–71.

Warren, Roland L. 1967. "The interorganizational field as a focus for investigation," *Administrative Science Quarterly* 12:396–419.

Waterman, R. H. 1990. *Adhocracy: The power to change.* Memphis, TN: Whittle D. Books.

Weich, K. E., Sutcliffe, K., and Obstfeld, D. 2005. "Organizing and the process of sense-making," *Organization Science* 16(4):409–21.

Weick, Karl. 1995. *Sensemaking in organizations.* Thousand Oaks, CA: Sage.

Weingast, Barry. 1996. "Political institutions: Rational choice perspectives," in *A new handbook of political science*, ed. Goodin, Robert and Klingemann, Hans-Dieter, 169–90. New York: Oxford University Press.

2002. "Rational choice institutionalism," in *The state of the discipline*, eds. Katznelson, Kra and Milner, Helen, 660–92. New York: W.W. Norton.

Weingast, Barry and Marshall, W. 1988. "The industrial organization of Congress," *Journal of Political Economy* 96:132–63.

Welch, L. S. and Luostarinen, R. 1988. Internationalization: Evolution of a concept," *Journal of General Management* 14:34–55.

Wells Jr., L. T. and Ahmed, R. 2006. *Making foreign investment safe: Property rights and national sovereignty.* Oxford University Press.

Westney, D. E. 1993. "Institutionalization theory and the multinational corporation," in *Organization theory and the multinational corporation*, eds. Ghoshal, S. and Westney, D. E., 53–76. New York: St. Martin's Press.

Whitley, R. 1991. *Business systems in East Asia: Firms, markets and societies*. London: Sage.

1992a. *European business systems: Firms and markets in their national contexts*. London: Sage.

1992b. "The social construction of organizations and markets: The comparative analysis of business recipes," in *Rethinking organizations: New directions in organization theory and analysis*, eds. Reed, M. and Hughes, M., 120–43. Newbury Park, CA: Sage.

1999. *Divergent capitalisms: The social structuring and change of business systems*. Oxford University Press.

2006. "Project-based firms: New organizational form or variations on a theme?" *Industrial and Corporate Change* 1:77–99.

Whitley, R. and Kristensen, P. H. 1997. *Governance at work: The social regulation of economic relations*. Oxford University Press.

Wickham, C. R. 2002. *Mobilizing Islam: Religion, activism and political change in Egypt*. Edinburgh University Press.

Wieland, G. F. and Ullrich, R. A. 1976. *Organizations: Behavior, design, and change*. Homewood, IL: Richard D. Irwin.

Williams, T. 1999. "The need for new paradigms for complex projects," *International Journal of Project Management* 17: 269–73.

2002. *Modeling complex projects*. Chichester: John Wiley & Sons.

Williamson, Oliver E. 1975. *Markets and hierarchies: Analysis and antitrust implications*. New York: Free Press.

1979. "Transaction cost economics: The governance of contractual relations," *Journal of Law and Economics* 22:233–61.

1985. *The economic institutions of capitalism*. New York: Free Press.

1994. "Transaction cost economics and organization theory," in *Handbook of economic sociology*, eds. Smelser, Neil J. and Swedberg, R.,77–107. New York and Princeton: Russell Sage Foundation and Princeton University.

Wilson, James Q., ed. 1980. *The politics of regulation*. New York: Basic Books.

Witt, M. A., and Lewin, A. Y. 2007. "Outward foreign direct investment as escape response to home country institutional constraints," *Journal of International Business Studies* 38: 579–94.

Wittenbaum, G. W., Vaughan, S. I., and Stasser, G. 1998. "Coordination in task-performing groups," in *Theory and research on small groups*, eds. Tindale, R. S., Heath, L., and Edwards, J. New York: Plenum Press.

Woodhouse, E. J. 2005. "The Experience with Independent Power Projects in Developing Countries: Interim Report" in http://crgp.stanford.edu/news/events.html Collaboratory for Research on Global Projects.

———. 2006. "The obsolescing bargain redux? Foreign investment in the electric power sector in developing countries," *The New York University Journal of International Law and Politics* 38:121–219.

Wooten, M., and Hoffman A. J. 2008. "Organizational fields: Past, present and future," in *Sage handbook of organizational institutionalism*, eds. Greenwood, R., Oliver, C., Sahlin, K., and Suddaby, R., 130–47. Los Angeles: Sage.

World Bank. 2005. "Development topics: Globalization."

Wright, R. W. 1994. "Trends in international business research: Twenty-five years later," *Journal of International Business Studies* 25:687–701.

Wright, T. P. 1936. "Learning curve," *Journal of the Aeronautical Science* 3:122–28.

Xu, D. and Shenkar, O. 2002. "Institutional distance and the multinational enterprise," *Academy of Management Review* 27:608–18.

Yaziji, Michael. 2004. "Turning gadflies into allies," *Harvard Business Review* 82(2):110–15.

Yin, R. 2003. *Case study research: Design and methods.* New York: Sage.

Zaheer, S. 1995. "Overcoming the liability of foreignness," *Academy of Management Journal* 38:341.

Zajac, E. J. and Olsen, C. 1993. "From transaction cost to transactional value analysis: Implications for the study of interorganizational strategies," *Journal of Management Studies* 30:131–45.

Zandamela, H. 2001. *Lessons from Mozambique: The Maputo water concession*: Available online at www.citizen.org.

Zeiss, C. C. 1998. "Noxious facilities and host community response: A causal framework." *Journal of Environmental Health* 61(1):18–29.

Zelner, Bennet A., Henisz, Witold J., and Holburn, Guy L.F. 2009. "Contentious implementation and retrenchment in neoliberal policy reform: The global electric power industry, 1989–2001," *Administrative Science Quarterly* 54:379–412.

Zhao, Dingxin. 1998. "Ecologies of social movements: Student mobilization during the 1989 prodemocracy movement in Beijing," *American Journal of Sociology* 103: 1493–529.

Znaniecki, F. 1934. *The method of sociology.* New York: Farrar & Rinehart

Zucker, Lynne G. 1977. "The role of institutionalization in cultural persistence," *American Sociological Review* 42:726–43.

# Index

adaptability, 237
adhocracy, 2
agency
  and institutions, 60–1
alternative dispute resolution (ADR),
  322, 329–30
  and rule of law, 346–7
approval processes, 261–3

bureacratic
  hierarchical vs. collegial orientation,
  120–3
  rules vs. results orientation, 116–18

Central Vigilance Commission (CVC),
  119–20
Chevron Texaco, 370–4
cognitive. *See also* cultural-cognitive
  elements
  liberation, 97–8
collective behavior
  and social movements, 88
conflict
  institutional, 113–14
  legal, 280, 298, 304
  political, 280, 298, 299–302
  resolution strategies, 123–9
constitutive processes, 57, 68
contingency
  plan, 233–7
  theory, 2, 4–6
contractors
  general, 199–200, 208–9, 214–16
  important knowledge for, 270–2
  on Indian railway projects, 117–18,
  120–1, 122–3
  systems, 201, 209–10, 212–13
contracts
  legalistic vs. relational, 314–15
  renegotiation of, 312–13, 320, 321, 355

coordination
  costs, 30, 37–8, *See also* transaction
  costs; institutional:costs
cultural-cognitive elements, 57–8, 251,
  *See also under* institutional
  defined, 57, 141
  knowledge of, 267–9, 274
culture
  Davos, 80–1
  dimensions, 317–19
  popular, 83
  professional, 81–2

Davos, 80–1
developers, 200–1, 209, 216–18
  important knowledge for, 270

embeddedness, 185
  local. *See* local embeddedness
engineers
  important knowledge for, 272
environments
  local, 64–5
  sectoral, 65–7
  societal, 67–8
  transnational, 69–71
European Union (EU), 66, 69
expatriates
  freelance consultants, 129–33, 134,
  212–18

field, organization, 21, 383–4
  and global projects, 73–8
  and institutional logics, 72, 388–9, 401
  and organizational archetypes, 72
  defined, 71–2
  dimensions of, 399–401
  governance systems in, 72–3, 388
  intermediaries in, 389
  sensemaking in, 390

field, organization (*cont.*)
  structuration of, 72–3
  types of actors, 385–7
firm
  decisions, 139
  structures, 139
framing processes, 96–7, 101

global projects
  and compensation, 293–4
  and human rights, 87, 281
  and local embeddedness, 195–9
  and political opportunities and
    threats, 107–9
  and public participation, 285–6, 306
  and risk, 355–6
  and social movements, 86–7,
    99–110, 279–89
  challenges of, 29–37, 247
  consultants to, 129–33, 134
  defined, 17
  drivers behind, 29, 90–9, 101–10,
    282–7, 289–98
  infrastructure construction.
    *See* infrastructure projects
  metrics for, 43–4
  modeling and analysis of, 41–3
  opposition to. *See* opposition to
    global projects
  theory and scholarship, 19–20, 27
  varieties of, 41
globalization
  and institutions, 79–84
  and organization theory, 24–5
governance
  systems, 66, 72–3, 388

human rights
  and global projects, 87, 281
  normative support for, 101–2, 106

identity
  collective, 99
Indian civil service, 119
infrastructure projects, 18, 192
  and local embeddedness, 65, 270
  distinctive features of, 44–7
  funding, 310, 377–8
  need for, 1, 87, 247, 280–1,
    310, 377

institutional
  conflicts, 115–16, 86–110, 135–82,
    279–309, 310–40
  costs, 37, 162, 174–7
  deviation, 159–60
  differences, 33–7, 83–4, 115–16,
    136–8, 247
  elements (pillars), 58, 140–1, 250–2
  exceptions, 136, 141–3, 155–7,
    175, 178
  ignorance, 153
  knowledge, 133, 189, 258–69,
    *See also* local knowledge
  learning, 252
  logics, 72, 388–9, 401
institutions
  and agency, 60–1
  and globalization, 79–84
  and rule of law, 55, 322–9
  and societal differences, 136–8
  construction of, 61–3
  defined, 54, 140
  transnational, 69–70
interdependence, 31
international business
  and foreignness, 135, 164, 178,
    186–7, 247
  and learning, 187–90, 240–1
  and local embeddedness, 195–9
  and need for local knowledge,
    247–8, 250
  risk, 249–50, 252–3
  strategies by firm, 211–18

knowledge
  business, 189
  institutional. *See under* institutional
  local. *See* local knowledge
  needed for different firms, 270–2
  types of, 258–69

labor law, 259
learning
  content-free, 188–9
  curve, 240–1
  deutero, 241
legal systems, 259–60
legalization, 70
legitimacy
  and institutional elements, 59–60

local embeddedness
  aligning strategy with, 218–20
  and coping strategies, 186, 220–39,
    239–40
  and need for local knowledge, 184,
    202, 203
  and uncertainty, 210
  by firm type, 199–201
  defined, 185
  factors affecting, 204–5
local knowledge. *See also* local
    embeddedness
  deficits and consequences, 202,
    203–4
  need for, 184, 202, 203, 247–8
  strategies, 221–8, 228–33, 233–8
logics. *See under* institutional

management
  advice for global projects, 147–80
  project, 21–3
  risk. *See* risk management
  supply chain, 16
markets, foreign. *See also* international
    business
  challenges of, 186
  strategies for entering, 211–18
multinational
  corporations (MNCs), 64, 73–4
  enterprise, 23–4

network
  approaches to information gathering,
    360–1
  forms, 3
NIMBY (not-in-my-backyard), 107,
    285
nongovernmental organizations
    (NGOs)
  and project conflict, 293, 304
  and public–private partnerships,
    386
  and risk analysis, 359
  international (INGOs), 70–1, 108,
    387
normative elements, 56–7, 251
  *See also under* institutional
  and institutional exceptions, 162
  defined, 56, 140–1
  knowledge of, 267

opposition to global projects
  and insurgent frames, 101–4
  causal conditions, 304–6, 294
  emergence of, 86–7, 107,
    280–96
organization
  archetype, 72
  field. *See* field, organization
  institutions-based approach to,
    7–8
  project-based, 3
  rationalization, 28–9
  set, 73
  theory, 4–8, 20–1, 24–5, 96

Partnerships British Columbia (PBC),
    392–4
pipeline projects, 288–9
  and conflict, 299–304
political opportunity and threat.
    *See under* social movement
professional associations
  and normative controls, 56, 66, 75,
    387, 388
project
  business, 40
  consultants, 74, 201, 209,
    213–14
  management, 21–3
  management unit (MU), 116–17,
    117–18, 121–2, 123, 78
  network, 40
Public and Private Infrastructure
    Investment Management Center
    (PIMAC), 396–7
public–private partnerships (PPP),
    310–11, 378–401
  and rule of law, 321–2
  challenges to, 378
  enabling organizations, 379–83
  in British Columbia, 392–5
  in Chile, 398
  in China, 399
  in India, 399
  in Korea, 395–7
  in Mozambique, 398
  in South Africa, 390–2
  project vs. program level, 379
  renegotiations in, 311–13, 347–9
  unit, 381–2

Qualitative Comparative Analysis
  (QCA), 288, 294–304, 330–2
  and consistency, 339–40
  and coverage, 340

regulative elements, 251, *See also under*
  institutional
  defined, 55, 140
  knowledge of, 258–63
research methods
  comparative case, 287–8, 306
  qualitative comparative.
    *See* Qualitative Comparative
    Analysis (QCA)
resource-based theory, 6–7
risk analysis, 354, 361–7
  and political and social actors, 356–7
  and sources of information, 358–60
  network approaches to, 360–1, 365–7
risk management. *See also* risk analysis
  and network structures, 353
  political and social, 353–4, 357–8,
    374–5

sensemaking processes, 163
  and local knowledge, 165, 167,
    389–90
social movement
  and anti-Western sentiment, 102–3,
    109
  and collective identity, 99
  and emotion, 98–9
  and framing processes, 96–7, 101
  and mobilizing structures, 94–6, 104–7
  and resources, 292–3
  and risk, 285
  organizations (SMOs), 70–1, 77,
    94–5, 100, 104–5, 108
  political opportunity and threat,
    90–2, 282, 289–92, 305–6
  political process models of, 95, 109,
    283

resource mobilization models of,
    94–5, 108, 283
  theory, 87–99, 279
  transnational, 104–5
strategies
  for managing political and social
    risk, 367–9
  institutions-based approach to, 8
  legalistic vs. relational, 314–16,
    343–4, 345
  network-based, 369–70
structuration
  processes, 72–3
  theory, 61
supply chain
  global, 17
  management, 16

transaction costs, 37, 113,
    *See also* coordination: costs;
    institutional: costs
transnational
  institutions, 69–70
  social movement organizations
    (TSMOs). *See under* social
    movement
  social movements, 104–5

uncertainty, 31–2, 116
  and predictablity, 206
  by firm type, 208–11
  insuring against, 238

Virtual Design Team (VDT), 38

World Bank, 73
  and anti-neo-liberal backlash, 103,
    109
  and Davos culture, 81
  and project conflict, 292
  and public–private partnerships,
    383, 398